Beginning
Ajax

Beginning
Ajax

Chris Ullman
Lucinda Dykes

Wiley Publishing, Inc.

Beginning Ajax

Published by
Wiley Publishing, Inc.
10475 Crosspoint Boulevard
Indianapolis, IN 46256
www.wiley.com

About the Authors

Chris Ullman is a freelance Web developer and technical author who has spent many years working with ASP/ASP.NET. Coming from a computer science background, he started initially as a UNIX/Linux guru, who gravitated toward Microsoft technologies during the summer of ASP (1997). He cut his teeth on Wrox Press ASP guides, and since then he has written and contributed to more than 25 books, most notably as lead author for Wrox's bestselling *Beginning ASP/ASP.NET 1.x* series. He has contributed chapters to books on PHP, ColdFusion, JavaScript, Web Services, C#, XML, and other Internet-related technologies. After he left Wrox as a full-time employee in August 2001, he branched out into VB.NET/C# programming and ASP.NET development, and he started his own business, CUASP Consulting Ltd, in April 2003. He maintains a variety of Web sites from `http://www.cuasp.co.co.uk` (his "work" site) to `http://www.atomicwise.com` (a selection of his writings on music and art). He now divides his time between his family and composing electronic sounds for his music project, Open E.

Lucinda Dykes is a freelance Web developer, teacher, and technical author who has been writing code and developing Web sites since 1994. She started her career in a high-tech area of medicine but left medicine to pursue her interests in technology and the Web. She has been involved in client-side development with JavaScript for many years through her company, Zero G Web, and teaches JavaScript courses online for an international group of students at `eclasses.org`. She has also authored numerous technical books about XML, XHTML, and Web application development with Dreamweaver.

Credits

All my love to my wife, Kate, and the boys.

—Chris Ullman

With love and thanks to Wali for putting up with being married to a writer; to my mother, Doris Dykes, for instilling a lifelong love of reading and books; and to all the Web pioneers and innovators who shared their knowledge with the rest of us.

—Lucinda Dykes

Acknowledgments

Thanks to my fellow author, Lucinda, for being available for queries and comments. Thanks to Kevin Shafer for his tremendously measured and consistent input on my text. Thanks to Alexei Gorkov for his excellent and incisive input on the chapters and code. And thanks to Jim Minatel for being there to field my numerous requests.

—*Chris Ullman*

Thanks to my fellow author Chris for everything I've learned about server-side development from him. Thanks to Kevin Shafer for tolerating all the quirks of working with two authors long distance. Thanks to Alexei Gorkov for an outstanding technical review and suggestions about the code. And thanks to Jim Minatel for always being there to answer our questions, for providing excellent suggestions, and for giving me the opportunity to be involved in this project.

—*Lucinda Dykes*

Contents

Contents

Contents

Contents

Contents

Contents

Introduction

Ajax has become a huge buzzword over the past two years, and it is often mentioned in the same breath as another buzzword — Web 2.0. Neither term refers to something concrete or downloadable, but they've both been coined to reflect the changing face of the Web. Web 2.0 is as much about an attitude and a mindset as it is about new developments. Several innovations have emerged concurrently to create this sea of change, such as wikis, blogs, newsfeeds, third-party application programming interfaces (APIs), and web services. Ajax is one of the prime enablers.

Ajax is not a technology in itself, but rather an umbrella term used to describe how several existing technologies such as JavaScript, the Document Object Model (DOM), and Extensible Markup Language (XML) can be used together to create Web applications that are more interactive and that remove the need for entire web pages to be refreshed when only part of the page is changing.

While the term "Ajax" appeared only fairly recently, the technologies used in Ajax applications have been around for several years, and some programmers have been using Ajax-style technologies and techniques for half a decade at least. In the past year, though, there has been a rapid increase in the number of Web sites that are using Ajax-style techniques. Furthermore, a lot of new job positions are requiring that programmers know how to program Ajax-style applications. This book helps programmers to understand the core technologies behind the term "Ajax" and to start building sites using Ajax techniques.

While many people have heard of Ajax, few understand how to write applications using these techniques. Ajax blurs the traditional boundaries between front-end developers and server-side developers, and it forces a new evaluation of the way applications should be created, as well as the kind of prerequisites a user interface should offer.

Ajax doesn't require new software, new servers, or tools. It's about making use of what is already available. It's about challenging perceptions that everything is necessarily done on the server. It's about going back to old ideas and breathing new life into them. It's about fundamentally changing the way in which the Web works.

Who Is This Book For?

This book teaches you how to create applications according to Ajax principles. This book takes no views on whether Internet Explorer (IE), Firefox, or Safari is a superior browser, and it offers examples that work across all major browsers. Because of the complexities involved, however, Ajax is not something a complete novice can expect to pick up. The reader is expected to be familiar with the following client-side technologies:

- ❑ HTML (and/or) XHTML
- ❑ JavaScript
- ❑ Cascading style sheets (CSS)

The reader will also need to be familiar with at least one of the two following server-side technologies:

❑ PHP

❑ ASP.NET

Server-side examples will be given in both PHP and ASP.NET/C#, but an extensive knowledge of either isn't expected.

The reader is *not* expected to know any of the following because full introductions to each technology will be given (although familiarity with one or many of them may be useful):

❑ Document Object Model (DOM)

❑ XML

❑ XPath

❑ Extensible Stylesheet Language Transformations (XSLT)

❑ Web services (REST and SOAP)

As with other Wrox Beginning books, you'll find that the concepts discussed in one chapter are then used and extended in other chapters.

What This Book Covers

This book discusses what Ajax is and what it means to Web developers, as well as the technologies behind Ajax applications. The early chapters of this book begin with a discussion of the pros and cons of Ajax techniques, and they provide a quick refresher of JavaScript techniques. Working through this book, you'll discover how Ajax applications cross between client-side and server-side development techniques, examine some common Ajax patterns, and see how Ajax links in to existing technologies such as XSLT, web services, and the DOM. The final chapter provides an in-depth case study in creating Ajax applications.

Here's a chapter by chapter breakdown of what to expect:

❑ **Chapter 1: "Introducing Ajax"** — This chapter provides an open-minded assessment of what Ajax is, what is good about it, and what is bad or potentially bad about it. This chapter examines the different technologies and starts you with a solid opening example of a dynamic menu that draws its display from an XML back end.

❑ **Chapter 2: "JavaScript Refresher"** — Before beginning to discuss the building of Ajax applications in any detail, all readers should be starting from the same level. This chapter provides a quick refresher of JavaScript techniques and talks about the DOM, including why it has such an important role in Ajax applications.

❑ **Chapter 3: "Ajax and Server-Side Technologies"** — While Ajax is primarily about building applications with JavaScript and calling the server under the covers, how the server receives, processes, and returns data is of great importance. This chapter introduces the XMLHttpRequest object and looks at how it can call ASP.NET, PHP, and Java applications. The discussion also examines the different ways and formats in which it can return information back to the client.

❏ **Chapter 4: "Ajax Techniques"** — This chapter delves into far greater detail about the `XMLHttpRequest` object. It discusses all the different techniques that can be considered Ajax techniques, regardless of whether they make use of the `XMLHttpRequest` object, hidden frames, hidden inline frames, dynamic image loading, and dynamic script loading. The discussion also considers some of the scenarios in which they might be used.

❏ **Chapter 5: "Working with XML"** — XML has become a de facto standard for storing data in a structured manner and transmitting it. One of the principle Ajax techniques involves using the `XMLHttpRequest` object. While this object isn't restricted to using only XML, it is primarily used with XML. This chapter digs into the rules for creating XML documents and how they can be efficiently navigated and queried.

❏ **Chapter 6: "Debugging and Error Handling"** — Integrated development environments (IDEs) such as Visual Studio, .NET, and Dreamweaver provide the user with a set of tools and a safety net from which to debug. Without them, however, locating errors can be a bind. This chapter talks about how best to debug your JavaScript applications manually and how to write error handlers that mean your Ajax applications can handle the results of any eventuality.

❏ **Chapter 7: "Web Services, APIs, and Mashups"** — Another piece in the Web 2.0 jigsaw puzzle has been the opening up of application functionality by large companies and corporations. Any developer is free to embed maps, photographs, weather forecasts, or music playlists in applications via either web services or APIs. This chapter looks at how these new features can be combined in Ajax applications to create mashups.

❏ **Chapter 8: "XSLT and XPath"** — XSLT and XPath are XML-based technologies that provide more efficient and flexible ways of querying and outputting XML documents (rather than using JavaScript and the DOM). This chapter provides quick tours through the syntax of using both and shows how they can be used to aid with the creation of a rich and seamless user interface.

❏ **Chapter 9: "Patterns"** — Programming is about the modularization and reuse of code. The same problems tend to emerge repeatedly in business, and solutions are created with tried-and-trusted techniques that are known as *patterns*. Ajax applications lend themselves to particular usages (such as page preloading and form validation). This chapter looks at some common patterns that Ajax can be used to implement.

❏ **Chapter 10: "Working with External Data"** — This chapter examines how to use external feeds such as RSS and Atom and how you can create applications to consume data sources that push data at regular intervals. The discussion talks about the structure needed for an example feed and what an application needs to be able to do to read such feeds.

❏ **Chapter 11: "JSON"** — This chapter examines JavaScript's alternative format for transmitting data, JavaScript Object Notation (JSON), which returns a set of array and object literals. The discussion examines what problems this format can be used to solve and how to build a component that returns this format.

❏ **Chapter 12: "In-Depth Example"** — The final chapter provides a large sample application that makes use of Scriptaculous and techniques learned throughout the book, including the `XMLHttpRequest` object, the DOM, and keyboard event handlers.

❏ **Appendix A: "Exercise Answers"** — Answers to the exercises from all of the chapters.

❏ **Appendix B: "Ajax Resources: Frameworks and Libraries"** — A guide on how to install and use some of the most common frameworks and libraries, such as Prototype, Scriptaculous, Dojo, and more.

❑ **Appendix C: "JavaScript Resources"** — A list of useful blogs, tutorials, articles, and web sites dedicated to JavaScript.

❑ **Appendix D: "JavaScript Language Reference"** — An overview of the objects and language constructs of JavaScript.

How This Book Is Structured

This book explains concepts step by step, using working examples and detailed explanations, to demonstrate how to create Ajax applications. Although not every chapter depends on knowledge developed in previous chapters, you will find that most chapters do, so most likely you will find that a front-to-back study approach works best to understand the concepts explained. Wrox Beginning books are developed with a narrative approach to provide users with a methodical and friendly approach. They pursue a philosophy of telling you what you are going to do, guiding you through an example, and then explaining what you have done. The authors of this book have worked closely together (with some great editorial support) to give you a steady and complete tutorial.

What You Need to Use This Book

To gain the most from this book, you should have the following software installed on your system:

❑ A minimum of Windows XP Professional or a version of Linux

❑ At least one of the following two web servers: IIS or Apache

❑ At least one of the following two server-side technologies: PHP (version 5) or ASP.NET (version 2.0)

❑ Internet Explorer version 6 or 7 and Mozilla Firefox version 2

❑ A text editor (such as Notepad or emacs)

Although Ajax applications do not have to call server-side pages, their usability and potential are greatly restricted if they don't. Many of the examples in this book require a web server running either PHP or ASP.NET. Each example is given in both versions, except in rare cases, where the reasons for not doing so will be stated beforehand.

Conventions

To help you get the most from the text and keep track of what's happening, a number of conventions have been used throughout the book.

Try It Out

The "Try It Out" sections are exercises you should work through, following the text in the book.

1. They consist of a set of steps.

2. Each step has a number.

3. Follow the steps with your copy of the code. You can either type in the code yourself or download it from the www.wrox.com web site. Occasionally, there maybe additional items on the web site that won't be available in the book (such as images). These are non-essential for making the examples work.

How It Works

After each "Try It Out" section, the code you've typed will be explained in detail.

> **Boxes like this one hold important, not-to-be forgotten information that is directly relevant to the surrounding text.**

Tips, hints, tricks, and asides to the current discussion are offset and placed in italics like this.

As for styles in the text:

❑ New terms and important words are *italicized* when introduced.

❑ Keyboard strokes are shown as Ctrl+A.

❑ Filenames, URLs, and code in the text appear like so:

`persistence.properties`

❑ Code appears in two different ways:

```
In code examples, new and important code is highlighted with a gray background.
```

```
The gray highlighting is not used for code that's less important in the
present context or has been shown before.
```

Source Code

As you work through the examples in this book, you may choose either to type in all the code manually or to use the source code files that accompany the book. All of the source code used in this book is available for download at www.wrox.com. When you are at the site, simply locate the book's title (either by using the Search box or by using one of the title lists), and click the Download Code link on the book's detail page to obtain all the source code for the book.

Because many books have similar titles, you may find it easiest to search by ISBN. For this book the ISBN is 978-0-470-10675-4.

After you download the code, just decompress it with your favorite compression tool. Alternately, you can go to the main Wrox code download page at www.wrox.com/dynamic/books/download.aspx to see the code available for this book and all other Wrox books.

Errata

Every effort has been made to ensure that there are no errors in the text or in the code. No one is perfect, though, and mistakes do occur. If you find an error in a Wrox book (such as a spelling mistake or a faulty piece of code), the authors and editors would be very grateful for your feedback. By sending in errata, you may save another reader hours of frustration, and at the same time, you will be helping us provide even higher quality information.

To find the errata page for this book, go to www.wrox.com and locate the title using the Search box or one of the title lists. Then, on the book details page, click the Book Errata link. On this page, you can view all errata that have been submitted for this book and posted by Wrox editors. A complete book list including links to each book's errata is also available at www.wrox.com/misc-pages/booklist.shtml.

If you don't spot "your" error on the Book Errata page, go to www.wrox.com/contact/techsupport.shtml, and complete the form there to send us the error you have found. We'll check the information and, if appropriate, post a message to the book's errata page and fix the problem in subsequent editions of the book.

p2p.wrox.com

For author and peer discussion, join the P2P forums at http://p2p.wrox.com. The forums are a Web-based system for you to post messages relating to Wrox books and related technologies and to interact with other readers and technology users. The forums offer a subscription feature to e-mail you topics of interest of your choosing when new posts are made to the forums. Wrox authors, editors, other industry experts, and your fellow readers are present on these forums.

At http://p2p.wrox.com, you will find a number of different forums that will help you not only as you read this book, but also as you develop your own applications. To join the forums:

1. Go to http://p2p.wrox.com, and click the Register link.

2. Read the terms of use, and click Agree.

3. Complete the required information to join, as well as any optional information you wish to provide, and click Submit.

4. You will receive an e-mail with information describing how to verify your account and complete the joining process.

You can read messages in the forums without joining P2P, but in order to post your own messages, you must join.

After you join, you can post new messages and respond to messages other users post. You can read messages at any time on the Web. If you would like to have new messages from a particular forum e-mailed to you, click the "Subscribe to this Forum" icon by the forum name in the forum listing.

For more information about how to use the Wrox P2P, be sure to read the P2P FAQs for answers to questions about how the forum software works, as well as many common questions specific to P2P and Wrox books. To read the FAQs, click the FAQ link on any P2P page.

Introducing Ajax

The path of history is littered with splits, branches, and what-if's. The pace of development of technology is relentless and often merciless. Past battles have seen VHS triumph over Betamax, PCs over microcomputers, Internet Explorer (IE) over Netscape Navigator, and plenty more similar conflicts are just waiting to happen in DVD formats. It doesn't mean that one technology was necessarily better than the other; it's just that one format or technology had the features and functionality required at that time to make it more popular. You'll still find enthusiasts now waxing lyrical about the benefits of Betamax tape, claiming that it was smaller, had better quality and such. It doesn't mean they were wrong. Perhaps they were being a little sad and obsessive, but beneath it all, they had a point.

The evolution of the Internet has had its own such forks. One that continues to rumble is the so-called "fat-client" versus "thin-client" debate. Briefly put, this is the choice between getting your browser to do most of the work, as opposed to getting a server at the other end to do the processing. Initially, in the mid-1990s, it looked as if the "fat-client" ideology was going to win out. The introduction of IE 4 and Netscape Navigator 4 brought with them the advent of Dynamic HTML, which used scripting languages to alter pages so that you could drag and drop items or make menus appear and disappear without requiring a page refresh. Within a year, though, there was a rush toward the "thin-client," with the introduction of server-side technologies such as Active Server Pages and PHP. The client-side techniques still exist, but the model of current Internet and web page usage is broadly based on the server-side method of "enter your data, send the page to the server, and wait for a response."

When one format predominates in the stampede to adoption, you can often forget what was good about the other format. For example, some aspects of page validation can be performed equally as well on the browser. If you were to type "fake e-mail" into an e-mail textbox, you wouldn't need to go to the server to check this. JavaScript can perform a check for you equally as efficiently, and also much more quickly. While plenty of people sensibly do validation on both client and server, many pages attempt to perform the processing only on the server. If there has been one continual bugbear about the Web, it is that it is slow. Timeouts, page-not-found errors, unresponsive buttons and links haven't gone away, despite the fact that bandwidth has increased tenfold. So, other ways of addressing this sluggishness are becoming more common.

Companies have begun to reevaluate the way they are doing things to see if they can improve the user experience on several levels — making pages faster and more responsive, but also offering a more seamless and richer experience. This often involved going back to old techniques. The first and best example of creating web applications in this "new" way was Google's Gmail. Google also used these techniques in the applications Google Suggest and Google Maps, although neither application showcases them quite in such an effective way or enjoys quite the same notoriety. Windows Live Mail (formerly named Kahuna), Amazon's search engine A9.com, Yahoo's flickr.com for organizing photos online all were lacking a common way of describing their features, until an online article in 2005 changed all that by christening these techniques *Ajax*.

What Is Ajax?

Ajax is the catchy term coined by Jesse James Garrett in his 2005 article for Adaptive Path called "Ajax: A New Approach to Web Applications," which can still be found at http://adaptivepath.com/publications/essays/archives/000385.php. You should read this article if you haven't already, although not before you finish this chapter, because it can be slightly misleading as to exactly what Ajax is! Ajax is also an acronym, but for the same reasons, let's defer explaining just what it stands for right now. Ajax didn't exist before this article, but the features the article described certainly did.

In short, Ajax is a set of programming techniques or a particular approach to web programming. These programming techniques involve being able to seamlessly update a web page or a section of a web application with input from the server, but without the need for an immediate page refresh. This doesn't mean that the browser doesn't make a connection to the web server. Indeed, the original article paints a slightly incomplete picture in that it fails to mention that server-side technologies are often still needed. It is very likely that your page, or data from which the page is drawn, must still be updated at some point by a rendezvous with the server. What differs in the Ajax model is that the position at which the page is updated is moved. We'll look at the two models in more detail shortly.

Garrett's article envisaged a world where web applications could be mirrored Windows applications in their functionality. "Richness," "responsiveness," and "simplicity" were the key words involved. He envisioned a new breed of applications, one that would close the gap between the worlds of Windows and web applications. He cited Gmail, Google Suggest, and Google Maps as key exponents of this new approach.

The article — and even the term "Ajax" — polarized people. While plenty of people loved it and took up its creed, many developers criticized aspects from the name "Ajax," calling it banal, to the techniques described, which weren't (by any stretch of the imagination) new. There was definitely a hint of the modern art hater's typical criticism about abstract art — "Hey, I could do that and so could my 10-year-old" — about the complaints. Just because people could have been using these techniques to create their web pages and applications didn't mean they had been. Unfortunately, jealousy and backbiting reigned.

What emerged, though, was a consensus that the techniques and ideas that Jesse James Garrett described really struck a chord (such as "*If we were designing the Web from scratch for applications, we wouldn't make users wait around*" and "*The challenges are for the designers of these applications: to forget what we think we know about the limitations of the Web and begin to imagine a wider, richer range of possibilities*"). It was a call to arms to use existing mature and stable methods to create web applications rather than the latest flaky beta. It invited developers to leverage the existing knowledge of JavaScript, style sheets, and the Document Object Model (DOM), instead of sweating blood to get up to speed on the latest tag-based page-building language. It was liberating, and overnight job ads were reworded — "Wanted: developers with five years JavaScript Ajax experience."

This doesn't really give you a feel for what Ajax does, and as always, the best way is to walk though some Ajax techniques currently being used on the Web.

Ajax in Action

Undoubtedly, the Ajax "killer" application is Gmail, which allows users to edit and update their e-mails and inbox without hundreds of page refreshes. Overnight, it convinced people who would use applications such as Outlook, Outlook Express, or Thunderbird on their own machines to use a web-based e-mail system instead. Unfortunately, Gmail can't easily be demonstrated without signing up, and currently signups are available only to a limited amount of countries. So, let's take a look at some other examples.

flickr

Yahoo's `flickr.com` is a photo-organizing site that lets you "sort, store, search and share photos online." Previously, flickr had used Flash as the main tool behind its photo display interface, but in May 2005 it announced that it was moving over to using Dynamic HTML and Ajax (`http://blog.flickr .com/flickrblog/2005/05/from_flash_to_a.html`). You have to sign up for an account to be able to see the tool in action, but because it's free and photo manipulation tools on web applications are a great way of demonstrating Ajax techniques, you should look into it.

Once you've logged in, you can access the tool via the Organize menu by selecting the Organize All Your Photos option (Figure 1-1). You can drag and drop photos into a single batch, and then you can rotate them and amend their tags.

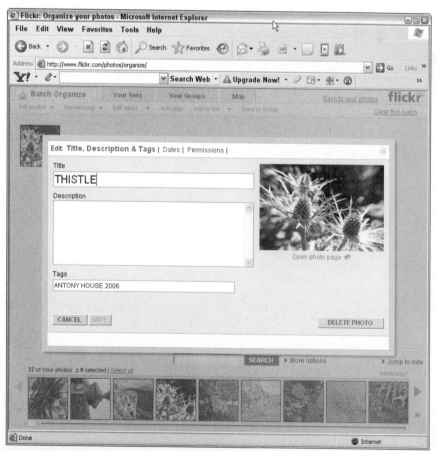

Figure 1-1: Organize your photos option.

This is all done seamlessly using Ajax techniques. In addition, the "Send to Group," "Add to Set," and "Blog this" buttons also perform their functionality right there on the page. flickr even talks about the fact that the pages use an "old technology" to achieve this. The Dynamic HTML techniques replaced Flash because Flash requires you to have the latest Macromedia plug-in installed and the wrapper for Flash can take a long time to load. Users complained about this. Flash is a great application, but here Ajax techniques prove more efficient.

Basecamp

Basecamp is a web-based tool for managing and tracking projects. You can find it at www.basecamphq.com. Once again, you have to sign up to use it, but there is a free sign-up option with a reasonable range of capabilities included.

Basecamp employs Ajax when adding people to a company, adding companies to a project, adding/editing/deleting/reordering/completing to-do items, adding/editing/deleting/reordering to-do lists, adding/editing/deleting time items, and renaming attachments to messages (Figure 1-2).

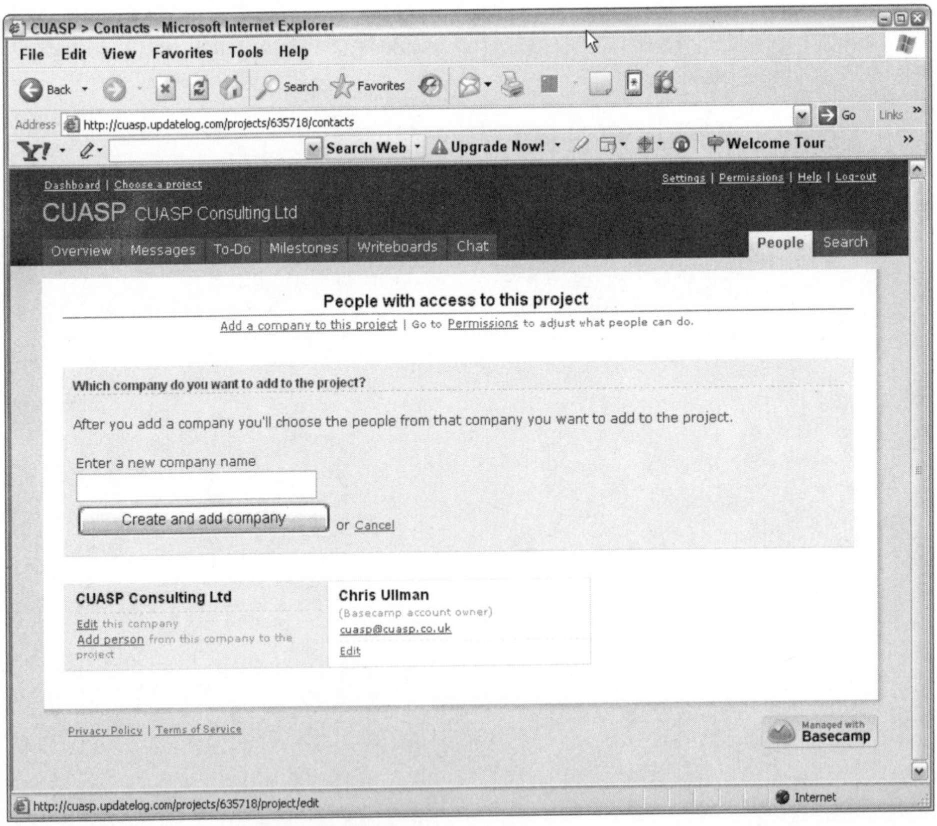

Figure 1-2: Adding people to a company.

When you click to add a person to the company, the dialog drops down smoothly without a screen refresh. Also, the hints and tips panel disappears when you select the button "Don't show this again."

Not all of Basecamp employs Ajax, but what makes it compelling is the mixture of server-side interaction and Ajax techniques that aren't overused, but are put into practice when they can be of benefit to the end-user experience.

Amazon (A9.com)

Amazon is well known for its store site, but less well known for its search engine, www.A9.com, which combines search results from a whole host of sources. Search engines have remained fairly static in terms of their user interface since their inception. You type a word and click on Search. What has changed is the complexity of the searches behind the engine and the different sources you can now interrogate. Amazon's A9 allows you to search on a single term across media such as movies, books, Wiki pages, and blogs. Figure 1-3 shows what a typical search on "Tour De France" would yield.

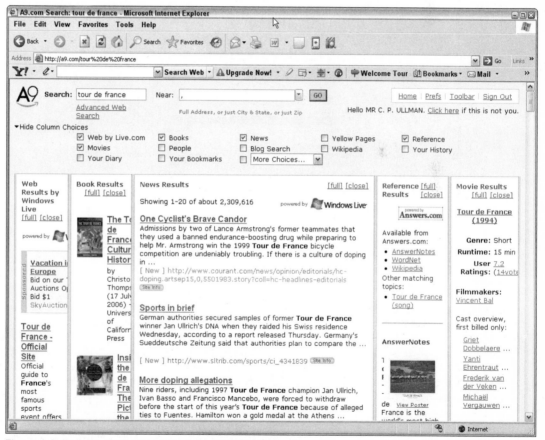

Figure 1-3: Results of a typical search on "Tour De France."

Ajax comes into play where you click on the check boxes to add or remove searches. You can click on the People link, and a box will appear without a refresh, even though you didn't include it in the original search. You can uncheck the References and Movies boxes, and immediately these links disappear. It's instantaneous and very much in the spirit of a rich and responsive user interface.

Google Suggest and Google Maps

Google Suggest and Google Maps were both mentioned in the Adaptive Path article as good examples. These are mentioned last, though, because their use of Ajax techniques is less pervasive than in the other web applications mentioned and because they are probably overfamiliar as examples. Google Suggest is a version of a search engine that attempts to offer suggestions as you type other similar searches. As shown in Figure 1-4, it can be found at `www.google.com/webhp?complete=1&hl=en`.

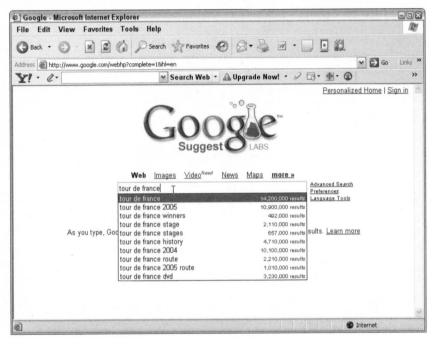

Figure 1-4: Google Suggest.

One thing that makes me slightly reluctant to recommend this site for Ajax techniques is that auto-suggest boxes have a bad press with some users. They can be seen as intrusive or confusing or both. Users of Short Message Service (SMS) text services on mobile phones will be only too familiar with the sense of frustration when words such as "no" are helpfully changed to "on." This has much to do with the code that does the "predicting" of what you're going to type. In Google Suggest, this is a good application of the technique, but when using something similar to perform form validation, you should be careful not to intrude on the usability of the form. A simple error message will often suffice.

Google Maps uses Ajax. When a location on the map is pinpointed it will load the relevant section of the map. If you then scroll along, rather than keeping the entire map in memory, it will load the map in blocks as and when you need them. You can see this in action in Figure 1-5; the loading is very fast indeed.

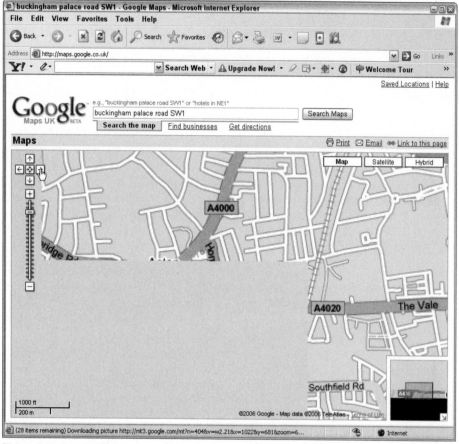

Figure 1-5: Google Maps.

This is another example of using just one technique to enhance the usability and end-user experience of a site.

Other Sites

Plenty of other sites employ Ajax techniques, and, of course, it's not possible to preview them all. A good place to start looking is A Venture Forth's list of the top 10 Ajax applications as created by start-ups. This can be found at: www.aventureforth.com/2005/09/06/top-10-ajax-applications/. Its list contains an online calendar, a word processor, an RSS reader, a project management tool and a version of Google Suggest for Amazon Suggest. This set gives a nice overview of the kinds of things you can put to use. You're limited only by your imagination.

Last, there is a good list of the kind of tasks you might use Ajax techniques to perform at the site http://swik.net/Ajax/Places+To+Use+Ajax. It's a Wiki, so it's interactive, and people are constantly adding suggestions. Here are some of the better suggestions:

❑ **Dynamic menus** — Web sites are constantly changing beasts, and having a rigid structure imposed on them only means more work when the structure changes. Menus are more responsive when handled by client-side code, and you can pull the data to fill them using Ajax.

❑ **AutoSave** — A good behind-the-scenes procedure is to save the contents of a textbox without a user's prompting.

❑ **AutoComplete** — Predictive text phrases, like Google Suggest, if done well, can speed up the process of typing.

❑ **Paginating or organizing large numbers of results** — When large amounts of data are returned by a query such as a search, then you could use an Ajax application to sort, organize, and display the data in manageable chunks.

❑ **User-to-user communication** — You would probably think twice about using MSN Messenger if you had to refresh the screen every time you sent or received a message. With online forums or chat areas on web applications, however, this can often be the case. Having communication come up instantly with another user in a web application is a good place where Ajax could be used.

You can see that these kinds of tasks are already achieved using server-side technologies. These tasks, though, could be better accomplished by reverting to the client to perform some of the processing, to achieve a faster and more responsive site.

Bad Examples

Of course, not all examples of Ajax in use on the Web are good ones. As already mentioned, not all areas are suitable for use with Ajax. In Alex Bosworth's list of Ajax mistakes at http://alexbosworth .backpackit.com/pub/67688, a new note has been appended to the list "Using Ajax for the sake of Ajax." Perhaps what irritates a lot of Ajax's detractors is that developers will take a cutting-edge technology or methodology and apply it, regardless of its suitability for a particular task.

So, what exactly makes for a bad Ajax example? Providing some URLs might be instructive and a little cheeky, but probably would encourage a lot of flames, not to mention lawsuits. It's also quite subjective. Let's define "bad" examples as sites that use Ajax and that are slower in what they achieve than they might be with a simple submit to the server.

For example, you may have seen a search engine paginator that, while it doesn't update the page, takes longer to return the results than it might otherwise do if it just sent the query off to the server. The problem is that by shifting the focus back to the client, you are also partially dependent on the user's machine resources and the browser involved. If you give them large amounts of data to process, then a Pentium 2 isn't going to process it as fast as Pentium 4.

Another bad example of Ajax would be in form validation if you actually interrupt what the users are typing before they've finished typing it. You don't want to interrupt the normal pattern of how a user types or enters data. One of the key aims of Ajax must be to improve the user's overall experience. In some cases, this might mean that the use of Ajax is very subtle or barely noticeable, but when it comes to user interfaces, that is a good thing.

Now it's time to talk about what Ajax stands for and why what it stands for isn't necessarily what Ajax is all about right now.

Ajax: The Acronym

If you read the Adaptive Path article, then you'll already know that Ajax the acronym stands for *Asynchronous JavaScript and XML*. Here's a curveball: Ajax doesn't have to use XML, and neither does it have to be asynchronous. Ajax applications can use XML, and they can be updated asynchronously. These are quite common tricks and techniques used to update the page, but they are not tied to these technologies.

To reiterate an earlier point, Ajax is "a set of programming techniques," "a particular approach to web programming." It isn't rigid; it isn't like a members-only club, if you don't use one technique then it isn't Ajax; it's an overall guiding philosophy. How you achieve these objectives on the client is up to you. The objectives, though, prove a good starting point. Jesse James Garrett mentioned in the article "several technologies... coming together in powerful new ways." Here are the technologies he specifically mentioned:

- ❑ XHTML and CSS
- ❑ The Document Object Model (DOM)
- ❑ JavaScript
- ❑ XML and XSLT
- ❑ The `XMLHttpRequest` object

In reality, to create an application using Ajax techniques you need only three of these: XHTML, the DOM, and JavaScript. If you do any amount of development with Ajax techniques, though, you will almost certainly need to use all of the technologies at some point.

You'll also probably need a server-side language to handle any interaction with the server. This is most typically one of the following three:

- ❑ PHP
- ❑ ASP.NET (Visual Basic.Net/C#)
- ❑ Java

When building a web page, you'll probably have encountered many or most of these technologies, but perhaps not all, so it's worth having a quick reminder of what each one is and does, its role in web development, and how it pertains to Ajax.

XHTML and CSS

You will be familiar with HyperText Markup Language (HTML), the lingua franca of the Web, but perhaps not so familiar with its successor, eXtensible HyperText Markup Language (XHTML). XHTML is the more exacting version of HTML. In fact, it is the HTML standard specified as an XML document. The main difference with this is that whereas HTML has been fairly easygoing and the browser will make a reasonable attempt to display anything you place in tags, XHTML now follows XML's rules. For example, XML documents must be well formed (tags are correctly opened and closed, and nested), and so must XHTML pages. For example, the following is correct nesting:

```
<div>
<h1>
```

```
                    This is a correctly nested H1 tag
    </h1>
    </div>
```

The following is incorrect nesting:

```
    <div>
    <h1>
                    This is an incorrectly nested H1 tag

    </div>
    </h1>
```

Although it might seem to go against the grain of HTML's easygoing and easy-to-code nature, if a page isn't correctly constructed, then you won't be able to perform the kind of Ajax techniques discussed in this book. To use the DOM, the page has to be correctly formed. Otherwise, you won't be able to access the different parts of the page.

Cascading Style Sheets (CSS) are the templates behind HTML pages that describe the presentation and layout of the text and data contained within an HTML page. CSS is of particular interest to the developer because changes made to the style sheet are instantly reflected in the display of the page. The style sheets are linked into the document commonly with the HTML <link> tag, although it is possible (but not preferable) to specify style attributes for each individual HTML tag on a page. You can also access CSS properties via the DOM.

In the design of any web site or web application, you should make the division between the content/structure of the page and the presentation as clear as possible. Suppose you have 100 pages and you specify the font size on all 100 pages as a style attribute. When you're forced to change the font size you will have to change it on each individual page, instead of changing it just once in the style sheet.

Having a style sheet isn't 100 percent essential, but to keep good organization, style sheets are an indispensable aid.

The Document Object Model (DOM)

The DOM is a representation of the web page as a hierarchy or tree structure, where every part of the page (the graphics, the text boxes, the buttons, and the text itself) is modeled by the browser.

Before IE 4 and Netscape Navigator 4, not every part of the web page was accessible to code. In fact, changing text on a web page had to be done by using server-side technologies or not at all. The whole page was termed a *document*, and that document contained all the HTML tags and text that made up the page. The DOM is specified as a standard by the World Wide Web Consortium, also known as W3C (www.w3.org), and so it is a standard way for all browsers to represent the page. You can pretty much guarantee that when you use JavaScript to alter the background color of a page in IE, it will correctly do so in Mozilla, Safari, or Opera as well. There are exceptions to the rule, though. There are several non-standard methods in IE, and items such as ActiveX controls can't be used in the other browsers.

You can add items to the DOM or alter them using a scripting language (such as JavaScript or VBScript), and they will appear on the page immediately. They are typically addressed in the format that addresses the page in hierarchical format, such as the following code, which addresses a button called "button" on a form and changes the text of that button. Note that in this code fragment, the form element has the name attribute set to form1:

```
document.form1.button.value = "Click Me";
```

Or, you can use methods that can access the specific elements or subsets of elements on the page, such as the `document.getElementById` method, which will return a specific instance of an element that matches the criteria:

```
var myTextBox = document.getElementById("myTextbox");
```

You can then assign values to the variable you have created to alter the values. To make the text box invisible, you could call the following:

```
myTextBox.style.visibility = "visible";
```

Another related method is the `getElementsByTagName` method. The `getElementsByTagName` method will return an array of elements on the web page of type `NodeList`, all with a given tag name, even if there is only one occurrence of that element on the page. The following code will return all the image elements on the page:

```
var imageElements = document.getElementsByTagName("img");
```

It is also possible to assemble the page by adding new sections to the document known as *nodes*. These can be elements, attributes, or even plain text. For example, you could create a span tag that contains a short message and add it to the page as follows:

```
var newTag = document.createElement("span");
var newText = document.createTextNode("Here is some New Text. Ho Hum.");
newTag.appendChild(newText);
document.body.appendChild(newTag);
```

All of these DOM techniques are applicable to the client side, and as a result, the browser can update the page or sections of it instantly. Ajax leans on these capabilities very heavily to provide the rich user experience. Also, as mentioned, these techniques have been around since version 4 of IE. It's just that they have been underused. The DOM is an important topic, and it is discussed in much more detail in Chapter 2.

JavaScript

JavaScript is the scripting language of choice of most web developers. You must know JavaScript to be able to use this book. This book doesn't teach JavaScript, although a quick refresher of the most salient points is available in Chapter 2.

Ajax techniques aren't solely the preserve of JavaScript. VBScript also offers the same capabilities for dynamic updates as well — albeit tied to IE only. While JavaScript has a standard specified in the ECMAScript standard, JavaScript was initially created in Netscape Navigator before such standards existed. Microsoft created its own version of JavaScript (called *JScript*) in parallel, and as a result, each browser's version of JavaScript is slightly different. Although JavaScript remains a very powerful method for updating your web pages, some amount of dual-coding is necessary to make sure that the web pages and applications function in the correct way across browsers, When not possible, some error-handling code will also be necessary.

A fair amount of Ajax code will deal with handling cross-browser code and handling errors if and when they arise, unless you can guarantee that your target audience will only ever use one browser (such as on a local intranet). This is an unfortunate set of circumstances that even new versions of IE and Firefox are not able to rectify. Later chapters address both of these dilemmas.

XML, XSLT, and XPath

XML is another familiar cornerstone, the language that is used to describe and structure data, to any web developer.

With XML comes a whole plethora of supporting technologies, each allocated its own individual niche. An XML document contains no information about how it should be displayed or searched. Once the data is rendered as an XML document, you typically need other technologies to search and display information from it. IE and Firefox both contain XML engines that can parse XML documents.

XSLT is a language for *transforming* XML documents into other XML documents. It isn't restricted to transforming XML documents into XML. You could also specify HTML or pure text as the output format. When you transform a document, you start with a source XML document, such as the following fragment:

```
<HotelList>
  <Hotel>
    <Name>Hotel Shakespeare</Name>
    <Rooms>50</Rooms>
    <City>Birmingham</City>
  </Hotel>
  <Hotel>
    <Name>Hotel Washington</Name>
    <Rooms>500</Rooms>
    <City>Chicago</City>
  </Hotel>
</HotelList>
```

You apply a second document in XSLT to the first document. The XSLT document contains a set of rules for how the transformation should be conducted, as shown here:

```
<xsl:stylesheet version="1.0"
    xmlns:xsl="http://www.w3.org/1999/XSL/Transform">

  <xsl:template match="/">
    <table>
    <tr>
        <td>
          Hotel Name
        </td>
        <td>
        Number of Rooms
        </td>
        <td>
        Location
        </td>
    </tr>
      <xsl:for-each select="//Hotel">
```

```
            <tr>
              <td>
                  <xsl:value-of select="Name" />
              </td>
              <td>
                  <xsl:value-of select="Rooms" />
              </td>
              <td>
                  <xsl:value-of select="City" />
              </td>
            </tr>
          </xsl:for-each>
        </table>
    </xsl:template>

</xsl:stylesheet>
```

And you get a resulting XML document (in this case, also an XHTML document) looking like this:

```
        <table>
        <tr>
            <td>
              Hotel Name
            </td>
            <td>
            Number of Rooms
            </td>
            <td>
            Location
            </td>
        </tr>
          <tr>
            <td>
                Hotel Shakespeare
            </td>
            <td>
                50
            </td>
            <td>
                Birmingham
            </td>
          </tr>
          <tr>
            <td>
                Hotel Washington
            </td>
            <td>
                500
            </td>
            <td>
                Chicago
            </td>
          </tr>
        </table>
```

You could then insert the XHTML document fragment into the HTML page dynamically to update the page.

XSLT is another standard maintained by W3C. Both IE and Mozilla have XSLT processors; however, they don't always treat their XSLT documents in the same way. XSLT uses another language, XPath, to query the XML document when applying its transformations. XPath queries are used to address elements within the original XML document, such as the following:

```
<xsl:for-each select="//Hotel">
```

The `//Hotel` statement instructs the browser's XSLT processor to look for elements called `<Hotel>` that are descendants of the root element `<HotelList>`. XPath queries can be used to locate specific items or groups of items within an XML document, using a syntax that is superficially similar to the way browsers can locate web pages, with the following as an example:

```
//HotelList/Hotel/Rooms
```

These techniques can be used to retrieve sections of data and display it on the page using the browser. Again, they are able to offer instantaneous updates without the need for a trip back to the server. Both XSLT and XPath are discussed in more detail in Chapter 8.

The XMLHttpRequest Object

If there's one thing you haven't come across before, it's likely to be the XMLHttpRequestObject. Microsoft introduced quite an obscure little ActiveX control in Internet Explorer version 5 (IE 5) called the `XMLHttp` object. Of course, ActiveX controls are tied to IE, so shortly afterward, Mozilla engineers followed suit and created their own version for Mozilla 1 and Netscape 7, the corresponding `XMLHttpRequest` object. The status of these objects was elevated considerably because of their inclusion in the original Ajax article. They are now more commonly referred to singularly as the `XMLHttpRequest` object, and, in IE 7, there is a native `XMLHttpRequest` object in addition to the ActiveX Control. Versions of this object have been included in Safari 1.2 and Opera as well.

But what does it do? Well, it allows a developer to submit and receive XML documents in the background. Previously, you could use hidden frames or IFrames to perform this task for you, but the `XMLHttpRequest` is rather more sophisticated in the ways in which it allows you to send and pick up data.

Unfortunately, because it isn't yet standard, that means there are still two separate ways of creating it. In versions of IE prior to version 7, it is created as an `ActiveXObject` in JavaScript as follows:

```
var xHRObject = new ActiveXObject("Microsoft.XMLHTTP");
```

> There are several versions of the MSXML library with respective `ProgIDs` to instantiate `XMLHttp` object. Specifically, you cannot instantiate any version of `XMLHttp` object higher than `'Msxml2.XMLHTTP.3.0'` with the given version independent `ProgID Microsoft.XMLHTTP`. For the examples in this book, though, this will be sufficient.

In Mozilla Firefox, IE 7, and other browsers, it is created as follows:

```
var xHRObject = new XMLHttpRequest();
```

In turn, this means that you have to do a little bit of browser feature detection before you can determine in which way the object needs to be created. Because ActiveX controls and objects are unique to IE, you can test for them by attempting to call the `ActiveXObject` method of the window object. For IE 7, Mozilla Firefox, Safari, and Opera, there is an `XMLHttpRequest` method. These calls use implicit type conversion to return `true` or `false`, depending on which browser is being used to view the page. In other words, if there is an `ActiveXObject` on that browser, it will return `true`. If not, it will return `false`.

Typically your browser feature detection and object creation code would look something like this:

```
var xHRObject = false;
if (window.XMLHttpRequest)
{
xHRObject = new XMLHttpRequest();
}
else if (window.ActiveXObject)
{
xHRObject = new ActiveXObject("Microsoft.XMLHTTP");
}
else
{
    //Do something to handle non-Ajax supporting browsers.
}
```

There are plans to standardize this functionality in level 3 of the DOM specification, but until then, you will need to make allowances for this fact.

The role the `XMLHttpRequest` object plays is a major one. It is used heavily in Google's Gmail to ferry the data backward and forward behind the scenes. In fact, it can provide the asynchronous part of the Ajax application. It uses the `onreadystatechange` event to indicate when it has finished loading information. You can tell it to get an XML document as shown here:

```
xHRObject.open("GET", "SuiteList.xml", true);
```

Then, at a later point, you can check the value of the `readyState` property to see if it has finished loading and, if it has, then extract the information that you need.

The `XMLHttpRequest` object is misleading in one sense, in that you don't have to transfer XML with it. You can quite happily use it to transfer HTML or just plain text back and forth as well. The `XMLHttp Request` is examined in more detail in Chapter 4. The difference between synchronous and asynchronous methods of data transfer is examined later in this chapter.

Server-Side Technologies

The last piece of this equation (and one not really touched on in Garrett's original article) is the server-side technologies that Ajax will need to use. This book uses PHP and ASP.NET (where appropriate) to service requests to the server. Any one method is not better than another; rather, you should use the one that you are most familiar with.

As with JavaScript, this book does not teach you how to use PHP and ASP.NET. It's expected that you will know either one or the other. Server-side technologies are examined more closely in Chapter 3, but the current discussion attempts to avoid going into them in too much detail because they provide the glue for Ajax, rather than the backbone.

With all the pieces of the Ajax puzzle in place, let's now look more closely at how Ajax changes the traditional method of web interaction.

The Ajax Application Model

At first, the Web intended to display only HTML documents. This means that the classic web application has an "enter your data, send the page to the server, and wait for a response" model, intended only for web pages. Second, there is the problem of synchronous communication. A good example of a real-world synchronous device is a public telephone booth. You have to call somebody, and that person has to be available to communicate with you. With many public telephone booths, you cannot get the receiver to call you back. You can only call the receiver and impart information. After the call you must leave the booth, as quite often there will be other people waiting to use it. If the receiver hasn't given you the information you need, then that is too bad. An example of asynchronous communication would be with your home phone where you phone someone, and they can't give you the information you need right now, so they agree to call you back when they do have the information, whenever that might be.

On the Web, synchronous means that the user requests an HTML page, and the browser sends an HTTP request to a web server on his or her behalf (Figure 1-6). The server performs the processing, then returns a response to the browser in the form of an HTML page. The browser displays the HTML page requested. The browser always initiates the requests, whereas the web server merely responds to such browser requests. The web server never initiates requests — the communication is always one way. The "request/response" cycle is synchronous, during which the user has to wait.

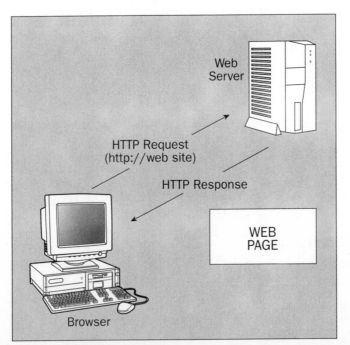

Figure 1-6: Synchronous model.

As mentioned, this model works for browsing web pages, but the development of more and more complex web applications means that this model is now breaking down. The first area in which it breaks down is that of performance. The "enter, send, and wait" approach means there is wasted time. Second, whenever you refresh a page, you are sending a new request back to the server. This takes up extra server processing, and it leads to time lost while waiting for a response and higher bandwidth consumption caused by redundant page refreshes. The underlying problem is that there is a complete lack of two-way, real-time communication capability, and the server has no way in which to initiate updates.

This scenario leads to slow, unreliable, low-productivity and inefficient web applications. You have two basic problems here: one of having to wait for a response for the server and one of the server not being able to initiate an update. The Ajax application model seeks to produce higher performance, thereby creating more efficient web applications by subtly altering the way in which this works.

Ajax introduces the idea of a "partial screen update" to the web application model. In an Ajax application, only the user interface elements that contain new information will be updated. The rest of the user interface should be unchanged. This means that you don't have to send as much information down the line, and you're not left waiting for a response because the previous page is already operational. This model enables continuous operation of a web page, and it also means that work done on the page doesn't have to follow a straight, predictable pattern.

Instead of a synchronous model, you can now have either an asynchronous model or a polling one. In an Ajax application, the server can leave a notification today when it's ready, and the client will pick it up when it wants to. Or, the client can poll the server at regular intervals to see if the server's ready, but it can continue with other operations in the meantime, as shown in Figure 1-7.

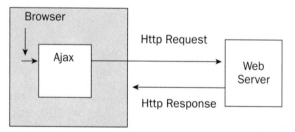

Figure 1-7: Model in Ajax application.

As a result, the user can continue to use the application while the client requests information from the server in the background. When the new data finally does turn up, only the related parts of the user interface need to be updated.

Why Should I Use Ajax?

We've looked at the model, but let's now spell out in real terms the advantages of using Ajax to create your applications. This is my equivalent of the second-hand car dealer's hard-sell.

Partial Page Updating

You don't have to update the data on an entire page. You can update only the portions of the page that require it. This should mean no full page refreshes, less data to be transferred, and an improved flow for the user experience. You don't have to stutter from page to page.

Invisible Data Retrieval

The longer you look at a web page, the greater its chance to go out of date. With an Ajax application, even though on the surface the web page might not be told to do anything, it could be updating itself behind the scenes.

Constant Updating

Because you're not waiting for a page refresh every time, and because Ajax can retrieve data under the covers, the web application can be constantly updated. A traditional software application such as Word or Outlook will alter the menus it displays or the views it shows, dependent on its configuration, or the data it holds or the situation or circumstances it finds itself in. It doesn't have to wait for a server or user to perform an action before it can download new mail or apply a new template. Ajax techniques enable web applications to behave more like Windows applications because of this.

Smooth Interfaces

An interface that doesn't have to be changed is almost inevitably a user interface that is easier to use. Ajax can cut both ways here in that you can use it to modify parts of the interface and simply confuse users by changing the ground beneath their feet. In theory, by making subtle alterations, you could aid the user's passage through an interface or wizard and speed up the process.

Simplicity and Rich Functionality

As shown in the previous examples, some of the most impressive Ajax applications are those where you had to look for the Ajax functionality, such as Basecamp. If Ajax can be used to make your applications simpler while improving the user's experience, then that must be an improvement.

Drag and Drop

Drag-and-drop functionality is one of the neatest features of most software applications, from Windows Explorer to Windows Desktop. It doesn't strictly qualify as Ajax functionality. It's something that's been possible for a great many years in web applications, even before the introduction of the XMLHttp Request object. Most developers seem to opt for Flash or some similarly heavyweight solution rather than using the JavaScript and DOM solutions. In the reassessment of user-interface creation techniques that Ajax has introduced, drag-and-drop functionality can be used to manage front-end changes, and then these changes are submitted via Ajax to the server. For example, you drag several items on the screen into new positions, and then you log out. Later, when you come back, those items are located in the same positions.

With such a host of benefits, it might be difficult to imagine why everyone isn't switching over to using Ajax applications. There are definitely quite a few pitfalls, though, to consider.

When Not to Use Ajax

Once you've learned Ajax techniques, you shouldn't go back and tear up all your old web pages and start again. Rather, you should consider how you could improve the usability of your pages and whether Ajax is a solution that will help improve them. Without advances in usability, you might as well not bother at all.

A considerable number of articles explain why you shouldn't use Ajax techniques in certain situations, such as those found at the following URLS:

❑ **Ajax sucks** — `http://www.usabilityviews.com/ajaxsucks.html` (a spoof article on Jakob Nielsen's why frames suck)

❑ **Ajax promise or hype** — `http://www.quirksmode.org/blog/archives/2005/03/ajax_promise_or.html`

❑ **Ajax is not cool** — `http://www.lastcraft.com/blog/index.php?p=19`

Poor Responsiveness

Perhaps the most glaring problem noticed with Ajax is when it is used in theory to speed up the interaction, and it actually slows down the page.

If you continually use Ajax to submit data to the server, then you could find that the page has slowed down. Alternately, if the server returns large datasets to the client, you can find that your browser will struggle to cope with the data in a timely manner. In theory, a search engine might seem like a good place to use Ajax to break up the data so that you don't have to refresh the page when you move from pages 1–10 to pages 11–20. In reality, you'd still be much better off, though, using the server to slice the dataset up into small chunks, rather than getting the browser to attempt to deal with a 1,000-record-plus dataset. Intelligent and judicious applications of Ajax techniques are the key here.

Breaks the Back Button on Your Browser

Ajax applications can, if not judiciously applied, break the Back button on your browser.

One of the prime examples of a great Ajax application, Gmail, uses the Back and Forward buttons very effectively. Also, there are plenty of web sites out there that don't use Ajax techniques that disable the Back button anyway. In my list of crimes, this one doesn't rate particularly highly.

Breaking Bookmarks and Blocking Search Engine Indexes

If you bookmark a page in an Ajax application, you could, of course, end up with a different page in your list of favorites. JavaScript creates a particular view of the page, and this "view" has no dependence on the original URL. Also, conversely, with a dynamic menu system, you might think you have shut off part of your site that is no longer accessible via the menu and regard it as defunct when, in fact, others can still access it. Plenty of sites have thousands of hits for old versions of pages that just cause errors on the server.

It is possible to create web applications that handle bookmarks and Back buttons correctly. A good example of how to handle both effectively can be found at `http://onjava.com/lpt/a/6293`.

Strain on the Browser

If you push the entire burden for processing data back to the browser, you then become more reliant on the browser and the user's machine to do the processing for you. Waiting for the browser to process a page is no better than waiting for a web server to get back to you with a response. In fact, in some cases, it could be worse if it is IE you're waiting for and it decides to hog all of the processing space on your machine while it's doing the processing and make the whole machine respond at a crawl.

You should be getting a feel by now that each of these reasons is qualified — the use of Ajax can hinder usability, not aid it; however, if development is considered, if you take steps to address the problems with Back buttons and bookmarks, then there's no reason why Ajax techniques shouldn't be used. It does raise a question, though.

If Garrett's seminal article was so flawed, then why is it so popular? This might be because it articulated what a lot of people were thinking and doing already, but didn't have a name for. It didn't matter that there were some inaccuracies about the methods of execution. It completely struck a chord with developers. You could liken it to some of the early Beatles recordings that weren't the best played, but they're rightfully remembered affectionately because the tunes always shone through. Even developers who had issues with the article agreed that it described a sensible approach to creating web applications and that it revisited old techniques that had been either ignored or forgotten.

Who Can/Can't Use Ajax?

It might go without saying that not everyone will be able to use Ajax. You should always be aware of any portion of your web site that might exclude some users by its use of a particular technology, and you should consider how to address that portion of the target audience.

Here are some of the main considerations:

❑   Users of reasonably modern versions of the main browsers (IE 4+, Mozilla Firefox/Netscape 7+, Safari, and Opera 5+) will find they can use Ajax applications just fine. Users of older browsers won't be able to.

❑   People who have scripting languages disabled won't be able to use Ajax (or indeed JavaScript applications). Before you scoff, just remember that after some of the recent vulnerabilities in both IE and Microsoft Outlook, the initial advice from Microsoft was to disable active scripting until a patch was in place to fix the vulnerability.

❑   People browse applications offline. Again, it might almost seem a prehistoric way of using the Web, but it is, in fact, a very modern way, too. Mobile communications charge a lot more for bandwidth and offer a lot less throughput, so it's very common to log in, download, and log out. Sites such as AvantGo allow you to browse a series of web pages offline that you have subscribed to. If Ajax were included in these pages, it would break them.

Once again, be aware of who your target audience is and what their needs are.

Create Your Own Example

You shouldn't come away from this chapter feeling "so why bother using Ajax?" This hasn't been the point. There is a time and a place for using Ajax correctly. Consider it like a fast car. Sure, it's capable of doing 0–60 mph in 7 seconds and can reach top speeds of 150 mph. But in town or on the freeway is not the place to demonstrate those capabilities. You will incur the wrath of the rest of the populace, not to mention the police. The same goes for Ajax. If you use it at every available opportunity, you won't find quite as many visitors to your site as you perhaps envisioned.

Creating an Ajax application is about the design and thinking about how the user interface and experience will be improved by your application. We're going to create a quick example that shows how you can use the XMLHttpRequest object and XML files to create a dynamic menu system for a business scenario.

The business scenario is this. You have a travel company whose web site displays information about hotels and suites. The hotels wish to display booking information about only those suites that currently are available. This information is published as an XML file. It is quite common for companies to publish data as text or XML files to the same location at a given interval because it can usually be generated automatically. This example does not create the facility to publish the XML file, but rather checks and fetches new data from a given location every 10 seconds. This, in turn, will have the effect of updating the options on the menu system without the need for a page refresh.

Note that this example is quite complex. It demonstrates a meaningful way in which Ajax can be used. You should skim over the code. Later chapters discuss the XMLHttpRequest object, the use of the DOM, and scenarios in which you can use XML and XSL in your applications.

Try It Out   **First Ajax Example**

1. Create a new folder in your web server's root directory called BegAjax. Inside that, create a folder called Chapter1.

2. You will start by creating the data file in XML. Save this as SuiteList.xml in the Chapter1 folder. Note that all of these files can be created in Notepad or your preferred text or web page editor. If you don't wish to type the code in, it can be downloaded from www.wrox.com in the Downloads section.

```
<?xml version="1.0" encoding="utf-8" ?>
<SuiteList>
  <Suite>
    <SuiteID>1001</SuiteID>
    <Name>Ponderosa</Name>
    <Size>2</Size>
    <Price>50</Price>
    <WeeksFree>10</WeeksFree>
  </Suite>
  <Suite>
    <ProductID>1002</ProductID>
    <Name>Colenso</Name>
    <Size>2</Size>
    <Price>30</Price>
    <WeeksFree>10</WeeksFree>
  </Suite>
  <Suite>
    <ProductID>1003</ProductID>
    <Name>Dunroamin
    </Name>
    <Size>2</Size>
    <Price>60.00</Price>
    <WeeksFree>10</WeeksFree>
  </Suite>
```

```
  <Suite>
    <ProductID>1003</ProductID>
    <Name>Family</Name>
    <Size>6</Size>
    <Price>90.00</Price>
    <WeeksFree>10</WeeksFree>
  </Suite>
</SuiteList>
```

3. Next, you must create a JavaScript script to handle the client-side processing. Save this as ajax.js, and, once again, in the Chapter1 folder.

```javascript
// Create the XMLHttpRequest
    var xHRObject = false;
    if (window.XMLHttpRequest)
    {
        xHRObject = new XMLHttpRequest();
    }
    else if (window.ActiveXObject)
    {
        xHRObject = new ActiveXObject("Microsoft.XMLHTTP");
    }
    function getData()
    {
        //Check to see if the XMlHttpRequest object is ready and whether it has
        //returned a legitimate response
        if (xHRObject.readyState == 4 && xHRObject.status == 200)
        {
            var xmlDoc = xHRObject.responseXML;

if (window.ActiveXObject)
            {
                //Load XSL
                var xsl = new ActiveXObject("Microsoft.XMLDOM");
                xsl.async = false;
                xsl.load("MenuDisplay.xsl");

                //Transform
                var transform = xmlDoc.transformNode(xsl);
                var spanb = document.getElementById("menuhere");

            }

            else
            {
              var xsltProcessor = new XSLTProcessor();

              //Load XSL
              XObject = new XMLHttpRequest();
              XObject.open("GET", "MenuDisplay.xsl", false);
              XObject.send(null);

              xslStylesheet = XObject.responseXML;
              xsltProcessor.importStylesheet(xslStylesheet);

              //Transform
```

```
        var fragment = xsltProcessor.transformToFragment(xmlDoc, document);

        document.getElementById("menuhere").innerHTML = "";
        document.getElementById("menuhere").appendChild(fragment);
        }
        if (spanb != null)
        {
            spanb.innerHTML = transform;
        }

        //Clear the object and call the getDocument function in 10 seconds
        xHRObject.abort();
        setTimeout("getDocument()", 10000);
    }
}


    function getDocument()
{
 //Reset the function
 xHRObject.onreadystatechange = getData;

 //IE will cache the GET request; the only way around this is to append a
 //different querystring. We add a new date and append it as a querystring
 xHRObject.open("GET", "SuiteList.xml?id=" + Number(new Date), true);

 xHRObject.send(null);

}
```

4. You will also need an XSL style sheet for this example. This handles the presentation of the data contained in the XML document. This will be the section that controls which items from the XML document are displayed and which items are not. Save the XSL style sheet as `MenuDisplay` `.xsl` to the `Chapter1` folder.

```
<?xml version="1.0" encoding="utf-8"?>

<xsl:stylesheet version="1.0"
    xmlns:xsl="http://www.w3.org/1999/XSL/Transform">

  <xsl:output method="html"/>

  <xsl:template match="/">
    <div onmouseout=" var submenu =
document.getElementById('romesubmenu');submenu.style.visibility = 'hidden';return
true;" >
      <table>
        <tr>
        <td id="td1" class="menublock"
onMouseOver="td1.style.backgroundColor='#cccccc';"
onMouseOut="td1.style.backgroundColor='#eeeeff';" >
          Hotel Paris
        </td>
      </tr>
      <tr>
```

```
            <td id="td2" class="menublock"
onMouseOver="td2.style.backgroundColor='#cccccc';"
onMouseOut="td2.style.backgroundColor='#eeeeff';"  >
            Hotel London
        </td>
    </tr>
    <tr>
        <td  id="td3" class="menublock"
onmouseover="td3.style.backgroundColor='#cccccc';var submenu =
document.getElementById('romesubmenu');submenu.style.visibility = 'visible';return
true;" onMouseOut="td3.style.backgroundColor='#eeeeff';" >
            Hotel Rome
        </td>
    </tr>
    <tr>
        <td id="td4" class="menublock"
onMouseOver="td4.style.backgroundColor='#cccccc';"
onMouseOut="td4.style.backgroundColor='#eeeeff';" >
            Hotel New York
        </td>
    </tr>
    <tr>
        <td id="td5" class="menublock"
onMouseOver="td5.style.backgroundColor='#cccccc';"
onMouseOut="td5.style.backgroundColor='#eeeeff';" >
            Hotel Montreal
        </td>
        </tr>
    </table>
    <xsl:call-template name="DynamicSubMenu"></xsl:call-template>

  </div>
 </xsl:template>


    <xsl:template name="DynamicSubMenu">
    <div id="romesubmenu" class="submenublock" onmouseover="var submenu =
document.getElementById('romesubmenu');submenu.style.visibility = 'visible';return
true;">
        <xsl:for-each select="//Suite">

         <xsl:if test="WeeksFree&gt;0">
           <a href="{Name}.htm">
             <xsl:value-of select="Name"/>
           </a>
           <br/>
         </xsl:if>

       </xsl:for-each>

    </div>
 </xsl:template>

</xsl:stylesheet>
```

5. Next is the CSS, which controls the switching on and off of the dynamic submenu and the presentation of the menu blocks, such as the colors and font size. Save this as `SuiteListStyles.css` in the `Chapter1` folder.

```css
td.menublock
{
        background-color:#eeeeff; width:120px;height:25px;border-style:ridge; border-
width:thin; border-color:gray; font-weight: bold; text-align:center;  font-family:
Arial; color:gray;
}
div.submenublock
{
        visibility:hidden; background-color:lightsteelblue; position:absolute; top:
70px; left: 133px; width:180px;border-style:ridge; border-width:thin; color:gray;
font-weight: bold; text-align:center; font-family: Arial;
}
a
{
        color: White; text-decoration: none;
}

a:hover
        {background-color: #28618E;
                    font-weight: bold;

}
```

6. Last is the HTML page that contains very little detail. It simply has links to the script and the CSS and a single placeholder `<span>` tag into which you write the menu information. Save this as `default.htm` in the `Chapter1` folder.

```html
<html>
<head>
    <title>Ajax First Example</title>
      <link rel="stylesheet" type="text/css" href="SuiteListStyles.css" />
        <script type="text/javascript" src="ajax.js"></script>
</head>
<body onload="GetDocument()">
    <span id="menuhere"></span>
</body>
</html>
```

> Note that in the code download for Chapter 1, there are some extra pages for each of the suites. These are for presentation only and are not needed for the example.

7. Open your browser and view the `default.htm` page. Ensure that you do this via your web server. For example, the following typed into the browser Address bar would be correct:

```
http://localhost/BegAjax/Chapter1/default.htm
```

If you were to browse via Windows Explorer directly to the file and click on it, then you would see the following and this would not work:

```
C:\Inetpub\wwwroot\BegAjax\Chapter1\default.htm
```

Just as with server-side technologies, the XMLHttpRequest object requires the server to work correctly. If it works correctly, you will see a page with five menu options on the left-hand side. Four of these options are inactive. The active option is Hotel Rome, and if you hover the mouse over it, you will see a blue menu appear (Figure 1-8).

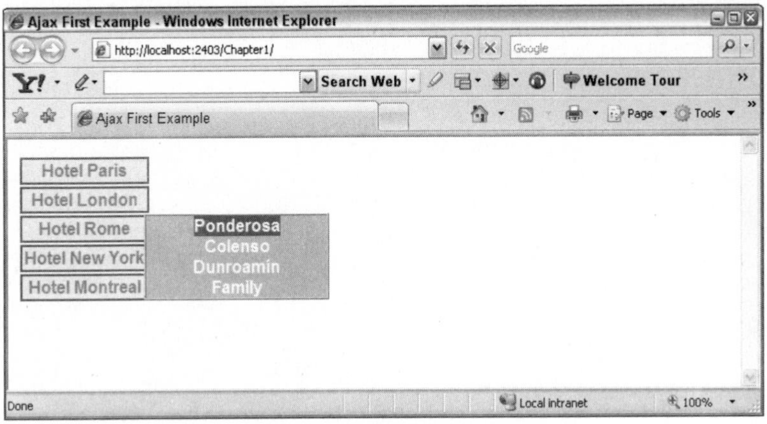

Figure 1-8: Hovering over the active option of Hotel Rome.

8. Now, this is the neat bit. Say that the XML document that you used has just been updated to reflect the fact that you have no availability on the Ponderosa suite. Go back to the SuiteList .xml file, and alter the weeks free to zero:

```
...
<Suite>
  <SuiteID>1001</SuiteID>
  <Name>Ponderosa</Name>
  <Size>2</Size>
  <Price>50</Price>
  <WeeksFree>0</WeeksFree>
</Suite>
...
```

9. Go back to the page, making sure you do not refresh it. Wait for about 10–15 seconds. Hover over Hotel Rome with the cursor once more, as shown in Figure 1-9.

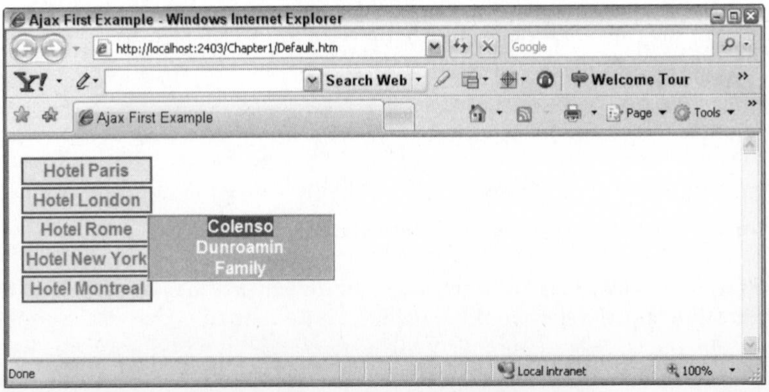

Figure 1-9: New results of hovering over Hotel Rome.

10. The top entry has disappeared.

How It Works

As mentioned previously, this discussion does not go into detail about this example because the techniques will be covered in later chapters. Instead, let's look at what the application is doing and how the different parts fit together. We've created a simple menu system in an XSL template. This consists of a table with five rows. The XSL template takes its data from the XML document SuiteList.xml. The middle row of the XSL template contains a JavaScript mouseover event, which turns on the visibility of the submenu. The XSL template contains a subtemplate, which is used to display the submenu:

```
<xsl:template name="DynamicSubMenu">
    <div id="romesubmenu" class="submenublock" onmouseover="var submenu =
document.getElementById('romesubmenu');submenu.style.visibility = 'visible';return
true;">
        <xsl:for-each select="//Suite">
          <xsl:if test="WeeksFree&gt;0">
            <div>
              <a href="{Name}.htm">
                <xsl:value-of select="Name"/>
              </a>
            </div>
            <br/>
          </xsl:if>
        </xsl:for-each>
    </div>
</xsl:template>
```

XSL statements are used in the template to iterate through the SuiteList.xml document. The xsl:for-each statement locates each element called <Suite> in the XML document. There are four elements in all:

```
...
    <Suite>
      <SuiteID>1001</SuiteID>
      <Name>Ponderosa</Name>
      <Size>2</Size>
      <Price>50</Price>
      <WeeksFree>0</WeeksFree>
    </Suite>
    ...
```

Then, the <xsl:if> statement is used to conditionally display the submenu item. You check the value of the <WeeksFree> element, and you say that, if this element is greater than zero, then you will display the <span> and <a> element's contained within. If not, you won't. This has the effect of showing only the suites on the submenu that have a WeeksFree value greater than zero, which corresponds with the requirement of the businesses that wish to display only the suites with available weeks.

What is happening behind the scenes is of most interest. Instead of waiting to go back to the server for a refresh, you are actually getting the code to reload the XML document every 10 seconds. This is all controlled in the JavaScript on the page. In four swift steps, you create an XMLHttpRequest object, you set the event to notify you when the XML document has been loaded, you get the XML document, and you send it. The creation of the XMLHttpRequest object is performed at the head of the code. It is browser independent, but you can add some code to make sure that this works on IE 6 as well. You create it at the head because you want the object to be accessible to all functions in your script.

```
// Create the XMLHttpRequest
var xHRObject = false;
if (window.XMLHttpRequest)
{
    xHRObject = new XMLHttpRequest();
}
else if (window.ActiveXObject)
{
    xHRObject = new ActiveXObject("Microsoft.XMLHTTP");
}
```

The other three steps are contained in the `getDocument()` function, which is loaded on startup, via the body element's onload event handler:

```
//Reset the function
    xHRObject.onreadystatechange = getData;

    //IE will cache the GET request; the only way around this is to append a
    //different querystring. We add a new date and append it as a querystring
    xHRObject.open("GET", "SuiteList.xml?id=" + Number(new Date), true);

    xHRObject.send(null);
```

When the `readystatechange` event is fired, it calls a function `getData`. `getData` checks to see whether the response (the XML) has been returned from the server and acts only if it has. It then performs three steps to load the XML document with the data, load the XSL style sheet (which controls which parts of the data are displayed on the menu), and then performs a transform on the XML document — meaning that the two are combined to produce an HTML document fragment.

```
        if (window.ActiveXObject)
            {
                //Load XSL
                var xsl = new ActiveXObject("Microsoft.XMLDOM");
                xsl.async = false;
                xsl.load("MenuDisplay.xsl");

                //Transform
                var transform = xmlDoc.transformNode(xsl);
                var spanb = document.getElementById("menuhere");

            }

        else
            {
              var xsltProcessor = new XSLTProcessor();

              //Load XSL
              XObject = new XMLHttpRequest();
              XObject.open("GET", "MenuDisplay.xsl", false);
              XObject.send(null);

              xslStylesheet = XObject.responseXML;
              xsltProcessor.importStylesheet(xslStylesheet);

              //Transform
```

```
var fragment = xsltProcessor.transformToFragment(xmlDoc, document);

document.getElementById("menuhere").innerHTML = "";
document.getElementById("menuhere").appendChild(fragment);
}
```

XSLT is browser-specific, so you have one branch for IE and one branch for Firefox, but they both do the same thing. They store the XML response, they load an XSL style sheet, and they perform a transform on it. The fragment is then inserted into the page at the <span> element with the ID "menuhere". When a change has been made to the document, you are no longer dependent on a page refresh. The XML document is being loaded and then placed into the DOM using the innerHTML property.

```
spanb.innerHTML = transform;
```

Last, you clear the XmlHttpRequest object with the abort method and then use the setTimeout to call another method getDocument(). getDocument performs the same processing on the XmlHttpRequest object, as you did at the beginning of the script, and it essentially sets up a cycle that loads the XML document every 10 seconds.

```
//Clear the object and call the getDocument function in 10 seconds
xHRObject.abort();
setTimeout("getDocument()", 10000);
```

Reloading a page every 10 seconds is definitely not the most efficient way of populating a dynamic menu system. You might wish to consider some alternatives. ASP.NET has a Cache object that allows you to create a dependency so that when the XML file is updated, the contents of the cache are automatically refreshed. You could shoehorn this into the application here, so that the menu updates every time the file is updated ; it is reloaded into the XMLHttpRequest. Currently, as it stands, if you were loading a large XML file every 10 seconds, you might end with the unresponsiveness you have been seeking to avoid. To demonstrate how this kind of updating works, though, it more than serves the purpose.

You have a flow — the data is contained in the XML document, and you use an XSL style sheet to interpret the document. You use the DOM and XMLHttpRequest to load the combined XML/XSL document into your HTML page every 10 seconds. You use the CSS to make the output look a bit more presentable.

If you feel this has been a bit fast, don't worry. Each individual aspect is examined in a later chapter. For now, you should see that you can have a model where you update a portion of the web page without ever having to refresh the page -- and without any delay. It's also worth noting that this is just one "view" of how Ajax might be used. Plenty of other techniques that use Ajax in radically different ways are explored throughout the book.

Summary

This chapter considered what Ajax is and some of the reasons you may have for using Ajax techniques. The chapter examined the original article by Jesse James Garrett and the different components that he described as going into an Ajax application. Because there has been a lot of contention over what is and what isn't an Ajax application, this chapter explained that not everything in the article has to be found in an Ajax application. The discussion looked at why indiscriminate use of Ajax could have the reverse effect to the desired one. Examples showed some good Ajax applications in action, and the chapter discussed their techniques. Last, you created your own Ajax application that used a lot of the technologies to be discussed and used in this book.

Exercises

Suggested solutions to these questions can be found in Appendix A.

1. What are the defining points that will make a web application into an Ajax application?

2. Why might Ajax be considered a misleading acronym?

2

JavaScript Refresher

JavaScript is an essential piece of the Ajax package. JavaScript serves as the intermediary between the browser (the client) and the server so that a web page can be dynamically updated without refreshing the entire page.

JavaScript was developed by Brendan Eich and introduced in the 1995 release of Netscape 2.0. Because JavaScript offered a means to add interactivity to HTML pages, it quickly became popular and widely used. Different versions were developed both by Netscape and other browser manufacturers, but eventually the JavaScript language was standardized by the European Computer Manufacturer's Association (ECMA) as ECMAScript.

The ECMAScript standard defines the core of the JavaScript language. Most browsers today support the third edition of the ECMA-262 standard.

This chapter provides a review of core JavaScript (ECMAScript), JavaScript objects, the Document Object Model (DOM), and event handling for readers who have some familiarity and experience with JavaScript and with basic programming constructs (variables, operators, functions). If you're new to programming and/or JavaScript, refer to books such as *Beginning JavaScript, Second Edition* (Indianapolis: Wiley Publishing, 2004) and *Professional JavaScript for Web Developers* (Indianapolis: Wiley Publishing, 2005) for more comprehensive information about JavaScript.

In this chapter, you learn about these topics:

- ❑ Core JavaScript (variables, operators, statements, functions)
- ❑ Object-oriented JavaScript (built-in objects, the Browser Object Model, user-defined objects)
- ❑ The Document Object Model (DOM)
- ❑ JavaScript and events

Core JavaScript

Core JavaScript (ECMAScript) provides everything you need to accomplish basic programming tasks: variables, operators that act on the variables, statements, and functions that provide reuseable blocks of code to accomplish a task. Objects are also part of ECMAScript, and they are discussed later in this chapter in the section, "Object-Oriented JavaScript."

Syntax

The ECMAScript standard specifies JavaScript's basic syntax rules. Using correct syntax is crucial. If your code has syntax errors, the browser's JavaScript interpreter stops processing your code until the error is corrected.

A few guidelines can help you follow good programming practices and avoid syntax errors:

- ❑ **JavaScript is case-sensitive** — Pay extra attention when using capital letters in the names of variables, functions, and objects. A variable named myVar is not the same as one named myvar.

- ❑ **Semicolons are optional** — Even though semicolons are not required at the end of every code statement, it's good practice to include them in your code to delineate where the line of code ends. They make the code easier to read, easier to debug, and they help decrease the number of errors generated when the browser reads your code.

- ❑ **Let the code wrap** — Don't insert line returns in the middle of a line of code. A line return character in the middle of a code statement is one of the most common errors in JavaScript, and line returns will make your code non-functional.

- ❑ **Add comments** — The syntax for JavaScript comments is // for a single-line comment and /* and */ for opening and closing multiline comments. Commenting your code makes it much easier for you or anyone else to understand your code when it's being updated or debugged. Remember, the person updating or debugging just might be you.

Variables

A *variable* is a temporary storage container for data. JavaScript variables can be declared using the var keyword. For example, the following declares a new variable named myColor:

```
var myColor;
```

This variable doesn't contain any information yet. If you included this variable in an alert message, such as the following, its value would be undefined, as shown in Figure 2-1:

```
alert ("myColor = " + myColor);
```

Figure 2-1: Undefined value.

You don't have to declare a variable as a separate step. Instead, you can *initialize* a variable—declare it and assign a value to it at the same time, as shown here:

```
var myColor = "green";
```

> You don't have to use the `var` operator to declare or initialize a variable. If you exclude it, though, the variable automatically has global scope. Using `var` also makes it obvious that you're declaring or initializing a new variable and makes debugging your code easier.

Variable names must start with a letter, an underscore (_), or a dollar sign ($). *Camel notation* is commonly used for variable names, although no specific notation is required. In camel notation, the first word is lowercase, and additional words start with a capital letter, as shown here:

```
var myFavoriteNumber;
```

Primitive Datatypes

Every JavaScript variable has a datatype that indicates the kind of data the variable contains. *Primitive datatypes* store data directly in a variable. There are five types of primitive datatypes:

- ❏ Number
- ❏ String
- ❏ Boolean
- ❏ Undefined
- ❏ Null

The *Number type* includes both integers and floating-point numbers. The *String type* includes any group of one or more characters. A string is distinguished from a number by enclosing it in quotation marks. For example, `"5"` is a string, while `5` is a number. The *Boolean type* has two values: `true` and `false`. The *Undefined type* has only one value: `undefined`. An `undefined` value occurs when a variable is declared but not assigned a value, as shown earlier for the `myColor` variable. The *Null type* also has only one value: `null`. A `null` value means that the object in question does not exist.

You don't have to include a datatype when you declare or initialize a JavaScript variable. JavaScript uses dynamic typing—the datatype is inferred from the context of the JavaScript statement. This also means that the same variable can be used for different types of data at different times, as shown here:

```
var myNumber = "lucky";
    // myNumber contains a string
myNumber = 3;
    // myNumber contains a number
```

Reference Datatypes

Reference datatypes in JavaScript contain a reference to a place in memory that holds the data, rather than the data itself. The `Object` type (as well as special categories of `Object` such as `Array` and `Function`) is a reference datatype.

It's important to be clear about whether you're using a primitive type or a reference type. If you use a reference type for a function parameter and then make changes to the data within the function, you can modify the original data in the reference type. Even though the change is made locally (within a function), the data is changed globally, as shown here:

```
function myArray(a) {
   var a[0] = 5;
}
var nextArray = [1, 2, 3];
myArray(nextArray);
alert ("nextArray = " + nextArray);
```

After the myArray function is called, the value of nextArray is 5,2,3.

Operators

Operators enable you to perform an action on a variable. The basic JavaScript operators include assignment, arithmetic, comparison, logical, and increment/decrement operators.

Assignment Operator

The *assignment operator* (=) is used for assigning a value to a variable, as shown here:

```
var myTree = "oak";
```

In this case, the value "oak" is assigned to the variable myTree.

Arithmetic Operators

JavaScript includes operators for all the basic arithmetic functions, including addition (+), subtraction (-), multiplication (*), and division (/).

> The addition operator and the string *concatenation* operator are the same character (+). If you use this operator with numeric values, the numbers are added together. If you use this operator with string values, the strings are joined together (concatenated) into a single string.

```
var a = 5;
var b = 10;
var c = a + b;
   // c = 15
a = "My";
b = " name";
c = a + b;
   // c ="My name"
```

JavaScript includes a modulus (%) operator, also known as the *remainder operator*. The modulus operator is used to calculate the value of the remainder after a number has been divided by another number, as shown here:

```
var myMod = 16%5;
   // myMod = 1
```

Using a modulus is an easy way to determine if an integer has an even or odd value. Calculate integer%2. *If the result is 0, then it's an even number.*

Comparison Operators

Comparison operators are used to evaluate an expression and return a Boolean value (true or false) indicating whether the comparison is true or false. For example, if a = 2 and b = 4, the expression a > b is false. The comparison operator in this case is the greater than (>) operator.

Table 2-1 shows JavaScript's comparison operators.

Operator	Meaning
>	Greater than
<	Less than
>=	Greater than or equal to
<=	Less than or equal to
==	Equal to
!=	Not equal to
===	Equal and the same type
!==	Not equal or not the same type

A common mistake is to confuse the assignment operator and the equality operator, as shown here:

```
var a = 1;
var b = 2;
a = b;
   // assigns the value contained in the variable b to the variable a, and evaluates
to true
a == b;
   // compares a and b and evaluates to false, since a and b are not equal
```

Logical Operators

In addition to the comparison operators, JavaScript also includes *logical operators* for more complex comparisons. The logical operators include && (AND), || (OR), and ! (NOT). These operators also return a Boolean value (true or false).

The easiest way to understand the logical operators is with a *truth table* (Table 2-2). A truth table shows whether a value or an expression is true or false. The following table shows the value of A, B, and expressions using the logical operators. As you can see, the && operator returns true only if both A and B are true. The || operator returns true if either A or B is true.

A	B	A && B	A || B	!A	!B
True	True	True	True	False	False
False	True	False	True	True	False
True	False	False	True	False	True
False	False	False	False	True	True

Increment and Decrement Operators

The *increment* and *decrement operators* provide a shortcut for adding or subtracting 1 from a value, as shown here:

```
var a = 1;
a++;
    // a = 2
var b = 45;
b-- ;
    // b = 44
```

Increment and decrement operators can appear before a variable (prefix) or after a variable (postfix). If a variable with a prefix operator is used in an expression, the value of the variable is incremented or decremented before the expression is evaluated. If a postfix operator is used, the value is incremented or decremented after the expression is evaluated. For example:

```
var a = 1;
alert(++a);
```

Figure 2-2 shows that the result is 2. The value of a is incremented before the expression is evaluated.

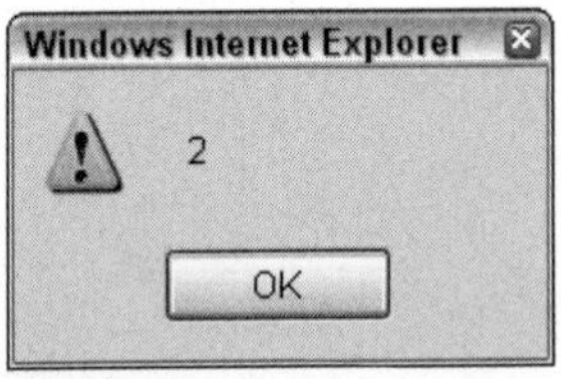

Figure 2-2: Incrementing a value before the expression is evaluated.

On the other hand, if you use a postfix operator, the value of a is incremented after the expression is evaluated:

```
alert (a++);
```

Figure 2-3 shows that the result is 1.

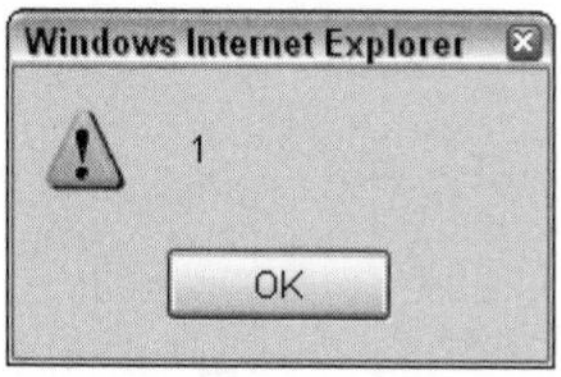

Figure 2-3: Incrementing a value after the expression is evaluated.

Statements

A JavaScript program is composed of *statements*. Variable declarations, assignments, and initializations are examples of JavaScript statements. JavaScript also includes a core set of programming statements similar to those used in other programming languages: conditionals (`if`/`else`, `switch`), loops (`for`, `while`), and flow controls (`break`, `continue`).

Conditional Statements

You can control the execution of code in your program with `if` statements or with `switch` statements.

An `if` statement evaluates the Boolean value of an expression (true or false), then executes code based on the result of that evaluation. If the expression in the parentheses evaluates to true, the block of code contained in the curly braces (`{}`) following the expression is executed. If the expression evaluates to false, the first code statement following the closing curly brace is executed:

```
if (myValue == "hedgehogs")
{
   var yourValue = "warthogs";
}
```

Note that there's no semicolon after the closing parenthesis or after the closing curly brace, but there are semicolons after each statement in the code block.

You can also evaluate additional expressions by adding `else if` and `else`:

```
if (myValue == "hedgehogs")
{
   var yourValue = "warthogs";
}
else if (myValue == "dragons")
{
   var yourValue = "dungeons";
}
else
{
   var yourValue = "centipede";
}
```

A switch statement can be used in place of a series of `if` statements:

```
switch (myValue)
{
  case 'hedgehogs':
    var yourValue = "warthogs";
    break;
  case 'dragons':
    var yourValue = "dungeons";
    break;
  default:
    var yourValue = "centipede";
}
```

Note that a `break` statement is used after each code block. The `break` is used to exit the `switch` once the code for that case has been executed. The first statement after the `switch` is then executed.

The `default` case plays a similar role to an `else` statement. If there is not a specific case for a value, the `default` is used.

Loops

Loops are a way to repeat a block of code based on conditions that you specify. The two major kinds of loops are `for` and `while`.

A `for` loop includes three components:

❑ Initialization

❑ Test condition

❑ Iterator (counter)

```
for (i=0; i<=10; i++) {
  document.write("i = " + i + "<br>");
}
```

Note the following in this code block:

❑ The initialization is `i = 0;`.

❑ The test condition is `i <= 10;`.

❑ The iterator is `i++`.

The code in this loop is executed 11 times and writes the current value of `i` to the page each time, as shown in Figure 2-4.

A `while` loop can be considered a reformulation of a `for` loop. It includes a test condition and an iterator. The loop continues as long as the test condition is true.

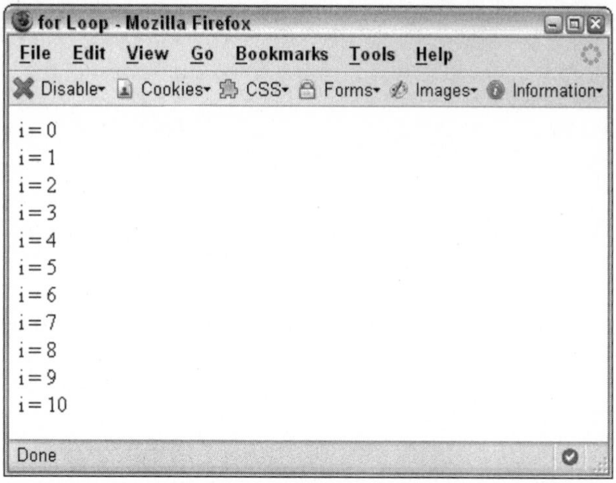

Figure 2-4: Executing the loop and writing the current value.

You can change the preceding `for` loop to a `while` loop:

```
var i=0;
while (i <= 10){
  document.write("i = " + i + "<br>");
  i++;
}
```

In this case,

❑   The initialization is `i = 0;`. The initialization occurs before the `while` loop starts.

❑   The test condition is `i <= 10`.

❑   The iterator is `i++`.

> **Be careful not to create an infinite `while` loop. Check to make sure that your test condition is not always true.**

A `do-while` loop is very similar to a `while` loop. The main difference is that the condition is tested at the end of the loop, which means that the loop will always execute at least once.

```
var i = 0;
do {
  document.write("i = " + i + "<br>");
  i++;
}
while (i <=10);
```

Two flow-control statements that can be used with loops are break (as you saw earlier in the switch statement) and continue. A break statement is a way to escape a loop and continue with the first statement after the loop. A continue statement allows you to skip the rest of the loop, but to continue with the next iteration of the loop.

Functions

A *function* is a reusable group of code statements that are treated as a unit. JavaScript includes many built-in functions, and you can also create your own functions for code blocks that you want to reuse.

Function definitions are usually included in script blocks in the head section of an HTML/XHTML page. A function must be defined before it can be used. Because the code in the head section of the page is read and interpreted before the code in the body section, functions are usually defined in the head section and called from the body section.

To create a function, you define it and give it a name:

```
function myCat (catname) {
  alert (catname + " is a great name for a cat!");
}
```

To call (invoke) a function, use the function's name in a code statement:

```
myCat("Jobo");
```

When the myCat function is called, the parameter catname is assigned the value Jobo.

A function includes the function keyword and the following:

❑   **A name** — myCat

❑   **A parameter in parentheses** — (catname)

❑   **A code block between curly braces** — {alert (catname + " is a great name for a cat!");}

Supplying a parameter for a function is optional. But even if there are no parameters for a function, you must include the parentheses after the function name. In general, the name you use for a parameter is entirely up to you. It will help you understand your code better if you use a name that has meaning (for example, a name that's related to what the parameter does).

You can return a value from a function by using a return statement:

```
function shopping (price) {
  var salesTax = price * .0625;
  var total = price + salesTax;
  return total;
}
```

> Unless an explicit value is returned from a function, a value of undefined will be returned.

Object-Oriented JavaScript

An *object* is a collection of properties and methods that are grouped together with a single name. Objects gather together everything needed for a particular task.

JavaScript uses four different types of objects:

❏ Built-in objects (such as Date and Math objects)

❏ Browser objects (such as the window, navigator, and history objects)

❏ Document objects (for example images, forms, and links)

❏ User-defined objects

There's no one standard that defines all the uses of JavaScript. For example, these four types of JavaScript objects are each derived from different sources. The built-in objects are part of core JavaScript, and they are defined in the ECMAScript standard. Both browser objects and document objects can be called *host objects* because they're part of the host environment and not defined by the ECMAScript standard. The browser objects aren't defined by any standards organization. They've been developed by browser vendors, and their use and support in any browser are determined by the browser vendor. Document objects are part of the Document Object Model (DOM), as defined by the W3C. User-defined objects are, of course, defined by the programmer.

Built-in Objects

When you use the new keyword and an object constructor function, you create a new instance of the object:

```
var myArray = new Array();
// creating a new instance of the Array object
```

In this case, the instance is a specific Array object that is assigned to a variable named myArray. This object has all the methods and properties of all Array objects. Whatever changes you make to this specific instance of the Array object affect only this instance. The changes don't affect the Array object itself.

Methods are the specific functions that belong to a particular type of object. The Array object, for example, includes a reverse() function that reverses the order of the members of the array:

```
var backwards = myArray.reverse();
```

Objects also include *properties*. Properties are attributes of an object. For example, the Array object includes a length property.

```
var howLong = myArray.length;
```

You can use dot notation to access either methods or properties of an object:

```
myArray.reverse();
myArray.length;
```

For more details about the nine JavaScript built-in objects, see Appendix D and the third edition of the ECMA-262 standard.

A PDF of the ECMA-262 standard can be downloaded at www.ecma-international.org/ publications/standards/Ecma-262.htm..

Browser Objects

The *Browser Object Model (BOM)* is a collection of objects that interact with the browser window. These objects include the window object, history object, location object, navigator object, screen object, and document object.

The window object is the top object in the BOM hierarchy. The window object can be used to move and resize windows as well as to create new windows. The window object also includes methods to create dialog boxes such as the alert dialogs shown earlier in Figures 2-1, 2-2, and 2-3. The window object is a unique object — you don't have to explicitly include a reference to it when you use its methods or properties. Consider the following example:

```
alert("Look! Is there a reference?");
```

This functions exactly the same as the following:

```
window.alert("Look! Is there a reference?");
```

The history object keeps track of every page the user visits. Methods of this object include forward, back, and go:

```
history.back(2);
// go back by 2 pages
```

The location object contains the URL of the page. You can use its href property to go to a new page:

```
location.href="myPage.htm";
```

The navigator object contains information about the browser name and version. Properties include appName, appVersion, userAgent.

> As browser detection became more complex, this object became less useful and reliable. Currently, object detection is preferred over browser detection. Object detection checks to see if a browser supports a particular feature, rather than detecting a browser name or version.

The screen object provides information about display characteristics such as screen height and width in pixels.

The document object is included in the window object. This object belongs to both the BOM and the Document Object Model (DOM). The document object in the BOM includes page properties such as background color (bgColor), and also includes arrays for all the forms, images, and links in a page.

You can access the individual items in these arrays by item name or by array index number:

```
document.form('myForm');
    // accessing a form by name
document.form[0];
    // accessing the first form on the page
```

User-Defined Objects

To create a *user-defined object*, you use a constructor function to create the new object, then add properties and methods to the new object.

Constructors

New user-defined objects are created with the Object constructor:

```
var member = new Object();
```

In this case, you're defining a new object, not a new instance of a built-in object.

You can then add properties to the object:

```
member.name = "Jobo";
member.address = "325 Smith Rd";
member.isRegistered = true;
```

You can also create methods for the object. You can do this by creating a named function:

```
function showMe()
{
alert("I'm here!");
}
```

Then you can assign this function as a property of the object:

```
member.present = showMe;
```

You call this function in the usual way:

```
member.present();
```

You can do this more efficiently by using a function literal:

```
member.present = function()
{
alert("I'm here!");
};
```

Note that in this case the function is anonymous — it has no name. Also note that there's a semicolon at the end of the function literal.

In this case, you can still call the function in the usual way:

```
member.present();
```

You can also create a new object by using an object literal:

```
var member =
{name: "Jobo",
 address: "325 Smith Road",
 isRegistered: true,
 present: function () {alert("I'm here!");}
};
```

Commonly you may want to create more than one instance of an object so that you can have objects with the same basic properties, but with different values for those properties. You can create a function that uses JavaScript's this keyword so that you can pass parameters when a new object is created and specify values for the properties for each new instance that's created:

```
function member (name, addr, reg)
{
  this.name = name;
  this.address = addr;
  this.isRegistered = reg;
  this.present = function () {alert("I'm here!");};
}
```

> **The this keyword always refers to the current object.**

You can then create new instances of the member object with the new keyword:

```
var member1 = new member ("Robert", "17 Cove Ct", true);
var member378 = new member ("Joan", "44 Redding Rd", false);
```

You can also add new properties that are specific to instances and not part of the original object definition:

```
member1.city = "Chicago";
```

Prototypes

Every object in JavaScript is based on a *prototype object*, and every object includes a prototype property that refers to the properties and methods of the prototype object. You can use this property to specify properties and methods for all objects of that type.

For example, as instances of the member object are created, multiple copies of the present function are created and stored in memory. You can avoid tying up memory but still give all member objects access to this function by using the prototype property and defining the present function outside of the constructor definition:

```
function member (name, addr, reg)
{
this.name = name;
this.address = addr;
this.isRegistered = reg;
}
member.prototype.present = function () {
  alert("I'm here!");
};
```

You can also use the `prototype` property to specify default values for an object:

```
member.prototype.isActive = true;
```

You can change the default values by specifying instance variables with a different value:

```
member378.isActive = false;
```

If a property is accessed by an instance object, the JavaScript interpreter checks to see if there's an instance property with that name. If not, it checks the prototype object for a property with that name, and on up the prototype chain. All objects in JavaScript are descended from a generic `Object`. If the property isn't found in the generic `Object`, the value is undefined

Prototypes in JavaScript are similar to, though not exactly the same as, classes in Java and C++.

Destroying Objects

Objects are reference types, so they may take up a lot of memory space. If you're finished with an object, destroy it so that the memory space can be reused.

To destroy an object, set it equal to `null`:

```
member378 = null;
```

Try It Out   Creating Objects

In this example, a new object is created. The properties are specified in a constructor function. A method is added to the object using the object's prototype property. This method enables you to pass parameters for different values for the position and background color when you create a new object. Type the following code into your text editor and save it as `ch2_examp1.htm`.

```
<!DOCTYPE html PUBLIC "-//W3C//DTD XHTML 1.0 Transitional//EN"
"http://www.w3.org/TR/xhtml1/DTD/xhtml1-transitional.dtd">
<html xmlns="http://www.w3.org/1999/xhtml">
<head>
<meta http-equiv="Content-Type" content="text/html; charset=iso-8859-1" />
<title>Address Book</title>
<style type="text/css">
.ab {
    font-family: Verdana, Arial, Helvetica, sans-serif;
    font-size: small;
```

```
      color: #993300;
      background-color: #CCFFCC;
      padding: 5px;
      height: 100px;
      width: 350px;
      border: thin dotted #993300;
}
</style>
<script type="text/javascript">
function addrBook (fname, lname, email) {
  this.fname= fname;
  this.lname = lname;
  this.email = email;
  var adrbook = "<p class='ab'>First Name: " + fname + "<br />";
  adrbook += "Last Name: " + lname + "<br />";
  adrbook += "Email Address: " + email + "</p>";
  document.write(adrbook);
}
</script>
</head>

<body>
<script type="text/javascript">
var aB1 = new addrBook('Roger', 'Williams', 'rwilliams@gmail.com');
var aB2 = new addrBook ('Rose', 'Schultz', 'rose_s@earthlink.net');
</script>
</body>
</html>
```

When you open this page in a browser, it should show two address book entries, as seen in Figure 2-5.

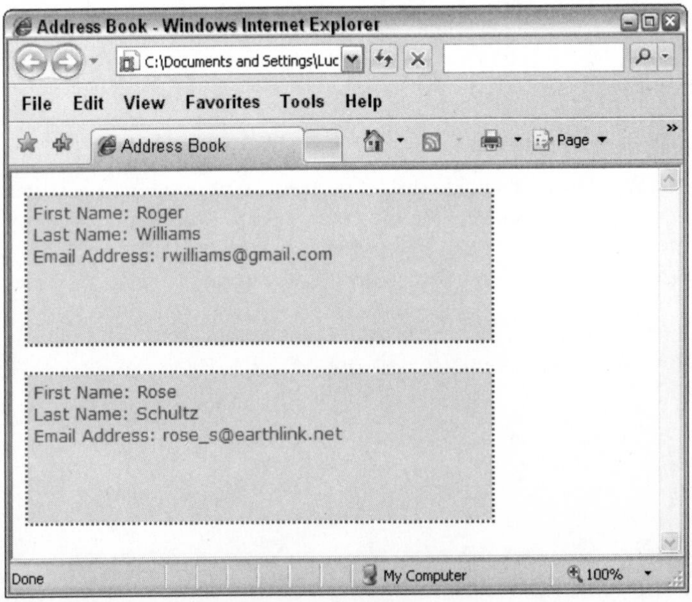

Figure 2-5: Address book entries in browser.

How It Works

The `addrBook` object constructor function is placed in the head section of the page. This function includes three parameters: `fname` for first name, `lname` for last name, and `email` for e-mail address.

```
function addrBook (fname, lname, email) {
```

The parameters that are passed to the `addrBook` function — `fname`, `lname`, and `email` — provide values for the address book entry. The `this` keyword indicates that these properties apply to the current instance of the `addrBook` object.

```
this.fname= fname;
this.lname = lname;
this.email = email;
```

All `addrBook` objects use the `ab` style class, defined in the head section of the page:

```
<style type="text/css">
.ab {
    font-family: Verdana, Arial, Helvetica, sans-serif;
    font-size: small;
    color: #993300;
    background-color: #CCFFCC;
    padding: 5px;
    height: 100px;
    width: 350px;
    border: thin dotted #993300;
}
</style>
```

This style is applied to the new instance of the `addrBook` object with the `adrbook` variable. This variable includes a `p` tag with the `ab` class and a line for each of the three parameters (`fname`, `lname`, `email`). The `+=` operator is used to build a value for this variable. The variable value is then written to the page using the `document.write` method.

```
var adrbook = "<p class='ab'>First Name: " + fname + "<br />";
adrbook += "Last Name: " + lname + "<br />";
adrbook += "Email Address: " + email + "</p>";
document.write(adrbook);
```

In a script block in the body section of the page, two new instances of the `addrBook` object are created.

```
var aB1 = new addrBook('Roger', 'Williams', 'rwilliams@gmail.com');
var aB2 = new addrBook ('Rose', 'Schultz', 'rose_s@earthlink.net');
```

The Document Object Model

The *Document Object Model* (*DOM*) is a tree-based representation of a document created by the World Wide Web Consortium (W3C) for XML and HTML/XHTML. The DOM provides a set of objects for representing the structure of a document, as well as methods for accessing those objects. The DOM is divided into three parts. The *Core DOM* includes objects that XML and HTML have in common, the *XML DOM* includes XML objects, and the *HTML DOM* includes HTML objects.

All of the elements in a page are related to the topmost object, the `document` object. Using this model, you can access *any* object in an HTML document with JavaScript and change its properties. For example, you can do the following:

❑ Change its position

❑ Change its source file

❑ Change its style properties

❑ Change its content

❑ Add new content

The Document as a Family Tree

To use the DOM effectively, it's important to understand the HTML/XHTML document as a family tree structure, as shown in Figure 2-6.

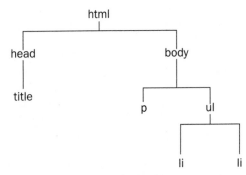

Figure 2-6: Document as a family tree structure.

Following are key components of the family tree structure:

❑ **html** — Every element in the page is contained in this element, so it's the root element. It's also the parent element of the head and body elements.

❑ **head, body** — These two elements are siblings. They are both children of the html element. They are also both parent elements and have their own children — head (title) and body (p and ul).

❑ **title** — This element is a child of the head element.

❑ **p, ul** — These two elements are siblings — they are both children of the body element.

The Document as a Node Tree

In addition to viewing a document as a family tree, a document can also be viewed as a node tree. In the node tree view, a document is a collection of *nodes*. The nodes are the branches and leaves on the document tree.

There are several types of nodes, but there are three main types: element nodes, text nodes, and attribute nodes.

This line of HTML can be viewed as a node structure, as shown in Figure 2-7:

```
<p class="intro">Welcome to my site.</p>
```

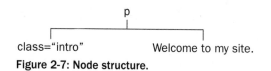

Figure 2-7: Node structure.

Following are key components of the node structure:

❑ **Element node** — p is an element node. Elements are the basic building blocks of documents and give them their structure. Elements can contain other elements.

❑ **Text node** — Welcome to my site. is a text node. In HTML/XHTML, text nodes are always contained in element nodes.

❑ **Attribute node** — class="intro" is an attribute node. Attributes provide more information about elements. Attribute nodes are always contained in element nodes.

DOM Methods for Accessing Objects

Once you understand the basic structure of the DOM tree, you can use it to access any element with DOM methods.

getElementById

If an element has an id, the simplest way to access it is getElementById.

```
<p id="myPara">Greetings, earthlings!</p>
...
var x = document.getElementById('myPara');
```

x is now a shortcut for accessing the unique element with the id value of myPara.

To change a property of this element, for example, the font weight, use the following:

```
x.style.fontWeight = "bold";
    // changes the font weight to bold
```

You can also use getElementById to access elements using family relationships and node properties. For example, if the head and body elements in Figure 2-6 include id values, such as the following, you can use these id values to access all the other elements in the page:

```
<head id="el1">
...
<body id="el2">
```

To access the parent node of the head and body elements, you can use either of the following:

```
document.getElementById('el1').parentNode;
document.getElementById('el2').parentNode;
```

Both of these access the html element.

To access all the children of the body element, use the following:

```
document.getElementById('el2').childNodes;
```

The child nodes are contained in an array. You can access individual child nodes by using the array index value:

```
document.getElementById('el2').childNodes[0];
```

This accesses the first child node of the body element — p — since array indexes start with 0.

You can also access the first child with this code:

```
document.getElementById('el2').firstChild;
```

If you want to access a sibling node, use the following:

```
document.getElementById('el2').previousSibling;
    // accesses the head element
document.getElementById('el1').nextSibling;
    // accesses the body element
```

getElementsByTagName

To use the getElementsByTagName method, you use a Tag name rather than an id. For example:

```
var y = document.getElementsByTagName('p');
```

y contains an array referencing all p elements in the document.

To change the text color of *all* paragraphs, use the following:

```
for (i=0; i < y.length; i++) {
y[i].style.color = "green";
}
```

If you want to change only the *first* paragraph, use the following:

```
var z = document.getElementsByTagName('p')[0];
```

z is now a shortcut for accessing the *first* p element in the document.

Creating Nodes

The DOM includes a number of methods for adding new nodes to the document object, such as `createElement` and `createTextNode`. To create a new paragraph, use the following:

```
var newNode = document.createElement('p');
```

To create a new text node, use the following:

```
var newText = document.createTextNode('Just to add one more thing on this
subject.');
```

To add the new text node to the paragraph, you need another DOM method, `appendChild`:

```
newNode.appendChild(newText);
```

This combines the two new nodes (paragraph and text node).

These DOM methods are a great way to add new content to a page after the input stream to the document is closed. Instead of writing to a new page, you can add new content to an existing page by using a `div` with an `id` as a placeholder for adding new content.

Try It Out   Adding New Elements to an Existing Page

In this example, you use a button to call a function that adds a new paragraph to an existing page. Type the following code into your text editor, and save it as `ch2_examp2.htm`:

```
<!DOCTYPE html PUBLIC "-//W3C//DTD XHTML 1.0 Transitional//EN"
"http://www.w3.org/TR/xhtml1/DTD/xhtml1-transitional.dtd">
<html xmlns="http://www.w3.org/1999/xhtml">
<head>
<meta http-equiv="Content-Type" content="text/html; charset=iso-8859-1" />
<title>Adding New Elements</title>
<style type="text/css">
body {
     font-family: Verdana, Arial, Helvetica, sans-serif;
     font-size: small;
     font-weight: bold;
}
.newDiv {
     background-color:#ffcccc;
}
</style>
<script type="text/javascript">
function newOne() {
  var newEl = document.createElement('p');
  var newTx = document.createTextNode('This is the new paragraph.');
  newEl.appendChild(newTx);
  var newPara = document.getElementById('newText');
```

```
        newPara.appendChild(newEl);
    }
    function newColor() {
        document.getElementById('newText').style.color="red";
    }
    </script>
</head>
<body>
<p>This is the first paragraph on the page.</p>
<div class="newDiv" id="newText"></div>
<p>This is the next paragraph on the original page.</p>
<form>
<input type="button" value="Add a new paragraph" onclick="newOne()" /><br /><br />
<input type="button" value="Make it red" onclick="newColor()" />
</form>
</body>
</html>
```

Open this page in a browser, click the button labeled "Add a new paragraph", and then click the button labeled "Make it red". A new paragraph will be added to the existing page, as shown in Figure 2-8.

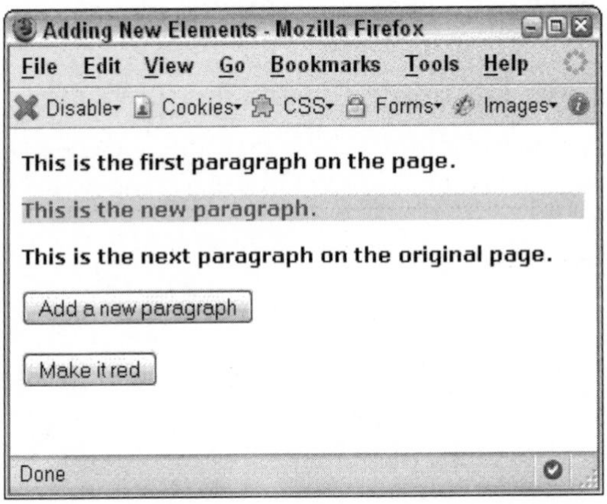

Figure 2-8: Paragraph added to existing page.

How It Works

The first step in adding new content to an existing page is to add a placeholder element so that you have a place to insert the new content. This element includes an `id` attribute to make it accessible with the `getElementById` method.

```
<div class="newDiv" id="newText"></div>
```

In a script block in the head section of the page, the `newOne` function contains the code to add the new paragraph to the page.

```
var newEl = document.createElement('p');
```

This code creates a variable named `newEl` to hold the new `p` element:

```
var newTx = document.createTextNode('This is the new paragraph.');
newEl.appendChild(newTx);
```

A variable named `newTx` contains the new text node. The `appendChild` method is used to add the text node to the new `p` element.

```
var newPara = document.getElementById('newText');
newPara.appendChild(newEl);
```

The `newPara` variable contains the element with the id `newText` — this is the placeholder element for the new element. Once the placeholder element is identified with the `getElementById` method, the `appendChild` property is used to add the new element to the placeholder element.

```
document.getElementById('newText').style.color="red";
```

The `newColor` function also uses `getElementById` to access the new element and change the text color in the new paragraph to red using the `style` property of the element.

```
<form>
<input type="button" value="Add a new paragraph" onclick="newOne()" />
<input type="button" value="Make it red" onclick="newColor()" />
```

Each function is invoked by clicking a button that includes an inline event handler (`onclick`) and a function name.

The innerHTML Alternative

The `innerHTML` property of all HTML elements is a somewhat controversial alternative to using DOM methods to change element content. It's very commonly used in callback functions in Ajax applications, and you'll see it used in many of the examples in this book.

The `innerHTML` property enables you to replace the content of any HTML element with a string. This string can include HTML elements, and so you can create new elements without using DOM methods.

In the previous example, the following code used DOM methods to add a new paragraph to the page after the page was fully loaded:

```
function newOne() {
  var newEl = document.createElement('p');
  var newTx = document.createTextNode('This is the new paragraph.');
  newEl.appendChild(newTx);
  var newPara = document.getElementById('newText');
  newPara.appendChild(newEl);
}
```

Using `innerHTML`, this task could be accomplished with much less code:

```
function newOne() {
    var newPara = document.getElementById('newText');
    newPara.innerHTML = "<p>This is the new paragraph.</p>";
}
```

The controversy about `innerHTML` arises because `innerHTML` is not part of any W3C or other standard. It is supported by most current browsers, including Firefox 2, Internet Explorer 6 and 7, and Opera 9.

In addition to requiring less code, `innerHTML` is also much faster than using DOM methods to generate new content. Peter-Paul Koch has created a benchmark test for `innerHTML` and shown that it is faster than DOM methods in all the browsers he tested. For more details, see www.quirksmode.org/dom/innerhtml.html.

JavaScript and Events

Browser *events* are key to running JavaScript code after a page is loaded. Once a web page has loaded in the browser window, all the JavaScript code has been read and executed. Events are necessary to create any further interaction between the JavaScript and HTML. Events occur either when a user does something (rolls the mouse over an element) or the browser does something (loads a page).

HTML attributes such as `onclick`, `onblur`, or `onload` are one way to bind an event to an event handler (JavaScript code). For example, in the following, when the user clicks the button, the `myResponse` function is invoked:

```
<input type="button" value = "Click Me" onclick="myResponse()">
```

The event is `click`, and the event handler is the `myResponse` function.

Event Models

Events continue to be a complicated part of scripting because of cross-browser differences in *event models*. An event model specifies how events are processed and which objects are involved. One of the main differences at this time is a difference in event flow between the Internet Explorer (IE) model and the W3C DOM event model. (The event model used in Mozilla-based browsers is similar to the W3C DOM model.)

There are two main techniques for dealing with event flow. In the *event bubbling* technique, an event fires from the most-specific target to the least-specific target. An *event target* is the element at which the event originally took place. In the *event capturing* technique, an event fires from the least-specific target to the most-specific target.

This is best illustrated by an example:

```
<div>
    <p>Event order</p>
</div>
```

As shown here, a child element (p) is nested in a parent element (div). If the user mouses over the child element, this creates a mouseover event for both the child element and the parent element. Which mouseover event fires first?

In event capturing, the mouseover event for the parent element (div) fires first. In event bubbling, the mouseover event for the child element (p) fires first.

Internet Explorer (including IE 7) uses the event bubbling technique. The W3C DOM model includes both event capturing and event bubbling.

Event Registration

The first step in using an event with JavaScript is to register an event handler so that the browser runs your script when the event takes place.

The most common way to register an event handler is by using an HTML attribute:

```
<a href="goThere.html" onclick="startNow()">
```

This method is called *inline event registration*.

To stop the default behavior for an event (for example, to prevent the link from being followed when the link is clicked in the previous code), use return false:

```
<a href="goThere.html" onclick="startNow();return false">
```

This method of registering event handlers is reliable and supported by all browsers that support events. It does, however, mix behavior (JavaScript) and structure (HTML/XHTML), rather than keeping them as separate layers in the document. Table 2-3 shows the web standards view of page layers.

Structure	HTML/XHTML
Presentation	CSS
Behavior	JavaScript

You can also register an event handler directly to an element using an event property and the function name:

```
var myElement = document.getElementById('1stpara');
myElement.onclick = startNow;
```

This method is known as traditional event registration. The startNow function is bound to the click event for myElement.

You can't register this event handler until after the code for the HTML element has been read, or you'll create a run-time error. To prevent this, you can place the JavaScript code for registering the event after the element, or you can place the registration code in a function that's called after the page has loaded.

Note that there are no parentheses after startNow. *If you include parentheses, the function is called and the result of the function is assigned to* myElement.onclick *rather than assigning the function itself.*

To remove the event registration, use the following:

```
myElement.onclick = null;
```

This method is reliable and cross-browser compatible, but it allows you to register only one event handler to an event on the same element. Internet Explorer and the W3C both include methods to register more than one event handler.

The Internet Explorer Event Registration Model

Internet Explorer includes two methods for registering and unregistering an event handler: attachEvent() and detachEvent():

```
var myElement = document.getElementById('1stpara');
myElement.attachEvent('onclick', startNow);
```

You can also register additional event handlers:

```
var myElement = document.getElementById('1stpara');
myElement.attachEvent('onclick', startNow);
myElement.attachEvent('onclick', startNow2);
```

To remove the registration, use the following:

```
myElement.detachEvent('onclick', startNow);
myElement.detachEvent('onclick', startNow2);
```

These methods are proprietary and work only in IE.

The W3C DOM Event Registration Model

The W3C DOM methods use three parameters: the event name, the function name, and a Boolean value (true or false). The Boolean value is set to true if the event registration should be used in the event capturing phase, and it is set to false if the event registration should be used in the event bubbling phase.

```
var myElement = document.getElementById('1stpara');
myElement.addEventListener('click', startNow, false);
```

You can also add additional event registrations:

```
var myElement = document.getElementById('1stpara');
myElement.addEventListener('click', startNow, false);
myElement.addEventListener('click', startNow2, false);
```

The event listener code is equivalent to the traditional event registration seen earlier:

```
myElement.onclick = startNow;
```

In traditional event registration, the event registration is added in the bubbling phase of the event.

To remove an event listener, use the following:

```
myElement.removeEventListener('click', startNow, false);
```

Event Objects

Event objects are used to access an event so that you can obtain information about its properties, such as which key a user pressed. Event objects are created when an event occurs.

There are two different models for event objects: the Internet Explorer model and the W3C DOM model.

In Internet Explorer, the event object is a property of the window object (`window.event`). In this model, the `window.event` property contains the last event that took place.

```
var myElement = document.getElementById('1stpara');
myElement.onclick = startNow;
function startNow () {
  // window.event gives access to the event
}
```

In the W3C DOM model, the event is passed to the event-handling function as an argument:

```
var myElement = document.getElementById('1stpara');
myElement.onclick = startNow;
function startNow (e) {
  // e gives access to the event
}
```

To access events in a way that's compatible with either model, you can use a function such as this:

```
var myElement = document.getElementById('1stpara');
myElement.onclick = startNow;
function startNow (e) {
  if (!e) {
  var e = window.event;
}
  // if e doesn't already exist, assign window.event to e
}
```

The Internet Explorer event object and the W3C DOM event object have different properties and methods. See Appendix D for more details.

Try It Out   **Cross-Browser Event Registration**

In this example, event registration to join an event (`click`) and a function (`addBord`) are added and removed from a paragraph. The function adds a border and a background color to a paragraph of text. Both Internet Explorer (`attachEvent`/`detachEvent`) and W3C DOM (addEventListener/removeEventListener) methods are included. Type the following code into your text editor and save it as ch2_examp3.htm.

```
<!DOCTYPE html PUBLIC "-//W3C//DTD XHTML 1.0 Transitional//EN"
"http://www.w3.org/TR/xhtml1/DTD/xhtml1-transitional.dtd">
<html xmlns="http://www.w3.org/1999/xhtml">
<head>
<meta http-equiv="Content-Type" content="text/html; charset=iso-8859-1" />
<title>Event Registration</title>
<script type="text/javascript">
function addHandler () {
  var addH = document.getElementById('p1');
  if (addH.addEventListener) {
    addH.addEventListener('click', addBord, false);
  }
  else if (addH.attachEvent) {
    addH.attachEvent('onclick', addBord);
  }
}
function detHandler () {
  var detH = document.getElementById('p1');
  detH.style.border = '';
  detH.style.backgroundColor = '#ffffff';
  if (detH.removeEventListener) {
    detH.removeEventListener('click', addBord, false);
  }
  else if (detH.detachEvent) {
    detH.detachEvent('onclick', addBord);
  }
}
function addBord () {
  var add = document.getElementById('p1');
  add.style.border = '1px dotted #ff0000';
  add.style.backgroundColor = '#ffff99';
}
</script>
</head>
<body onload="addHandler()">
<p id='p1'>Lorem ipsum dolor sit amet, consectetuer adipiscing elit. Sed
scelerisque odio non ligula. </p>
<p>Integer mollis, libero et facilisis hendrerit, tellus dui porttitor quam, vitae
iaculis nisi mauris ac dui. Vivamus volutpat sollicitudin est. </p>
<form>
<input type='button' value='No border, please!' onclick='detHandler()'>
</form>
</body>
</html>
```

When you open this page in a browser and click the first paragraph, it should display a border and a background color, as shown in Figure 2-9.

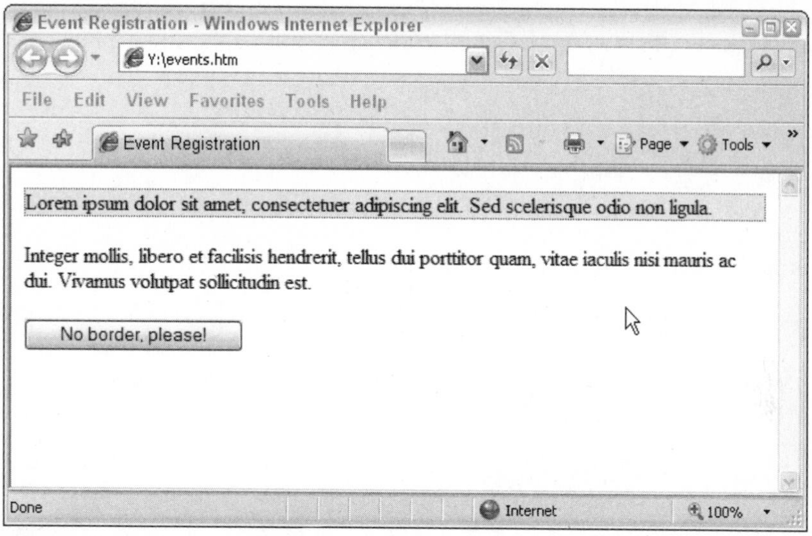

Figure 2-9: Border and background on first paragraph in browser.

How It Works

When the page is loaded, the `addHandler` function is called.

```
<body onload="addHandler()">
```

This function identifies the paragraph with an ID equal to `p1`.

```
function addHandler () {
var addH = document.getElementById('p1');
```

If the browser supports the `addEventListener` method, the W3C DOM method is used to add an event listener — event handler — to the click event. The third parameter is `false` to specify the event bubbling phase.

```
if (addH.addEventListener) {
addH.addEventListener('click', addBord, false);
}
```

If the browser supports the `attachEvent` method, the Internet Explorer method is used to add an event handler to the click event. The event name includes an `on` prefix. Only two parameters are used in the `attachEvent` method.

```
else if (addH.attachEvent) {
addH.attachEvent('onclick', addBord);

}
```

When the user clicks the paragraph, the addBord() function is called. The paragraph is identified using getElementById, then formatting is applied to the paragraph via the style property.

```
function addBord () {
   var add = document.getElementById('p1');
   add.style.border = '1px dotted #ff0000';
   add.style.backgroundColor = '#ffff99';
}
```

A button is used to call the detHandler() function.

```
<input type='button' value='No border, please!' onclick='detHandler()'>
```

Once the paragraph is identified with getElementById, the styles are removed.

```
function detHandler () {
   var detH = document.getElementById('p1');
   detH.style.border = '';
   detH.style.backgroundColor = '#ffffff';
```

If the browser supports the removeEventListener method, the W3C DOM method is used to remove the event listener from the click event. The third parameter is false to specify the event bubbling phase.

```
if (detH.removeEventListener) {
   detH.removeEventListener('click', addBord, false);
}
```

If the browser supports the detachEvent method, the Internet Explorer method is used to remove the event handler from the click event. The event name includes an on prefix. Only two parameters are used in the detachEvent method.

Once the button is clicked and the event handler removed, the addBord() function is no longer called when the user clicks the paragraph.

Summary

JavaScript is a large topic, and this chapter touched on only the basic features of JavaScript as it's used in current browsers. For more detailed information on JavaScript syntax, see Appendix D.

Because JavaScript is a core component of Ajax, additional JavaScript code and concepts are included throughout this book.

This chapter included the following points:

❑ The ECMA-262 standard provides the rules for the core JavaScript language, including variables, operators, statements, functions, and objects.

❑ JavaScript's built-in objects include the String object, Date object, Math object, and Array object.

- ❑ The browser includes a set of objects such as the `window` object, the `history` object, and the `location` object that can be accessed with JavaScript to create interactivity in the browser window.

- ❑ User-defined objects are created using an object constructor function and then adding methods and properties to the object definition.

- ❑ The prototype property of objects can be used to add new methods and properties to an object that are inherited by every new instance of that object.

- ❑ The Document Object Model (DOM) is a representation of the document that includes objects and methods to access those objects.

- ❑ The document can be viewed as a tree made up of different types of nodes that have family relationships with the other nodes in that tree.

- ❑ DOM methods can be used to identify specific elements and to create new elements.

- ❑ Browser events provide a way to create interactivity on a page. JavaScript code can be called in response to a browser event.

- ❑ Event models are not yet standardized in today's browsers. Internet Explorer uses a different event model and event object than Mozilla-based browsers.

Exercises

Suggested solutions to these questions can be found in Appendix A.

1. Use a `for` loop to create a running total of numbers from 1 to 10. Display the subtotals on the page using `document.write`.

2. Create a function to change the `backgroundColor` style of the page. Call the function using a button.

Ajax and Server-Side Technologies

You'd be forgiven at this point for thinking that Ajax is all about what happens on the client side. In the initial definition of Ajax, the term "with input from the server" was the important caveat. In fact, many Ajax developers would consider an application that uses `XMLHttpRequest` to update the page without any input from the server not to be an Ajax application at all. So far, the discussions have avoided talking about the other side of the client/server communication — the server side. In reality, though, this is like having a phone call and conducting a conversation without being able to hear the other person speak. In fact, the first two chapters of this book have not used any server-side code. This is a state of affairs that cannot continue.

One of the initial goals of this book has been to remain agnostic and ambivalent about telling you which server-side technology to use. In fact, the discussion in this chapter assumes that you already have made your choice; therefore, telling you which one the authors prefer is only going to antagonize. One of the great advantages of using Ajax techniques is that you should be able to fit any server-side technology into your Ajax applications with ease. This chapter demonstrates this.

The way in which Ajax (read the `XMLHttpRequest` object) communicates with the server is fundamentally the same for each technology. But once the information has arrived, the way in which it is dealt with differs a little for each technology. It's evident that it's not possible to touch on all server-side technologies in this chapter, so the authors selected the three considered to be the most common and most pertinent to the Ajax developer: ASP.NET, PHP, and Java. If you work with another technology, then you should be able to look at the patterns here and glean how you might get the information back.

This discussion does not go into massive detail about how each of these technologies works, nor does it teach you the ins and outs of syntax or usage. Rather, this chapter cuts to the chase and provides an example of how an Ajax application can mesh with each technology and how that particular server-side technology can relay information and data, which can be used in the application, back to the client.

This chapter examines the following:

- ❏ Ajax and the server-side technologies
- ❏ ASP.NET
- ❏ PHP
- ❏ Java servlets

Ajax and the Server-Side Technologies

Thus far, this book has already established that the major difference between the way server-side technologies normally work (the "add data-send-wait" model) and the way in which Ajax works (by calling the server asynchronously) is the primary way in which Ajax alters the traditional pattern of web page usage.

Ajax isn't restricted to just one pattern of usage, and in Chapter 9 you will see how there are varying patterns by which Ajax can alter the flow of data from the client to the server. The one similarity all these patterns share is that you are no longer tied to having to explicitly submit a form and then wait for its response. Let's talk a little about how forms and HTML controls are used in the page.

Forms and HTML Controls

Ajax doesn't alter the fundamental way in which HTML controls work and the way in which data is retrieved from them. You still have a set of HTML controls (such as drop-down lists, radio buttons, check boxes, text boxes, and text areas), and these are still submitted to the server. The server picks them up in the same way.

There are two big changes, however. The first is the way in which the server-side page is called, and the second is the fact that the HTML form can be completely removed from the page or doctored to such an extent that it doesn't work in the expected way. Let's explain this by first taking a closer look at how the existing model of submitting a form to the server side works.

The Forms Model of Submission

With any server-side technology, the normal way of submitting a form is to have a form with a button that is submitted to the server when the user clicks the button.

Classic ASP and PHP would use the form's ACTION attribute to redirect the user from an original page to a response page. The processing is done on the server before the user is redirected to a new page, and the new page is used to display the data (Figure 3-1).

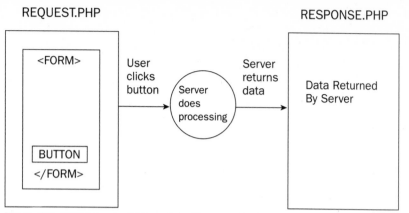

Figure 3-1: PHP/classic ASP model of forms submission.

ASP.NET subtly altered this model by removing the ACTION method and including a RUNAT=" SERVER " attribute. Rather than moving to another page, the page would then post back to itself. Once again, though, the page is acting on the intervention of the user (Figure 3-2).

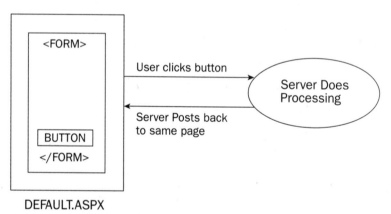

Figure 3-2: ASP.NET model of forms submission.

In ASP.NET model, the navigation between pages is more commonly performed by Response.Redirect or Server.Transfer methods. One of the biggest obstacles faced by novices who were moving from classic ASP to ASP.NET was getting over this conceptual difference. This remained the common mode of usage until Ajax, which reintroduced the idea of getting the script to submit the page instead, arrived.

The Ajax/JavaScript Model of Submission

The JavaScript model of submission that Ajax uses changed the model again. The form can be (although it doesn't have to be) completely removed from the model.

This model uses JavaScript to intercept a call to an event, and when this event happens (such as the user clicking a button or making a selection in an HTML control), then the call is passed to the script. It is then left to the script to initiate the call to the server (Figure 3-3).

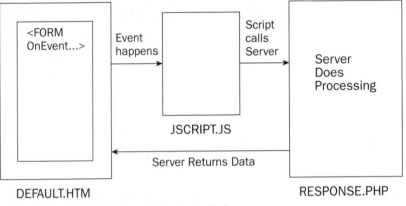

Figure 3-3: JavaScript/Ajax model of submission.

Of course, the script doesn't have to immediately submit the data. It can wait for other conditions and criteria to be satisfied before submitting the data. Also, in this model, because the script can respond immediately to the event and doesn't have to wait to be explicitly submitted, the return of data from the server doesn't have to be immediately visible to the user either. The script isn't tied down by having to wait for the response.

From the Server Side Onward

JavaScript is used to commence the client/server interaction. Let's now move over the divide and talk about what happens to the data when it arrives at the server. Because each section of the process is handled quite distinctly, you can slice up each section and examine it almost independently from the other sections. You can think of the sections as black boxes. They require a particular input, and they will provide a particular output, although what goes on inside can be completely different.

For example, consider a cash-point or ATM. You insert your card into it, you enter a personal identification number (PIN), and then you expect to get money (and possibly a receipt) out of the machine. There are thousands of ATMs across the country, belonging to many different banks. Some will charge fees, some will provide you with the ability to check your banking details, others won't do more than just provide cash. They work in many different ways, but they have the same interface through which you can communicate.

The server-side section of a client/server transaction works in much the same way as this hypothetical black box or ATM. It will receive the data from the HTTP request and, ultimately, after processing this data, it must provide data back in terms of a server response.

Submitting Data to the Server

While there are several methods for submitting data to the server, let's focus only on the `XMLHttpRequest` object. To submit data to the server using this object, there are three steps involved:

1. Set the event that triggers when the data is received.
2. Call the `open` method along with the request.
3. Send the request.

The `open` method is the only one to be discussed here.

```
XMLHttpRequestObject.open(method, URL to call, asynchronous or synchronous);
```

It submits it in one of two ways. First can be via the HTTP GET method, where the message is sent, as follows:

```
XMLHttpRequestObject.open("GET", "response.aspx?value=1", "true");
```

Or, it can be via the HTTP `Post` method. In the following code fragment a variable data is URI encoded, wrapped in the request body, and the request is sent across:

```
var argument = "value=";
argument += encodeURIComponent(data);
XMLHttpRequestObject.open("POST", "response.aspx", "true");
xHRObject.send(bodyofrequest);
```

This allows you to send the values of HTML controls and form data across to the server in exactly the same way and format as you might do if you were submitting a page via PHP or ASP.NET.

The Server Receives the Request

What happens once the server receives the data? The JavaScript has already specified the GET or POST method to post the data as either part of the URL or part of the `Request` body. In classic ASP and ASP.NET, you can use the `QueryString`, `Form` or `Params` collections to pick up these items. In PHP, you can use the $_GET, $_POST, or $_REQUEST collections to pick them up.

There is no observable difference because you can observe between receiving data from a HTML form or from a JavaScript-originated request. For example, you could have a text box called `"MyTextbox1"` created by the following code in your HTML page:

```
<input type="text" id="MyTextbox1" name="MyTextbox1" />
```

This will appear in the `QueryString` collection in ASP.NET using C# when submitted by the GET method.

```
string TextBox = Request.QueryString["MyTextbox1"].ToString();
```

Or, it can appear in the `Form` collection when submitted by the `POST` method.

```
string TextBox = Request.Form["MyTextbox1"].ToString();
```

Or, to pick up an item of that name from either the `QueryString` or `Form` collection, you could use the following:

```
string TextBox = Request.Params["MyTextbox1"].ToString();
```

In PHP, the equivalent is the `REQUEST` collection. For example, you could use the following:

```
$TextBox = $_REQUEST["MyTextbox1"];
```

In PHP, you also pick up the values of these collections separately via the `GET` or `POST` collections, which are analogous to the `QueryString` and `Form` collections of ASP.NET.

```
$TextBox = $_GET["MyTextbox1"];

$TextBox = $_POST["MyTextbox1"];
```

Once you've picked up the data, the server is free to process it and then return it to the client.

Writing the HTTP Response

What differs from the normal sequence of events you would get with the server-side technology is that the information you wish to display can't be immediately written back to the page. Instead, you're in the position of having to package up the information in the HTTP `Response`. This is a lot more straightforward than it sounds.

In ASP and ASP.NET, you simply write your data using the `Response.Write` method.

```
string data = "This is our data";
Response.Write(data);
```

In PHP, you use the `echo` command.

```
$data = "This is our data";
echo $data
```

You can create more complex structures (such as XML documents or other structures) as long as they can be parsed as text. This could be implemented in ASP.NET as follows:

```
XmlDocument XmlDoc = new XmlDocument();
XmlNode versionNode = XmlDoc.CreateXmlDeclaration("1.0","ISO-8859-1","yes");
XmlNode mainNode = XmlDoc.CreateElement("root");
XmlDoc.AppendChild(mainNode);
XmlNode childNode = XmlDoc.CreateElement("child");
childNode.AppendChild(XmlDoc.CreateTextNode("Data"));
mainNode.AppendChild(versionNode);
mainNode.AppendChild(childNode);
```

```
string strXml = XmlDoc.InnerXml;
Response.Write(strXml);
```

Or, in PHP, this could be as follows:

```
$doc = new DomDocument('1.0');
$root = $doc->createElement('root');
$root = $doc->appendChild($root);
$child = $doc->createElement('child');
$child = $root->appendChild($child);
$value = $doc->createTextNode("Data");
$value = $child->appendChild($value);
$strXml = $doc->saveXML();
echo $strXml;
```

This would produce the following XML document:

```
<?xml version="1.0"?>
<root>
<child>Data</child>
</root>
```

The string is appended to the HTTP Response and sent back to the client ready for retrieval. While this section of the process is simple, when the response gets back to the client, it's a slightly more complex matter to retrieve the data.

The XMLHttpRequest Object

As you will see in Chapter 4, the XMLHttpRequest object isn't the only means you have at your disposal for performing client/server interaction using Ajax techniques. It, however, is probably the most widely favored.

This chapter doesn't discuss the workings of this object in any detail, so imagine it as another black box that expects its input from the HTTP Response.

The Callback Function

The first stage of receiving the data is known as the *callback function*. This is simply a JavaScript function that is run when the data has been completely downloaded from the server. You can call the callback function something generic like getData(), and the function will look fairly similar in most Ajax applications. Inside the callback function, the first task to perform is to check that the data is ready for retrieval. This is done by checking to see if the XMLHttpRequest object's readyState property equals 4 (which stands for complete). So far, the typical callback function looks like this:

```
function getData()
{
  if (xHRobject.readystate == 4)
  {

  //Do our processing here

  }
}
```

Once you've ascertained that the data is ready, you are in a position to retrieve it using one of two properties of the `XMLHttpRequest` object:

❑   `responseText`

❑   `responseXML`

The responseText Property

The `responseText` property is the most common approach to retrieving data from the HTTP `Response`, and it is also the simplest. You can create a new JavaScript variable to collect the contents of the `Response`, and it will be returned as a string.

```
var text = xHRobject.responseText;
```

If, in your ASP.NET page, you create the following, then `responseText` method would contain `"This is our data"`:

```
string data = "This is our data";
Response.Write(data);
```

In PHP, you would create the following:

```
$data = "This is our data";
echo $data
```

That's all there is to it. You can also use it to retrieve HTML/XHTML. But what happens if you want to retrieve XML data? Well, you can still use the `responseText` method. It's just that it will return the XML data as a string. Consider the following ASP.NET code:

```
string data = "<?xml version=\"1.0\" encoding=\"ISO-8859-1\"
standalone=\"yes\"?><root><child>Data</child></root>";
Response.Write(data);
```

And consider the following PHP code:

```
$data = "<?xml version=\"1.0\" encoding=\"ISO-8859-1\"
standalone=\"yes\"?><root><child>Data</child></root>";
echo $data
```

These would return the following data:

```
<?xml version="1.0" encoding="ISO-8859-1"
standalone="yes"?><root><child>Data</child></root>
```

Returning the XML document as strings, however, can remove a lot of the benefits of using XML. Hence, there is a `responseXML` method.

The responseXML Property

The `responseXML` property intuitively looks to be a better bet if you want to start passing XML documents back to your client. It allows you to treat the response as an XML document object and iterate through the different elements, attributes, and text nodes using the DOM. As usual with Ajax, though, you need to be aware of quite a few problems when using it.

Say that you had the following server-side code to read in an XML document:

```
string data = "<?xml version=\"1.0\" encoding=\"ISO-8859-1\"
standalone=\"yes\"?><root><child>Data</child></root>";
Response.Write(data);
```

And then you changed your JavaScript code to read as follows.

```
var document = xHRobject.responseXML;
```

If you expected to get back a fully working XML document, you might be a little surprised. You would get back an object, but it would be empty, with no sign of the XML that you've transmitted. This happens because the ContentType of the Response must be set as "text/xml" before you write the Response.

```
string data = "<?xml version=\"1.0\" encoding=\"ISO-8859-1\"
standalone=\"yes\"?><root><child>Data</child></root>";
Response.ContentType = "text/xml";
Response.Write(data);
```

Unfortunately, Internet Explorer (IE) is particularly intolerant of this. If you don't set this on the server, then you won't be able to use responseXML on the browser. In Firefox, it's possible in JavaScript to use the overrideMimeType method before the code is invoked to override and set the type to text/xml on the client in the JavaScript, as shown here:

```
xHRobject.overrideMimeType("text/xml");
xHRobject.send(null);
var document = xHRobject.responseXML;
```

This property isn't present in IE. The problems, though, don't just end there. If you make a mistake in your XML document so that it isn't well formed, then you'd also get back an empty object from IE, without an immediately obvious error message.

Debugging responseXML

You can use four methods when determining just why you are not getting anything back from responseXML. The first is to check responseText to see if there is any content returned in this. Say that you run an alert message, as follows:

```
var text = xHRobject.responseText;
alert(text);
```

You would expect to see something like this:

```
<?xml version="1.0" encoding="ISO-8859-1"
standalone="yes"?><root><child>Data</child></root>
```

If you're not seeing this, then the response isn't being correctly transmitted by the server, and you need to check your server-side code. More than likely, though, you will see the correct data.

If you don't see the correct data, then the next step is to check the error code.

Debugging responseXML in IE

To find more information about the error in IE, you should then use the following code to return a more instructive error message and advise you on what needs correcting with the XML document:

```
var errorcode = xHRobject.responseXML.parseError.errorCode;
```

In normal situations, the code returned by IE should be zero. Most likely, if you have definitely set the `ContentType` to `"text/xml"` and the `responseXML.xml` is empty, then the code will be something other than zero.

You can retrieve further information about what the code returned from the `responseXML` property means as follows:

```
var errormessage = xHRobject.responseXML.parseError.reason;
```

Debugging responseXML in Firefox

While there is no equivalent object to parseError in Firefox, via the tools menu of Firefox is the "Javascript Console" that will allow you to examine meaningful error messages that include the type of object causing the error. If you have an XML formatting problem in your AJAX response, the Javascript Console provides information like the following and requires no changes or additions to the Javascript code:

```
Error: mismatched tag. Expected: </error>.
Source File:
http://localhost:8080/Company/WebPages/framed.jsf?com.asparity.AJAX_CLIENT_ID=
_idJsp0%3AmasterTree&com.company.AJAX_REQUEST=true&oracle.adf.faces.STATE_TOKEN=3&
nodeString=%3A%3AdomainModel%3A1&clientNodeId=%3A%3AdomainModel%3A1%3Aawaiting
AjaxData
Line: 1, Column: 6905
Source Code: [...]
```

In addition, there is an easy-to-install extension called 'firebug' that will allow the developer to examine the XHR traffic in real time, both request and response.

Using the Data

Once you've returned the data successfully from the `responseXML` property, you can retrieve the data as though it were a DOM object. For example, say that you had the following document:

```
<?xml version="1.0" encoding="ISO-8859-1" standalone="yes"?>
<cart>
 <book>
    <Title>Beginning ASP.NET with C#</Title>
     <Quantity>1</Quantity>
  </book>
</cart>
```

Then you could return the `<cart>` element in the XML document as follows:

```
var XMLDoc = xHRobject.responseXML;
var book = XMLDoc.getElementsByTagName("book");
```

You could also navigate to the first element contained in book like this:

```
var title = book[0].firstChild;
```

There is a notable difference between the two main browsers, IE and Mozilla, in terms of how text content is returned from the XML document.

IE will return it using the text property, as shown here:

```
var title = book[0].firstChild.text;
// title will equal "Beginning ASP.NET with C#"
```

Mozilla will return it using the textContent property, as shown here:

```
var title = book[1].firstChild.textContent;
// title will equal "Beginning ASP.NET with C#"
```

Also, you'll notice that with IE, book[0] is used to refer to the first node, while with Firefox it's book[1]. This happens because in Firefox book[0] would contain a text node with a newline character because Firefox doesn't skip whitespace characters; it treats them as separate nodes, whereas IE does not.

Once again, some cross-browser coding is needed to access data returned from the server.

The Server-Side Technologies

The discussion thus far has talked about the process by which data can be sent and received from the server, but not about what happens on the server itself. The server-side technologies are a separate entity to Ajax, and they must be learned separately. Let's assume that you already have working knowledge of one of these technologies because without being able to perform some basic processing on the server, you won't get too far. What follows now is a very brief introduction to each technology, followed by an example Ajax application that makes use of that technology.

If you are familiar with ASP.NET but not familiar with PHP or Java, don't feel that you need to skip these sections. Familiarity with other languages and technologies alien to the one you feel most comfortable working with is what gives any developer not only a good grounding, but future-proofing as well. Quite often, you will see jobs or contracts available that involve porting an application from one language to another, and this requires good knowledge of both languages.

Classic ASP and PHP share quite a few similarities, and you will soon see how one resembles the other. The following discussion dips briefly into Java to show how it can dovetail neatly into the Ajax philosophy, but let's start with Microsoft's current flagship: ASP.NET.

ASP.NET

ASP.NET is Microsoft's technology for creating dynamic web pages. It has two prerequisites for it to run on a computer: the installation of the .NET Framework and a compatible web server, usually Internet Information Server (IIS).

.NET has been around since 2000, but the most recent major revision, .NET 2.0, was made available in late 2005. You can obtain the latest version from http://update.microsoft.com. Be sure you select the Custom option rather than Express, and search under Optional Software Updates.

IIS, on the other hand, is available only as part of the Windows operating system. It is not installed by default on many versions of Windows, and furthermore, it is not available on Windows XP Home Edition. You can add it by going to the Control Panel and selecting the Add/Remove Windows Components icon.

ASP.NET is supposed to be language agnostic. The idea is that you can use any .NET implementation of a language in which to create your applications. In reality, it usually boils down to your having one of two choices of language, Visual Basic.NET and C#. For this book, let's create the ASP.NET examples in C# because C# shares structural similarities with JavaScript and features such as case sensitivity. It is also closer in keeping to PHP, as well.

To deploy an application in ASP.Net, you place it in the C:\inetpub\wwwroot\application_name folder (or wherever you might have chosen to locate the application) and then use IIS to create this as a virtual directory. This can be done by running IIS and right-clicking the directory you wish to enable, then selecting Properties, as shown in Figure 3-4.

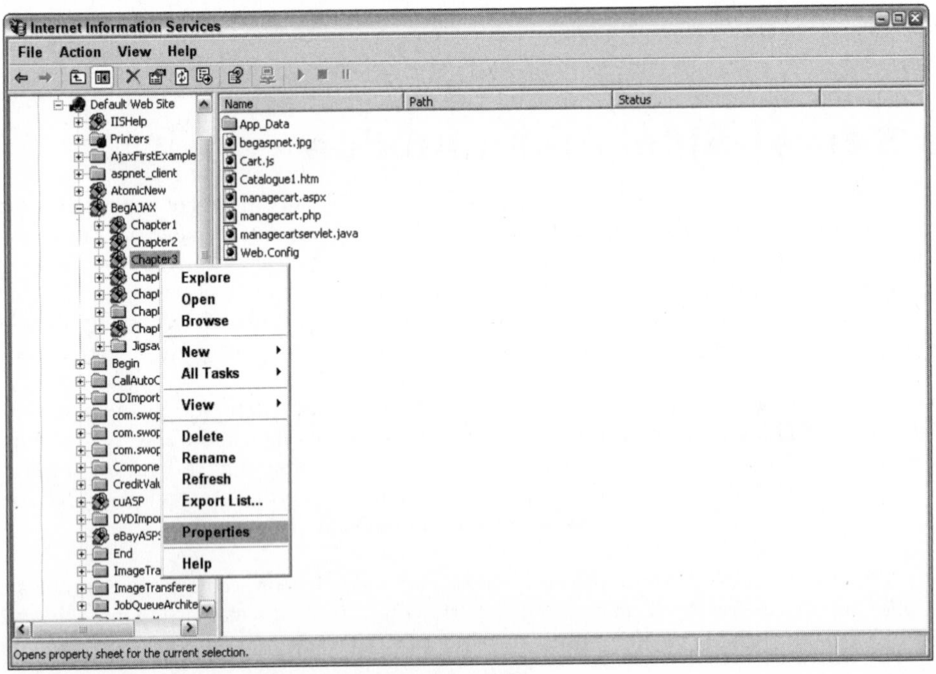

Figure: 3-4: Selecting properties of a directory in IIS.

Then, click on the Create button in the dialog that appears to create a new application, as shown in Figure 3-5.

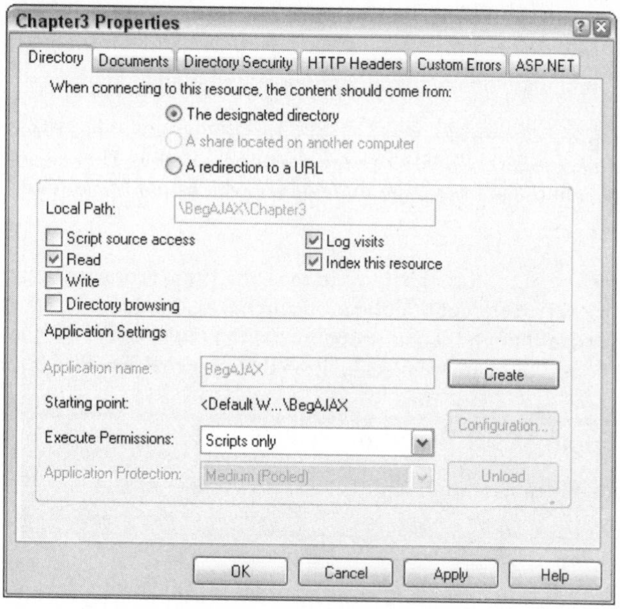

Figure: 3-5: Create button in Properties dialog.

If you then go into your browser to your new application (in this example, `http://localhost/BegAjax/chapter3`), then you will receive a `HTTP 403, view a directory is forbidden` error, which will indicate that you have created it successfully.

Once the application has been correctly deployed on the web server, you can call it from JavaScript by passing a reference to the ASP.NET page you want to call, in the `Open` method of the `XMLHttpRequest` object, as shown here:

```
XMLHttpRequestObject.open("POST", "response.aspx?value=1", "true");
```

Example Using AJAX and ASP.NET

Let's create a dummy catalogue page for a book seller using a shopping cart. You will allow users to place items in the shopping cart and to update the shopping cart without the need for a page refresh. Let's assume that the user has already been identified, to keep the example as simple as possible.

The shopping cart will have three pieces of functionality:

❑   You can add new items to it.

❑   If you add a second item to it, the quantity will increase by one.

❑   You can remove items from it.

Now, this evidently is not something that can be achieved entirely on the client side, although it can be initiated on the client side. The application will scoop the book title from the client page and pass that on to the server. This is used to identify the book when you place it in the shopping cart.

On the server, a shopping cart must keep track of which items a user has placed in the cart and the number of items. To do this, the cart will be stored in a session variable. This means that, in a large catalogue, the user would be able to move from page to page, without losing track of what has been placed in the basket.

Let's use an XML document to store the items in the cart. There is one single cart element, and inside this is a book element for every different title the user purchases. The book element contains a title element and a quantity element (although there is scope to add the ISBN, price, authors). Although you have only one catalogue page, this example is scalable so that you could run it off many catalogue pages.

Try It Out   Shopping Cart Example in ASP.NET

1.   Create a new file called `Catalogue1.htm`.

```
<html xmlns="http://www.w3.org/1999/xhtml" >
<head>
  <script type="text/javascript" src="Cart.js"></script>
</head>
<body >
<br/>
<img id="cover" src="begaspnet.jpg" />
<br />
<br />
<b>Book:</b><span id="book">Beginning ASP.NET with C#</span><br />
<b>Authors: </b><span id="authors"> Hart, Kauffman, Sussman, Ullman</span>
<br /><b>ISBN: </b><span id="ISBN">0764588508</span>
<br /><b>Price: </b><span id="price">$39.99</span>
<br /><br />
<a href="#" onclick="AddRemoveItem('Add');" >Add to Shopping Cart</a>
<br /><br />
<span id="cart" ></span>
</body>
</html>
```

2.   Create a script called `Cart.js`.

```
var xHRObject = false;
if (window.XMLHttpRequest)
{
xHRObject = new XMLHttpRequest();
}
else if (window.ActiveXObject)
{
xHRObject = new ActiveXObject("Microsoft.XMLHTTP");
}

function getData()
{
```

```
if (xHRObject.readyState == 4 && xHRObject.status == 200)
    {
        var serverResponse = xHRObject.responseXML;
        var header = serverResponse.getElementsByTagName("book");
        var spantag = document.getElementById("cart");
        spantag.innerHTML = "";
        for (i=0; i<header.length; i++)
        {

        if (window.ActiveXObject)
        {
            spantag.innerHTML += " " + header[0].firstChild.text;
            spantag.innerHTML += " " + header[0].lastChild.text + " " + "<a
href='#' onclick='AddRemoveItem(\"Remove\");'>Remove Item</a>";
        }
        else
        {
            spantag.innerHTML += " " + header[0].firstChild.textContent;
            spantag.innerHTML += " " + header[0].lastChild.textContent + " " + "<a
href='#' onclick='AddRemoveItem(\"Remove\");'>Remove Item</a>";
        }
        }

    }
}

function AddRemoveItem(action)
{
        var book  = document.getElementById("book").innerHTML;

        if(action=="Add")
        {
          xHRObject.open("GET", "managecart.aspx?action=" + action + "&book=" +
encodeURIComponent(book)+ "&value=" + Number(new Date), true);          }
        else
        {
          xHRObject.open("GET", "managecart.aspx?action=" + action + "&book=" +
encodeURIComponent(book)+ "&value=" + Number(new Date), true);          }
        xHRObject.onreadystatechange = getData;
        xHRObject.send(null);
}
```

3.   Create a page called `ManageCart.aspx`.

```
<%@Page Language = "C#" Debug="true" %>

<%@ import Namespace="System.Xml" %>
<script language="C#" runat="server">
    void Page_Load()
    {
        string newitem = Request.Params ["book"];
        string action = Request.Params ["action"];
        Hashtable ht = new Hashtable();
        if (Session["Cart"] != null)
```

```
        {
        ht = (Hashtable)Session["Cart"];
        if (action == "Add")
        {
            if (ht.ContainsKey(newitem))
            {
                int value = int.Parse(ht[newitem].ToString());
                ht.Remove(newitem);
                value++;
                ht.Add(newitem, value);
                Session["Cart"] = ht;
                Response.ContentType = "text/xml";
                Response.Write(toXml(ht));
            }
            else
            {
                ht.Add(newitem, 1);
                Session["Cart"] = ht;
                Response.ContentType = "text/xml";
                Response.Write(toXml(ht));
            }
        }
        else
        {
            ht.Remove(newitem);
            Session["Cart"] = null;
            Response.ContentType = "text/xml";
            Response.Write(toXml(ht));
        }
    }
    else
    {
        ht.Add(newitem, 1);
        Session["Cart"] = ht;
        Response.ContentType = "text/xml";
        Response.Write(toXml(ht));

    }

}

string toXml(Hashtable ht)
{
    XmlDocument XmlDoc = new XmlDocument();
    XmlNode versionNode = XmlDoc.CreateXmlDeclaration("1.0","ISO-
8859-1","yes");
    XmlNode mainNode = XmlDoc.CreateElement("cart");
    XmlDoc.AppendChild(versionNode);
    XmlDoc.AppendChild(mainNode);

    foreach (string key in ht.Keys)
```

```
        {
            XmlNode childNode = XmlDoc.CreateElement("book");
            XmlNode TitleNode = XmlDoc.CreateElement("Title");
            XmlNode QuantityNode = XmlDoc.CreateElement("Quantity");
            TitleNode.AppendChild(XmlDoc.CreateTextNode(key));
            QuantityNode.AppendChild(XmlDoc.CreateTextNode(ht[key].ToString()));
            childNode.AppendChild(TitleNode);
            childNode.AppendChild(QuantityNode);
            mainNode.AppendChild(childNode);
        }

        string strXml = XmlDoc.InnerXml;

        return strXml;
    }
</script>
```

4. Start `Catalogue1.htm` in your browser, and select the "Add to Shopping Cart" link, as shown in Figure 3-6.

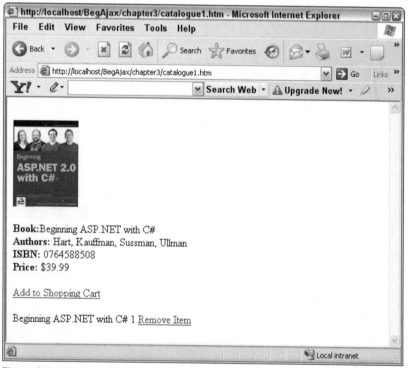

Figure 3-6: "Add to Shopping Cart" link.

5. Click "Add to Shopping Cart" again and the item quantity goes up by one, as shown in Figure 3-7.

6. Now, click Remove Item and the Item disappears from your cart, as shown in Figure 3-8.

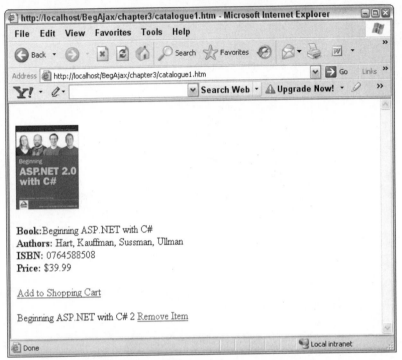

Figure 3-7: Item quantity going up by one.

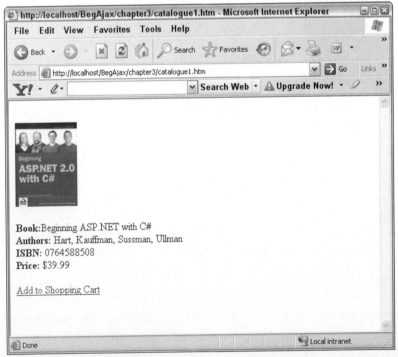

Figure 3-8: Item disappearing from cart.

How It Works

The three-page cycle exactly mirrors the JavaScript model discussed earlier. The HTML page is a "dummy" page that displays one item from a catalogue. In reality, this page would be a server-side page that would pull the details of a single book onto the screen from a database. This catalogue page includes the script cart.js in the page. The script is called via the "Add to Shopping Cart" link:

```
<a href="#" onclick="AddRemoveItem('Add');" >Add to Shopping Cart</a>
```

You use the same function in your script to perform both the addition and removal of items from the shopping cart. You just pass a string variable as the argument to the script, indicating whether you want to "Add" or "Remove" an item. Let's not linger on what this function does because talking about XMLHttpRequest isn't the purpose of this exercise.

The function extracts the book from the page using document.getElementById and creates one of two requests to the server, depending on whether an Add or Remove Item task has been called. It assembles a querystring and calls the server-side page.

```
function AddRemoveItem(action)
{
        var book  = document.getElementById("book").innerHTML;

        if(action=="Add")
        {
          xHRObject.open("GET", "managecart.aspx?action=" + action + "&book=" +
encodeURIComponent(book)+ "&value=" + Number(new Date), true);
        }
        else
        {
          xHRObject.open("GET", " managecart.aspx?action=" + action + "&book=" +
encodeURIComponent(book)+ "&value=" + Number(new Date), true);
        }
        xHRObject.onreadystatechange = getData;
        xHRObject.send(null);
}
```

There are two methods in the server-side code managecart.aspx. The first section is in the Page_Load method and is executed as soon as the page is called. The second, toXml, serializes the shopping cart as XML and gets it ready to send back to the client. You start in Page_Load by creating three variables: The first two are for storing the book title you extracted from the page on the client side, and the third is the action that the user selected (which can be Add or Remove). You then create a hash table to store the items in the shopping cart. Store the title of the item in the cart, alongside the quantity that the user has selected.

```
void Page_Load()
{
    string newitem = Request.Params["book"];
    string action = Request.Params["action"];
    Hashtable ht = new Hashtable();
```

Next, check to see if your `Session` variable that holds your shopping cart is empty. If it isn't empty, then you know the user has been here before, and that leaves one of four possible actions:

❑   The user is adding an item, and that item is already present in the cart.

❑   The user is adding a new item that isn't already in the cart, but there is already a cart.

❑   The user is removing an item.

❑   The user is adding an item and there is no cart present, so one must be created.

If the user is adding an item, and that item is already present in the `hashtable ht`, then you execute the following code:

```
if (Session["Cart"] != null)
{
    ht = (Hashtable)Session["Cart"];
    if (action == "Add")
    {
        if (ht.ContainsKey(newitem))
        {
            int value = int.Parse(ht[newitem].ToString());
            ht.Remove(newitem);
            value++;
            ht.Add(newitem, value);
            Session["Cart"] = ht;
            Response.ContentType = "text/xml";
            Response.Write(toXml(ht));
        }
```

Whichever action you are performing, you ensure that you get the most up-to-date version of the shopping cart from the `Session` variable and store it in the `Hashtable ht`. You check to see if your action variable is equal to `Add` and also check to see if your item is present in the hash table. Next, you create a variable value that stores the quantity associated with the item in the hash table. The item is removed from the hash table. You add one to the value and add the new item to the hash table. You read the updated hash table into the `Session` variable.

The next step is vital. You set the `content-type` to `Xml`. If you don't do this, then the `responeXML` will not function correctly. Last, you write the hash table to the `Response` stream, via the function `toXML` (discussed shortly).

If the hash table doesn't contain the item, you must add a new item, so you run the following code.

```
        else
        {
            ht.Add(newitem, 1);
            Session["Cart"] = ht;
            Response.ContentType = "text/xml";
            Response.Write(toXml(ht));
        }
    }
```

You add the item to your hash table and assign it the value 1. You also set the `Content-Type` to `text/xml` and then write it to the `response` stream. At the end of each possible scenario, you must do this to ensure that the client displays the correct information.

The third scenario is that the `Action` variable wasn't equal to `Add`, so you assume that it must be `Remove`. To remove an item, you run the following section:

```
else
{
    ht.Remove(newitem);
    Session["Cart"] = null;
    Response.ContentType = "text/xml";
    Response.Write(toXml(ht));
}
}
```

You remove the item from hash table. You set the `Session` variable containing the cart to zero, and you set the `ContentType` to `text/xml` and write the hash table to the `Response` stream.

The last scenario will look fairly familiar. It's basically the same as the second scenario. You add an item to the hash table, you store the hash table in the `Session` variable, you write the `ContentType` as `"text/xml"`, and you write the hash table to the `Response` stream.

```
else
{
    ht.Add(newitem, 1);
    Session["Cart"] = ht;
    Response.ContentType = "text/xml";
    Response.Write(toXml(ht));

}
}
```

At the end of each scenario, you call the `toXML` function to serialize the hash table into XML. Chapter 5 goes into more detail about XML, so let's not spend too much time on the structure of the document here.

```
XmlDocument XmlDoc = new XmlDocument();
        XmlNode versionNode = XmlDoc.CreateXmlDeclaration("1.0","ISO-
8859-1","yes");
        XmlNode mainNode = XmlDoc.CreateElement("cart");
        XmlDoc.AppendChild(versionNode);
        XmlDoc.AppendChild(mainNode);
```

You create a new document, and you create a declaration node. You create a root node and call it `cart`. You then append the root node and the declaration to your document.

Next, you iterate through each key in the hash table. You stored the `Title` of the book as a key in the table and the `Quantity` the user wishes to purchase as the value. For each item in the table, you create a book `Title` and `Quantity` element. Because `Title` and `Quantity` are subelements of book, you must be careful about the order in which you append them and to which items.

```
foreach (string key in ht.Keys)
{
    XmlNode childNode = XmlDoc.CreateElement("book");
    XmlNode TitleNode = XmlDoc.CreateElement("Title");
    XmlNode QuantityNode = XmlDoc.CreateElement("Quantity");
```

First, though, you must add the text values from the hash table to the elements. You append the key of the hash table to the Title element and the value of the hash table's key to the Quantity element:

```
TitleNode.AppendChild(XmlDoc.CreateTextNode(key));
QuantityNode.AppendChild(XmlDoc.CreateTextNode(ht[key].ToString()));
```

Then you append the two subelements to the child element <book>. Last, you append the book to the cart element to complete the document.

```
childNode.AppendChild(TitleNode);
childNode.AppendChild(QuantityNode);
mainNode.AppendChild(childNode);
}
```

All that must be done is to get the text version of this document, using the innerXml method and return it to the calling method:

```
string strXml = XmlDoc.InnerXml;

return strXml;
```

Of course, your work still isn't completed here. You've managed to send the data to the server, and, on the server, you have packaged up the data and sent a response back as an XML document. You must still disentangle the XML and display it on the page. This is back to your JavaScript, and the function getData(), which is called when the readystatechange event is triggered.

Inside the callback function, you retrieve the data from the responseXML property of the XMLHttpRequest object. You isolate a subset of your XML using the DOM's getElementsByTagName method to retrieve an array of book elements.

```
var serverResponse = xHRObject.responseXML;
var header = serverResponse.getElementsByTagName("book");
```

At the same time, you must also retrieve information about the HTML element that will be displaying the shopping cart. You have created an empty <span> tag in Catalogue1.htm. Here, you retrieve it using the DOM's getElementById method, and you ensure that its innerHTML property is set to zero.

```
var spantag = document.getElementById("cart");
spantag.innerHTML = "";
```

Now that you have retrieved all of the book elements and stored them in an array, it's time to unpack them. You create a loop and set its maximum to be the number of items in the array. You then check to see if the user is using IE or Mozilla. If the user is using IE, then use the text property to display each book element. If the user is using Mozilla, then you use the textContent property. The firstChild of the book element is the Title element; the lastchild of the book element is the Quantity element.

```
for (i=0; i<header.length; i++)
{

if (window.ActiveXObject)
{
```

```
                spantag.innerHTML += " " + header[0].firstChild.text;
                spantag.innerHTML += " " + header[0].lastChild.text + " " + "<a
        href='javascript:AddRemoveItem(\"Remove\");'>Remove Item</a>";
            }
            else
            {
                spantag.innerHTML += " " + header[0].firstChild.textContent;
                spantag.innerHTML += " " + header[0].lastChild.textContent + " " + "<a
        href='javascript:AddRemoveItem(\"Remove\");'>Remove Item</a>";
            }
        }
```

After you have displayed the book element's title and quantity, you also create a dynamic link that allows the user to remove an item. This hooks back into the JavaScript with a call to AddRemoveItem and passing "Remove" as an argument. This completes the circuit.

The ASP.NET page has a fair amount of code, but as you can see, there is nothing particularly difficult about the code it contains. You will see the same with the PHP version of the code.

PHP

PHP is an acronym that has been rumored to have several meanings. The commonly accepted one is simply "Hypertext PreProcessor," although others include "Personal Home Pages" and "PHP Hypertext PreProcessor" (a potentially recursive acronym). PHP is perhaps the simplest alternative to ASP.NET. Unlike ASP.Net (which leverages existing programming languages), PHP is a programming language in its own right. It can run on both major web servers (IIS and Apache) and doesn't get tied to the Windows platform. It has managed to maintain a lot of the simplicity that first brought developers to use classic ASP, in that you don't require strong typing of variables or have to package everything up in a separate procedure or method.

PHP is an Open Source product that is commercialized by the company Zend Technologies. It can be downloaded from www.php.net. The current version as of this writing is 5.1.6. Whereas ASP.NET theoretically requires you to have at least purchased a Windows operating system somewhere down the line, PHP is totally free because it can run on an Open Source operating system (such as Linux). It also runs on the very widely used Apache web server (www.apache.org), which boasts the same kind of flexibility and multiple platform support as PHP.

PHP resembles two main languages. It was created in PERL by Rasmus Lerdorf, and also in C. It, however, has removed much of the complexity of both of these languages. It has a set of objects that ape the classic ASP/ASP.NET objects with Request and Session as well, so that it will be not be too alien to ASP and ASP.Net developers.

Despite previous incarnations of PHP having reputations as being awkward to install, the latest version of PHP 5 is now very easy to put on IIS. If you create a directory on your hard drive and extract the contents of the Windows-installer ZIP file to here from www.php.net/downloads.php#v5, all you need to do is register the ISAPI filter via IIS. To do this, go to IIS and right-click your Default Web Site and select Properties. Choose the ISAPI Filters tab, as shown in Figure 3-9. Click Add, and create the filter name as PHO and point the executable to the location of php5isapi.dll.

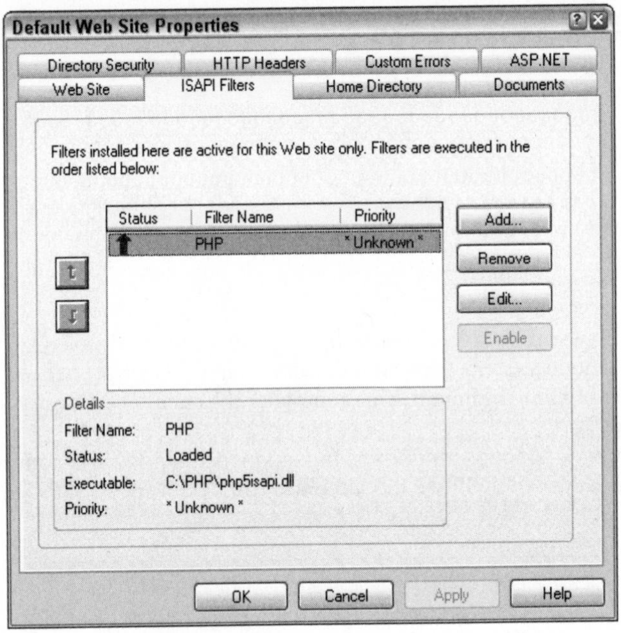

Figure: 3-9: ISAPI Filters tab.

Once the application has been correctly deployed on the web server, you can call it from JavaScript by passing a reference to the PHP page you want to call in the same way as you did with ASP.NET, via the `Open` method of the `XMLHttpRequest` object, as shown here:

```
XMLHttpRequestObject.open("POST", "response.php?value=1", "true");
```

In fact, PHP can run alongside ASP/ASP.Net without any hassle.

Example Using AJAX and PHP

Let's convert this chapter's example now to use PHP in place of ASP.NET. It's a relatively simple task in terms of how you must engineer the client-side code. You just change the calls from the ASP.NET page to a PHP page.

Note that if you don't want to create the ASP.NET example first, then follow Steps 1 and 2 in that "Try It Out" section, and jump to Step 1 in the following "Try It Out" section.

Then you follow the same pattern in the PHP code as you did in the ASP.NET code. You have two sections of code — one that performs the actions of the shopping cart (adding and removing items) and one that serializes the contents of the shopping cart into an XML document.

Try It Out   **Shopping Cart Example in PHP**

   1.   Open `Catalogue1.htm`, change the following line, and save it as `catalogue1PHP.htm`:

```
...
<head>
```

```
<script type="text/javascript" src="cartPHP.js"></script>
</head>
...
```

2. Change the following highlighted lines in cart.js in the function AddRemoveItem so that they read as follows, and save it as cartPHP.js:

```
if(action=="Add")
{
    xHRObject.open("GET", "managecart.php?action=" + action + "&book=" +
book + "&value=" + num, true);
}
else
{
    xHRObject.open("GET", "managecart.php?action=" + action + "&book=" +
book + "&value=" + num, true);
}
```

3. Now, create a new page called managecart.php, and add the following:

```
<?php
session_register('Cart');
header('Content-Type: text/xml');
?>
<?php
    $newitem = $_GET["book"];
    $action = $_GET["action"];
    if ($_SESSION["Cart"] != "")
    {
        $MDA = $_SESSION["Cart"];
        if ($action == "Add")
        {
            if ($MDA[$newitem] != "")
            {
                $value = $MDA[$newitem] + 1;
                $MDA[$newitem] = $value;
                $_SESSION["Cart"] = $MDA;
                ECHO (toXml($MDA));
            }
            else
            {
                $MDA[$newitem] = "";
                $_SESSION["Cart"] = $MDA;
                ECHO (toXml($MDA));
            }
        }
        else
        {
            $MDA= "";
            $_SESSION["Cart"] = "";
            ECHO (toXml($MDA));
        }
    }
    else
```

```
        {
            $MDA[$newitem] = "1";
            $_SESSION["Cart"] = $MDA;
            ECHO (toXml($MDA));
        }


    function toXml($MDA)
    {
        $doc = new DomDocument('1.0');
        $cart = $doc->createElement('cart');
        $cart = $doc->appendChild($cart);

        foreach ($MDA as $Item => $ItemName)
        {

        $book = $doc->createElement('book');
        $book = $cart->appendChild($book);

        $title = $doc->createElement('title');
        $title = $book->appendChild($title);
        $value = $doc->createTextNode($Item);
        $value = $title->appendChild($value);

        $quantity = $doc->createElement('quantity');
        $quantity = $book->appendChild($quantity);
        $value2 = $doc->createTextNode($ItemName);
        $value2 = $quantity->appendChild($value2);

        }

        $strXml = $doc->saveXML();
        return $strXml;
    }
?>
```

4. Now, run the example again viewing `Catalogue1.htm`. It should work in exactly the same way as before.

How It Works

You've changed almost nothing in the client-side code other than making the references point to the PHP code. So, how is the PHP code different? Well, PHP has no native support for hash tables as a data structure; instead, you are forced to use a multidimensional array in which to store the `Session` variable. Apart from that, however, the code almost directly corresponds to the ASP.NET code.

Once again, you have four scenarios to deal with:

❑ User adding an item, and that item is already present in the cart

❑ User adding a new item that isn't already in the cart, but there is already a cart

❑ User removing an item

❑ User adding an item and there is no cart present, so one must be created as well

Because PHP doesn't require you to strongly type your variables, it makes the code you must provide slightly shorter and simpler than the ASP.NET code. Because a specific on_load event is not required, the PHP code you want to run every time the page is called is just placed at the head of the page.

You start by registering a Session variable called Cart, which holds the shopping cart. You set the Content-Type of the response to be text/xml, so that it can be used by the responseXML method.

```
session_register('Cart');
header('Content-Type: text/xml');
```

You create two variables to store the book title and the action the user has chosen to perform. These are taken from the GET collection, which has been appended as a querystring to the request made by the JavaScript:

```
$newitem = $_GET["book"];
$action = $_GET["action"];
```

You query the $_Session["Cart"] variable to see if it is empty or not. If it isn't empty, then you create a variable called $MDA to store the Session variable. Because you are not using strong typing, you don't have to worry about casting the PHP variables from one type to another. This is all handled automatically.

```
if ($_SESSION["Cart"] != "")
        {
            $MDA = $_SESSION["Cart"];
```

You check to see if the $action variable contains the word "Add," which has been passed from the JavaScript originally. If it does, then you have one of two scenarios to deal with.

The first one is where you already have an item in the cart and you simply add one to the value, store the new value in the array, store the array in the Session variable, and then serialize the array, as follows:

```
if ($action == "Add")
{.
    if ($MDA[$newitem] != "")
    {
        $value = $MDA[$newitem] + 1;
        $MDA[$newitem] = $value;
        $_SESSION["Cart"] = $MDA;
        ECHO (toXml($MDA));
    }
```

The array works in a very similar way to ASP.NET's hash table. Each element is referenced by the book title stored in it. The index value of the array is simply the book title. If there isn't an item in the cart, then you set the value to nothing, store the array in the Session variable, and serialize the array to XML.

```
else
    {
        $MDA[$newitem] = "";
        $_SESSION["Cart"] = $MDA;
        ECHO (toXml($MDA));
    }
}
```

In scenario three, you remove an item by setting the array and `Session` variable to be empty strings, and then you serialize that to XML:

```
else
{
    $MDA= "";
    $_SESSION["Cart"] = "";
    ECHO (toXml($MDA));
}
```

Last, the fourth scenario (where there is no cart in existence) uses the same code as the second one.

```
$MDA[$newitem] = "1";
$_SESSION["Cart"] = $MDA;
ECHO (toXml($MDA));
```

You set the value to 1. You create the `Session` variable cart and assign it the array. Then you serialize the array to XML.

While PHP doesn't natively have a set of methods specifically for dealing with the creation of XML documents, it does have a `DomDocument` method. In this example, let's create the XML document as a DOM document, and create and append the XML elements to the document and the text nodes as with the ASP.NET. You have a root element <cart>, and inside that you create a `book` element for each separate title in the cart. The `book` element contains a `<title>` element and a `<quantity>` element and you assign text nodes to these to store the data.

```
function toXml($MDA)
    {
        $doc = new DomDocument('1.0');
        $cart = $doc->createElement('cart');
        $cart = $doc->appendChild($cart);

        foreach ($MDA as $Item => $ItemName)
        {

        $book = $doc->createElement('book');
        $book = $cart->appendChild($book);

        $title = $doc->createElement('title');
        $title = $book->appendChild($title);
        $value = $doc->createTextNode($Item);
        $value = $title->appendChild($value);

        $quantity = $doc->createElement('quantity');
        $quantity = $book->appendChild($quantity);
        $value2 = $doc->createTextNode($ItemName);
        $value2 = $quantity->appendChild($value2);

        }

        $strXml = $doc->saveXML();
        return $strXml;
    }
```

You use the `saveXML` function to compile the document as a single entity. You store this as a string and return this to the `ECHO` function. The `ECHO` function writes to the `Response` stream and passes the information back from the server to the client-side script, where the XML document is used in the assembling of the HTML page.

Java Servlets

The last server-side technology involves using Java. While the Java run-time environment can be present on the client, this discussion looks at Java on the server, with the use of servlets. *Servlets* are server-side applications written in the Java programming language. They are used to create interactive Web pages, and they provide the kind of functionality you would expect from PHP or ASP.NET (such as form processing, session and cookie management, and membership and login handling).

Again, as with PHP, while the Java technology is proprietary, it is distributed freely by Sun and available from `http://java.sun.com`.

Ironically, Ajax is now being used to fill the gap that Java aimed to fill a decade or so ago. Originally Java used the Java Virtual Machine (JVM) to run applications on the client side that were more interactive and boasted a richer functionality.

Several problems have hamstrung this particular use of Java. The first was that the `<applet>` tag was a Netscape approved addition (which was standardized in HTML 3.2) from the running Java applets was quickly deprecated in HTML 4.0 and treated as a bit of an aberration. In fact, the whole HTML 3.2 standard was seen as slightly wayward.

The approved replacement was the `<object>` tag, which was only present for a long while in Internet Explorer, and so you had no effective standard way of adding Java applications. On top of this, the JVM that was required to run Java was regularly updated, while the ones distributed with the browsers were stuck at the same version unless they were updated separately. In reality, this meant that in order to run the more "modern" Java applets, you often had to download an entire new version of the JVM first.

The last reason was that Java shifted almost the whole burden of processing back to the client. Java applets were frequently slow to download and even slower to start running, depending on the user's processing power. While Java continues to thrive as a programming language and development environment, Ajax has most definitely usurped it on the client side.

Just because Ajax has usurped Java in its role on the client, this doesn't mean that Ajax techniques can't be employed very successfully in tandem with Java running on the server.

Example Using AJAX and Java Servlets

You should be getting used to the pattern now. Let's now adapt this chapter's example so that it uses the servlet technology in the Ajax application.

To develop and run servlets, you will need the following:

❑ J2EE SDK, version 2 (`http://java.sun.com/products/servlet/download.html`) — This is the actual Java programming language.

❑   Tomcat@Jakarta (`http://tomcat.apache.org/`) — This is the server on which you can run servlets

The servlets require a Java technology-enabled server with the Tomcat-embedded servlet engine. You must install the J2EE SDK following the instructions provided and deploy the Java Application server. The Java Application server typically runs off of `http://localhost:8080`, `http://localhost:8081`, or `http://localhost:4848`. Next, you must install Tomcat and start the service that runs it, following the instructions given on installation.

When the application has been correctly deployed on the web server, you can call it from JavaScript, in a similar but slightly different way as before. Servlets must be compiled before they can be referenced, so you compile a Java class into a `.class` file. Then you reference the `.class` file via the `Open` method of the `XMLHttpRequest` object as follows:

```
XMLHttpRequestObject.open("POST", "response?value=1", "true");
```

Once again, the example requires minimal intervention to the client-side code; it is just the code on the server that will be changed, and because this example uses Tomcat as a server, then the location where you place your files must be changed. Tomcat also requires you to perform an extra bit of configuration to get the servlet working, too.

Try It Out   Shopping Cart Example in Java

1. Place all files in the `C:\Program Files\Apache Software Foundation\Tomcat 5.5\webapps\ROOT` folder, unless otherwise specified. Open `Catalogue1.htm`, change the following line, and save it as `catalogue1Java.htm`:

```
...
<head>
    <script type="text/javascript" src="cartJava.js"></script>
</head>
...
```

2. Change the following highlighted lines in `cart.js` in the function `AddRemoveItem` so that they read as follows, and save it as `cartJava.js`:

```
        if(action=="Add")
        {
            xHRObject.open("GET", "ManageCartServlet?action=" + action + "&book=" +
book + "&value=" + num, true);
        }
        else
        {
            xHRObject.open("GET", "ManageCartServlet?action=" + action + "&book=" +
book + "&value=" + num, true);
        }
```

Change these lines as well:

```
    if (window.ActiveXObject)
            {
                spantag.innerHTML += " " +header[0].firstChild.text;
```

```
                     spantag.innerHTML += " " + header[0].lastChild.text + " " + "<a
href='#' onclick='AddRemoveItem(\"Remove\");'>Remove Item</a>";
                }
else
                {
                     spantag.innerHTML += " " + header[0].childNodes[1].textContent;
                     spantag.innerHTML += " " + header[0].childNodes[3].textContent
+ " " +

"<a href='#' onclick='AddRemoveItem(\"Remove\");'>Remove Item</a>";

                }
```

3. Next, create a text file called `ManageCartServlet.java`, and add the following:

```java
import javax.servlet.http.HttpServlet;
import javax.servlet.http.HttpServletResponse;
import javax.servlet.http.HttpSession;
import javax.servlet.http.HttpServletRequest;
import javax.servlet.ServletException;
import java.io.IOException;
import java.util.Hashtable;
import java.util.Iterator;

public class ManageCartServlet extends HttpServlet {

    public void doGet(HttpServletRequest req, HttpServletResponse  res)
        throws IOException, ServletException {

String newitem = req.getParameter("book");
String action = req.getParameter("action");
Hashtable ht = new Hashtable();
HttpSession session = req.getSession(true);
if (session.getAttribute("cart") != null)
{
    ht = (Hashtable) session.getAttribute("cart");
        if ("Add".equals(action))
    {
        if (ht.containsKey(newitem))
          {
                int value= 1;
                if (ht.containsKey(newitem))
                {
                  Integer currentQuantity = (Integer)ht.get(newitem);
                  value += currentQuantity.intValue();
                }
                ht.put(newitem, new Integer(value));
                session.setAttribute("cart", ht);
                String cartXml = toXml(ht);
                res.setContentType("text/xml");
                res.getWriter().write(cartXml);
            }
            else
            {
                ht.put(newitem, 1);
```

```
                                session.setAttribute("cart", ht);
                                String cartXml = toXml(ht);
                                res.setContentType("text/xml");
                                res.getWriter().write(cartXml);
                        }
                }
                else
                {
                        ht.remove(newitem);
                        session.setAttribute("cart", null);
                                String cartXml = toXml(ht);
                                res.setContentType("text/xml");
                                res.getWriter().write(cartXml);   ;
                }
        }
        else
        {
                        ht.put(newitem, 1);
                        session.setAttribute("cart", ht);
                        String cartXml = toXml(ht);
                        res.setContentType("text/xml");
                        res.getWriter().write(cartXml);
        }
}

    public String toXml(Hashtable ht)
    {
     StringBuffer xmlDoc = new StringBuffer();
     xmlDoc.append("<?xml version=\"1.0\" encoding=\"UTF-8\"
standalone=\"yes\"?>\n");
     xmlDoc.append("<cart>\n");

        for (Iterator<String> x = ht.keySet().iterator() ; x.hasNext() ; )
        {
            String item = x.next();
            int Quantity = ((Integer)ht.get(item)).intValue();
            xmlDoc.append("<book>\n");
            xmlDoc.append("<title>");
            xmlDoc.append(item);
            xmlDoc.append("</title>\n");
            xmlDoc.append("<quantity>");
            xmlDoc.append(Quantity);
            xmlDoc.append("</quantity>\n");
            xmlDoc.append("</book>\n");
        }
        xmlDoc.append("</cart>\n");
        return xmlDoc.toString();

    }
}
```

4. Compile the application to a class file. The Sun JDK includes the `javac` command-line compiler. You will need to include the servlet API as follows when compiling it (note the following URL may vary depending on your installation of Tomcat). For the sake of expediency, the `ManageCartServlet.java` file has been placed in the same folder as the `javac.exe` compiler in the following command.

```
javac -classpath ".;C:\Program Files\Apache Software Foundation\Tomcat
5.5\common\lib\servlet-api.jar" ManageCartServlet.java
```

5. In the default configuration of Tomcat, compiled servlets are placed in the `webapps\ROOT\WEB-INF\classes` folder of the Tomcat installation directory to deploy them. Place the `ManageCartServlet.class` file in that directory. If you are running Tomcat for the first time, then you must create this folder.

6. Create a `web.xml` file as follows, and save it in the `WEB-INF` folder, just below the `ROOT` folder:

```
<?xml version="1.0" encoding="ISO-8859-1"?>
<web-app xmlns="http://java.sun.com/xml/ns/j2ee"
    xmlns:xsi="http://www.w3.org/2001/XMLSchema-instance"
    xsi:schemaLocation="http://java.sun.com/xml/ns/j2ee
http://java.sun.com/xml/ns/j2ee/web-app_2_4.xsd"
    version="2.4">

    <display-name>ManageCartServlet Application</display-name>
    <description>
Beg Ajax
    </description>

    <servlet>
        <servlet-name>ManageCartServlet</servlet-name>
        <servlet-class>ManageCartServlet</servlet-class>
    </servlet>

  <servlet-mapping>
    <servlet-name>ManageCartServlet</servlet-name>
    <url-pattern>/ManageCartServlet</url-pattern>
  </servlet-mapping>

</web-app>
```

7. Now, run the example again viewing `http://localhost:8080/Catalogue1Java.htm`, but this time using Java. It will work in exactly the same way as with ASP.NET and PHP.

How It Works

This example mirrors the previous two examples, although it has required some extra configuration to get it working. Once again, you use two methods that carry out all of the work.

The `doGet` method resembles the ASP.NET `OnLoad` method in that it is the method that is called each time the page is executed. If you are not familiar with ASP.NET, then this is the method that is called whenever a page starts running. Typically, in the PHP file, this is code that isn't enclosed within a function.

You are back to your four scenarios again. Let's not reiterate them a third time, nor go over the code in too much detail. Instead, let's note the fundamental differences.

Once again, you are able to use a hash table to store the cart information, and this table is stored in a `Session` variable. Semantically speaking, Java's session handling is slightly wordier than its ASP.NET and PHP brethren, but it works in much the same way. You set the values and store them in the hash table. You use the key of the hash table to store the title of the book name. You set the contents of the `session` variable, the `Content-Type` of the response, and you write the serialized hash table (via the `toXML` method) in an almost identical way as you have done in the ASP.NET and PHP examples.

The `toXML` method is rather more rudimentary than either the ASP.Net or PHP, and to keep the example simple, a `StringBuffer` object is created and a string with the XML document is dynamically created in the following code:

```java
public String toXml(Hashtable ht)
    {
            StringBuffer xmlDoc = new StringBuffer();
            xmlDoc.append("<?xml version=\"1.0\" encoding=\"UTF-8\"
standalone=\"yes\"?>\n");
            xmlDoc.append("<cart>\n");

            for (Iterator<String> x = ht.keySet().iterator(); x.hasNext(); )
            {
                String item = x.next();
                int Quantity = ((Integer)ht.get(item)).intValue();
                xmlDoc.append("<book>\n");
                xmlDoc.append("<title>");
                xmlDoc.append(item);
                xmlDoc.append("</title>\n");
                xmlDoc.append("<quantity>");
                xmlDoc.append(Quantity);
                xmlDoc.append("</quantity>\n");
                xmlDoc.append("</book>\n");
            }
            xmlDoc.append("</cart>\n");
            return xmlDoc.toString();

    }
```

This is returned to the `doGet method()` with the serialized XML document, and from there back to the client. Because you've set the `Content-Type` of the response to `"text/xml"`, this will still be processed correctly by the `XMLHttpRequest` object, despite the fact that you have created it as a string on the server.

Which One Should You Use?

We hope that you now have a feel for all of the most common server-side technologies available. ASP.NET and PHP can be run on IIS. PHP can also be run on Apache, while Java servlets require their own application server. None of the examples is dramatically different from each other, and the more complex aspects probably involve actually installing the server-side technologies and getting them to work.

The purpose of this discussion is not to judge the pros and cons of one technology over another. Necessity is what normally drives developers, and either you will have been instructed to use one particular technology by your client or you will be sufficiently familiar with only one of the technologies to develop the full-blown solution in it.

Of course, there will be times when one technology is better suited to a particular implementation than another. ASP.NET boasts much more complex and robust state handling than PHP, and it offers an alternative way of managing state that doesn't involve using cookies. PHP and Java can work on more platforms than ASP.NET can, but ASP.NET is becoming increasingly ubiquitous. In terms of answering the question, "Does any particular one work better with Ajax or is more suited to Ajax?" the answer is "no." In fact, it's better to look at it in reverse. Ajax plugs a hole that each of the server-side technologies needed to fill.

The choice is completely up to you, and you shouldn't be deterred from using Ajax techniques because you might be tied to a particular development platform or technology; Ajax works equally well with all of them.

Summary

This chapter has been a brief look over the wall at the role of the server in Ajax applications. If you came to Ajax expecting not to have to use the server at all, then you may well be feeling a little dismayed, and there's probably no getting over it for the majority of applications. You started by examining the role of the server in the traditional web programming request/response cycle, and then you compared it to the way Ajax and JavaScript can make calls to the server. You then extended the coverage of each step in this cycle.

Next, you took a very brief look at each of the three server-side technologies. You created a single shopping cart example and slotted in a server-side page in ASP.NET, PHP, and Java into the Ajax application to see how few differences there were between each of them. You spent little time on the client side, but we were forced to talk a little about how the XMLHttpRequest object is used to initiate requests and receive data.

Chapter 4 examines this in a lot more detail, as well as the methods Ajax uses to create a request and handle the results.

Exercises

Suggested solutions to these questions can be found in Appendix A.

1. Add the ISBN to the XML document. Why might this be useful?
2. Amend the cart so that the ISBN is now visible in the cart display.

Ajax Techniques

Chapter 1 discussed how when people mention Ajax, they are usually referring to the use of the XMLHttpRequest object and client-side script to perform interaction behind the scenes in a web page. That discussion also mentioned that the XMLHttpRequest object doesn't have to be the only way in which you can instigate client/server communication. Some techniques have predated the XMLHttpRequest object involving hidden frames and hidden inline frames, and some alternative techniques to using XMLHttpRequest use either dynamic script loading or preloading images and cookies. This chapter takes a brief look at all of these techniques, which broadly fit under the Ajax umbrella.

While it sounds as if there could be a lot of ground to cover, most of these techniques are fairly simple, and they are all worth looking at. The examination begins with the XMLHttpRequest object and spends the most time looking at it because it's central to a lot of Ajax applications. Also, it's the most widely applicable solution for most developers. The discussion looks at how to use it with the POST and GET methods because, unlike with an ASPX or PHP page, the way in which it must be used with these two methods varies quite widely. Also considered are some of the most common mistakes and issues people run into when they start using this object. Some of the problems you might run into when trying to get your page to run on all browsers are discussed; this will become a recurring theme for later chapters as well. Then the chapter looks at each of the alternative Ajax techniques and provides a quick example of how they might be used.

In this chapter, you learn about the following:

- ❑ The XMLHttpRequest object
- ❑ Hidden frames
- ❑ Hidden iframes
- ❑ Dynamic script loading
- ❑ Preloading images and cookies

The XMLHttpRequest Object

The XMLHttpRequest object started life as an ActiveX control in Internet Explorer 5.0 (IE 5), although the actual concept can be dated back to Outlook Web Access 2000. Outlook Web Access 2000 was an Outlook web-mail service that was used to allow people to access e-mail functionality (such as download e-mail, check calendars, and update contacts) while on the go. It did this by allowing the application to issue its own client-side HTTP requests. It was quickly drafted into IE 5 for the same purpose.

ActiveX controls have the awkward distinction of being able to run only on Internet Explorer. The object immediately gained popularity, though, and was later included in Mozilla 1.0, Netscape 7, Safari 1.2, and Opera 7.60.

> Although Opera implemented the object in 7.60, there were some bugs that weren't ironed out until version 8.0. So, if you have version 7.6, you should download a more recent version from www.opera.com/, which is currently at version 9.02.

This meant that the implementation of the object differed between the version used in IE and the version used in all the other main browsers, which ran as part of the window object. In practice, this means you have to use browser-detecting script to discover which browser is being used before you can create an instance of the object. The World Wide Web Consortium (W3C) standards organization took over the implementation of the object with the intent of creating a common subset of properties and methods that can be used on all browsers, the second working draft of which can be found at www.w3.org/TR/XMLHttpRequest.

As a result, the XMLHttpRequest is now included in IE 7 as a native object (which means it works in the same way as it does on Firefox), and the XMLHTTP object is still present as an ActiveX Control. With IE 6 being an integral part of the Windows XP operating system, you are likely to have to make arrangements for it in your applications, for a long time yet.

This explains a bit about the history of the object, but not what the object does. According to working draft two of the XMLHttpRequest object standard, the object may be used "to allow scripts to program-matically connect to their originating server via HTTP." In other words, it allows scripts to communicate with the server, outside of the normal HTTP request/response scenario.

The main purpose of the XMLHttpRequest object is to be able to use just HTML and script to connect directly with the data layer that is stored on the server. It allows you to bypass the need for the server-side scripting in many instances. Chapter 1 discussed how you could use the DOM to create a dynamic menu system and where the menu options were entirely populated by data derived from an XML file. The benefit of using the XMLHttpRequest is that you don't have to send the page or refresh it because changes to the underlying data (such as the text in the menu) are immediately reflected in the web page displayed by the browser. It is integral to creating the seamless and rich user interfaces that Ajax applica-tions strive for. Let's take a look at how to use it.

Creating an XMLHttpRequest Object

Chapter 1 discussed how you can create the XMLHttpRequest object in both Firefox and IE. Just in case you've forgotten (or in case you're the type of person who skips over Chapter 1 in any book), here's the JavaScript code needed to do it. In IE 7, Firefox, Safari, and Opera, the syntax needed to create an object is as follows:

```
var xmlRequest = new XMLHttpRequest();
```

In IE 5 and IE 6, the code looks like this:

```
var xmlRequest = new ActiveXObject("Microsoft.XMLHTTP");
```

Because JavaScript is case sensitive, you must ensure that you get the rather odd case correct. Otherwise, you'll find that nothing is created.

Of course, just creating the object on your web page won't produce anything visible or make the object work straight off. You can use the XMLHttpRequest in two ways: synchronously or asynchronously.

Synchronous Usage

You can use the XMLHttpRequest object synchronously with the following pattern:

1. Create the object.
2. Create a request.
3. Send the request.
4. Hold processing until you get a response.

This corresponds to what you normally do when you send a request to the server and wait for a response. The real power, though, comes from using it asynchronously.

Asynchronous Usage

When you use the object asynchronously, you must call the object using the onreadystatechange event. When this event is triggered, you must check the contents of the readystate property before your application can act. This means you will conform to the following pattern:

1. Create the object.
2. Set the readystatechange event to trigger a specific function.
3. Check the readyState property to see if the data is ready. If it isn't, check again after an interval. If it is, then carry on to the next step.
4. Open the Request.
5. Send the Request.
6. Continue processing, only interrupting it when you get a response.

The whole operation of the readystatechange event is performed behind the scenes and enables you to use the XMLHttpRequest object asynchronously.

It might sound strange, but the way in which the object works is similar to going on car journeys with your children. When children reach five years old, every five minutes of the journey they'll always ask the classic question, "Are we nearly there yet?" It doesn't matter how close you are to the destination, the only thing that changes is your answer in response to their question. Early on, you will say something like, "There are miles to go." Then, in the middle of the journey, you'll say, "We're half way there." Near the end, it will be, "Not much longer." At the end, it will be "Phew, here we are." Of course, only the latter response is in any way effective for preventing tantrums.

The XMLHttpRequest object is similar in that it keeps on telling you about its state, via the readyState property, yet you really want to know only when it's finished loading the data because you can't use its properties and methods until that happens.

The readyState Property

The readyState property indicates at what point the XMLHttpRequest object is with regard to sending/receiving data. The XMLHttpRequest object goes through five possible state changes. The codes are as follows and indicate the cycle in which data is loaded:

❑ **0 – Uninitialized** — This is when the object has been created but has not yet been initialized. In other words, the open method has yet to be called.

❑ **1 – Open** — This is when the object has been created and initialized, but the send method has not been called.

❑ **2 – Sent** — This is when the send method has been called, but the object is waiting for the return of the status code and the headers.

❑ **3 – Receiving** — This is when some of the data has been received, but not all of it. You won't be able to use the properties of the object to view partial results because status and response headers are not fully available.

❑ **4 – Loaded** — This is the final stage where all of the data has been received and the complete data is available. This is normally the readyState code you will be checking for.

Once the data has been loaded, you are able to use the other properties and methods to get back the data from the response to your request.

XMLHttpRequest Properties and Methods

As shown in Table 4-1, the XMLHttpRequest object has a fairly small selection of methods and properties that are used in its operation.

Property	Description
onreadystatechange	Returns or sets the event handler for asynchronous requests.
readyState	Returns a code representing the state of the request. This can be one of the following:
	0 – Uninitialized
	1 - Open
	2 – Sent
	3 – Receiving
	4 – Loaded

Property	Description
responseBody (IE 7 only)	Returns the HTTP response as an array of unsigned bytes.
responseText	Returns the HTTP response as a string.
responseXML	Returns the HTTP response as an XML DOM object.
status	Returns the HTTP status code.
statusText	Returns the text that describes what a particular HTTP status code means.

Table 4-2 shows the methods that are used to perform the various functions.

Method	Description
abort	Cancels the request in progress.
getAllResponseHeaders	Gets the entire list of HTTP response headers.
getResponseHeader	Gets only the specified HTTP response header.
open	Takes several arguments. The first assigns the method attribute, the second assigns the destination URL, and the third specifies whether the request is sent synchronously (false) or asynchronously (true).
send	Sends the request to the server.
setRequestHeader	Adds a custom HTTP header to the request.

You can see that you will use the onreadystatechange event handler to indicate which code should be run, the open method to create a request, and the send method to send the request. The readyState property helps us to know when exactly to run the code that will act on the response, and the responseText or responseXML properties can be used to retrieve the response. Last, the abort method is used to cancel the particular request that is in progress. Although there are other methods and properties in the tables, as you can see, it is on these seven properties and methods that the majority of your applications will be based. Let's now take a look at a very simple example of the object being used that will work with all browsers.

Try It Out   **Dynamic Display Using the XmlHttpRequest Object**

In Chapter 1, one of the example sites mentioned was Basecamp, which used Ajax techniques in a very unobtrusive way to dynamically display sections of the page on demand. Let's now look at an example that uses the XMLHttpRequest object to ape this kind of technique and to display sections of the page on demand, when you click a link. You will add a little server-side script into this page, and you will have the opportunity to use either ASP.NET or PHP, depending on which you prefer.

1. Locate the folder in your web server's root directory called BegAjax. Inside that, create a folder called Chapter4.

2. Create a client-side script as follows, and save it as `XmlHttpRequest.js`:

```
var xHRObject = false;
if (window.XMLHttpRequest)
{
 xHRObject = new XMLHttpRequest();
}
else if (window.ActiveXObject)
{
 xHRObject = new ActiveXObject("Microsoft.XMLHTTP");
}

function sendRequest(data)
{
    xHRObject.open("GET", "display.php?value=" + data, true);
    xHRObject.onreadystatechange = getData;
    xHRObject.send(null);
}

function getData()
{
  if (xHRObject.readyState == 4 && xHRObject.status == 200)
  {
    var serverText = xHRObject.responseText;

    if(serverText .indexOf('|' != -1))
    {
      element = serverText.split('|');
      document.getElementById(element[0]).innerHTML = element[1];
    }
  }
}
```

> Note that if you want to do this example in ASP/ASP.NET, then change the line highlighted in bold type to the following:
>
> ```
> xHRObject.open("GET", "display.aspx?value=" + data, true);
> ```

3. Create an HTML page as follows, and save it as `display.htm`:

```
<html>
<head>
  <script type="text/javascript" src="XmlHttpRequest.js"></script>
</head>
<body>
<a href="#" onclick ="sendRequest('Contacts');return false;"">Contacts</a>
<a href="#" onclick ="sendRequest('Calendar');return false;">Calendar</a>
<a href="#" onclick ="sendRequest('Adverts');return false;">Adverts</a><br/>
<div id="box1">
</div>
<div id="box2">
</div>
<div id="box3">
```

```
</div>
</body>
</html>
```

4. Last, if you want to use PHP, then add the following, and save it as `display.php`:

```php
<?php
switch($_REQUEST['value']) {
case 'Contacts':
echo "box1|<br><b>Contacts</b><br>John Doe 1, Acacia Avenue<br>Jane Doe, 2 Willow
Tree Lane";
break;
case 'Calendar':
 $dt = gmdate("M d Y H:i:s");
 echo "box2|<br><b>Calendar:</b><br> $dt";
break;
case 'Adverts':
 $source = "wrox_logo.gif";
 echo "box3|<br><b>Advert:</b><br><img src='$source '>";
break;
   }
?>
```

Or, if you want to use ASP.NET, then add the following, and save it as `display.aspx`:

```aspx
<%@Page Language = "C#" Debug="true" %>
<script language="C#" runat="server">
    void Page_Load()
    {
        switch (Request.Params["value"])
        {
            case "Contacts":
                Response.Write("box1|<br><b>Contacts</b><br>John Doe 1, Acacia
Avenue<br>Jane Doe, 2 Willow Tree Lane");
                break;
            case "Calendar":
                string dt = DateTime.Now.ToString();
                Response.Write("box2|<br><b>Calendar:</b><br>" + dt);
                break;
            case "Adverts":
                string source = "wrox_logo.gif";
                Response.Write("box3|<br><b>Advert:</b><br><img src='" + source +
"'>");
                break;
        }
    }
</script>
```

5. Now, run the view `display.htm` in your browser, and click each of the links and the corresponding text will appear, as shown in Figure 4-1.

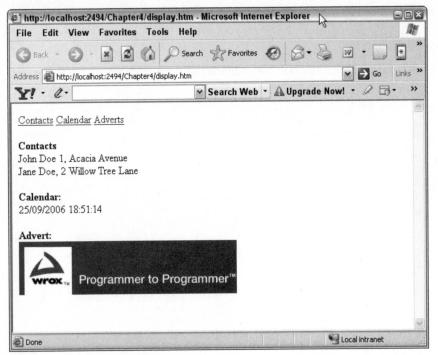

Figure 4-1: Text corresponding to link.

How It Works

You can see that the example works on a very basic level by using the `XMLHttpRequest` object to create and send requests that are acted on by the server. The server here returns a couple of lines of HTML for each option, but it should be easy to extrapolate from this the kind of data that it could return. The code that it uses might be getting quite familiar by now. Start by detecting the browser and creating a browser-specific instance of the `XMLHttpRequest` object.

```
var xHRObject = false;
if (window.XMLHttpRequest)
{
   xHRObject = new XMLHttpRequest();
}
else if (window.ActiveXObject)
{
   xHRObject = new ActiveXObject("Microsoft.XMLHTTP");
}
```

Next, create a function, `sendRequest`, that sets the `onreadystatechange` event handler and opens a request to the server page `display.php` (or `display.aspx`, if you are using this one). Last, it sends the object.

```
function sendRequest(data)
{
    xHRObject.open("GET", "display.php?value=" + data, true);
```

```
        xHRObject.onreadystatechange = getData;
        xHRObject.send(null);
    }
```

This function is called in the three anchor <a> tags on the HTML page:

```
...
<a href="#" onclick ="sendRequest('Contacts');return false;"">Contacts</a>
<a href="#" onclick ="sendRequest('Calendar');return false;">Calendar</a>
<a href="#" onclick ="sendRequest('Adverts');return false;">Adverts</a>
...
```

Pass a single parameter to the sendRequest method. This is, in turn, used by the server to determine which branch of code to run.

```
switch($_REQUEST['value']) {
case 'Contacts':
echo "box1|<br><b>Contacts</b><br>John Doe 1, Acacia Avenue<br>Jane Doe, 2 Willow
Tree Lane";
break;
case 'Calendar':
 $dt = gmdate("M d Y");
 echo "box2|<br><b>Calendar:</b><br>" + dt;
break;
case 'Adverts':
 $source = "wrox_logo.gif";
 echo "box3|<br><b>Advert:</b><br><img src='" + $source + "'>";
break;
    }
```

Each condition in the switch statement just prints out a relevant line of data. To keep this example simple, you don't actually retrieve any data. The execution of the PHP page finishes, but nothing is displayed on the page until the onreadystatechange event is fired. If you go back to XmlHttpRequest.js and look at the sendRequest method again, you can see that you have set the getData function to be run every time this event is fired with the following line of code:

```
xHRObject.onreadystatechange = getData;
```

The event fires several times during the loading of the data. You're interested in running the final code to display the items on the screen only when you know that the data has finished loading fully. This, as you may recall, happens when the readyState property of the XMLHttpRequest object returns a code of 4.

```
if (xHRObject.readyState == 4 && xHRObject.status == 200)
{
  var serverText = xHRObject.responseText;

  if(serverText .indexOf('|' != -1))
  {
    element = serverText.split('|');
    document.getElementById(element[0]).innerHTML = element[1];
  }
}
```

Inside the condition, create a variable `serverText`, and assign it the value of whatever is contained in the `xHRObject`'s `responseText` property. This method will return exactly what you have told the PHP/ASP.NET program to return to the screen. So, for `contacts`, it would contain this:

```
"box1|<br><b>Contacts</b><br>John Doe 1, Acacia Avenue<br>Jane Doe, 2 Willow Tree Lane"
```

Next, create an array called `element`. Then check to see if there is a | symbol in your output. You have used the pipeline | symbol simply as a delimiter to indicate that your line of data contains two pieces of information.

The first piece of information, `box1`, is the name of the element you want to dynamically populate; the second is the actual HTML you want to populate it with. So, the array now has two items:

- ❑ `element[0] = box1`
- ❑ `element[1] = <br><b>Contacts</b><br>John Doe 1, Acacia Avenue<br>Jane Doe, 2 Willow Tree Lane`

Last, use `getElementById` to identify the element with the ID `box1`, and set its `innerHTML` property to contain the HTML and text you want to display. You have a line of execution that runs as follows for the Contact link:

1. When the link in the page is clicked, it runs `sendRequest('Contacts')` via the `click` event.

2. The `XmlHttpRequest.js` script creates an `XMLHttpRequest` object.

3. The `sendRequest` method creates a request on the object with the `querystring` `display.php?value=Contacts`.

4. The `send` method is called.

5. The `onreadystatechange` event fires. It is set to 1, and the `getData` function is run but does nothing.

6. The method calls the `display.php` page and runs it.

7. In the first case (in the PHP page), `Contacts` is triggered, which runs the following line:

    ```
    echo "box1|<br><b>Contacts</b><br>John Doe 1, Acacia Avenue<br>Jane Doe, 2
    Willow Tree Lane";
    ```

8. The execution of the PHP page completes.

9. The `onreadystatechange` event fires. It is set to 3. The page is still loading, and the `getData` function is run but does nothing

10. The `onreadystatechange` event fires, it is set to 4, and the `getData` function is run, but this time the conditions are met.

11. The `getData` function changes the `innerHTML` property of the `div` that it received to display the HTML.

The whole cycle involves the creation of a request and the sending of a request without a page submission being required. This pattern of usage is going to be repeated each time you use the XMLHttpRequest object. It can seem quite fiddly, but you will get used to it.

Common Mistakes

If you didn't get the previous example to work the first time, then you might consider the following common pitfalls discovered when creating the example:

❑ Double-clicking on the HTM file in Windows Explorer and expecting it to run.

❑ Not setting up the folder on IIS as applications.

❑ Getting the case of XMLHttpRequest wrong:

   ❑ Right — XMLHttpRequest

   ❑ Wrong — XmlHttpRequest

   ❑ Wrong — XMLHTTPRequest

❑ Writing the line with parentheses:

   ❑ Right — xHRObject.onreadystatechange = getData;

   ❑ Wrong — xHRObject.onreadystatechange = getData();

In JavaScript, if you include the parentheses after the function name in this line of code, you're assigning the result of the function to onreadystatechange rather than the function itself. The difference between the two is as follows:

```
// this assigns the function to onreadystatechange

xHRObject.onreadystatechange = getData;

// this calls the function and then assigns the result of the function to
// onreadystatechange

xHRObject.onreadystatechange = getData();
```

Most of these mistakes can be put down to absent-mindedness or following your normal practices and habits. Not all problems, though, are fixed so easily. Articles have been published saying that Ajax techniques are easy and that unnecessary "scare-mongering" is going on. The truth is that many times you can find a page with Ajax techniques not functioning in the way that is expected, and there may not being anything obviously wrong with it. Let's take a look at some of the more complex issues that can dog Ajax applications.

More Complex Issues

In the last example, you shouldn't have run into the more difficult problems examined in this section, so let's look at them now because there's a good chance you could run into them later in this book. It's a good idea to be prepared and forewarned.

Same Origin Issues

The `XMLHttpRequest` object has some problems with same origin issues. It used to be possible in earlier versions of the browsers to run any script from any source, but it became obvious that this invited too many possible security hazards. A "same origin policy" is generally enforced where only scripts that originate from the same domain, the same protocol, and the same port can be run. If any of these values differ, then the script will not be run.

IE actually goes one step further with the notion of security zones. Unfortunately, though, IE doesn't actually validate the fields that it gets back from the `XMLHttpRequest` object. One of these is the `HTTPPREFERER` value, which contains the URL/domain name of the page that referred the user to a particular page. (Note there isn't always one.) What this means is that the `Referer` can be completely faked on the client and that pages and images can be retrieved and displayed using a spoofed `Referer` value.

This security hole means that the `Referer` value shouldn't be trusted. When writing cookies, it's a good idea to add the domain name/server to the cookie, as well to verify that the correct one is being sent and received.

Cache Control: IE Aggressive Caching

One problem that you might come across (although you shouldn't in this example) is that when the data behind the page is updated, the page doesn't reflect the update. It shows the old data because, to save on reload time, the browser will cache the page locally, and it will then pull the page from the cache rather than reload it. This particular problem is more common with IE, which has a tendency to cache pages unless you specifically force it not to do so.

Typically, to cure the problem, you would insert the following code into the HTML page:

```html
<meta http-equiv="Pragma" CONTENT="no-cache" />
<meta http-equiv="Expires" CONTENT="-1" />
```

This should be enough to force it to reload the page. When using the GET directive as part of a request using the `XMLHttpRequest` object, then, unfortunately, IE will always cache the page and never reload it.

Try It Out   Aggressive Caching in Internet Explorer

Let's demonstrate this by making a quick tweak to the example you've just run.

1. Run the `display.htm` program from the previous example in IE.

2. Open `display.php` and change the name in the following line:

```php
switch($_REQUEST['value']) {
case 'Contacts':
echo "box1|<br><b>Contacts</b><br>William Woe 1, Acacia Avenue<br>Jane Doe, 2
Willow Tree Lane";
break;
```

3. Now, go back and click Contacts again. Nothing changes, as shown in Figure 4-2.

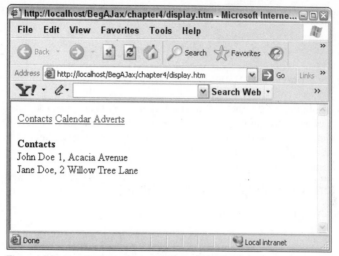

Figure 4-2: No change after clicking on Contacts link.

How It Works

Something, however, should change. Let's just consider what happens again from the cycle of execution point of view:

1. When the link in the page is clicked, it runs the sendRequest('Contacts') function.

2. The XmlHttpRequest.js script creates an XMLHttpRequest object.

3. The sendRequest method creates a request on the object with the querystring display.php?value=Contacts.

4. The send method is called.

You call up display.php, and it should use a new page, given that you've just changed the contents of the page and this is a brand new request. Wrong! Even if you added the no-cache <meta> tag, IE will still cache the page and produce the same page as previously. If you're trying to create a dynamically updated web site with Ajax, this one can be incredibly annoying.

There are three solutions to this problem. The first is that you add a querystring to the end of your GET request that you can guarantee will be different each time you run it. A date would be a good choice, for example, as shown here:

```
xHRObject.open("GET", "display.php?id=" + Number(new Date) +"&value=" + data,
true);
```

The "different each time" querystring solution is conceptually a bit of a copout (it creates a redundant item on the querystring). Imagine it as being like a competition where it says you can't enter twice, but there's nothing to stop you from entering your auntie's name, your cat's name, your dog's name, or even your goldfish's name on a second entry. This is where the second solution comes in.

The second solution is to set the HTTP header `If-Modified-Since` to reference a date in the past:

```
xHRObject.open("GET", "display.php? value=" + data, true);
xHRObject.setRequestHeader("If-Modified-Since", "Sat, 1 Jan 2000 00:00:00 GMT" );
```

In this way, caching is prevented.

The third solution is to use a `POST` request instead. It is common for browsers and servers to vary their behavior, so good practice would be to combine techniques. The third solution avoids the problem completely, but the first two are simpler and can be combined without fuss. Let's take a look at how to do that now.

Try It Out   Correcting the Aggressive Caching Problem

This example involves some "to-ing" and "fro-ing" of the code in `display.php`. Unfortunately, this is unavoidable.

1. Open `display.php`, and change the name back to the following:

```
switch($_REQUEST['value']) {
case 'Contacts':
echo "box1|<br><b>Contacts</b><br>John Doe 1, Acacia Avenue<br>Jane Doe, 2
Willow Tree Lane";
break;
```

2. Open `XmlHttpRequest.js`, locate function `sendRequest`, and amend the code as follows:

```
function sendRequest(data)
{
xHRObject.open("GET", "display.php?id=" + Number(new Date) +"&value=" + data,
true);    xHRObject.setRequestHeader('If-Modified-Since', 'Sat, 1 Jan 2000
00:00:00 GMT' );xHRObject.onreadystatechange = getData;
xHRObject.send(null);
}
```

3. Start a new instance of IE, or, if the browser from the previous example is still open, click the Refresh button. This is to ensure that the browser is using the updated version of `XmlHttpRequest.js`. Leave this browser open, and do not press Refresh. If it has worked, you will see the results shown in Figure 4-3.

4. Open `display.php`, and change the name back to the following once again:

```
switch($_REQUEST['value']) {
case 'Contacts':
echo "box1|<br><b>Contacts</b><br>William Woe 1, Acacia Avenue<br>Jane Doe, 2
Willow Tree Lane";
break;
```

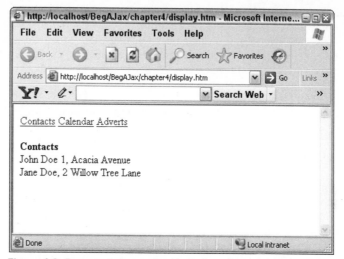

Figure 4-3: Browser using updated version of `XmlHttpRequest.js`.

5. Now, go back to your open browser, and click Contacts again. This time, it updates the page, as shown in Figure 4-4.

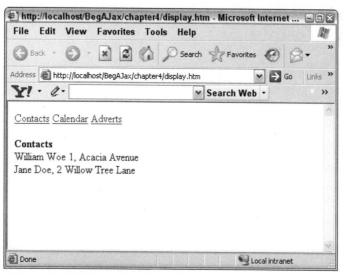

Figure 4-4: Updated page in browser.

How It Works

The first line of code appends a date as a number to the querystring. Because the date is constantly changing, this will be guaranteed to be unique:

```
xHRObject.open("GET", "display.php?id=" + Number(new Date) +"&value=" + data,
true);
```

As mentioned before, think of this like filling in your dog's name for a competition when you are s upposed to enter only once. This trick fools IE into thinking that this is actually a new request and reloading it properly, rather than using a cached version. Of course, Mozilla doesn't employ the same aggressive caching policy, and so it isn't affected by this problem. You can run the first version of this example using Mozilla and change the data, and it will be immediately effective when you click the Contacts link.

The second line of code that has been added simply appends a request header that has been set in the past.

```
xHRObject.setRequestHeader('If-Modified-Since', 'Sat, 1 Jan 2000 00:00:00 GMT' );
```

Request headers are extra information sent along with the request. The If-Modified-Since header is normally used with the GET method to make it conditional. In other words, if the requested document has not changed since the time specified, then the document won't be sent. It's another way of tricking the browser into resending the request.

A discussion on using the POST method should be deferred because using the POST method is a bit more complex and really a separate topic. Instead, let's consider another thorny issue for Ajax developers.

Cross-Browser Implications

Perhaps the most difficult issue to solve when using Ajax is that of ensuring that your application works in IE, Mozilla, Safari, and Opera. In fact, sometimes it just isn't practical to support all browsers. Unless you can be sure that your target audience won't be using a particular browser, or that only a tiny minority will, then you really should try to accommodate them if at all possible.

In the XmlHttpRequest example, the problem of whether the user was using IE or Mozilla was minimal because it boiled down to which version of the XMLHttpRequest object you needed to create. There are some things to remember:

❑   No ActiveX controls can be used outside of IE.

❑   The dynamic HTML collection document.all works only on IE.

❑   Synchronous XMLHttpRequests crash some versions of Firefox.

❑   IE doesn't cache images when inserting images into HTML using JavaScript.

The case of the ID attribute/case sensitivity of element names can make a difference as to whether a script works. IE can be tolerant of this, but Mozilla will take exception to different cases being used in the attribute names. For example, Box1 and box1 would be treated as two different elements.

Depending on which version of IE you are using, you might have to call different versions of MSXML.

This examination isn't exhaustive because there are an endless number of tics and idiosyncrasies in each browser.

There is no guarantee that the solution presented here will solve all of the problems, but it certainly solves the most common ones. Ajax isn't difficult to learn, but it can take a little tweaking to get it to work sometimes.

The POST Method

As was mentioned, using the POST method instead of GET is another solution to IE aggressively caching each page and thereby preventing you from using Ajax techniques to provide a more seamless front end.

Let's go back and amend the previous example to use the POST method. It isn't just a case of using POST instead of GET in the sendRequest method; life would be a lot easier if it were that simple. You need to remove the querystring, and then you encode the data you want to send yourself and send it across to the server as a parameter to the send method. The parameter is still a name/value, just like a querystring, in the format value=Contacts. But it is no longer appended to the URL, and instead it travels in the body of the request. It is also URL-encoded.

Try It Out   Using the Post Method

Rather than amending the existing example, let's clone parts of it and use new versions of the pages.

1.   First, start by copying the file display.htm into a new file displaypost.htm, and then amend the following line in it:

```
<html>
<head>
    <script type="text/javascript" src="XmlHttpRequest2.js"></script>
</head>
<body>
<a href="javascript:sendRequest('Contacts')">Contacts</a>
<a href="javascript:sendRequest('Calendar')">Calendar</a>
<a href="javascript:sendRequest('Adverts')">Adverts</a>
<br/>
<div id="box1">
</div>
<div id="box2">
</div>
<div id="box3">
</div>
</body>
</html>
```

2.   Next, copy across XmlHttpRequest.js into a file called XmlHttpRequest2.js, and change the code in the sendRequest method so that it reads as follows:

```
function sendRequest(data)
{
var bodyofrequest= getBody(data);
xHRObject.open("POST", "display.php", true);
xHRObject.setRequestHeader("Content-Type", "application/x-www-form-urlencoded");
xHRObject.onreadystatechange = getData;
xHRObject.send(bodyofrequest);
}
```

3. Next, add a new function to the script called `getBody()`:

```
function getBody(data)
{
    var argument = "value=";
    argument += encodeURIComponent(data)
    return argument;
}
```

4. Now, open `displaypost.htm` in your browser, and click Contacts. The example performs in exactly the same way it did before, as shown in Figure 4-5.

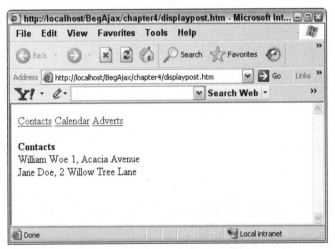

Figure 4-5: Browser performing as it did previously.

5. If you're viewing this in IE, and you change the name in the server-side code to "John Doe" once more and click Contacts, the change is made instantaneously.

How It Works

You amended the example to use the POST method. The same method to submit the data was used, via the `<a>` tag links, which called the JavaScript `sendRequest(method)`, so you didn't have to amend the HTML apart from pointing it at the new script

In the `sendRequest` method, quite a bit had changed:

```
var bodyofrequest= getBody(data);
xHRObject.open("POST", "display.php", true);
xHRObject.setRequestHeader("Content-Type", "application/x-www-form-urlencoded");
xHRObject.onreadystatechange = getData;
xHRObject.send(bodyofrequest);
```

You started by creating the body of the request that you were sending. Once again, this took the form of the name/value pair:

```
value=Contacts
```

The getBody function created this for you, which will be discussed shortly. You then passed the name of the PHP page to the Open method to determine the location of the server-side page you were calling, along with the method "POST" and the asynchronous parameter set to true. You created a request header and indicated that this data was form-URL-encoded. You set the onreadystatechange method just as you did with the GET method. Instead of sending the null value with the send method, though, you sent the variable bodyofrequest that was constructed by the getBody function.

The getBody function was used to URLEncode the variable you passed across:

```
var argument = "value=";
argument += encodeURIComponent(data)
return argument;
```

The argument variable is constructed using the name "value" and the contents of the data variable, which is URL-encoded. In truth, you didn't actually need to do this because you've hard-coded the value in the HTML page. Because the data needs to be form-URL-encoded, and in more complex applications you would have to ensure that this happens, this extra step was added anyway. If you have more than one value to pass, then you could use a loop to append each item that has been URL-encoded into an array and then return the whole array.

Overall, the changes required to the code weren't radical, but they did add a little bit of complexity. Let's briefly discuss the merits of using either the POST or GET methods.

Advantages and Disadvantages of Using the POST and GET Methods

Although the two methods can often be seen as interchangeable, there are several subtle differences between them that are worth noting.

querystrings used by the GET method are restricted in length depending on which browser you are using. In IE it's 2083 characters, in Opera it is 4050, in Netscape versions up to 4 it's 8192, in Netscape 6 it's 2000; in Mozilla it doesn't specify, although it is longer than the others.

Another restriction of using the GET method is that the data sent is restricted to using only ASCII codes. Also, the GET request is cacheable (as you've seen with IE) while POST requests never are.

There are also recommended guidelines for when you should choose the usage of one method over the other. GET requests are intended for queries that don't cause changes; if the submission of the form or the data will cause changes, then the POST method is to be preferred.

You will see that throughout this book there are differences required in the code as a result of using one or another of these methods.

Other Ajax Techniques

While the XMLHttpRequest object is likely to be a linchpin in many Ajax applications, you might choose plenty of other techniques to develop with that also provide similar functionality. Let's start by looking at a couple of old techniques that developers have used since before the birth of the XMLHttpRequest object.

117

Hidden Frames

The hidden frames technique is a longstanding trick of developers to return information from the server but keep it invisible to the user. It uses a standard frameset with two frames to open two separate pages (or more if required), the first being visible to the user and the second being made invisible by setting its width or height to zero. The hidden frame can be used to send requests and retrieve data from the server, but the data is placed in the visible frame only when needed.

Hidden frames can be commonly used to reduce the amount of times the server is accessed, and they can be used to preload or cache data. A particularly good application of hidden frames occurs with file uploading. Once the user has selected which file to upload, you could begin immediate uploading of the file behind the scenes. Once again, the aim is to provide a more seamless user experience.

The Concept

Hidden frames work as follows:

1. The script makes a call to the hidden frame.

2. The request is made to the server via the hidden frame.

3. The response received from the server goes to the hidden frame.

4. On the triggering of an event (normally `onload`), the data is transferred from the hidden frame to the visible frame.

The concept is quite a simple one, but the passing of the data from the visible frame to the hidden frame, to the server and back again, can prove a little fiddly. There's some debate as to whether this truly qualifies as an Ajax technique, but as you'll see from the next example, the way it can be used to update the page using data on the server is undoubtedly something in common with Ajax applications.

Try It Out   Using Hidden Frames to Pass Information

Let's create a quick example now. In this example, you have a web page from a travel agent's application that displays hotels from each city from a particular price range. Rather than waiting for the user to submit the page, the information is drawn from an XML file each time the user makes a selection from the drop-down list of hotels or from the radio button list of price ranges.

> A note to the purists: Technically speaking, this doesn't reduce the amount of hits to the server. In fact, it increases them. But, in an effort to keep this example relatively short, and to demonstrate a point, let's live with this one.

1. Create a page called `frameset.htm`, and add the following code:

```
<html>
<head>
</head>
<frameset rows="100%,*">
<frame name="currentframe" src="current.htm">
<frame name="hiddenframe" src="about:blank">
</frameset>
</html>
```

2. Add another HTML page. This will be the page that shows the visible frame. Call this one `current.htm`.

```html
<html>
<head>
<script type="text/javascript" src="HiddenFrame.js"></script>
</head>
<body>
Destination:
<br />
<select id="selectCity" onchange="retrieveInformation()">
 <option value="London" selected="true">London</option>
 <option value="Paris">Paris</option>
 <option value="New York">New York</option>
 <option value="Chicago">Chicago</option>
 <option value="Seattle">Seattle</option>
</select> <br />
<br />
Price Range:
<br />
Budget<input name="type" value="1" type="radio" onchange="retrieveInformation()"/>
Standard<input name="type" value="2" type="radio" onchange="retrieveInformation()"
checked="true"/>
Luxury<input name="type" value="3" type="radio" onchange="retrieveInformation()"/>
<div id="information">
</div>
</body>
</html>
```

3. Now, create a script called `HiddenFrame.js`.

```javascript
function initialize()
{
    var hiddenForm = document.getElementById('displayinfo');
    if(hiddenForm != null)
    {
        parent.frames[0].document.getElementById('information').innerHTML =
        hiddenForm.innerHTML;
    }
}

function retrieveInformation()
{
     var city = document.getElementById("selectCity").value;
    var type = "";
    var input = document.getElementsByTagName("input");
    for (var i=0; i < input.length; i++)
    {
      if (input.item(i).checked == true)
      {
        type = input.item(i).value;
      }
    }
     top.frames["hiddenframe"].location = "retrieveHotelInformation.aspx?city="
      + city + "&type=" + type;
}
```

Alternatively, change the line in bold to the following if you want to use ASP.NET:

```
top.frames["hiddenframe"].location = "retrieveHotelInformation.aspx?city="
        + city + "&type=" + type;
```

4. The last page is the server-side one. The PHP is as follows. Save this as
   `retrieveHotelInformation.php`.

```php
<?php
$xmlFile = "C:\\inetpub\\wwwroot\\BegAjax\\Chapter4\\hotel.xml";
$HTML = "";
$count = 0;
$dt = simplexml_load_file($xmlFile);
$dom = DOMDocument::load($xmlFile);
$hotel = $dom->getElementsByTagName("hotel");

foreach($hotel as $node)
{
     $city = $node->getElementsByTagName("City");
     $city = $city->item(0)->nodeValue;

  $type = $node->getElementsByTagName("Type");
  $type = $type->item(0)->nodeValue;

  $name = $node->getElementsByTagName("Name");
  $name = $name->item(0)->nodeValue;

  $price = $node->getElementsByTagName("Price");
  $price = $price->item(0)->nodeValue;

  if (($type == $_GET["type"]) && ($city == $_GET["city"]) )
     {
         $HTML = $HTML."<br><span>Hotel: ".$name."</span><br><span>Price:
".$price."</span><br>";
         $count++;
  }
}
  if ($count ==0)
  {
     $HTML ="<br><span>No hotels available</span>";
  }

  echo "<div id='displayinfo'>".$HTML."</div>";
?>
<html>
<script type="text/javascript" src="HiddenFrame.js"></script>
<body onload="initialize()">
</body>
</html>
```

The ASP.NET version is as follows. Save this one as `retrieveHotelInformation.aspx`.

```
<%@ Page Language="C#" %>
<%@ Import Namespace="System.Data" %>
<%@ Import Namespace="System.Xml" %>
```

```
<html>
<script type="text/javascript" src="HiddenFrame.js"></script>
    <script language="c#" runat="server">
        void Page_Load()
        {
            string xmlFile = @"C:\inetpub\wwwroot\BegAjax\Chapter4\hotel.xml";
            string HTML = "";
            DataSet ds1 = new DataSet();
            ds1.ReadXml(xmlFile);
            DataTableReader dt = ds1.CreateDataReader();
            int count = 0;
            while (dt.Read())
            {
                if ((dt["City"].ToString() == Request.Params["city"].ToString()) &&
(dt["Type"].ToString() == Request.Params["type"].ToString()))
                {
                    HTML += "<br><span>Hotel: " + dt[1].ToString() +
"</span><br><span>Price: " + dt[3].ToString() + "</span><br>";
                    count++;
                }
            }
            if (count ==0)
            {
                HTML ="<br><span>No hotels available</span>";
            }
            Response.Write("<div id='displayinfo'>" + HTML + "</div>");
        }
</script>
<body onload="initialize()">
</body>
</html>
```

5. Next, to create the data, make a small XML file. Save this as `hotels.xml`.

```
<hotels>
<hotel>
    <City>Paris</City>
    <Name>La Splendide</Name>
    <Type>Budget</Type>
    <Price>100</Price>
</hotel>
<hotel>
    <City>London</City>
    <Name>The Rilton</Name>
    <Type>Luxury</Type>
    <Price>300</Price>
</hotel>
</hotels>
```

6. Open `frameset.htm` in your browser, and select the option London from the drop-down list box and the option Luxury from the radio buttons, as shown in Figure 4-6.

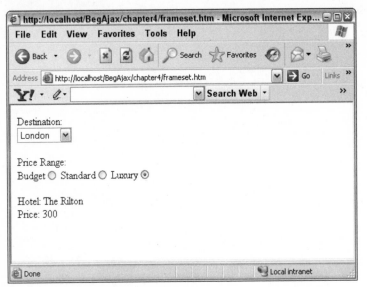

Figure 4-6: Selecting London and Luxury.

7.   Now, select the Budget button radio button. The text changes underneath to reflect the non-availability in the data, as shown in Figure 4-7.

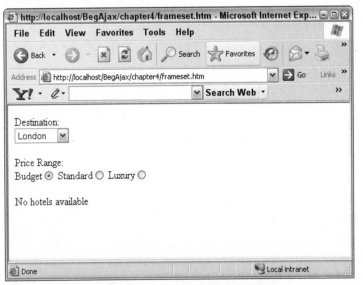

Figure 4-7: Text change after selecting Budget radio button.

How It Works

This example uses hidden frames. You created two frames in `frameset.htm`:

```
<frame name="currentframe" src="current.htm">
<frame name="hiddenframe" src="about:blank">
```

The first referred to `current.htm`, the visible page. The second was left blank. The first page just contained the drop-down list box, radio buttons, and the `div` element to display the hotel information.

```
<select id="selectCity" onchange="retrieveInformation()">
     <option value="London" selected="true">London</option>
 <option value="Paris">Paris</option>
 <option value="New York">New York</option>
 <option value="Chicago">Chicago</option>
 <option value="Seattle">Seattle</option>
</select>
<br />
<br />
Price Range:
<br />
Budget<input  name="type" value="1" type="radio" onchange="retrieveInformation()"/>
Standard<input  name="type" value="2" type="radio" onchange="retrieveInformation()"
checked="true"/>
Luxury<input  name="type" value="3" type="radio" onchange="retrieveInformation()"/>
<div id="information">
</div>
```

The `dropdownlist` called the `retrieveInformation()` method in the `HiddenFrame.js` script via the `onchange` method, while the radio buttons called the same method via the `onclick()` event. The `retrieveInformation` method set up two variables, `city` and `type`, which recorded the values of the items in the visible frame selected by the user. The radio buttons all have the same name, and the `document.getElementsByTagName` is used to retrieve all three, and then the checked value of each one is iterated through until one is found set to `true`. Its value is assigned to the `type` variable.

```
var city = document.getElementById("selectCity").value;
var type = "";
var input = document.getElementsByTagName("input");
for (var i=0; i < input.length; i++)
{
  if (input.item(i).checked == true)
  {
     type = input.item(i).value;
  }
}
```

Then you assigned a location to your blank hidden frame appending the `type` and `city` variables to a querystring.

```
top.frames["hiddenframe"].location = "retrieveHotelInformation.aspx?city="
  + city + "&type=" + type;
```

Because the server-side code isn't integral to the hidden frames technique, it is not addressed in detail here. The server-side code loads the XML file, takes the `querystring` values, and then decides which elements to display, depending on whether the values for the `city` and the `type` elements match the values the user has selected. It then dynamically writes them to a `div` tag in the hidden frame called `displayinfo`.

At the end of the server-side code is a `body` tag with an `onload()` event, which calls the `initialize` function back in your JavaScript. This searches for the dynamically created `<div>` tag in the hidden frame.

```
function initialize()
{
    var hiddenForm = document.getElementById('displayinfo');
    if(hiddenForm != null)
    {
        parent.frames[0].document.getElementById('information').innerHTML =
        hiddenForm.innerHTML;
    }
}
```

If this tag exists on the page, then you access the corresponding `<div>` tag called `'information'` on the visible page `current.htm` and transfer across the information using the `innerHTML` property.

As you can see, it's a relatively simple technique, but it allows you potentially to store information in the hidden frame and call on it only when it is needed.

Advantages and Disadvantages

One obvious advantage of this technique is that you don't need browser-specific code because all modern browsers support frames. Also, with regard to the uploading of files, this is something that is actually not possible to achieve with the `XMLHttpRequest` object, but it could be done with hidden frames.

The main disadvantage of this technique is that not all of the older browsers can properly hide frames. Despite setting the frame's height and width to zero, there would still be some unsightly borders left over. Also, it introduces an extra layer of complexity into the client/server interaction that might not be desirable.

Hidden Inline Frames

The HTML 4.0 standard introduced a new element — the *inline frame* or, to give it its more familiar name, the `<iframe>` element. Inline frames are floating frames that work in the same way as images, in that text will wrap around them, but they can contain separate web pages, just like normal frames. Unlike traditional frames, they don't have to be placed in a specific frameset. They were introduced in IE 3 but weren't supported until version 6 of Netscape Navigator. They can be created dynamically by scripting and is accessed in the same way as normal frames.

The Concept

The way in which an `iframe` is used is the same as a hidden frame:

1. The script makes a call to the hidden frame.
2. The request is made to the server via the hidden frame.

3. The response received from the server is transferred to the hidden frame.

4. On the triggering of an event (normally `onload`), the data is transferred from the hidden frame to the visible frame.

Inline frames can be used as a direct replacement for hidden frames. Because they have the advantage of not having to be placed in a frameset, you can use JavaScript to add them dynamically into a page at any point. Inline frames are a better alternative to hidden frames, and you'd choose to use them every time because of their greater flexibility, except that they aren't as well supported by browsers and there are some differences in their implementation between Firefox and IE.

Try It Out   Using Hidden Inline Frames to Pass Information

Let's go back and remove the frameset from the hidden frames example and instead dynamically create an `iframe` that will perform the task. It's fairly simple to do, but it's not as clean as you might like it to be.

1. Open the file `current.htm`. Copy it to a document called `currentiframe.htm`, and add the following highlighted lines:

```
<html>
<head>
<script type="text/javascript" src="HiddenIFrame.js"></script>
</head>
<body onload="createiframe()">
Destination:
<br />
...
```

2. Next, copy the file `HiddenFrame.js`, and call it `HiddenIframe.js`. Now, add the following function to it:

```
function createiframe()
{

        var iframe = document.createElement("iframe");
        iframe.style.border = "0px";
        iframe.style.width = "0px";
        iframe.style.height = "0px";
          document.body.appendChild(iframe);

}
```

3. Still in the same file, locate the `initialize` function, and amend the following line in it:

```
function initialize()
{
    var hiddenForm = document.getElementById('displayinfo');
    if(hiddenForm != null)
      {
          parent.currentframe.document..getElementById('information').innerHTML =
hiddenForm.innerHTML;
      }
}
```

4. In function `retrieveInformation`, change the following line:

```
function retrieveInformation()
{
    var city = document.getElementById("selectCity").value;
var type = "";
var input = document.getElementsByTagName("input");
for (var i=0; i < input.length; i++)
{
    if (input.item(i).checked == true)
    {
        type = input.item(i).value;
    }
}
    top.frames[1].location = "retrieveHotelInformation2.aspx?city="
      + city + "&type=" + type;
}
```

5. Go to the server-side page (whether PHP or ASP.NET), and amend the script line to read as follows and save it as: `retrieveHotelInformation2.`(`.aspx` or `.php`):

```
<script type="text/javascript" src="HiddenIFrame.js"></script>
```

6. Run `currentiframe.htm` in your browser. It works identically to the hidden frames example, as shown in Figure 4-8.

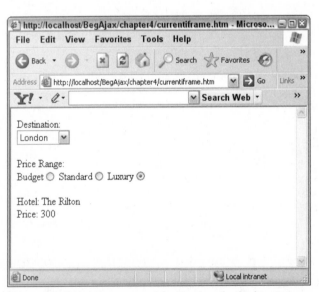

Figure 4-8: Running `currentiframe.htm` in the browser.

How It Works

The original hidden frame example works as follows:

❑ The visible frame passes information to the hidden frame, which is, in fact, a call to the server.

❑ The server returns information to a `<div>` tag in the hidden frame.

❑   The contents are transferred from the `<div>` tag in the hidden frame to the `div` tag in the visible frame.

What we do in this example now is a little more complex (but only a little); we have to create the iframe dynamically and set the border, height, and width properties to zero to ensure that it is effectively invisible on the page. Then you append the element to your HTML page as follows:

```
function createiframe()
{

        var iframe = document.createElement("iframe");
        iframe.style.border = "0px";
        iframe.style.width = "0px";
        iframe.style.height = "0px";
          document.body.appendChild(iframe);


}
```

You altered your HTML page to call the `createiframe()` function when the page first loads. And you amended the `initialize` function so that when it writes the information back to `<div>` tag on the page, it no longer has to go through a `frameset` to access it.

```
        parent.document.getElementById('information').innerHTML =
hiddenForm.innerHTML;
```

You also changed the reference to the frame in your `retrieveInformation` function. Next you assigned the results from your server side page to your hidden iframe as follows:

```
top.frames[1].location = "retrieveHotelInformation2.aspx?city="
        + city + "&range=" + range;
```

In this example, what you've done is remove the `frameset` page, dynamically create an `iframe` to replace it, and used the inline frame to pass the information to and from the server instead. Nothing else has had to change.

If you want to dynamically retrieve the contents of the form, in IE you can use the `contentWindow.document` property to retrieve the `document` element of the `iframe`, while with Firefox you must use the `contentDocument` property:

```
doc = iframe.contentDocument || iframe.contentWindow.document;
```

When using more complex examples than this, one problem might be that your browser can take longer to load the document. So, you can query the document's `readyState` property before you access the document content as follows:

```
doc = iframe.contentDocument || iframe.contentWindow.document;
        if (typeof doc.readyState!="undefined" && doc.readyState!="complete") {
            doc.onreadystatechange = function() {
                if (doc.readyState == "complete") {
                    ...
                }
            }
        }
```

```
    } else {
            . . .
    }
```

Then your `iframe` is guaranteed to be fully loaded, before you start using it.

Advantages and Disadvantages

The example is straightforward enough, although for more complex examples you must be aware of browser compatibility. In fact, you could end up using different methods for IE 5, IE 5.5, IE 6/7, and Firefox if you're not careful. Also, it isn't possible to dynamically create `iframes` in IE 5 at all.

Despite these minor hiccups, iframes represent a definite improvement on hidden frames. Let's consider another technique.

Dynamic Script Loading

Professional Ajax author Nicholas Zakas talks about another trick in an article online at www. webreference.com/programming/ajax_tech/, which has been in use for a while as a good alternative to the XMLHttpRequest object. This is *dynamic script loading*. This is where a JavaScript script can be created dynamically using the DOM, and the SRC attribute is also assigned dynamically. The JavaScript source file is downloaded and executed only when you add it to the page.

The Concept

The concept is very simple indeed:

1. You add a script to your page.

2. This script dynamically adds another script to the page, appending the SRC tag at a later point.

3. The script initiates dialog with the server.

Try It Out   **Dynamic Script Loading**

Let's look at an example now. Let's create a very short and rudimentary example that takes a single script and dynamically creates one of three other scripts, depending on which radio button the user selects on the web page. To keep this example short, let's not initiate any dialog with the server because there are some pitfalls to this method, to be discussed later.

1. Create an HTML page called `ScriptLoader.htm`.

```html
<html xmlns="http://www.w3.org/1999/xhtml" >
<head>
  <script type="text/javascript" src="ScriptLoader.js"></script>
</head>
<body>
Which script do you want to load?
<br/>
<br/>
Script 1<input id="range" name="range" value="1" type="radio"
onclick="retrieveInformation('1')" /><br/>
```

```
Script 2<input id="Radio1" name="range" value="2" type="radio"
onclick="retrieveInformation('2')" /><br/>
Script 3<input id="Radio2" name="range" value="3" type="radio"
onclick="retrieveInformation('3')"/><br/>
</body>
</html>
```

2. Next, create the script `ScriptLoader.js`.

```
function retrieveInformation(data)
{
        var newScript = document.createElement("script");
        newScript.src = "script" + data + ".js";
        document.body.appendChild(newScript);
}
```

3. Now, create another script, `script1.js`.

```
alert ("Are you sure you wanted to load script one?");
```

4. Now, create another script, `script2.js`.

```
alert ("Script two is no picnic either!");
```

5. Create a final script as follows, and call this `script3.js`.

```
alert ("This is the ultimate in scripts, script three");
```

6. Now, open `ScriptLoader.htm` in your browser, and click on the first radio button, as shown in Figure 4-9.

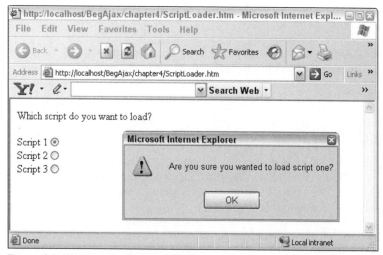

Figure 4-9: Clicking the first radio button in `ScriptLoader.htm`**.**

7. Clicking on the other radio buttons will run the other scripts.

How It Works

This is a fairly whimsical example, but it goes to show that it's very easy to load a second script in your program and dynamically determine its attributes. There were just three lines of code in the script that did this:

```
var newScript = document.createElement("script");
newScript.src = "script" + data + ".js";
document.body.appendChild(newScript);
```

The first line creates a `script` element. The second line sets the `src` attribute. You load a different script, depending on which radio button was selected by the user. The final line appends the new element to the `body` element. At this point, the script will then be run.

Even though you didn't use the second script to communicate with the server in any way, it wouldn't be too great a task to add in each of the scripts a separate call to the server, and either call different pages on the server or pass different information to the server.

Advantages and Disadvantages

The advantages of this technique are that you can have several different scripts, and, depending on the circumstances, you can dynamically load the one that you need. It provides another opportunity to instigate a call to the server.

There are, however, some fairly hefty disadvantages. The first is that you can't tell if the script has loaded correctly, because there is no return from the second script. The second problem is that in IE, the dynamic loading of scripts stops all other processing. One possible application of this method could have been to dynamically load an animated gif while a file was being uploaded. Unfortunately, in IE, it stops processing even animated gifs! Also, this method is limited to the GET method, and you can't use the POST method with it. Because it uses the DOM, you are restricted slightly to the more recent set of browsers from versions 4 and up.

Perhaps the most serious disadvantage is that using this technique with IE 5 and IE 6 causes a potential memory leak. Although it looks like quite an attractive method on the surface, it is definitely less common because of its unpredictable outcomes across different browsers. There's no such problem with the final technique.

Images and Cookies

The use (or rather misuse) of images in web pages and e-mails has caused even major applications such as Microsoft's Outlook to alter the way in which they behave. You might notice now in many e-mail clients that when you receive an HTML e-mail, you are prompted on whether you wish to download the images. If you choose to download the images, then it is more than likely you will be passing data back to the server containing information about yourself. Normally, this will be of a fairly benign nature, designed to let the application know how many people have opened a particular e-mail and which users, in particular, have.

This falls under the umbrella of Ajax because, once again, it allows calls to be made to the server, separate to the submit request/receive response model. In this case, it is done via the `src` attribute of the `<img>` tag. The `<img>` that is typically displayed is 1 pixel by 1 pixel so that the user doesn't notice it on the page. The server can then act on this information to write a cookie on the user's computer.

Of course, cookies receive a lot of bad press without actually doing any harm. They're simply small files of text, and the information they store is small and not directly associated with information stored on a user's machine. What they can contain is a unique ID, which a server can retrieve each time the user comes back to a page.

Recently, there was a scandal involving search engines recording everything some users typed in. From recognizing the cookie each time a user made a search, information could be deduced such as where the user lived and what they did for a living; in some cases, the information could be connected to a specific individual.

The kind of technique described here is less prying. If you were to apply this to a catalogue of products, with a graphic on each page relaying information, you would be able track the patterns of which products a user looked at, and you could do things such as recommend related products or make recommendations based on the viewing patterns of other users who had looked at that same product.

The Concept

This pattern works as follows:

1. The `<img>` element wraps a request to the server in the `src` attribute, passing any extra information appended to a `querystring`.

2. The server stores the information and writes some uniquely identifiable information that is stored in a cookie on the client.

This pattern is very similar in implementation to the dynamic script-loading example. It doesn't have the same drawbacks, however, and it is in widespread use for the users of bulk e-mails or web sites that wish to track their users' viewing habits.

Try It Out   Images and Cookies

Let's create an example that mimics a single page on a bookseller's web site. When the user views the page, the information about what page he or she is viewing is sent as part of the image to the server; the server then writes a unique identifier to the cookie and displays the information contained in the cookie in a message box to the user.

1. Create an HTML page, and call it `Catalogue.htm`. You will need a couple of images for this example. They can be downloaded (along with the code for this book) from `www.wrox.com`.

```
<html xmlns="http://www.w3.org/1999/xhtml" >
<head>
  <script type="text/javascript" src="ImageLoader.js"></script>
</head>
<body onload="createImage()">
<b>Book:</b>
<br/>
<img id="cover" src="begaspnet.jpg" />
<br />
<br />
<b>Authors: </b><span id="authors"> Hart, Kauffman, Sussman, Ullman</span>
<br /><b>ISBN: </b><span id="ISBN">0764588508</span>
<br /><b>Price: </b><span id="price">$39.99</span>
```

```
<img id="secret" src="onebyone.gif" /><br /><br />
<input type="button" onclick="showCookie()" value="Click to see Cookie" />
</body>
</html>
```

2.   Create a script called `ImageLoader.js`, and add the following code:

```
function createImage()
{
        var bookid  = document.getElementById("ISBN").innerHTML;
        var img = document.getElementById("secret");
        img.src = "relayInformation.aspx?bookid=" + bookid;
        img.width = 0;
        img.height = 0;


}

function showCookie()
{
        var cookie = document.cookie;
        alert(cookie);
}

function getCookieInfo(cookie)
{
        RegularXp = "(?:; )?" + cookie + "=([^;]*);?";
        var RegularXpExtract = new RegExp(RegularXp);
        if (RegularXpExtract.test(document.cookie))
        {
            return decodeURIComponent(RegExp["$1"]);
        }
        else
        {
            return null;
        }
}
```

3.   Now, create a server-side page to set the cookie. If you are using PHP, then add the following, and call it `relayInformation.php`:

```
<?php
  if ($_COOKIE[AnonymousID])
          {
              $tempCookie = $_COOKIE["AnonymousID"];
              setcookie("AnonymousID", $tempCookie."|BOOKID:".$_GET["bookid"],
time()+3600);
          }
          else
          {
              $random_id = (rand()%9999999);
              $tempCookie = "USERID:" .$random_id."|BOOKID:" . $_GET["bookid"];
              setcookie("AnonymousID", $tempCookie."|BOOKID:".$_GET["bookid"],
time()+3600);
          }
  ?>
```

If you want add ASP.NET, call it `relayInformation.aspx`, and add the following:

```
<%@ Page Language="C#" %>
<script language="c#" runat="server">
        void Page_Load()
        {
            if (Request.Cookies["AnonymousUser"] == null)
            {
                HttpCookie userCookie = new HttpCookie("AnonymousID");
                Guid userguid = System.Guid.NewGuid();
                userCookie.Value = "USERID:" + userguid.ToString() + "|BOOKID:" +
Request.QueryString["bookid"].ToString();
                userCookie.Expires = DateTime.Now.AddYears(1);
                Response.Cookies.Add(userCookie);
            }
            else
            {
                HttpCookie userCookie = Request.Cookies["AnonymousID"];
                userCookie.Value += "|BOOKID:" +
Request.QueryString["bookid"].ToString();
                userCookie.Expires = DateTime.Now.AddYears(1);
                Response.Cookies.Add(userCookie);
            }
        }
</script>
```

4. Now, open `catalogue.htm` in your browser, and click to see the cookie, as shown in Figure 4-10.

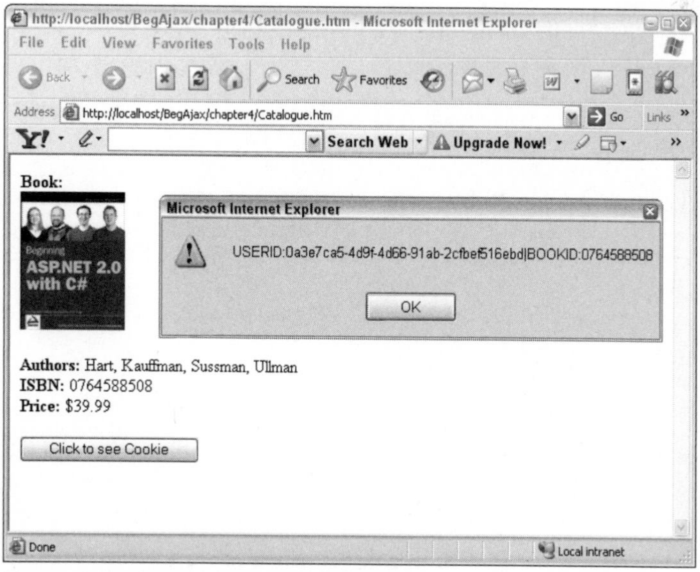

Figure: 4-10: Cookie displayed in browser.

5. Close the browser, and go back to the page. You will see it has appended the `bookid` to the cookie for a second time, as shown in Figure 4-11. If you were to change the value in the HTML page of the ISBN number, then the new value would be stored.

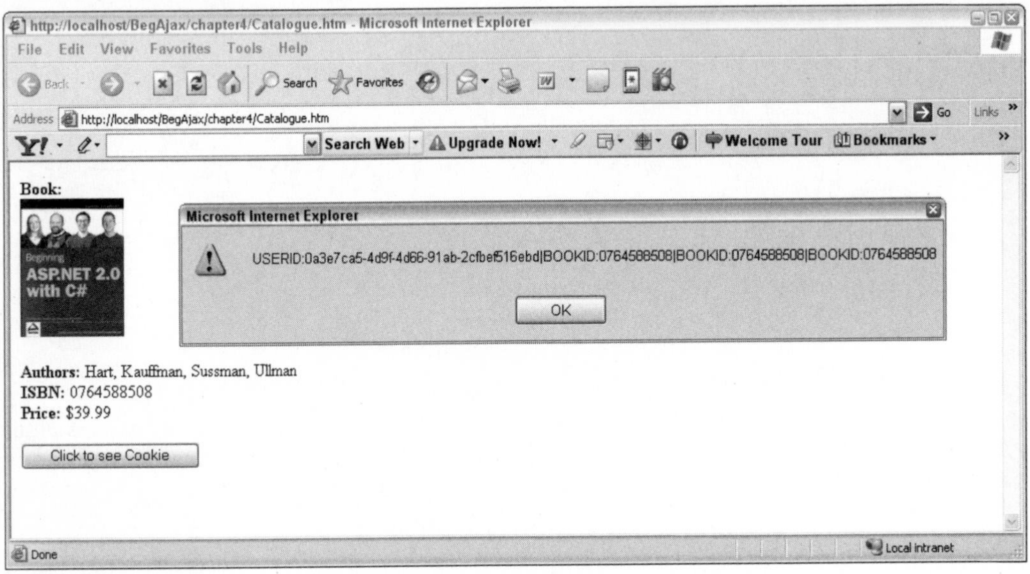

Figure: 4-11: Appending `bookid` to the cookie a second time.

How It Works

This example has shown how you can dynamically alter the SRC attribute of an image, so that it makes a call to the server instead. You load `createImage` on the start of the page, and then you locate the contents of the `<span>` element that contains the book ISBN, to be stored in the cookie, and also the image that displays the `onebyone.gif`.

```
var bookid  = document.getElementById("ISBN").innerHTML;
var img = document.getElementById("secret");
```

You dynamically replace its `src` attribute with one that points to the server-side page and passes the book ISBN as a `querystring`. Then you set the height and width to zero and append it to the document `body`.

```
img.src = "relayInformation.aspx?bookid=" + bookid;
img.width = 0;
img.height = 0;
```

The server-side code simply checks for the existence of a cookie. If there is a cookie, it adds a unique ID (in ASP.NET this is generated using a GUID, while in PHP GUID support is not native, so you just generate a random number for the sake of this example) and the ISBN of the book:

```
if (Request.Cookies["AnonymousUser"] == null)
{
    HttpCookie userCookie = new HttpCookie("AnonymousUser");
    Guid userguid = System.Guid.NewGuid();
    userCookie.Value = "USERID:" + userguid.ToString() + "|BOOKID:" +
Request.QueryString["bookid"].ToString();
```

```
        userCookie.Expires = DateTime.Now.AddYears(1);
        Response.Cookies.Add(userCookie);
    }
```

Or, if the cookie already exists, you append the ISBN information to the end of the cookie.

```
    else
    {
        HttpCookie userCookie = Request.Cookies["AnonymousUser"];
        userCookie.Value += "|BOOKID:" +
Request.QueryString["bookid"].ToString();
        userCookie.Expires = DateTime.Now.AddYears(1);
        Response.Cookies.Add(userCookie);
    }
```

You then use the `showCookie()` function to display the contents. Here, you can use Ajax techniques to quite quickly pick up the viewing patterns of one "anonymous" user. Because GUIDs are always unique, it would be no trouble to store this in a database. You could then amass over time a picture of where a user was going on a web site.

Advantages and Disadvantages

The main problem with this is that in an application such as an e-mail client (or it used to be common in the browser), the user can choose to have image downloading switched off. (Indeed, in Outlook it is switched off by default.) There is also a restriction on the amount of information that can be stored in a cookie, which is about 4KB (depending on how much of that is taken up by the cookie's unique transaction ID). The example here would quickly run into problems, even though you were storing the information on the cookie only to show how it could be done.

The other drawback is that, once again, this is restricted to the GET method only, and it cannot be used with the POST method.

You should now have a broad overview of a lot of popular techniques that can be used to create a client/server communication and where these techniques or tools might be applied.

Summary

This chapter has featured a broad overview of five different Ajax techniques. Most of this discussion has been devoted to the XMLHttpRequest object because this is the one that developers are most likely to use. You saw some of the reasons you might not be able to get the XMLHttpRequest to work correctly. The examination scratched the surface of some of the most common problems, and you saw that browser incompatibilities often lay at the heart of the problems. Next, the discussion examined four alternative techniques and found that hidden frames, hidden iframes, dynamic scripting loading, and preloading images techniques were not immune to these kinds of problems.

The message to take home from this chapter is that there are no quick shortcuts when using Ajax techniques. While all the techniques offer the developer practical and usable ways to communicate with the server, you will find yourself having to pay close attention to the responses you get in different browsers. Ultimately, the XMLHttpRequest object is the most flexible and powerful way of creating Ajax applications. You can derive more information from the object itself about the state of the data sending and receiving, and with the `onreadystatechange` event handler, you can also get it to work in a more truly asynchronous manner.

XML has been used a fair bit in the examples thus far in the book, so now it's time to look at XML itself and how it is used with Ajax techniques. This is discussed in Chapter 5.

Exercises

Suggested solutions to these questions can be found in Appendix A.

1. Amend the `XMLHttpRequest` object example so that it "works" synchronously. How does its behavior change (if at all)? Why do you think this is?

2. Change the example that uses hidden frames to utilize the `POST` method instead.

    Hint: You will need to trick the browser into submitting the hidden frame.

5

Working with XML

When you use an `XMLHttpRequest` object to make a request to a server, the server returns the requested data to you in one of two formats: text or XML. Text data is a string of characters and is easy to add to a page. It's a very limited format for data exchange, however. There are no elements, datatypes, or other differentiations between the characters. XML is a much more useful format for exchanging data between the client (browser) and the server. XML is a markup language that employs user-defined tags to organize data in a specific way.

When the browser receives an XML document from a server in response to an Ajax request, you need a way to extract the XML data and a way to display the data. JavaScript can use nodes, node properties, and DOM methods to retrieve data from an XML document. Once the XML data is extracted, it can be displayed on the page using CSS and/or XSLT.

This chapter provides a review of basic XML concepts and syntax, presents a variety of methods for using JavaScript to extract data from an XML document, and explores techniques for displaying XML data using CSS and for using JavaScript to create dynamic styles for data returned from the server.

In this chapter, you learn about the following:

❑ Basic XML (creating tags, XML syntax, well-formed and valid XML documents)

❑ Extracting XML data with JavaScript (nodes, node properties, DOM methods)

❑ Using CSS (CSS and XML data, using JavaScript with CSS)

XML Basics

XML is a very popular language for data exchange. It's well suited for organizing data and for sharing data because it allows you to classify data, create very specific rules for the format of the data, and output the data to a variety of places. For example, the same data could be used in a database, a web page, and a printed form. XML is not proprietary and is not limited to any particular platform or device.

Creating Tags

When you build a new XML document from scratch, you create your own set of custom tags. These tags provide the underlying structure of the document. You structure the document to meet your needs for using the data. Following is an example:

```
<classes>
  <class>
    <classID>CS255</classID>
    <department>ComputerScience</department>
    <title>JavaScript</title>
    <credits>3</credits>
    <instructor>Dykes</instructor>
  </class>
</classes>
```

In this code, the `classes` element contains all the other elements. The `class` element is a child of the `classes` element, and it contains five other elements (`classID`, `department`, `title`, `credits`, and `instructor`).

> **An element includes tags as well as any content. For example, in the previous code, `<classID>` is an opening tag, while the `classID` element includes the opening and closing `classID` tags, as well as the content contained between them.**

XML tag names must start with a letter or an underscore. They can include letters, digits, periods, hyphens, or underscores, but they can't include any spaces.

XML Syntax

XML is very flexible, but XML syntax is very rigid. All XML documents need to follow these basic rules:

❑   An XML document starts with an XML declaration:

```
<?xml?>
```

This declaration is the first line in the document, and it simply states that this is an XML document. The declaration should also include a version number, as shown here:

```
<?xml version="1.0">
```

❑   An XML document includes a root element that contains all the other elements:

```
<classes>
  <class>
    <classID>CS255</classID>
    <department>ComputerScience</department>
    <title>JavaScript</title>
    <credits>3</credits>
    <instructor>Dykes</instructor>
  </class>
</classes>.
```

In this case, the `classes` element is the root element.

> **The root element is also known as the *document element*.**

❑   An XML element must include an opening and a closing tag:

```
<title>JavaScript</title>
```

The exception to this rule is *empty elements*. Empty elements don't contain any content, although they can include attributes, as shown here:

```
<catalog id="1428"/>
```

❑   This empty element includes an `id` attribute with a value of `1428`. Note that this element also includes a `/` before the closing angle bracket to indicate that this is an empty element. You don't need to include a space before the forward slash — the XML processor will recognize that this is an empty element.

❑   Tags must be properly nested:

```
<classes>
  <class>
  </class>
</classes>
```

The last tag opened is the first tag closed.

Indenting your code helps you keep the nesting hierarchy clear.

❑   All attribute values must be in quotation marks:

```
<warehouse group="downtown">Grant Street</warehouse>
```

Regardless of the type of information contained in an attribute value, the value must be enclosed in single or double quotation marks.

Of course, there are many other rules for XML documents in addition to this basic set of syntax rules. For all the details, see the W3C XML 1.0 Specification at `www.w3.org/TR/xml/`.

Well-Formed and Valid XML Documents

A *well-formed* XML document is an XML document that follows XML syntax rules. A valid XML document is a well-formed XML document that also follows the rules specified in a *Document Type Definition* (*DTD*) or *XML Schema* document. DTDs and schemas provide descriptions of the XML document, such as what elements must be included, the order of the elements, the number of times each element can occur in the document, any attributes of the elements, and what types of data can be contained in an element.

A major advantage of using XML for data exchange is that XML document descriptions (especially XML schema) can include very specific information about the types and format of data that can be included in the document. Validating XML documents helps ensure the quality of the data that you collect and share with those documents.

Try It Out   Requesting XML Data

In this example, you create an XMLHTTPRequest object to retrieve an XML document (classes.xml) from the server. Type the following code into your text editor, and save it as ch5_examp1.htm. When the user clicks the "Make Request" button, an alert displays, as shown in Figure 5-1.

```html
<!DOCTYPE html PUBLIC "-//W3C//DTD XHTML 1.0 Transitional//EN"
"http://www.w3.org/TR/xhtml1/DTD/xhtml1-transitional.dtd">
<html xmlns="http://www.w3.org/1999/xhtml">
<head>
<meta http-equiv="Content-Type" content="text/html; charset=iso-8859-1" />
<title>Requesting XML</title>
<script language = "javascript">
    function getDoc()
    {
    if (window.XMLHttpRequest) {
      request = new XMLHttpRequest();
    }
    else if (window.ActiveXObject) {
      request = new ActiveXObject("Microsoft.XMLHTTP");
    }
    if (request.overrideMimeType) {
      request.overrideMimeType("text/xml");
    }
    if(request) {
      request.open("GET", "classes.xml", true);
      request.onreadystatechange = function()
        {
        if (request.readyState == 4 && request.status == 200) {
          var xmlDocument = request.responseXML;
          alert('XML Document Retrieved');
        }
        request.send(null);
        }
    }    }
</script>
</head>
<body>
<h1>Requesting XML</h1>
<form>
<input type = "button" id="reqDoc" value = "Make request">
</form>
<script type="text/javascript">
var myDoc = document.getElementById('reqDoc');
myDoc.onclick = getDoc;
</script>
</body>
</html>
```

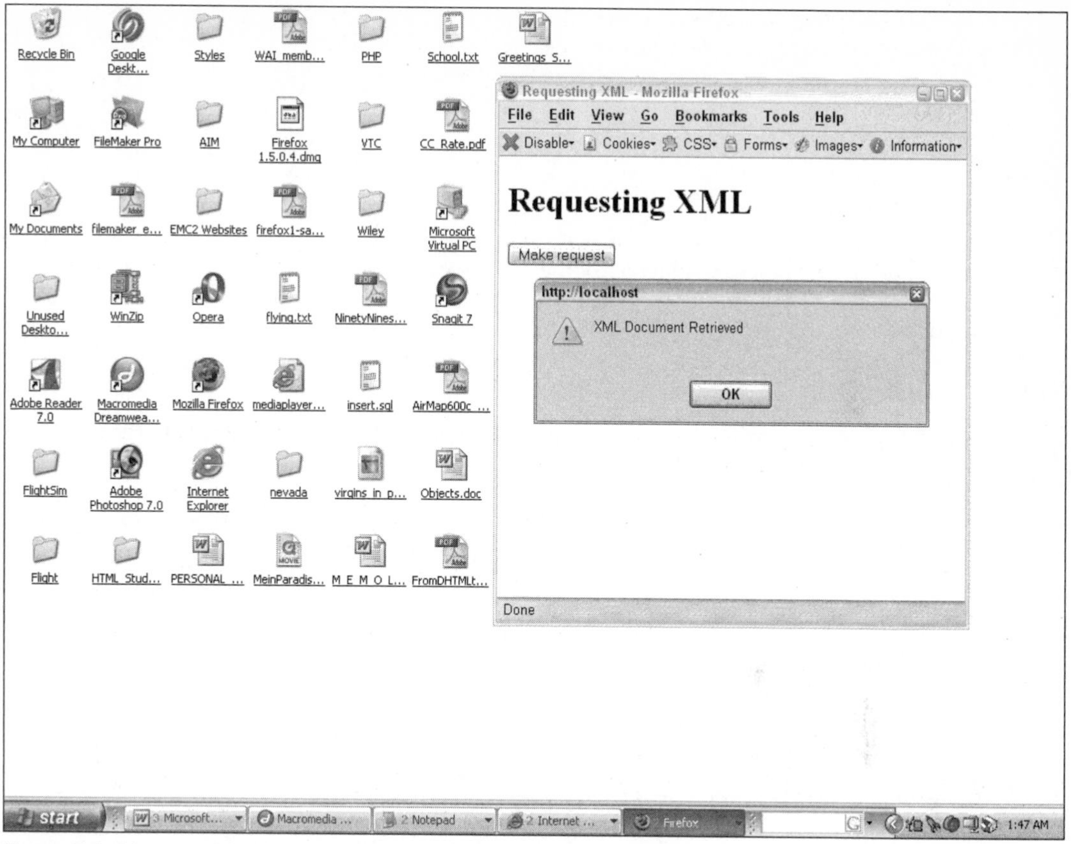

Figure 5-1: Alert resulting from clicking the "Make Request" button.

Type the following code into your text editor, and save it as `classes.xml`:

```
<?xml version="1.0"?>
<classes>
  <class>
    <classID>CS115</classID>
    <department>ComputerScience</department>
    <credits req="yes">3</credits>
    <instructor>Adams</instructor>
    <title>Programming Concepts</title>
  </class>
  <class>
    <classID semester="fall">CS205</classID>
    <department>ComputerScience</department>
    <credits req="yes">3</credits>
    <instructor>Dykes</instructor>
    <title>JavaScript</title>
  </class>
  <class>
```

```
        <classID semester="fall">CS255</classID>
        <department>ComputerScience</department>
        <credits req="yes">3</credits>
        <instructor>Brunner</instructor>
        <title>Java</title>
    </class>
</classes>
```

Both Ch5_examp1.htm and classes.xml need to be on your server for the Ajax request to work. Copy both these files to the Chapter5 subfolder of the BegAjax folder in the root folder of your web server (for example, the root folder is the wwwroot folder if you're using IIS, or the htdocs folder if you're using Apache).

How It Works

This page includes a form with a button labeled "Make Request." When the user clicks the button, the getDoc() function is called.

```
<form>
<input type = "button" id="reqDoc" value = "Make request">
</form>
```

Traditional event registration is used to register the click event, rather than including an onclick attribute in the input tag.

```
<script type="text/javascript">
var myDoc = document.getElementById('reqDoc');
myDoc.onclick = getDoc;
</script>
```

The getDoc() function uses an if statement to test if the browser supports XMLHttpRequest directly. If so, a new XMLHttpRequest object is created and stored in the variable named request.

```
    if (window.XMLHttpRequest) {
       request = new XMLHttpRequest();
    }
```

If the browser is Internet Explorer 5 or 6, a new ActiveXObject is created and stored in the request variable.

```
    else if (window.ActiveXObject) {
       request = new ActiveXObject("Microsoft.XMLHTTP");

    }
```

Internet Explorer 7 supports XMLHttpRequest directly, at least in so far as the ability to create a new XMLHttpRequest object without using ActiveX. For additional details on IE 7 and the XMLHttpRequest object, see "IE7 XMLHttpRequest — Native or Not?" at http://ajaxian.com/archives/ie7-xmlhttprequest-native-or-not.

The properties and methods of the XMLHttpRequest object are slightly different in different browsers. Mozilla-based browsers (Mozilla, Firefox, Netscape Navigator), Safari, and Internet Explorer each support different properties and methods. Chapter 4 provides more information.

The overrideMimeType method is supported in Mozilla-based browsers. The overrideMimeType method is used to override any problems with the Content-Type header and ensures that the Mime type for the document returned by the server is "text/xml". An if statement is used to check if this method is supported in the browser, and, if so, the method is applied to the object.

```
if (request.overrideMimeType) {
    request.overrideMimeType("text/xml");
}
```

If the object has been created, the open method of the XMLHTTPRequest object is used to request data from the XML document, classes.xml. This method uses three parameters: the HTTP method used for the request ("GET"), the URL of the document ("classes.xml"), and a Boolean value of true to indicate that the call is asynchronous.

```
if(request) {
    request.open("GET", "classes.xml", true);
```

The open method can also include two additional parameters for username and password, if required for the server connection.

When the readyState property of the XMLHttpRequest object changes (that is, when the data starts to download), an anonymous function is called.

```
request.onreadystatechange = function()
    {
    if (request.readyState == 4 && request.status == 200) {
```

If the readyState property is equal to 4, the download is complete. As an additional check, a status property equal to 200 also indicates that the request was processed successfully.

```
var xmlDocument = request.responseXML;
alert('XML Document Retrieved');
}
```

Once the download is complete, the responseXML property is used to store the data as XML in a variable named xmlDocument. An alert displays to show that the document was successfully retrieved.

The send method is used to make the actual request to the server. When you use the GET method, you send a value of null.

```
request.send(null);
```

This file uses several methods and properties of the XMLHTTPRequest object to make a request and retrieve XML data from the server. The send method is used to make the request and start the data download, the open method is used to configure the object, and the responseXML property saves the data in the response from the server as XML.

If you want to view the data that's retrieved with responseXML, you can use the xml property of responseXML in Internet Explorer to view the document. Add this code directly after the first alert in the anonymous function:

```
alert(request.responseXML.xml);
```

Figure 5-2 shows the XML document displayed in an alert box in Internet Explorer.

In the next section of this chapter, you learn how to use JavaScript to extract the data from the XML document returned by the server.

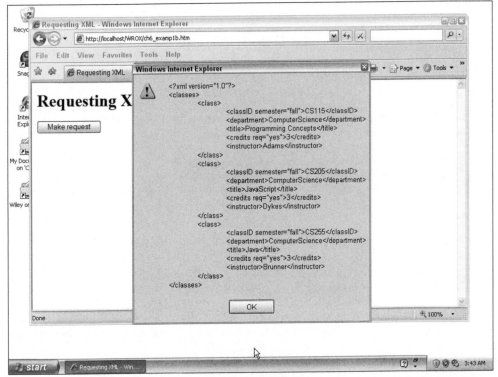

Figure 5-2: Viewing the XML document in Internet Explorer.

Extracting XML Data with JavaScript

Once you've retrieved the XML document from the server, the next step is to extract the XML data from the document using JavaScript. You can use nodes and node properties or DOM methods to do this. In addition to extracting the value of XML elements, you can also extract the value of XML attributes.

Using Nodes

JavaScript includes built-in node properties that you can use to access the nodes in an XML document. The `documentElement` property can be used to access the root element of the XML document. Other node properties include family relationships such as the following:

- ❑ `firstChild` — First child node
- ❑ `lastChild` — Last child node
- ❑ `nextSibling` — Next sibling node
- ❑ `previousSibling` — Previous sibling node
- ❑ `childNodes` — Array of child nodes

Other node properties give information about the node itself:

- ❑ `nodeName` — Name of the node
- ❑ `nodeValue` — Value of the node
- ❑ `nodeType` — Type of the node

The `nodeType` is useful for checking for a specific type of node. The 12 node types are shown in Table 5-1.

For more information on viewing a document as a family tree and viewing a document as a node tree, see Chapter 2.

nodeType	Description
1	Element
2	Attribute
3	Text
4	CDATA section
5	XML entity reference
6	XML entity
7	XML processing instruction

Table continued on following page

nodeType	Description
8	XML comment
9	XML document
10	XML DTD
11	XML document fragment
12	XML Notation

You can use the family relationships to access the nodes in an XML document. For example, if you want to access the title of the first course in the classes.xml document, you can add additional code to ch5_examp1.htm to traverse the nodes of the XML document using family relationships. You can access the root element of classes.xml by using the documentElement property:

```
var rootNode = xmlDocument.documentElement;
```

xmlDocument is the name of the variable that contains the requestXML property of the XMLHTTPRequest object. The rootNode is the classes element.

You can continue to traverse the document using family relationships:

```
var classNode = rootNode.firstChild;
var titleNode = classNode.lastChild;
var titleText = titleNode.firstChild;
```

The classNode is the class element, the first child of the classes element. The last child of the class element is the title element, stored in the titleNode variable. The first child of the title element is the text node that contains the title data, stored in the titleText variable. Now you can obtain the value of the text node that contains the course title:

```
var titleValue = titleText.nodeValue;
```

This works fine in Internet Explorer; however, Mozilla-based browsers treat white space in XML documents as text nodes. When you access the firstChild of the classes element in a Mozilla-based browser, you access the white space text node instead of the class element. You can take the white space into account and skip over these white space text nodes using family relationships. For example, to access the class element, instead of:

```
var classNode = rootNode.firstChild;
```

you can add a nextSibling property to skip over the white space text node:

```
var classNode = rootNode.firstChild.nextSibling;
```

You can add code to remove all the white space from the XML document rather than dealing with these increasingly cumbersome family relationships. Or you can take a different approach altogether and access the elements by name, as shown in the following section.

Accessing XML Elements by Name

JavaScript includes a `getElementsByTagName` method that you can use to extract specific elements from an XML document using the name of the XML element.

For example, if you want to extract the value of the first `title` element, use the name of the element:

```
var titleNode = xmlDocument.getElementsByTagName('title');
```

Because there is more than one `title` element in the `classes.xml` document, `titleNode` consists of an array. Use the following to access the first value in the array:

```
var firstTitle = titleNode[0];
```

Once you've accessed the first `title` element, you can use `firstChild` and `nodeValue` to extract the value of the text node:

```
var titleValue = firstTitle.firstChild.nodeValue;
```

You can display this value on the page by adding a `div` with an `id` value at the place on the page where you want to display the text.

```
<div id="title"></div>
```

Create a new element and text node to display the title value within the `div` element:

```
var myEl = document.createElement('p');
var newText = "The first course listing is " + titleValue + ".";
var myTx = document.createTextNode(newText);
myEl.appendChild(myTx);
var course = document.getElementById('title');
course.appendChild(myEl);
```

For more information on using JavaScript to add new elements to an existing page, see Chapter 2.

Figure 5-3 shows that the first course title is displayed on the page after the user clicks the button and sends a request to the browser for the XML document.

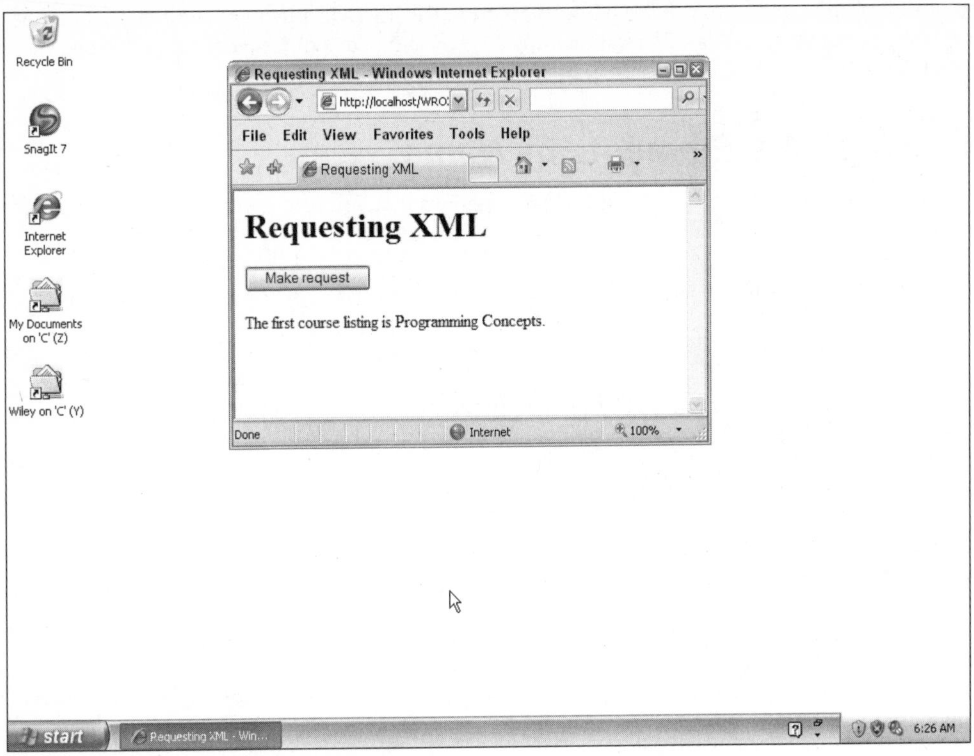

Figure 5-3: Displaying the first course title.

Accessing Attribute Values

You can also use JavaScript to extract the values of attribute nodes in XML documents. Attribute nodes are contained within element nodes, so you need to start by accessing the element that contains the attribute you're interested in. For example, in the `classes.xml` document, the `credits` elements include an attribute named `req` that indicates whether a course is required for a Computer Science degree. You can easily access the `credits` element using `getElementsByTagName`:

```
var creditStatus = xmlDocument.getElementsByTagName('credits');
```

You can then use the `attributes` property to access the attribute. Because there's more than one `credits` element, the `creditStatus` variable contains an array. Use the following if you want to know the value of the attribute for the third `credits` element in the document:

```
var creditAttr = creditStatus[2].attributes;
```

The `getNamedItem` method allows you to access the attribute node using the name of the attribute:

```
var reqAttr = creditAttr.getNamedItem('req');
```

Finally, you can use the `nodeValue` property to get the value of the `req` attribute:

```
var reqVal = reqAttr.nodeValue;
```

Try It Out   Extracting XML Element and Attribute Values

In this example, you create an `XMLHttpRequest` object to download an XML document. You then extract XML element and attribute values from this document and add them to the existing page. Type the following code into your text editor, and save it as `ch5_examp2.htm`. Copy it to the `Chapter5` subfolder of the `BegAjax` folder in the root folder of your web server (for example, the root folder is the `wwwroot` folder if you're using IIS or the `htdocs` folder if you're using Apache).

Figure 5-4 shows the element and attribute display in Firefox.

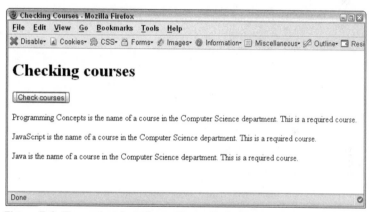

Figure 5-4: Element and attribute display in Firefox.

```
<!DOCTYPE html PUBLIC "-//W3C//DTD XHTML 1.0 Transitional//EN"
"http://www.w3.org/TR/xhtml1/DTD/xhtml1-transitional.dtd">
<html xmlns="http://www.w3.org/1999/xhtml">
<head>
<meta http-equiv="Content-Type" content="text/html; charset=iso-8859-1" />

<title>Checking Courses</title>
<script language = "javascript">
   function getDoc()
   {
   if (window.XMLHttpRequest) {
     request = new XMLHttpRequest();
   }
   else if (window.ActiveXObject) {
     request = new ActiveXObject("Microsoft.XMLHTTP");
   }
   if (request.overrideMimeType) {
     request.overrideMimeType("text/xml");
   }

   if(request) {
```

```
      request.open("GET", "classes.xml", true);

      request.onreadystatechange = function()
   {
        if (request.readyState == 4 && request.status == 200) {
          var xmlDocument = request.responseXML;
          findClass(xmlDocument);
        }
   }
      request.send(null);
   }
}

function findClass(doc) {
    var titleNode = doc.getElementsByTagName('title');
      for (i=0; i < titleNode.length; i++) {
        var title = titleNode[i];
        var titleValue = title.firstChild.nodeValue;

        var myEl = document.createElement('p');
        var newText = titleValue + " is the name of a course in the Computer Science
department.";
        var myTx = document.createTextNode(newText);
        myEl.appendChild(myTx);
        var course = document.getElementById('title');
        course.appendChild(myEl);

        var creditStatus = doc.getElementsByTagName('credits');
        var creditAttr = creditStatus[i].attributes;
        var reqAttr = creditAttr.getNamedItem('req');
        var reqVal = reqAttr.nodeValue;

          if (reqVal == 'yes') {
            var addlText = " This is a required course.";
            var addlText2 = document.createTextNode(addlText);
            myEl.appendChild(addlText2);
          }
      }
}
 </script>
 </head>
 <body>
   <h1>Checking courses</h1>
   <form>
     <input type = "button" id="reqDoc" value = "Check courses">
   </form>
<script type="text/javascript">
var myDoc = document.getElementById('reqDoc');
myDoc.onclick = getDoc;
</script>
<div id="title"></div>
</body>
</html>
```

How It Works

This file adds to the file you created in the previous example. You create an XMLHttpRequest object, as in the previous example. After retrieving the XML document from the server, you call the findClass function to extract XML element and attribute data and add it to your page.

```
if (request.readyState == 4 && request.status == 200) {
    var xmlDocument = request.responseXML;
    findClass(xmlDocument);
```

This function starts by searching for the title elements in the XML document using the getElementsByTagName method.

```
function findClass(doc) {
    var titleNode = doc.getElementsByTagName('title');
```

Because there is more than one title element, the titleNode variable contains an array. A for loop is used to iterate through each member of the titleNode array. The length of this array (titleNode.length) is used as the test condition for continuing the for loop.

```
for (i=0; i < titleNode.length; i++) {
    var title = titleNode[i];
    var titleValue = title.firstChild.nodeValue;
```

The value of the title text node is added to the existing page using createElement, createTextNode, and appendChild.

```
    var myEl = document.createElement('p');
    var newText = titleValue + " is the name of a course in the Computer Science
department.";
    var myTx = document.createTextNode(newText);
    myEl.appendChild(myTx);
    var course = document.getElementById('title');
    course.appendChild(myEl);
```

The value of the req attribute of the credits elements is extracted using getElementsByTagName, attributes, and getNamedItem.

Because there is more than one credits element, creditStatus contains an array. The value of i in the for loop is used to specify each member of the creditStatus array and apply the attributes property.

```
    var creditStatus = doc.getElementsByTagName('credits');
    var creditAttr = creditStatus[i].attributes;
    var reqAttr = creditAttr.getNamedItem('req');
    var reqVal = reqAttr.nodeValue;
```

The value of reqVal is used in an if statement. If the value is 'yes', an additional text node is added to the myEl element.

```
if (reqVal == 'yes') {
    var addlText = " This is a required course.";
    var addlText2 = document.createTextNode(addlText);
    myEl.appendChild(addlText2);
    }
```

Using CSS with XML Data

XML files are text files and don't contain any formatting information. If the XML document is well formed and you open it in Internet Explorer, you'll see a display of the elements, attributes, and content, as shown in Figure 5-5.

If you open the same document in Firefox, the display is similar to the one in Internet Explorer, but if you open the document in Netscape, the only display is a string containing the data in the document, as shown in Netscape 7 in Figure 5-6.

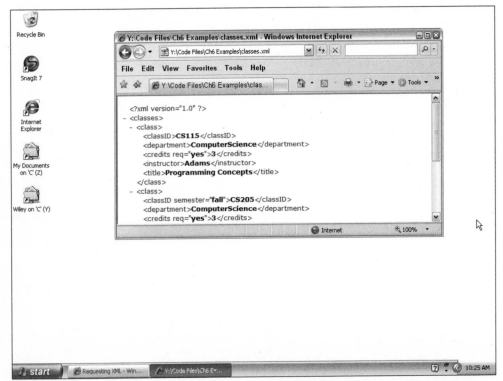

Figure 5-5: Display of elements, attributes, and content in an XML document in Internet Explorer.

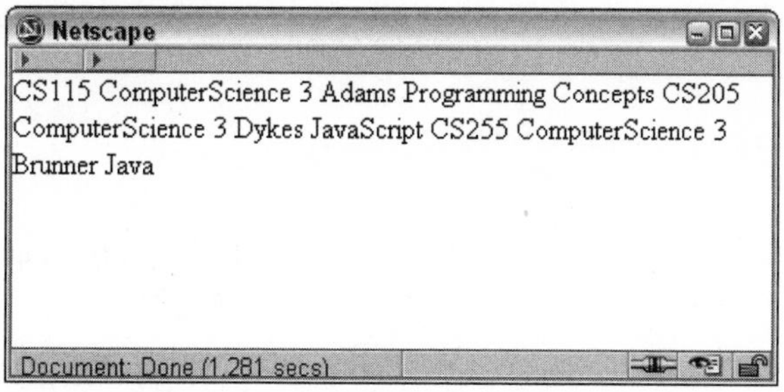

Figure 5-6: Display of an XML document in Netscape.

Using CSS with XML Documents

You can apply Cascading Style Sheet (CSS) styles directly to an XML document by adding a CSS style sheet to the document. You link the style sheet to the XML document by adding a processing instruction to the document that references the URL of the style sheet:

```
<?xml-stylesheet type="text/css" href="classes.css"?>
```

This processing instruction is added to the page right after the XML declaration:

```
<?xml version="1.0"?>
<?xml-stylesheet type="text/css" href="classes.css"?>
```

You can use XML element names as CSS selectors. For example, if you wanted to display the `classID`, `title`, and `credits` elements in `classes.xml` with a maroon-colored text set in Arial, you could create the following style:

```
classID, title, credits{
display: block;
color: maroon;
font-size: small;
font-family: Arial;
font-weight: bold;
}
```

Using CSS with Ajax

Because Ajax is used to update a page without reloading the entire page, it can also be used to apply styles dynamically to page elements, including any XML data you add to a page. You can apply styles dynamically using JavaScript and CSS. JavaScript's `style` and `className` properties can be used to do this.

The style Property

JavaScript's `style` property enables you to set the value of any CSS style. The format is as follows:

```
element.style.property = "value"
```

For example, if you have a paragraph with an `id` equal to `p1`, the code sets the text color in the `p1` paragraph to purple:

```
var myPara = document.getElementById("p1");
myPara.style.color = "purple";
```

Most hyphenated CSS property names are a single word in JavaScript, using camel notation (for example, `border-right` becomes `borderRight` and `padding-top` becomes `paddingTop`).

You can add CSS formatting to the display of any XML data you extract and add to your page. For example, in the `ch5_examp2.htm` file, you can apply a color to the XML data you add to the page by adding this line of code. This displays all the text in the `myEl` element in red.

```
myEl.style.color = 'red';
```

> **The `style` property can't access the value of properties that have been set in an external CSS style sheet or embedded in the head section of a document. What it can do, though, is define inline styles that override any external or embedded styles except for those marked as `!important`.**

The className Property

JavaScript's `className` property provides a quick way to switch the CSS class that's applied to an object. For example, say you've defined two CSS class selectors, `.red` and `.blue`, and initially assigned the red class to a paragraph:

```
<p id="first" name="first" class="red">
```

You can change that assignment with the following JavaScript:

```
document.getElementById("first").className="blue";
```

The `className` property is not subject to the limitations of the `style` property. You're not using JavaScript to change style properties directly; you're using JavaScript to change the CSS class that's applied to an object.

Summary

Data returned from an Ajax request is in text or XML format. XML is generally a much more useful format than plain text for exchanging data.

This chapter included the following points:

❑ XML allows you to create your own set of custom tags to organize and format your data in whatever way works best for your needs.

❑ When you download XML documents with an Ajax request, it's important that those documents follow XML syntax rules. It's also useful if the documents have been validated with a document description such as a DTD or XML Schema document. This ensures that the data is in the format and datatype that you need to use in your application.

❑ When you extract data from an XML document, you have access to the entire document, including elements, attributes, and content.

❑ You can use nodes and node properties to extract data from an XML document with JavaScript. This method works reasonably well in Internet Explorer, but it can be cumbersome in browsers that treat white space as text nodes.

❑ The fastest and simplest way to extract XML element data is with the `getElementsByTagName` method. This method can be used with XML element names, as well as HTML/XHTML element names.

❑ CSS can be used to supply formatting information for XML documents, whether those documents are viewed directly in a browser or the XML data is extracted first and then added to an existing page.

❑ CSS and JavaScript can be used together to apply dynamic formatting when you display data returned from an Ajax request.

Exercises

Suggested solutions to these questions can be found in Appendix A.

1. Create an XML document that organizes sales data for one day into three categories: `date`, `amount`, `salesperson`. Include a `salesID` attribute in the `salesperson` element. Once you've created the document structure (elements and attributes), add the following content to the document:

❑ `date` — Today's date

❑ `amount` — Any amounts from $20 to $500

❑ `salesperson` — Marie (`salesID = 225`), Joan (`salesID = 198`), and Ron (`salesID = 304`)

2. Use JavaScript's style property to apply a dynamic style to a paragraph that consists of a single word (`flower`). Change the background color and text color, and specify the Arial font family with a bold font weight.

Debugging and Error Handling

When the code for your Ajax application doesn't work as expected, you need a way to debug the code and find the source of the problem. The two most likely sources are errors in the JavaScript code and problems with the Ajax request.

JavaScript syntax errors occur when the code is interpreted. A syntax error occurs when the JavaScript interpreter parses an unexpected character, such as an extra angle bracket. If a syntax error is found, code parsing stops at that point and no code is executed. JavaScript runtime errors occur when the code is executed. For example, if the code includes a function call for a nonexistent function, a runtime error will occur when the function call is executed. If a runtime error occurs, code execution stops for that thread of code, but other code will still be executed. Runtime errors are also called *exceptions*.

JavaScript now includes built-in exception handling with the `try` statement, and additional tools such as the Mozilla JavaScript console, Microsoft Script Debugger, and the Firebug extension for Firefox can be used to identify errors.

You can also troubleshoot the Ajax request to determine if the `XMLHttpRequest` object is being created and if the request is actually being made. There may be problems with either the browser request or the server response. Because the Ajax request occurs in the background, special tools such as DOM inspectors and the Firebug console can be used to view what's happening at run time.

This chapter provides a review of tools and techniques for debugging Ajax applications, including troubleshooting JavaScript using consoles and debuggers, using a DOM inspector, and viewing live HTTP headers.

In this chapter, you learn about the following:

❑   **JavaScript error handling** — `try` statement, Mozilla JavaScript console, Microsoft Script Debugger, Firebug Console and Debugger

❑ **DOM inspectors** — Firefox DOM Inspector, IE DOM Inspector, MODI (Mouseover DOM Inspector)

❑ **Tools for troubleshooting Ajax** — Firebug Console, Firefox Live HTTP Headers extension, `ieHTTPHeaders` Explorer Bar

JavaScript Error Handling

JavaScript has a reputation as an error-prone language that's difficult to debug. Although this reputation may be appropriate for early versions of JavaScript in older browsers, changes in both JavaScript and newer browsers now make it much easier to find and correct errors. Although there is not yet a full-fledged Integrated Development Environment (IDE) for JavaScript, browser tools and add-ons such as consoles and debuggers can help you find errors and exceptions in your JavaScript code.

Handling Exceptions

The third edition of ECMAScript adapted the Java `try` statement and added it to JavaScript. The `try` statement can help you test your code and identify errors.

The `try` statement is used with `catch` and/or `finally` clauses, as shown here:

```
try {
// execute this block of code
}
catch (err) {
// if the try code can't be executed, execute this code
}
```

If an error occurs when the block of code in the `try` statement is executed, execution of that code stops at that point, and the code after the `catch` statement is executed.

A `finally` clause can be added to a `try` statement or to a `try` statement with a `catch` clause. A `finally` clause contains code that is always executed whether or not an exception occurs, as shown here:

```
try {
var x;
x[1] = 3;
}
catch (err) {
alert ('An error occurred: ' + err.message);
}
finally {
alert('try/catch test is complete');
}
```

The following line of the code creates an error because a value for array index position 1 in the x array is assigned, but no x array has been created:

```
x[1] = 3;
```

Figure 6-1 shows the error message displayed in Firefox when this code is executed, and Figure 6-2 shows the corresponding error message for IE 7. As you can see in the figures, the content of the error message is different in each of these browsers.

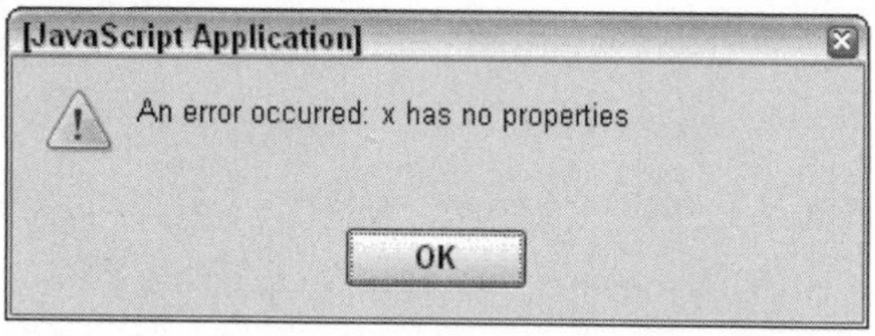

Figure 6-1: Error message displayed in Firefox.

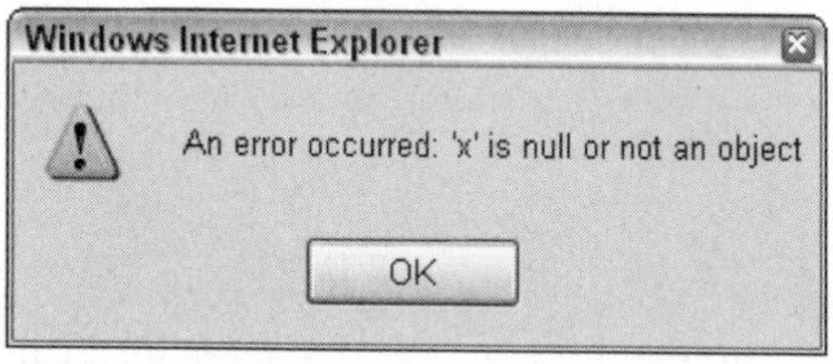

Figure 6-2: Error message displayed in IE 7.

The `catch` clause catches the JavaScript `Error` object that's created by the `try` code. The `Error` object includes a `message` property that contains the actual error message. The `Error` object also includes a `name` property that specifies the type of the error. In this case, a `TypeError` is created because the type of the variable `x` is not an array. You can add code to show both the name and the type of the error, as shown here:

```
catch (err) {
alert ('A ' + err.name + ' occurred: ' + err.message);
}
```

Figure 6-3 shows this alert message as displayed in Firefox.

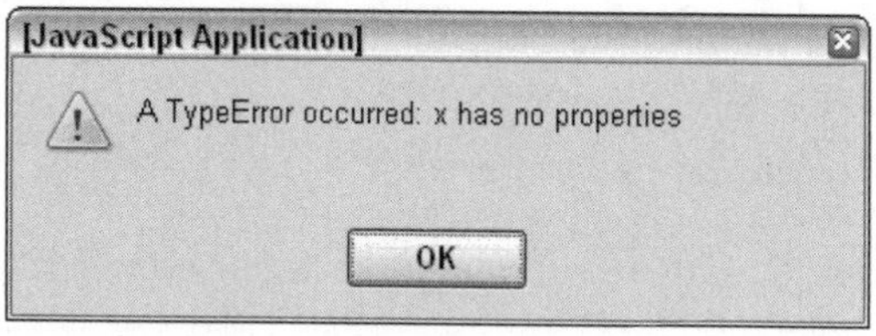

Figure 6-3: Alert message as displayed in Firefox.

A `TypeError` is one of six possible error types, as shown in Table 6-1.

Name	Description
EvalError	An error occurred in the code contained in an `eval()` function.
RangeError	A value is outside the allowable range of values.
ReferenceError	An illegal reference was used.
SyntaxError	A parsing error occurred in the code contained in an `eval()` function.*
TypeError	The type of a variable is different than expected.
URIError	A URI function (`encodeURI()` or `decodeURI()`) was used incorrectly.**

* Syntax errors occurring outside of `eval()` functions can't be handled with a `try` statement.

** The `encodeURI()` and `decodeURI()` functions are used to replace special characters, such as spaces, in a Uniform Resource Identifier (URI). A URL is a type of URI.

For additional details on error handling in JavaScript, see *Professional JavaScript for Web Developers* (Indianapolis: Wiley, 2005) and *Beginning JavaScript, Second Edition* (Indianapolis: Wiley, 2004).

The onerror Event Handler

An `error` event is fired in a browser when a script generates an error. You can use this event to identify errors by creating an `onerror` event handler that's called when an error event occurs:

```
function handleIt (msg, url, line) {
alert ('An error occurred:\nmessage: ' + msg + '\nurl: ' + url +'\nline: ' + line);
return true;
}
```

Three items of information about an error are created when an `error` event is fired on the `window` object:

❑ The browser's standard error message for this error

❑ The URL of the page that generated the error

❑ The line number where the error occurred

You can access these details to get more information about the error. In the `handleIt` function, parameters are passed to the function for each of these three items (`msg`, `url`, `line`). The browser error message will still display when an error occurs unless the `onerror` event handler returns a value of `true`, so `return true` should be included in the function code:

```
function handleIt (msg, url, line) {
alert ('An error occurred:\nmessage: ' + msg + '\nurl: ' + url +'\nline: ' + line);
return true;
}
```

Try It Out   Using an onerror Event Handler

In this example, a JavaScript error is generated with a block of code in the body of the page. The
onerror event handler is assigned to the handleIt() function, which displays an alert with the error
message, URL, and line number of the error. Type the following code into your text editor and save it as
ch6_examp1.htm. Figure 6-4 shows the alert message displayed in IE 7 when this page is loaded.

```
<!DOCTYPE html PUBLIC "-//W3C//DTD XHTML 1.0 Transitional//EN"
"http://www.w3.org/TR/xhtml1/DTD/xhtml1-transitional.dtd">
<html xmlns="http://www.w3.org/1999/xhtml">
<head>
<meta http-equiv="Content-Type" content="text/html; charset=iso-8859-1" />
<title>Accessing the error event</title>
<script type="text/javascript">
  function handleIt (msg, url, line) {
    alert ('An error occurred:\nmessage: ' + msg + '\nurl: ' + url +'\nline: ' +
line);
    return true;
  }
</script>
</head>
<body>
<script type="text/javascript">
  onerror = handleIt;
  var x;
  x[3] = 3;
</script>
</body>
</html>
```

Figure 6-4: Alert message displayed in IE 7.

How It Works

The script block in the body of the page registers the handleIt() function as the event handler for the
error event.

```
onerror = handleIt;
```

When the two lines of code following the event registration are executed, an error is created and an error
event occurs:

```
var x;
x[3] = 3;
```

When the error event occurs, the `handleIt()` function is called and displays an alert with the error message, URL of the page with the error, and line number of the error, as shown in Figure 6-4. The newline character (\n) is used to create line breaks in the display of the alert.

```
alert ('An error occurred:\nmessage: ' + msg + '\nurl: ' + url +'\nline: ' + line);
```

The main issue with using the error event for error handling is that it's part of the Browser Object Model (BOM). There may be major differences in the way different browsers deal with errors using this event.

> In addition to the `window` object, the `image` object also supports the use of the `error` event. For example, an `error` event occurs when an image file fails to load. Additional information about the message, URL, or line number of an error is not available when it occurs with an image, though.

Mozilla JavaScript Console

The JavaScript console is a tool that's available in Mozilla-based browsers. It's used for reporting JavaScript errors in the page that's currently loaded in the browser. It also reports CSS errors and messages from the browser's *chrome* — the browser border and objects that surround the browser window.

The JavaScript console keeps track of every error that occurs during an entire browser session and logs them in the console. For example, if you start your browser session by opening a page that includes the following JavaScript code, an error will be generated:

```
var x = 3;
alert ("x = + x);
```

To view the error in the JavaScript console, type `javascript:` in the browser address bar once the page has loaded. The console opens in a separate window, as shown in Figure 6-5. The option All is selected, so all errors, warnings, and messages are displayed in the console.

In some versions of Netscape, the JavaScript console can't be opened from the browser address bar. Instead, choose Tools → JavaScript Console or Tools → Web Development → GET
`http://webmail.att.net/wmui/images/icon_folder_closed.gif`

HTTP/1.0

*Accept: */**

Refere: http://we

The error message is "unterminated string literal" because there is only one quotation mark rather than a set of quotation marks in the alert code. Deciphering the error messages created by the console can take some practice; a good way to learn the common error messages is to deliberately create errors in your code and then open the console to see which error message displays.

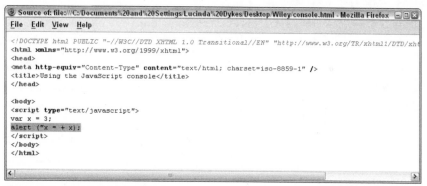

Figure 6-5: JavaScript console window.

If you click the file link that's displayed after the error message, a new window opens that displays the source code for the page and highlights the line with the error, as shown in Figure 6-6. If the error is not obvious in the highlighted line, though, look at the preceding line of code to see if that's where the actual error occurs. This is especially likely if the error occurs in code nested in braces and brackets.

Figure 6-6: Error line highlighted.

Click the Clear button in the console once an error displays so that the console then displays only new error messages rather than an ongoing log of all the errors that have occurred since you opened the browser. Once you've found and corrected the error, save and reload the page, and open the console again to ensure that the error is corrected and that there are no other errors in the page.

You can also use the console to evaluate JavaScript expressions by typing in the text box at the top of the console and then clicking the Evaluate button to the right of the text box. This enables you to test a block of code for errors without creating a page. For example, if you type the following in the text box, an alert message displays 7, as shown in Figure 6-7:

```
var x = 5; var y = x + 2; alert (y);
```

You can keep the console open as the browser loads new pages and view the error messages as they're logged to the console.

The console is a very useful tool for finding JavaScript syntax errors and exceptions, but it doesn't allow you to debug code by using breakpoints or stepping through the source code line by line. For that, you need to use a debugger such as Microsoft Script Debugger or the Firebug extension for Firefox.

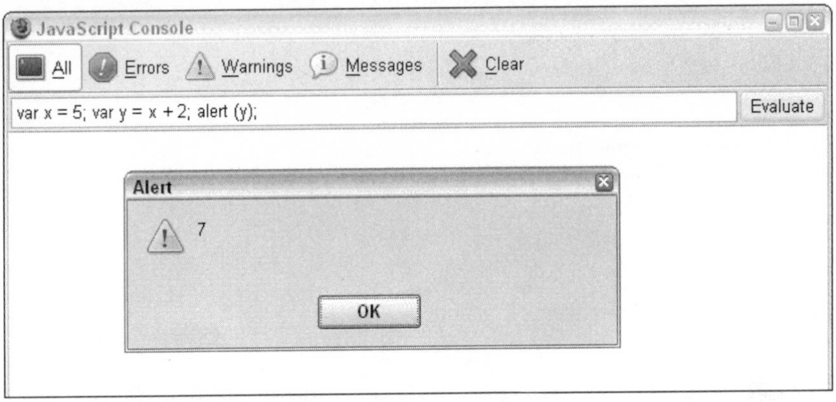

Figure 6-7: Alert message displaying "7".

Microsoft Script Debugger

The Microsoft Script Debugger is a free tool available for Internet Explorer in Windows NT, Windows 2000, Windows XP, and Windows Server 2003. It can be downloaded from the Microsoft site at www.microsoft.com/downloads/details.aspx?FamilyID=2f465be0-94fd-4569-b3c4-dffdf19ccd99&DisplayLang=en. After you install the debugger, restart Internet Explorer. The Script Debugger can then be accessed from the View menu.

> Although Microsoft Script Debugger is still available for free download, Microsoft no longer supports Script Debugger and recommends Visual Studio .NET 2003 as a debugging tool.

Ensure that script debugging is enabled in IE. From the main menu, choose Tools → Internet Options and then click on the Advanced tab. In the Browsing list, ensure that the check box labeled Disable Script Debugging (Internet Explorer) is not checked.

When you load a page with a JavaScript error in Internet Explorer, an error message displays, as shown in Figure 6-8. If you click the Yes button, the Microsoft Script Debugger opens. You can also open the Script Debugger by choosing View → Script Debugger from the main IE menu bar.

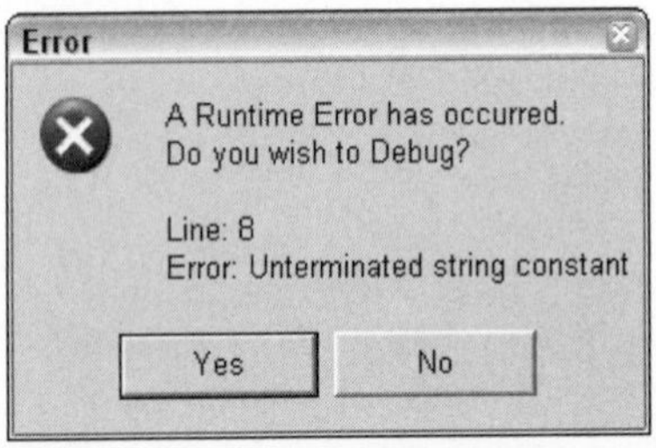

Figure 6-8: JavaScript error in Internet Explorer.

Figure 6-9 shows the Script Debugger window for the following code:

```
<script type="text/javascript">
function debugIt() {
var x = 3;
alert ('x = x);
}
</script>
</head>
<body>
<script type="text/javascript">
debugIt();
</script>
```

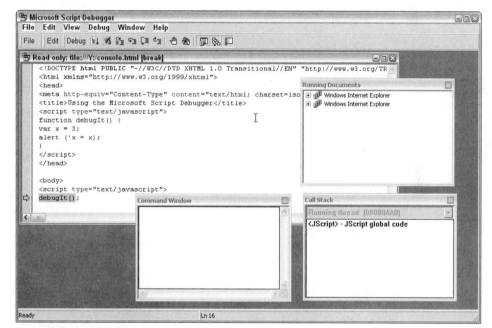

Figure 6-9: Script Debugger window.

The debugIt() function contains an error in this line of code:

```
alert ('x = x);
```

This line includes an unterminated string, as indicated in the error message in Figure 6-8. The debugger is highlighted at line 15:

```
debugIt();
```

The unterminated string in line 8 creates an error, so the debugIt() function is not created. When line 15 is parsed, the debugIt() function is still undefined and a second error is generated.

The Script Debugger window includes three other view windows that can be opened from the View menu. The Running Documents window displays all the documents open in IE. The Call Stack window displays the list of function calls leading up to the error. The most recently called function is at the top of the list. The Command Window can be used to enter commands to display current values of variables and properties, change variable and property values, or create new objects.

The Debugger also includes options for setting breakpoints and stepping through the code. These options can be accessed through the Debug menu on the main menu bar or the Debug section of the toolbar above the source code window. A *breakpoint* stops code execution at that point. You can then step through the code line by line to follow the course of the code as it's executed.

To edit a source file once an error is identified, choose File → Open and select the file. This opens a second copy of the source code in a new window. Unlike the read-only source code in the main debugger window, this code can be edited and saved. Once the error is corrected and the changes saved, refresh the document in the browser window. If no error messages appear this time, the error has been corrected and no other errors have been found.

Firebug

The Firebug add-on to Firefox combines the best features of the Mozilla JavaScript console and the Microsoft Script Debugger into one easy-to-use tool. Firebug is available for Firefox 1.5 and later versions. It can be downloaded at `https://addons.mozilla.org/firefox/1843/`. After installing Firebug, a green checkmark appears at the bottom-right corner of the browser window. Clicking on this checkmark opens a Firebug window in the bottom of the browser, as shown in Figure 6-10.

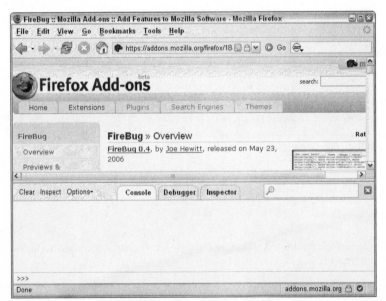

Figure 6-10: Firebug window in the bottom of the browser.

The Firebug menu includes three tabs: Console, Debugger, and Inspector.

The Console tab displays error messages, similar to the display in the JavaScript console. A link to the right of the error message shows the line of code where the error occurred. If you click on the link, the source code is displayed in a new window with that line highlighted. When the Console tab is selected, the Clear button at the top left of the Firebug window can be clicked to clear the console messages. The Options button displays options for the type of messages that you want to view in the console (such as JavaScript errors and warnings, CSS errors, or XML errors). The contents of the Options menu vary, depending on the tab that's selected. The Firebug console can also be used for troubleshooting XMLHttp requests, as shown in the "Troubleshooting Ajax" section, later in this chapter.

The Debugger tab allows you to step through the code line by line. The Debugger tab displays a marker at the line where code execution stops. You can set a breakpoint at a different point in the code by adding this code to the JavaScript at the point where you want code execution to stop:

```
debugger;
```

Save the file, and then refresh the file in the browser.

The Debugger tab also includes a call stack that displays the list of function calls leading up to the error and a list of properties for the current selection in a frame to the right of the tabs. You can click the buttons below the code display on the left to step through the code. When an error is generated, the green checkmark in the bottom-right corner of the browser changes to a red X, and the number of errors is displayed next to the X. You can then click on the Console tab for more information about the error.

When the following code blocks are parsed and executed in the browser, two errors are generated. Figure 6-11 shows the error messages displayed in the Console tab.

```html
<html>
<head>
<title>Firebug Debugger</title>
<script type="text/javascript">
function debugIt() {
var x = 3;
alert ('x = x);
}
</script>
</head>
<body>
<script type="text/javascript">
debugIt();
</script>
</body>
</html>
```

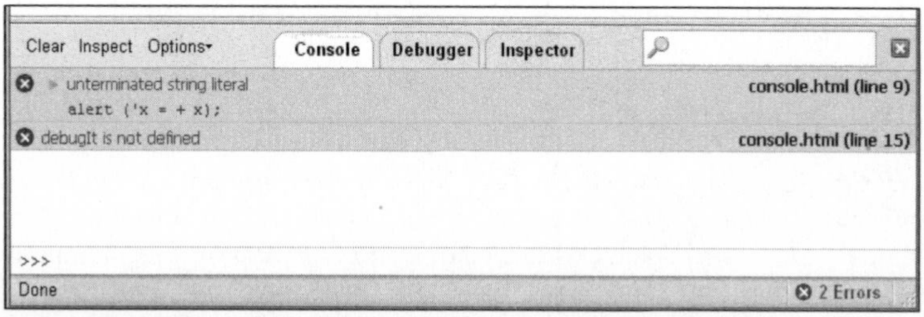

Figure 6-11: Error messages displayed in the Console tab.

If you view the code in the Debugger tab, a breakpoint is indicated at line 15, as shown in Figure 6-12. If you then click the Step Into button in the Debug toolbar at the bottom of the window, two errors are generated with one click of the Step Into button. As soon as the `debugIt()` function is called, the unterminated string literal error is generated, the `debugIt()` function is not created, and the function call in line 15 generates the second error because the function that's being called is not defined.

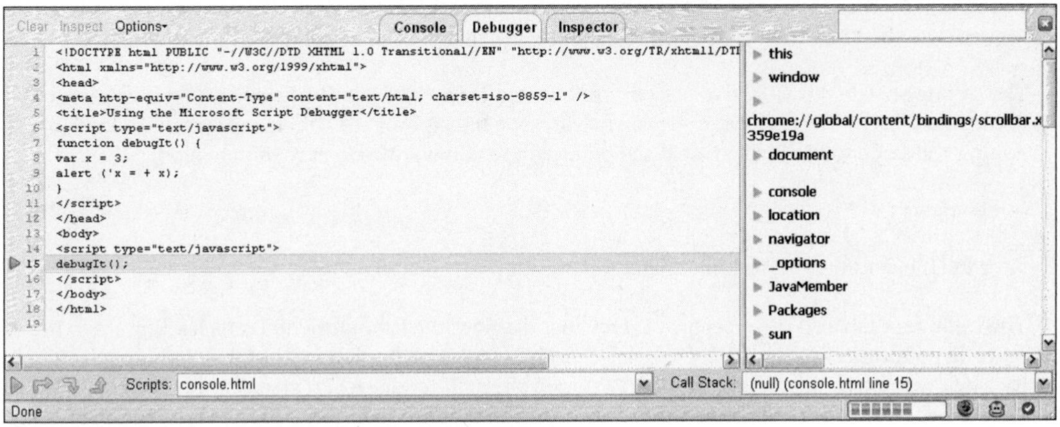

Figure 6-12: Breakpoint displayed in the Debugger tab.

The Inspector enables you to inspect the properties of the HTML elements in the currently loaded document. The Inspector includes additional options at the bottom of the window for the page source (Source) and Style, Layout, Event, and DOM properties.

You can add console commands to your JavaScript source code to include additional features such as a timer to calculate how long it takes a block of code to execute. Just add `console.time('code1');` at the beginning of the code block and `console.timeEnd('code1');` at the end of the code block. The value in the parentheses can be any unique identifier. Save the file, and refresh the file in the browser. The console displays the time that it took for the browser to execute the code.

For more information on Firebug, see the documentation at `www.joehewitt.com/software/firebug/docs.php`.

DOM Inspectors

DOM inspectors enable you to check a dynamic model of the DOM. A DOM inspector traverses the browser's current DOM model and displays the current state of the DOM.

Firefox DOM Inspector

The Firefox DOM inspector is installed with the Firefox installation only if you choose a Custom Installation and select the Developer Tools option. You can check if it's installed by opening the Tools menu from the main menu bar. The DOM inspector option displays in this menu if it has been installed. If you don't see this option, reinstall Firefox. Your current settings will be maintained, and the DOM inspector will be added.

When you open the DOM inspector, the DOM Inspector window opens and displays a DOM tree for the currently loaded document. For example, if you open the ch5_examp2.htm file in Firefox, the DOM tree displays in the left pane of the DOM Inspector window (Figure 6-13). If you select a node in the DOM tree, the node name, type, and value are displayed in the right pane in the DOM Inspector. If you click the window icon at the top of the right pane, you can choose other options in the menu including the following:

❏ **Box model** — Displays the values for properties of the box model that represents the selected element.

❏ **XBL bindings** — Displays bindings for Firefox's XML-based User Interface Language (XUL).

❏ **CSS style rules** — Displays the CSS rules that are applied specifically to the selected element.

❏ **Computed style** — Displays the CSS styles that are applied to the selected element, including inherited styles.

❏ **JavaScript object** — Displays all properties of the JavaScript object that represents the selected element.

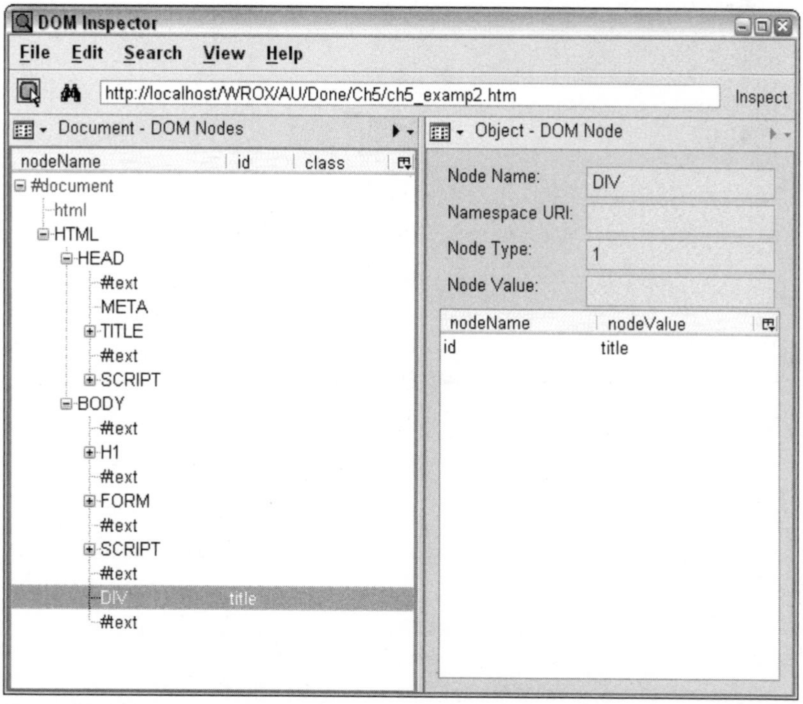

Figure 6-13: DOM tree displayed in the left pane of the DOM Inspector window.

When you click the Inspect button at the upper right of the DOM Inspector window, the browser window displays in the lower half of the DOM Inspector. If you click the Check Courses button when ch5_examp2.htm is displayed, an Ajax request is created, and three new paragraphs of text are added within the div element. The DOM Inspector then displays these additional elements and text nodes (Figure 6-14).

You can find specific nodes by selecting Search → Find Nodes from the main menu. In the Find Nodes dialog, you can search by ID, tag name, or attribute value.

IE DOM Inspector

The IE DOM inspector is included as part of the IE Developer Toolbar that's available for Internet Explorer 6.0 and later. You can open the DOM inspector by clicking the View DOM button on the Developer Toolbar (Figure 6-15). The DOM tree, node name and attributes, and current style properties are displayed in the three panes of the DOM inspector. The inspector displays in the bottom of the browser window.

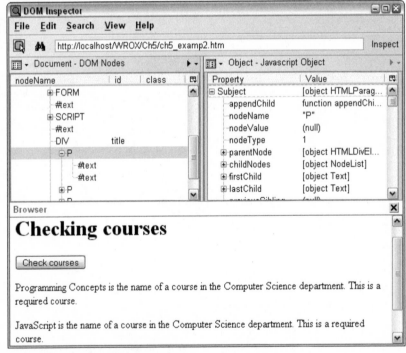

Figure 6-14: Firefox DOM Inspector.

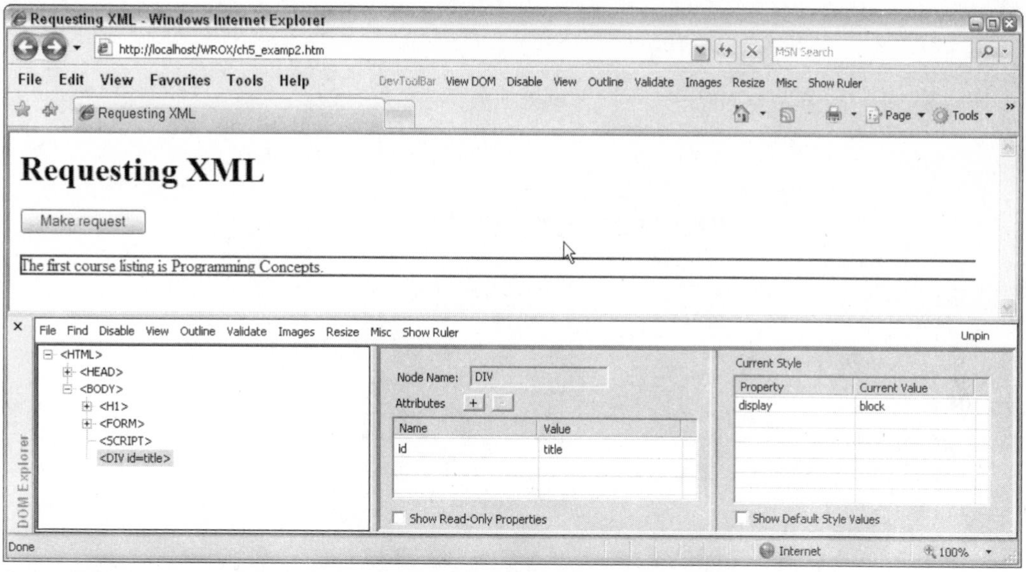

Figure 6-15: Clicking the View DOM button on the Developer toolbar in IE 7.

At the top of the DOM Inspector window is a toolbar that includes all the buttons of the Developer Toolbar, plus two additional buttons: File and Find. The File menu includes options for refresh and for undo. The Find menu includes options for finding an element by class, ID, or name value, and for selecting an element by clicking on it in the browser window.

To download the IE Developer Toolbar, go to www.microsoft.com/downloads/, and enter **Developer Toolbar** in the search box.

Mouseover DOM Inspector (MODI)

The Mouseover DOM Inspector (MODI) bookmarklet is a DOM inspector that can be used in Firefox, Mozilla, Opera 7.5 and later, Netscape 8, and Internet Explorer 6 and later.

To use MODI, go to http://slayeroffice.com/tools/modi/v2.0/modi_help.html and bookmark the page. Then, open the page you want to inspect, and open the MODI bookmark. A MODI pop-up window appears and displays DOM information about the area of the page that the mouse is over (Figure 6-16).

MODI includes keyboard commands such as selecting the parent element of the current selection by entering a **W**. MODI also includes additional features such as the Keep in View feature that adjusts the position of the MODI window when you scroll vertically. The full list of keyboard commands and additional features is available on the MODI Help page.

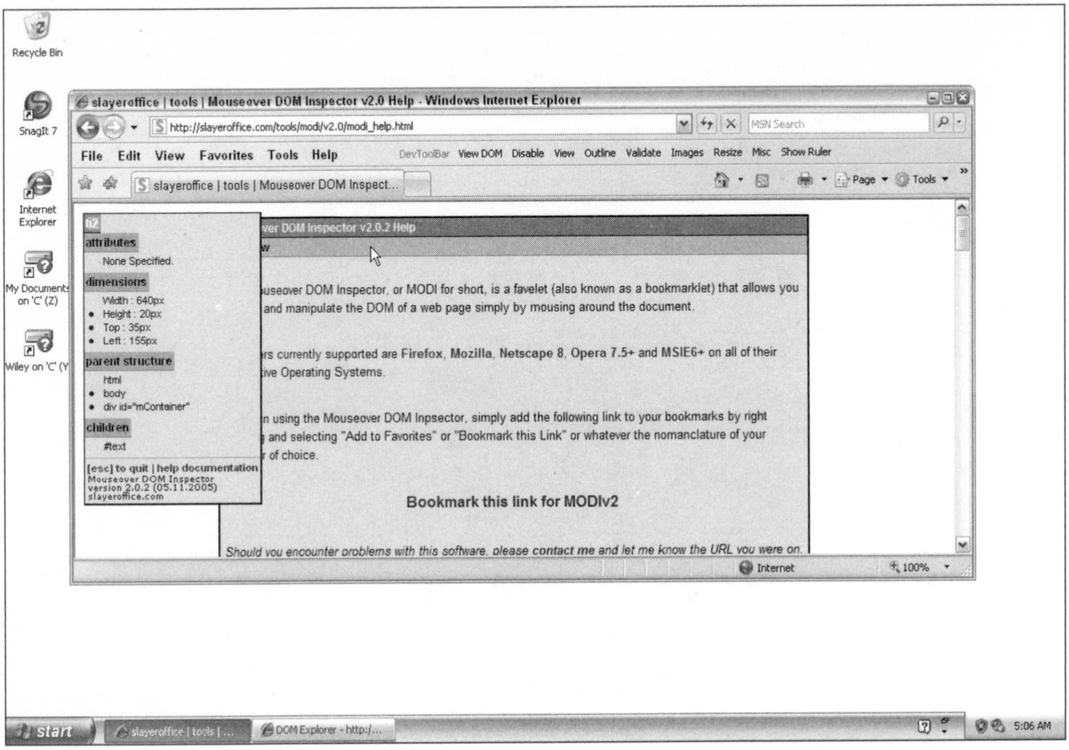

Figure 6-16: MODI pop-up window.

Troubleshooting Ajax

Ajax applications can be difficult to troubleshoot because the browser request and server response occur in the background and because errors aren't generated when something isn't working correctly. Tools for troubleshooting Ajax are beginning to appear. Firefox supports two Ajax troubleshooting tools: the Firebug console and the LiveHTTP Headers extension. A LiveHTTP Header bookmarklet is also available for IE.

Using the Firebug Console with XMLHttpRequest

The Firebug console is an extremely useful tool for troubleshooting an XMLHttpRequest. The Firebug console logs the XMLHttpRequest, and you can view both the response and the headers in the console. If your Ajax application is not displaying the response you expected, check the console to see the content of the server response. Figure 6-17 shows the XML that's returned from the XMLHttpRequest in Ch5_examp2.htm.

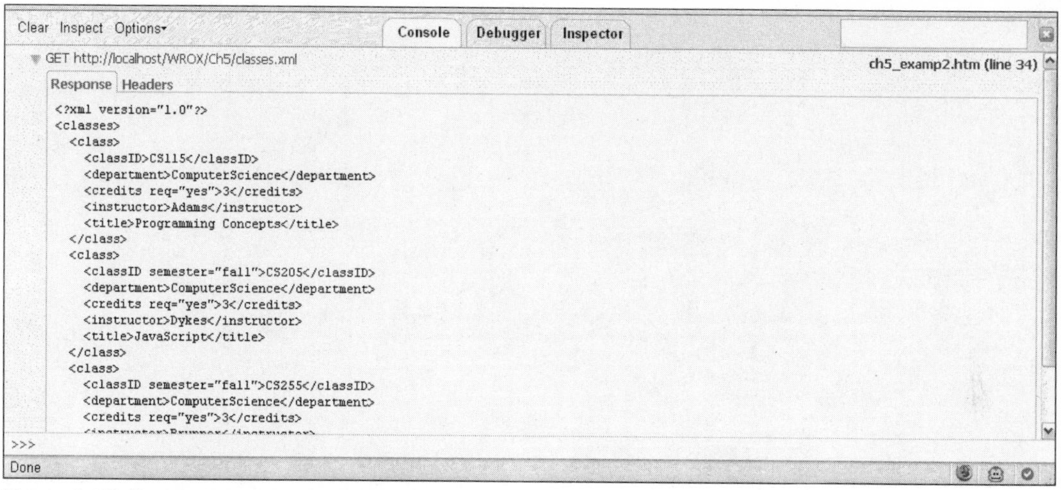

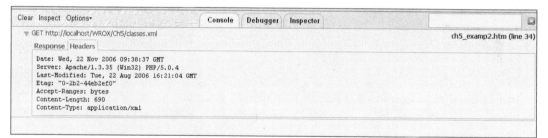

Figure 6-17: Response tab in the Firebug console.

You can also inspect the headers of the XMLHttpRequest, as shown in Figure 6-18.

Figure 6-18: Headers tab in the Firebug console.

Viewing the response and headers is an easy way to view what's actually happening "behind the scenes" with an XMLHttpRequest.

Live HTTP Headers

Live HTTP Headers is a Firefox extension that shows HTTP Headers in real time and enables you to track HTTP requests and responses. The extension can be downloaded at http://livehttpheaders.mozdev.org/.

Once the extension is installed, you can access it from the main Firefox menu bar by choosing Tools → Live HTTP Headers. The Live HTTP Headers window appears and logs HTTP activity. An HTTP request is shown in the Live HTTP Headers window in Figure 6-19.

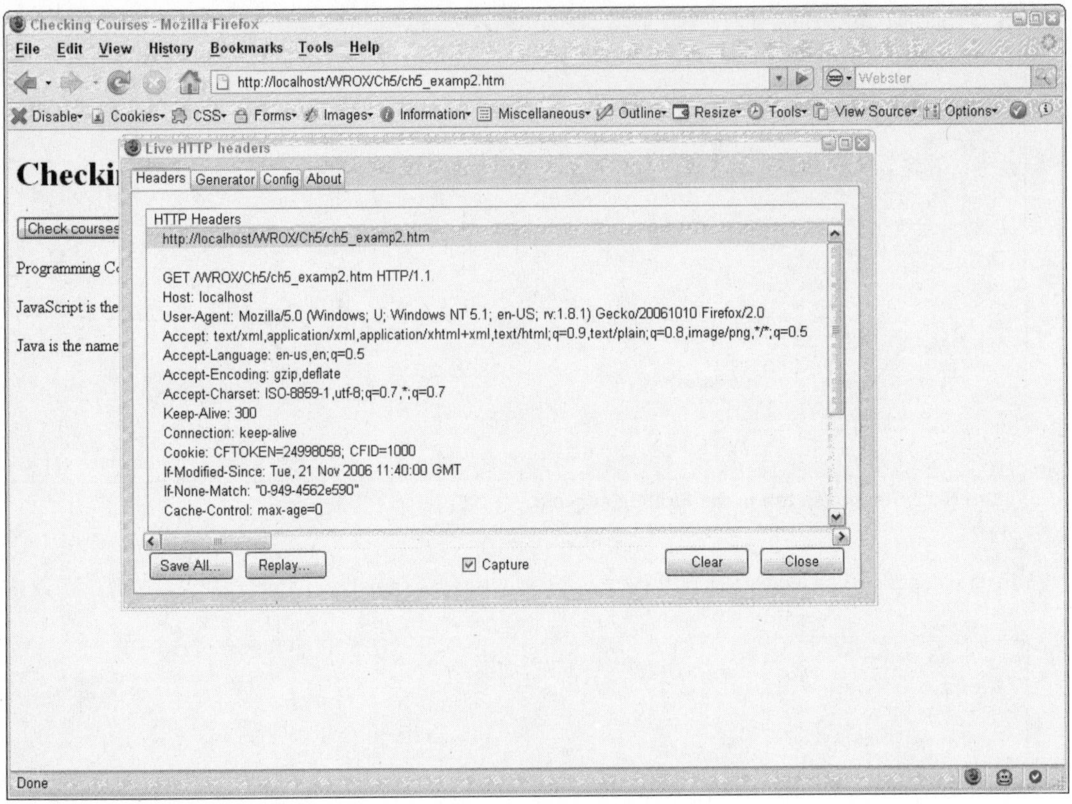

Figure 6-19: HTTP request shown in the Live HTTP Headers window.

The first line of the request indicates that this is a GET request using HTTP 1.1.

```
GET/WROX/ch5_examp2.htm HTTP/1.1
```

The second line shows the target of the request, a local web server.

```
Host: localhost
```

The third line shows the user-agent string for the browser that sent the request.

```
User-agent: Mozilla/5.0 (Windows;U;Windows NT 5.1;en-US; rv:1.8.1) Gecko/20061010
Firefox/2.0
```

Figure 6-20 shows an HTTP response. The main difference between the request and the response is that the response shows the status of the request in the first line.

```
HTTP/1.x 304 Not Modified
```

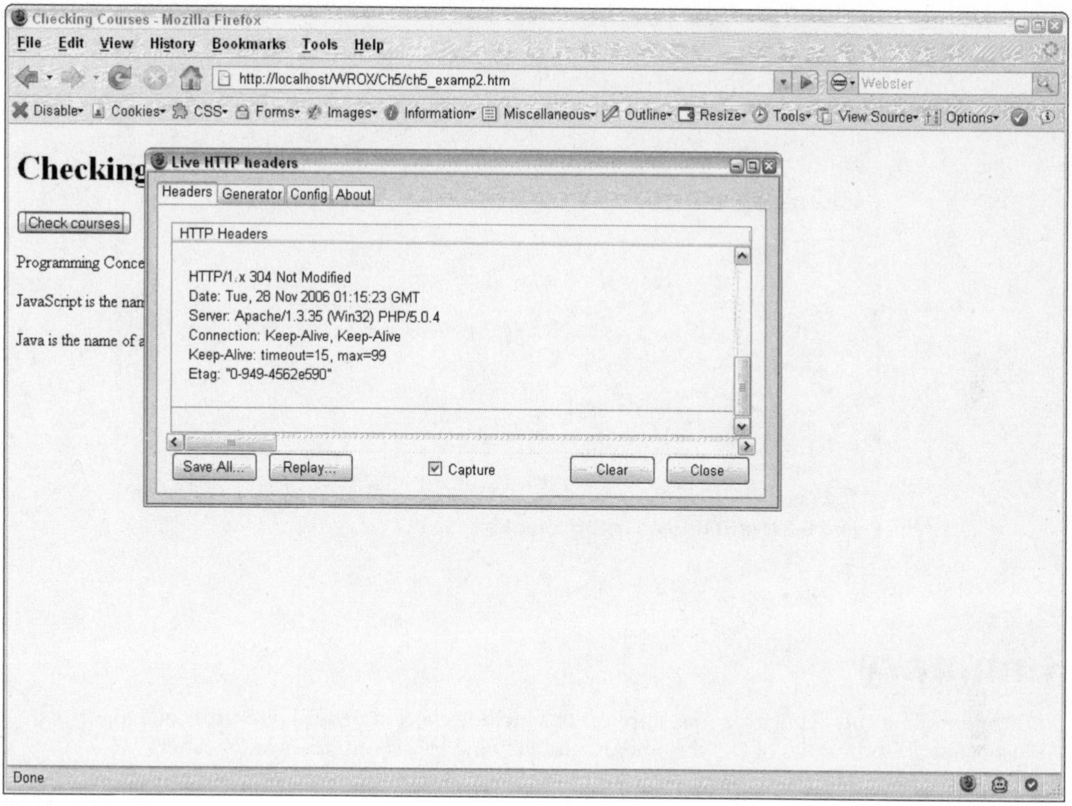

Figure 6-20: HTTP response.

A 304 status code indicates that the requested page has not been modified since the last request.

ieHTTPHeaders Explorer Bar

The ieHTTPHeaders Explorer Bar is a free toolbar for IE that displays HTTP headers in real time. This toolbar can be downloaded at www.blunck.info/iehttpheaders.html. Once you download and install the toolbar, you can access it in IE 7 by clicking on the Tools icon to the right of the document tabs, then selecting Toolbars → Explorer Bar → ieHTTPHeaders from the menu.

This tool is very similar to the Firefox Live HTTP Headers extension. It appears in a split-screen view at the bottom of the browser page, and it displays a log of HTTP headers for the current browser session (Figure 6-21).

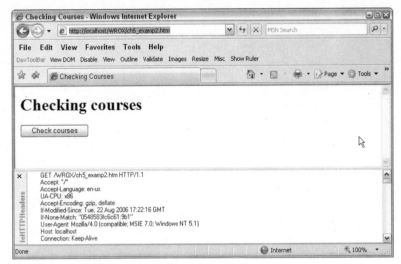

Figure 6-21: ieHTTPHeaders Explorer Bar.

Summary

Error handling and debugging Ajax applications include checking your JavaScript code for errors, inspecting the properties of DOM elements, and viewing HTTP responses and headers.

This chapter included the following points:

❑ Because Ajax requests are written in JavaScript, error handling and debugging JavaScript are integral parts of troubleshooting an Ajax application.

❑ Several tools are available for identifying JavaScript errors, including the JavaScript `try` statement, the Mozilla JavaScript console, and the Microsoft Script Debugger.

❑ The Firebug extension to Firefox combines the best features of a console and a debugger, and it is currently the most useful and easy-to-use tool for identifying and correcting JavaScript errors.

❑ DOM inspectors enable you to inspect the current state of DOM elements in your Ajax applications. Most DOM inspector tools show the current DOM tree and provide information about the properties of DOM elements.

❑ The MODI bookmarklet is an easy-to-use DOM Inspector tool that works in most current browsers.

❑ Viewing the headers of HTTP requests and responses provides information about the current state of Ajax requests and server responses. The Firebug console allows you to inspect the content of the server response as well as the HTTP request headers. You can also view the headers using the Firefox Live Headers extension or the ieHTTPHeaders Explorer toolbar.

In Chapter 7, you'll learn about using Ajax with Web services, application program interfaces (APIs), and *mashups*. A mashup is a hybrid application that's created from combining two sources, usually web services.

Exercises

Suggested solutions to these questions can be found in Appendix A.

1. Use the tools of your choice to find the four errors in the JavaScript code in the following document:

```
<!DOCTYPE html PUBLIC "-//W3C//DTD XHTML 1.0 Transitional//EN"
"http://www.w3.org/TR/xhtml1/DTD/xhtml1-transitional.dtd">
<html xmlns="http://www.w3.org/1999/xhtml">
<head>
<meta http-equiv="Content-Type" content="text/html; charset=iso-8859-1" />
<title>Debugging JavaScript</title>
<script type="text/javascript">
  function myErrors () {
    alert ("There's an error!');
  }
</script>
</head>

<body>
<script type="text/javascript">
onerror=myErrors;
var x = a;
x = x * 3;
alert ('x = ' + x;
</body>
</html>
```

2. Create an HTML file with JavaScript code that uses a `try` statement and a `catch` clause. Include an error in the block of code in the `try` statement. The code in the `catch` clause should consist of one line only, and it should consist of an alert that displays the error name and message.

Web Services, APIs, and Mashups

One of the problems that a novice developer might face when creating Ajax applications is being forced to become an expert in both the client-side and the server-side languages. Even throughout the early chapters in this book, the use of server-side code has been inescapable. But what happens if you simply hook up your page to someone else's server-side code? Good programming practice has always promoted componentization of common functions from calendars and ad rotators through to content management systems (CMSs) and e-commerce shopping cart and checkout systems and the reuse of such components. The Web really shouldn't be any different.

In fact, web services have been enabling this kind of functionality for a good while now. These are applications that make data available in a standard way over the Web. Weather forecasts, stock quotes, music CD image and product information, and news feeds are all examples of the types of information that can be made available through a web service. All your application needs to do is to know where to look for the information and what variables it is expecting to be able to pick up.

Ajax gives an interesting new spin on web services. As a client-side technology that facilitates interaction with the web server, you are not thinking about what web services you can create, but rather how best to consume them. In fact, consuming web services is the one area of web services that is often overlooked. It's seen as trivial or simple by developers. But perhaps this is one of the main reasons why web services aren't as ubiquitous as they otherwise might be: They aren't always as straightforward as they first appear. With a web service, the information is always there, readily available. It's up to you to decide just how often you pick up the information and how to put it into your application. That can be where the problems start.

Web services aren't the only way of making data available over the Web. Major companies such as Amazon and Google have gone further and exposed a set of APIs to developers that allow them to add sections of the Amazon and Google sites to their own applications. You can now bolt in a shopping cart from the Amazon site or the list of customer reviews for a particular product, or you can even add the Google map to your application in JavaScript. What's more, these APIs are offered free of charge.

The popularity of web services and APIs might be about to undergo a further increase with the invention of mashups. *Mashups* occur where information from two sources (typically web services) are combined to create a new application, such as taking maps and photos and using the image location from the photos to locate it on a map. With an increasing number of companies looking to make the functionality of their web sites available (via either web services or APIs), a lot of sites are appearing that are based on unusual hybrids.

This chapter takes a slightly unusual tact, in that you will not spend any time creating web services. This chapter doesn't really discuss what they do. What is important is consuming the service. The discussion in this chapter extends this to using some of the common APIs in your programs. This chapter concentrates on looking at web services, APIs, and mashups from the Ajax point of view, in terms of providing a rich and seamless user experience.

The discussion in this chapter examines the following:

❏ Understanding what a web service is

❏ Consuming a web service

❏ Consuming a web service in an Ajax application

❏ Using APIs

❏ Understanding what a mashup is

❏ Creating a mashup

What Is a Web Service?

A web service is a way of making data available from a web application over a network or the Internet to another application. Because there are possibly infinite ways of doing this, web services have been standardized by the World Wide Web Consortium (W3C) organization. If you look at the W3C standards on web services at `www.w3.org/2002/ws/` for too long, you'll probably get a headache. W3C describes a mountain of acronyms such as SOAP, WSDL, and UDDI; however, you don't need to know about any of these if you just want to get information back from a preexisting web service.

The great thing about web services is that they can be practically invisible. Some good examples of this are current flight simulator programs that are able to mimic the weather. They are able to go online, download a weather forecast, and transpose those conditions into the flight simulator as the player is flying the virtual craft.

This invisibility can equally be their downfall. If you're not aware of an application that is using a service, then you'll also be ignorant of what that service provides. In fact, so far, there has been no single "killer" application of web services, no Google or Internet Explorer (IE). Another problem is that web services are seen as too complex. Also, they encourage the exchange of free information, which means that they end up being the preserve of companies large enough to disseminate free goods. There's no point in a small single-person consultancy spending hours building services that he or she has to give away. On the other hand, if you charge for a service, you must guarantee its availability. To make it available 24/7, 365 days a year is expensive, both for the developer and for the customer.

Last, web services return information in XML format that requires extra processing and can slow down the performance of applications. Despite these drawbacks, though, web services are gaining a definite hold. The whole Web 2.0 culture is centered on the provision of web services. It's no surprise that major players such as Google, Yahoo!, eBay, and Amazon have all been at the forefront of enabling suites of web services that others can hook into. Web 2.0 isn't so much a new set of software or applications as it is a set of principles and practices that people are employing when building applications or sites.

Web services are about content delivery, and here is where Ajax fits into the pattern. Ajax principles can be applied by integrating that content into applications to provide the rich and seamless user experience. In fact, there has been a marked swing away from creating new content and a move toward consuming existing content in new ways. Because web services provide their output as XML, it isn't just a case of receiving the information and being done with it. Your application will have to work hard to glean the relevant content, ignore extraneous information, and position it in your web pages using style sheets, JavaScript, and XSLT.

Public Web Services

To hone in on the consumption of web services, you need some repositories of web services that are freely available to use. The following sites all provide a varying degree of free web services:

❑ WebServiceX.Net (www.webservicex.net)

❑ Yahoo Web Services (http://developer.yahoo.com)

❑ Amazon Web Services (http://aws.amazon.com)

❑ Last.FM (www.audioscrobbler.net/data/webservices/)

❑ eBay (http://developer.ebay.com/developercenter/rest/)

Of course, you'll quickly see that the boundary between APIs and web services gets blurred. The definition of a web service for purposes of this discussion is something that you can access by sending either a URL and querystring, or an XML document, and you can receive back as an XML document. APIs, as you will see, are more nebulous, and you don't necessarily get back the information in such a structured or predictable way.

Consuming a Third-Party Web Service

Let's start this chapter by launching immediately into a practical example of consuming a service. At the most basic level, all it involves is starting your browser and typing in the name of a preexisting web service. The URL of the service is known as the service *endpoint*. This is an .asmx file

Try It Out   Consuming an Example Web Service

A typical usage of a web service is to supply a stock quote, and, indeed, some stock ticker applications will be making good use of web services under the hood. Some examples of free public web services have already been presented, so let's consume one now.

1. First, you will need a web service endpoint. Go to www.webservicex.net/stockquote.asmx, and you should see the set of methods available for that particular service. In this case, there is only one, GetQuote, as shown in Figure 7-1.

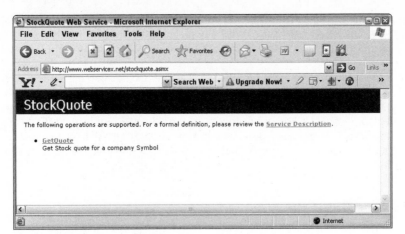

Figure 7-1: Locating a web service.

2.　Click on the GetQuote link. As shown in Figure 7-2, you will see a page that asks you to supply some parameters and displays the sample request/response that will be returned by the web service as a SOAP request/response, an HTTP-GET request/response, or an HTTP-POST request/response.

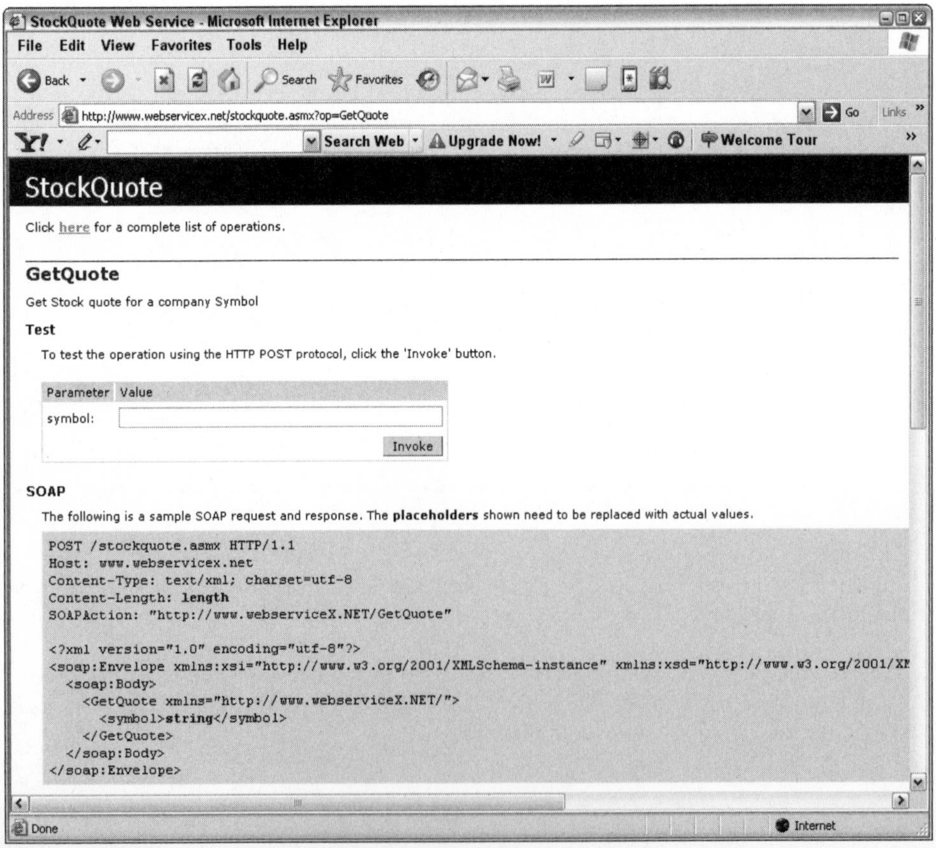

Figure 7-2: Result of clicking the GetQuote link.

3. Enter the symbol **MSFT** (the abbreviation for Microsoft) in the "symbol" text box, and click Invoke. You should see the result shown in Figure 7-3.

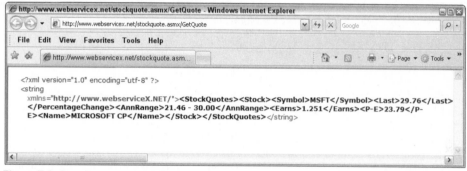

Figure 7-3: Result of entering MSFT.

How It Works

You sent a request to the web service, and the web service returned an XML document packaged up inside a string element, which can then be extracted and manipulated, just like a normal XML document. The XML information is encapsulated in a <string> element, which means the contained XML information isn't necessarily well formed, although it should be. If you want to use this information in an application, you will need to read it into a corresponding XML parser and check the syntax first. At the moment, all you have is the raw information that the web service has delivered.

Before discussing that, though, let's delve a little deeper into the whole process behind the send/receive cycle.

The Structure of a Web Service

The structure of a web service can be seen as the following cyclical four-step process:

1. The client calls the web service over a protocol. This is normally HTTP, but it doesn't have to be because you are equally able to work with other protocols, such as Simple Mail Transfer Protocol (SMTP) and Secure HTTP (HTTPS).

2. The client sends a method to the server, which contains instructions on what is needed from the web service.

3. The server returns values and/or an acknowledgment that it has received the method.

4. The client gets the result and acts on the received information. This may involve calling the web service again or a different web service, with the results received, or doing nothing further.

In this first example, you performed Step 1 when you clicked on the Invoke button to call the web service. The following information was sent to the web service as part of the request:

❑ The protocol (in this case HTTP)

❑ Parameters to send to the web service (in the first example, these were sent in the body of the request, but could equally have been sent in the form of querystrings attached to the URL)

- ❑ The method of transmission (HTTP-GET, HTTP-POST or SOAP)

- ❑ The amount of information being sent

- ❑ The type of document required from the web service (possibly XML, or it might also be in JavaScript Object Notational, or JSON, format)

- ❑ Information about the client (such as type of browser)

- ❑ The date of the request

You used HTTP-POST to send the request, and the server returned the values as an XML document. The one slight problem with this model is that it is a simplistic approach to the task of using web services.

The web services standards have long specified using SOAP (nominally, it stood for Simple Object Access Protocol, but these days isn't considered an acronym) to send and receive data from a web service. The problem is that you can't just attach data to a query string, or stuff it in the body of the document with SOAP. You have to create a specific SOAP document first. SOAP messages are normal XML documents. They have particular tags indicating which section of the XML document is the header and which section of the document body of the message. Also, if you send SOAP messages to a web service, then you get back messages in a SOAP format from the web service, and disentangling the response can be a bit more complex than with just a straightforward XML document.

The advantage of SOAP is that it allows the document to contain more instructions than it typically could otherwise. When you are learning about web services, though, SOAP introduces a layer of obfuscation that you're better off without.

SOAP has actually sparked off another heated set of debates on the Web, where people espouse using the HTTP-GET/POST methods coining the term REST (short for Representational State Transfer) against the more convoluted SOAP approach.

The REST Approach

With REST, you supply a URL, and you assume that the web service will return an XML fragment, as you did in the first example. In other words, you follow the normal HTTP-GET/HTTP-POST model of posting to a web server. The following request is a REST query:

```
http://www.webservicex.net/StockQuote.asmx/GetQuote?symbol=MSFT
```

In return, you will get back an XML fragment:

```
<?xml version="1.0" encoding="utf-8" ?>
<string xmlns="http://www.webserviceX.NET/">
<StockQuotes><Stock><Symbol>MSFT</Symbol><Last>28.52</Last><Date>10/18/2006</Date><
Time>4:00pm</Time><Change>0.00</Change><Open>N/A</Open><High>N/A</High><Low>N/A</Lo
w><Volume>0</Volume><MktCap>284.3B</MktCap><PreviousClose>28.52</PreviousClose><Per
centageChange>0.00%</PercentageChange><AnnRange>21.46 -
28.70</AnnRange><Earns>1.196</Earns><P-E>23.85</P-E><Name>MICROSOFT
CP</Name></Stock></StockQuotes>
</string>
```

There's nothing more to it than that. The benefits of the REST approach are as follows:

❏ Gets messages stored in XML

❏ Uses HTTP to transfer

❏ Uses HTTP verbs GET/POST/PUT

❏ Uses URIs for identification

❏ Can use HTTP authentication to provide security

❏ Is easy to use

The main problems with using it are as follows:

❏ Security isn't as robust as in SOAP.

❏ The length of the URI is limited when using GET.

Both Amazon and eBay offer REST access to their web services for product information, while news feeds such as Atom and RSS are also designed around REST, so that multiple calls or multiple failed calls by a device or process don't cause larger problems. Despite being seen as a bit of a "dirty" shortcut in the early days of web services, it is now a valid and popular approach for calling a web service.

The SOAP Approach

SOAP is something this discussion doesn't go into too much detail about. Otherwise, you'll be rapidly building up a large list of acronyms and specifications that you might not need to know about and work with. But it does merit a quick discussion if you want to use web services to deliver heavy-duty and sensitive data.

For starters, REST encourages a purely client/server view of web services, yet there may be many hops along a route that a web service takes. SOAP also takes care of important features such as priority of the message, expiration of the message, security credentials and their encryption, routing of the message, and the use of critical data.

When using SOAP, the message is sent to the server as a SOAP document. The SOAP document contains a <SOAP:Envelope> element. This envelope element, in turn, contains a <SOAP:Header> element and a <SOAP:Body> element. The <SOAP:Envelope> element specifies a namespace, and all elements in the document must be qualified by this namespace. The <SOAP:Header> element is similar to HTTP headers and can be used to convey information such as authorization information (like a user ID and password). The <SOAP:Body> element will contain the name of the web service to be called, along with the parameters and information about how you want the response to be returned.

Instead of calling the web service via a URL as you did in the first example, you could construct the following SOAP document in ASP.NET or PHP and send it to the server:

```
POST /stockquote.asmx HTTP/1.1
Host: www.webservicex.net
Content-Type: text/xml; charset=utf-8
Content-Length: length
SOAPAction: "http://www.webserviceX.NET/GetQuote"
```

```
<?xml version="1.0" encoding="utf-8"?>
<soap:Envelope xmlns:xsi="http://www.w3.org/2001/XMLSchema-instance"
xmlns:xsd="http://www.w3.org/2001/XMLSchema"
xmlns:soap="http://schemas.xmlsoap.org/soap/envelope/">
  <soap:Body>
    <GetQuote xmlns="http://www.webserviceX.NET/">
      <symbol>MSFT</symbol>
    </GetQuote>
  </soap:Body>
</soap:Envelope>
```

This, in turn, would lead to your receiving a result along the following lines:

```
HTTP/1.1 200 OK
Content-Type: text/xml; charset=utf-8
Content-Length: length

<?xml version="1.0" encoding="utf-8"?>
<soap:Envelope xmlns:xsi="http://www.w3.org/2001/XMLSchema-instance"
xmlns:xsd="http://www.w3.org/2001/XMLSchema"
xmlns:soap="http://schemas.xmlsoap.org/soap/envelope/">
  <soap:Body>
    <GetQuoteResponse xmlns="http://www.webserviceX.NET/">
<GetQuoteResult>&lt;StockQuotes&gt;&lt;Stock&gt;&lt;Symbol&gt;MSFT&lt;/Symbol&gt;&l
t;Last&gt;28.34&lt;/Last&gt;&lt;Date&gt;10/27/2006&lt;/Date&gt;&lt;Time&gt;3:00pm&l
t;/Time&gt;&lt;Change&gt;-
0.01&lt;/Change&gt;&lt;Open&gt;28.48&lt;/Open&gt;&lt;High&gt;28.79&lt;/High&gt;&lt;
Low&gt;28.25&lt;/Low&gt;&lt;Volume&gt;89061592&lt;/Volume&gt;&lt;MktCap&gt;282.5B&l
t;/MktCap&gt;&lt;PreviousClose&gt;28.35&lt;/PreviousClose&gt;&lt;PercentageChange&g
t;-0.04%&lt;/PercentageChange&gt;&lt;AnnRange&gt;21.46 -
28.79&lt;/AnnRange&gt;&lt;Earns&gt;1.196&lt;/Earns&gt;&lt;P-E&gt;23.70&lt;/P-
E&gt;&lt;Name&gt;MICROSOFT CP&lt;/Name&gt;&lt;/Stock&gt;&lt;/StockQuotes&gt;
</GetQuoteResult>
    </GetQuoteResponse>
  </soap:Body>
</soap:Envelope>
```

This all implies a lot of extra work on top. You must construct the document and adhere not only to the laws of XML, but also to the laws of SOAP. The document that is returned is encoded as well, so that the special characters in XML are correctly rendered. Of course, you must then write an application to retrieve the significant data from the SOAP document, and this will be less simple than retrieving a plain old XML fragment. Therefore, in this chapter, you will use REST to call and consume web services.

Integrating a Web Service into Your Ajax Application

Adding web services to Ajax applications should be disarmingly easy. The XMLHttpRequest object has the open method that takes three arguments, one of which is a URL. Instead of passing on a URL, you can place the web service's endpoint as the argument. If only life were that simple.

Consuming a Service with XMLHttpRequest

The main problem with consuming a service using XMLHttpRequest is that you have to host it in the same domain as your application. This is fine if you want to consume web services that you, yourself, or a colleague have created. Then this method will work satisfactorily, and there is precious little difference between an application that calls a resource on your server and one that calls a web service. For example, the following code fragment would call a web service endpoint called stockquote with the symbol MSFT:

```
var url = "stockquote.asmx/GetQuote?symbol=MSFT";
xmlhttp.open("GET", url, true);
```

This would make the call to the server and receive the data in exactly the same way as with any other request. But what happens if you want to integrate a weather forecast or stock quote from an outside source? For example, consider the following:

```
var url = "http://www.webservicex.net/stockquote.asmx/GetQuote?symbol=MSFT";
xmlhttp.open("GET", url, true);
```

If you are using IE, then one of three possible behaviors will occur, depending on the settings you have under the settings Tools → Internet Options → Security (tab) → Trusted sites (assuming your script is running in document loaded from Trusted sites zone) → Custom level ... → Miscellaneous section → "Access data sources across domains" option. If you have the default setting "Prompt," then IE will allow you to perform this after first displaying a rather clunky, cautionary dialog, as shown in Figure 7-4.

Figure: 7-4: Cautionary dialog in IE.

You can change this to "Enable" to get rid of this dialog. If you have it set to "Disable," though, an "Access denied" error will be displayed.

Firefox won't even let you get this far. The script will just fall over at this point, without even bothering to inform you, although you can see the error message, "Error: uncaught exception: Permission denied to call method XMLHttpRequest.open," in an Error Console in Firefox.

Same Origin Policy

What you've actually run into isn't really a problem, though. It's a sensible security restriction. This is a *same origin security policy*, and this policy is designed to stop your browser from loading one script that would be passed as fit by your anti-virus software and then (unbeknownst to you) loading a malicious script on another server. The Mozilla web site has a clear statement of allowed and disallowed cross-loading policies at the following URL:

```
www.mozilla.org/projects/security/components/same-origin.html
```

Of course, this means that consuming someone else's web services in your applications (a perfectly legitimate activity) becomes a lot more difficult.

Creating an Application Proxy

Currently, there are several workarounds, none of them particularly neat and tidy. Bear in mind that these are workarounds (or hacks, to give them another name), and they could open up holes in your security if you don't use them wisely.

The most common workaround involves creating a page on the server to do this for you. The page is known as a *proxy* — an intermediary, in other words. This works as follows. The XMLHttpRequest object calls the page on the server, and the page on the server then relays the call on to the web service. Of course, it removes one of the benefits of using third-party web services — namely, that you don't need to use server-side code. But, fortunately, the server-side code required in this case is relatively small.

For example, in PHP you could use the following:

```php
$url = 'http://www.webservicex.net/stockquote.asmx/GetQuote?symbol=';
$qs = $_GET["symbol"];
$url = $url.$qs;
$url = DOMDocument::load($url);
echo $url->saveXML();
```

In ASP.NET, it would be as follows:

```
XmlDocument Dom = new XmlDocument();
string url = "http://www.webservicex.net/stockquote.asmx/GetQuote?symbol="
+ Request.QueryString["symbol"].ToString();
Dom.Load(url);
```

Let's put this into operation in an example now.

Try It Out   Consuming a Web Service via a Proxy

You've already looked at the stock quote web service. Now, let's integrate this web service into an application that will allow the user to dynamically build a "portfolio" of quotations by supplying the symbol in a text box. You'll return each item in a table.

You've seen the problem with calling the XMLHttpRequest object from a different domain, and you've seen how you can work around it. You will use this as part of the solution.

1.   Create an HTML file, and call it webservice.htm:

```html
<html xmlns="http://www.w3.org/1999/xhtml" >
<head>
    <title>Untitled Page</title>
    <script type="text/javascript" src="webservice.js"></script>
</head>
<body>
<form id="form1" name="form1">
Enter Symbol: <input type="text" name="stocksymbol"  id="stocksymbol" />
```

```
<input type="button" onclick="sendData()" value="Click button to add quote" />
<br /><br />
<table id="table1">
</table>
</form>
</body>
</html>
```

2. Create a JavaScript file, and call it `webservice.js`:

```javascript
var xmlhttp = null;
if (window.XMLHttpRequest) {
  xmlhttp = new XMLHttpRequest();
} else if (window.ActiveXObject) {
  xmlhttp = new ActiveXObject("Microsoft.XMLHTTP");
}

function sendData()
{
 xmlhttp.abort();
 var url = "applicationproxy.aspx?symbol=" + document.form1.stocksymbol.value;
 xmlhttp.open("GET", url, true);
 xmlhttp.onreadystatechange = getData;
 xmlhttp.send(null);
}


function getData()
{
  if ((xmlhttp.readyState == 4) &&( xmlhttp.status == 200))
  {
    var myXml = xmlhttp.responseXML;
    var XMLDoc = null;
    var xmlobject = null;

    if (window.ActiveXObject)
    {
        XMLDoc = myXml.childNodes[1].firstChild.nodeValue;
        var xmlobject = new ActiveXObject("Microsoft.XMLDOM");
        xmlobject.async="false";
        xmlobject.loadXML(XMLDoc);
    }
    else
    {
        XMLDoc = myXml.childNodes[0].firstChild.nodeValue;
        var parser = new DOMParser();
        var xmlobject = parser.parseFromString(XMLDoc, "text/xml");
    }

    var table = document.getElementById("table1");
    var row = table.insertRow(table.rows.length);

    var cell1 = row.insertCell(row.cells.length);
    cell1.appendChild(getText("Name",xmlobject));
    var cell2 = row.insertCell(row.cells.length);
```

```
        cell2.appendChild(getText("Last",xmlobject));
        var cell3 = row.insertCell(row.cells.length);
        cell3.appendChild(getText("Date",xmlobject));

        table.setAttribute("border", "2");
    }
}


function getText(tagName, xmlobject)
{
 var tags = xmlobject.getElementsByTagName(tagName);
        var txtNode = null;
        if (window.ActiveXObject)
        {
                txtNode = document.createTextNode(tags[0].firstChild.text);
        }
        else
        {
                txtNode = document.createTextNode(tags[0].firstChild.textContent);
        }
        return txtNode;
}
```

3. Create the Application Proxy next. In ASP.NET, create the following, and save it as `ApplicationProxy.aspx`:

```
<%@Page Language = "C#" Debug="true" %>
<%@ import Namespace="System.Xml" %>
<script language="C#" runat="server">
    void Page_Load()
    {
        XmlDocument Dom = new XmlDocument();
        string url = "http://www.webservicex.net/stockquote.asmx/GetQuote?symbol="
+ Request.QueryString["symbol"].ToString();
        Dom.Load(url);
        string abc = Dom.InnerXml;
        Response.ContentType = "text/xml";
        Response.Write(abc);
    }
</script>
```

Or, in PHP, you could use the following:

```
<?php
header('Content-Type: text/xml');
?>
<?php
  $url = 'http://www.webservicex.net/stockquote.asmx/GetQuote?symbol=';
  $qs = $_GET["symbol"];
  $url = $url.$qs;
  $url = DOMDocument::load($url);
  echo $url->saveXML();
?>
```

4. Now, start `webservice.htm` in your browser. Enter **MSFT**, and click the button, as shown in Figure 7-5.

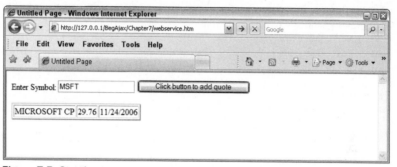

Figure 7-5: Starting `webservice.htm` **with input for Microsoft.**

5. Next, enter **ORCL** (short for Oracle), and click again. The screen is updated without a refresh, and the details about both stocks are shown in an HTML table, as seen in Figure 7-6.

Figure 7-6: Adding Oracle information to `webservice.htm`.

How It Works

The HTML page contains a `<script>` tag that loads the script `webservice.js`. It also contains a button that calls the function `sendData()` when clicked. The first part of the script creates an instance of the `XMLHttpRequest` object, one for IE 7, Firefox, and other browsers that support `XMLHttpRequest` and one for IE 5 and IE 6. There's absolutely nothing unusual here worth remarking on.

The `sendData` function should be similarly familiar:

```
function sendData()
{
 xmlhttp.abort();
 var url = "applicationproxy.aspx?symbol=" + document.form1.stocksymbol.value;
 xmlhttp.open("GET", url, true);
 xmlhttp.onreadystatechange = getData;
 xmlhttp.send(null);
}
```

You start by clearing the contents of the previous request using the `abort()` method because the `XMLHttpRequest` will be called each time the user makes a request. You create a URL that will call either a PHP or ASP.NET proxy page, and it will pass it the name of the symbol the user wants to submit to the web service. The last three lines open the object, set the `onreadystatechange` event handler to run the `getData` function, and send the request.

The server-side code is short and to the point. It's pretty much identical in both PHP and ASP.NET. In PHP, it is as follows:

```
$url = 'http://www.webservicex.net/stockquote.asmx/GetQuote?symbol=';
$qs = $_GET["symbol"];
$url = $url.$qs;
$url = DOMDocument::load($url);
echo $url->saveXML();
```

You create a variable to hold the URL of the web service. You append the querystring to the URL, then you perform a static invocation of the `load` method of the `DOMDocument`, passing the full URL of the web service and symbol to it. You then write the results of the `saveXML` method to the response stream.

The ASP.NET code uses the `XmlDocument` object instead of the `DOMDocument`, uses the `InnerXml` property in place of the `SaveXml` one, and writes the content type in the code rather than at the top of the page. Otherwise, it is identical.

```
XmlDocument Dom = new XmlDocument();
string url = "http://www.webservicex.net/stockquote.asmx/GetQuote?symbol="
+ Request.QueryString["symbol"].ToString();
Dom.Load(url);
string abc = Dom.InnerXml;
Response.ContentType = "text/xml";
Response.Write(abc);
```

The JavaScript code that processes the return call is a little more complex. You still must extract the data from the XML that is returned, and, as noted in the first example, when using HTTP GET or HTTP POST, the XML document wraps the response in a single `<string>` element. This means that you must delve into the document to get the elements you want. The function `getData()` starts with the callback and reads the contents of the `responseXML` method to obtain the XML returned by the web service:

```
if ((xmlhttp.readyState == 4) &&( xmlhttp.status == 200))
  {
    var myXml = xmlhttp.responseXML;
```

If you typed in MSFT, then the XML document you will have received back from the web service will be this:

```
<?xml version="1.0" encoding="utf-8" ?>
<string xmlns="http://www.webserviceX.NET/">
        <string
xmlns=\"http://www.webserviceX.NET/\">&lt;StockQuotes&gt;&lt;Stock&gt;&lt;Symbol&gt
;MSFT&lt;/Symbol&gt;&lt;Last&gt;29.76&lt;/Last&gt;&lt;Date&gt;11/24/2006&lt;/Date&g
t;&lt;Time&gt;1:00pm&lt;/Time&gt;&lt;Change&gt;0.00&lt;/Change&gt;&lt;Open&gt;N/A&l
t;/Open&gt;&lt;High&gt;N/A&lt;/High&gt;&lt;Low&gt;N/A&lt;/Low&gt;&lt;Volume&gt;0&lt
;/Volume&gt;&lt;MktCap&gt;292.6B&lt;/MktCap&gt;&lt;PreviousClose&gt;29.76&lt;/Previ
ousClose&gt;&lt;PercentageChange&gt;0.00%&lt;/PercentageChange&gt;&lt;AnnRange&gt;2
```

```
1.46 - 30.00&lt;/AnnRange&gt;&lt;Earns&gt;1.251&lt;/Earns&gt;&lt;P-
E&gt;23.79&lt;/P-E&gt;&lt;Name&gt;MICROSOFT
CP&lt;/Name&gt;&lt;/Stock&gt;&lt;/StockQuotes&gt;
</string>
```

There is a lot of extraneous information in here. In this example, you have honed in on the <last> price, the <date>, and the <name> elements. You are also confronted with a more immediate problem: In which browser is the user viewing the page? You must create the XML document in a slightly different way. If it's IE, then the XML you need is stored in the childNodes[1]. You must load the ActiveXObject XMLDOM and use an instance of that to store the XML document.

```
if (window.ActiveXObject)
{
    XMLDoc = myXml.childNodes[1].firstChild.nodeValue;
    xmlobject = new ActiveXObject("Microsoft.XMLDOM")
    xmlobject.async="false";
    xmlobject.loadXML(XMLDoc);
}
```

Otherwise, you must use childNodes[0] because, when using IE, an XML declaration will automatically be returned with the document. In Firefox, the first element will be <string>. In Firefox, you use the DOMParser and call the parseFromString method to return the XML document.

```
else
{
    XMLDoc = myXml.childNodes[0].firstChild.nodeValue;
    var parser = new DOMParser();
    xmlobject = parser.parseFromString(XMLDoc, "text/xml");
}
```

What you're left with in the variable xmlobject is an XML document shorn of the XML declaration and the <string> element, starting with the <StockQuotes> element. The last section of this function is concerned with dynamically creating a table in which to display the information:

```
var table = document.getElementById("table1");
var row = table.insertRow(table.rows.length);

var cell1 = row.insertCell(row.cells.length);
cell1.appendChild(getText("Name",xmlobject));
var cell2 = row.insertCell(row.cells.length);
cell2.appendChild(getText("Last",xmlobject));
var cell3 = row.insertCell(row.cells.length);
cell3.appendChild(getText("Date",xmlobject));

table.setAttribute("border", "2");
```

The <table> element is already present in the page, and you use the getElementById method to return a reference to it. You then create a table row <tr> and append that to the table. Next, you create three cells: one each for the name, last price, and date. You append these with the value returned from the getText function. You append these cells to the same row and set the table's border attribute to 2, to improve the presentation.

The `getText` function performs a repetitive task. It searches for a specified XML tag and adds the text contents of that tag to the `<td>` element. It has a different branch, depending on whether IE or Firefox is being used:

```
function getText(tagName, xmlobject)
{
 var tags = xmlobject.getElementsByTagName(tagName);
        var txtNode = null;
        if (window.ActiveXObject)
        {
              txtNode = document.createTextNode(tags[0].firstChild.text);
        }
        else
        {
              txtNode = document.createTextNode(tags[0].firstChild.textContent);
        }
        return txtNode;
}
```

It returns a `textNode` to the `getData` function. The table is then displayed showing the information from the web service embedded into a table.

There are times when this solution might not be applicable. For example, if you were going through a Corporate Proxy server, or need to communicate over HTTPS using security certificates, then our basic scripts might not be up to the job. There is then a more complex solution (devised by Jason Levitt and referenced by many developers) that uses the cURL (client library URL available via `http://uk.php.net/curl`) functions in PHP to open and close the session, which calls the web service for you. *Curl* is a PHP library of calls to fetch data from remote sites. By default, this library isn't installed and must be installed separately from PHP.

Once installed, you call the server-side proxy with a querystring `ws_path` and provide the name of the web service and the data that you wish to pass with it. For example, you could make the following call in your script to the server-side proxy on your server to call the `stockquote` service you saw in the first example, with the symbol MSFT:

```
var path = 'http://www.webservicex.net/stockquote.asmx/GetQuote?symbol=' +
document.getElementById("stocksymbol").value;
var url = 'http://localhost/curl_proxy.php?ws_path=' + encodeURIComponent(path);
xmlhttp.open('GET', url, true);
```

Because the path contains a question mark and your call to the server also contains a question mark, you must encode the path to ensure that you don't break the querystring.

Then, your server-side code would make the call on behalf of the script, adding on the `hostname` to your URL, and using Curl to perform the calling of the web service:

```
define ('HOSTNAME', 'http://www.webservicex.net/');

$path = ($_POST['ws_path']) ? $_POST['ws_path'] : $_GET['ws_path'];
$url = HOSTNAME.$path;

// Open the Curl session
```

```
$session = curl_init($url);

if ($_POST['ws_path']) {
    $postvars = '';
    while ($element = current($_POST)) {
        $postvars .= key($_POST).'='.$element.'&';
        next($_POST);
    }
    curl_setopt ($session, CURLOPT_POST, true);
    curl_setopt ($session, CURLOPT_POSTFIELDS, $postvars);
}

// Return the call not the headers
curl_setopt($session, CURLOPT_HEADER, false);
curl_setopt($session, CURLOPT_RETURNTRANSFER, true);

// call the data
$xml = curl_exec($session);

header("Content-Type: text/xml");

echo $xml;
curl_close($session);
```

With ASP.NET you would most likely use the HttpWebRequest class to retrieve the text instead.

The Script Tag Hack

A second alternative is the script tag "hack." In Chapter 4, the last method you looked at involved the dynamic creation of a `<script>` tag and the dynamic allocation of the src attribute. Using this Ajax pattern, you can fashion a simpler alternative to the application proxy method for calling web services. The method works as follows:

❑ You remove the XMLHttpRequest object, and you make the call to the web service in the src attribute of the `<script>` tag.

❑ The web service must be able to return output in the JSON format (covered in Chapter 11).

❑ You retrieve the JSON format data.

This discussion doesn't go into too much detail, but let's create a quick example of a web service that can return its output in JSON format, such as the Yahoo! TimeService, to demonstrate how this might be achieved.

Try It Out   Calling a Web Service via the Script Tag

1. Create a file called webservicescriptag.htm as follows:

```
<html xmlns="http://www.w3.org/1999/xhtml" >
<head>
    <title>Web Service example using Dynamic Script Tag</title>
<script type="text/javascript" src="webservice2.js"></script>
```

```
</head>
<body>
<form id="form1" name="form1">
<input type="button" onclick="dynamicTag();" value="Click button to use web
service" />
</form>
</body>
</html>
```

2. Create a script called `webservice2.js` as follows:

```
function getTime(JSONData) {
    if (JSONData != null)
    {
        alert(TimeStampToDate(JSONData.Result.Timestamp));
    }
}

function TimeStampToDate(xmlDate)
{
    return new Date(xmlDate);
}

function dynamicTag()
{
    request =
"http://developer.yahooapis.com/TimeService/V1/getTime?appid=YahooDemo&output=json&
callback=getTime&format=ms";
    var head = document.getElementsByTagName("head").item(0);
    var script = document.createElement("script");
    script.setAttribute("type", "text/javascript");
    script.setAttribute("src", request);
    head.appendChild(script);
}
```

3. View `webservicescripttag.htm` in your browser, and click on the button (Figure 7-7).

Figure 7-7: Viewing `webservicescripttag.htm` **in the browser.**

How It Works

This is a fairly trivial usage of a web service, but unfortunately there aren't too many around that are guaranteed to return JSON format instead of standard XML. If your web service returns just a standard XML document, then this will cause an error in your script because you have assigned the `src` attribute of the script to the output of the web service. Therefore, the browser is expecting to receive a JavaScript script of some sort.

You start by creating a `request` variable:

```
var request =
"http://developer.yahooapis.com/TimeService/V1/getTime?appid=YahooDemo&output=json&
callback=getTime&format=ms";
    var head = document.getElementsByTagName("head").item(0);
    var script = document.createElement("script");
    script.setAttribute("type", "text/javascript");
    script.setAttribute("src", request);
    head.appendChild(script);
```

The `request` variable calls the web service and appends three extra query strings. The first is that the output from the service should be in JSON format and not XML, and the second is the name of the function in the script that you want to call when the web service returns its result. The third is to set the format of the returned result to milliseconds. The Yahoo! Time web service returns a timestamp in milliseconds since 1970. By default, the web service returns a time in seconds. If you remove this query-string, then you will find a date from somewhere in 1970 being displayed, rather than the present day.

Then, you retrieve the `head` element of the document and append a `script` tag to it, with the `src` attribute assigned to the URL of the web service. You might want to consider two extra points. The first is that if you don't want IE to cache the script, then you can append a unique variable to the end of the `src` attribute. The second is that when using JSON, you should generate a unique script tag ID.

The callback function will then have an object returned as a parameter:

```
function getTime(JSONData) {
    if (JSONData != null)
    {
       alert(TimeStampToDate(JSONData.Result.Timestamp));
    }
}
```

You name this parameter `JSONData` and check to see if it is null. The result of this web service is a timestamp. To convert it to a readable date, you must perform a little conversion, and this is done in the `TimeStampToDate` function:

```
function TimeStampToDate(xmlDate)
{
    return new Date(xmlDate);
}
```

Here, you create a new date and then assign to the `timestamp` method the value you retrieved from the web service. You return the whole `Date` object to display in the alert box. It would be simpler just to call the JavaScript `Date` object, but because this example demonstrates web services that return JSON, this rather more prosaic solution is used.

Future Alternatives

The cross-domain browsing of web services is a problem that isn't going to go away in a hurry, and the result is that there are several new solutions in development:

❑ `FlashXMLHttpRequest` — Flash already allows you to create a file `crossdomain.xml`, which specifies a list of allowable domains that can be called. Julian Couvreur proposes a solution where Flash can then be called on your behalf to make cross-domain web service requests. More details on this can be found at www.xml.com/lpt/a/1662.

❑ `ContextAgnosticXMLHttpRequest` — Chris Holland's proposal is the creation of a header "Allow Foreign Hosts" and a new additional object `ContextAgonsticXMLHttpRequest`, which would expose information only if this header is present. More details can be found at: http://chrisholland.blogspot.com/2005/03/contextagnosticxmlhttprequest-informal.html

❑ `JSONRequest` — Getting more web services to return JSON as XML means that you can use the dynamic `script` tag workaround to return data. Doug Crockford's proposal accepts that you don't just need a workaround to return JSON, but indeed a new browser service that will initiate a two-way data exchange between the browser and a JSON data server. More details can be found at: http://json.org/JSONRequest.html

These are all indications that, while there are important ramifications for security, there is a very definite need to address the problem of calling a web service across domains. It isn't just something a few enthusiasts might want to attempt. It is something any serious developer might end up having to consider, as you'll see when this discussion evolves into the subjects of using company APIs and using mashups.

Using APIs

The next progression after web services has been the introduction of publicly accessible *application programming interfaces* (*APIs*). If you are familiar with programming a language such as Visual Basic, C#, Java, or even JavaScript, these APIs are just like the ready-made APIs and functions such as the `Date` or `Math` statements you will find in many of those languages.

Most of the large web companies (think Amazon, Google, Microsoft, eBay, Yahoo!) have not only made information available via web services, but they have created APIs that you can call from within your JavaScript to access functionality from their web sites.

In the very simplest of cases, you can just add HTML tags that render objects such as music playlists, book reading lists, or recent photographs; however, you're limited to the constraints of the embedding tag that does this. More impressive is the ability to run queries against some company's applications and lists of products. These are done in the form of APIs made freely available to independent developers.

Following are some of the most common examples of APIs available to developers:

❑ Flickr (www.flickr.com/services/)

❑ YouTube (www.youtube.com/dev)

❑ Google Maps (www.google.com/apis/maps/)

❑ eBay (http://developer.ebay.com/)

❏ del.icio.us (`www.programmableweb.com/api/del.icio.us`)

❏ Virtual Earth (`www.viavirtualearth.com`)

There are many more examples. If you search on the site `www.programmableweb.com`, you will find a list that is updated daily. If you browse these, you'll find them fairly similar to (if not the same as) the list of web services presented earlier in the chapter.

The Difference Between Web Services and APIs

What is the difference? The immediate answer is not a lot; it is fairly arbitrary. An API is the way in which a program can make requests for a particular set of services. APIs are essentially user-friendly wrappers for a set of services. These services, as you can probably guess, can just as easily be web services as they can be services running on your machine somewhere.

Recall the following distinction made at the beginning of this chapter:

❏ A web service, as discussed in this chapter, is something that takes an HTTP-GET/HTTP-POST (also known as a REST request) and returns an XML document, or takes a SOAP request document and returns a SOAP response document. Web services comply with the standards specified by `W3C.org`.

❏ An API is a specification of a set of methods to interact with a given application via a programming language. This might be implemented as a C++ library, a set of TCP/IP commands, or even as a web service. Here we're talking about Web APIs which in this particular case use JavaScript to call a method. APIs don't have to conform to any standards because, by their nature, they are proprietary.

There aren't hard-and-fast differences between them, though. For example, Last.fm categorizes its services as web services APIs, suggesting they are both. Of course, it's confusing to differentiate between them distinctly because an API could simply be a call to a web service under the covers (and many times it will be). It's the unpredictability of APIs that needs emphasizing. Because you are using a proprietary mechanism, you can't be sure what you're going to get back from it. In fact, to use each company's own API, you will find yourself having to learn one thing for Google Maps, another thing for Flickr, and another thing for YouTube. This doesn't mean that they don't all share similarities because they do. Also, this doesn't mean they are vastly complex and difficult to use. Again, a lot of the APIs are relatively simple to use. What you will be confronted with is at least some learning curve each time you pick up a new set of APIs. You will also find that, in most cases, you will have to register for some sort of key or developer account before you can use an API.

Let's look at a particular API now, the Google Maps API (because it's simple to use, and it's also one of the easier APIs to integrate in your applications). There are relatively few hurdles and hoops to overcome to get access to the API. Google Maps has been chosen as an example API because Google Maps already exports a ready-made method for using the XMLHttpRequest object (in other words, it's a ready-made Ajax application).

The Google Maps APIs

Google Maps is a large online map of the world. The Google Maps API makes much of the Google Maps application functionality available to your own web sites. You can show specific areas on a map and place markers on the map. The Google Maps API is freely usable and embeddable in your web sites as long as your web site is free for everyone to use. The URL is `www.google.com/apis/maps/`.

You need to sign up to be able to use it, and this requires you to have a Google account. Then you must specify the URL of the site on which you wish to use the maps. If you don't have a web site, don't worry, because you can develop an example on your local web server if you register the local URL. The registration of the local URL enables Google to supply you with a developer key.

Google Maps API Key

The Google Maps API key must be inserted into your HTML page. This is an example of what one looks like:

```
<script
src="http://maps.google.com/maps?file=api&amp;v=2&amp;key=ABQIAAAA2VWtIiYkkrFt6uptB
ppqpRQ-nq7HHFDIgV4kpixi_vFUjvLLkxTADPZASa_8fbnH5iUxIH47AOnELA"
    type="text/javascript"></script>
```

Each key is uniquely created for that developer, so don't embed this one and expect it to work in your code.

Google isn't the only company that requires a special key. It's quite commonplace for other companies to require such an item before making their APIs accessible. Flickr, for example, requires the presence of an application API key.

The Map Object

The simplest use of the Google Maps API is to embed a map in your web page. After adding the API key to your page, you must add a `<div>` tag to your HTML page with the ID `map`, and the width and height set to your preferred size. You must also prime two events in the `<body>` tag: `load()` and `GUnload()`:

```
<body onload="load()" onunload="GUnload()">
    <div id="map" style="width: 500px; height: 300px"></div>
</body>
```

The `GUnload()` function is a Google-provided one that you don't need to worry about. You provide only the `load()` code. Next, you must create a `map` object in JavaScript. This is contained in the `load()` function. It is a three-step process:

❑ Check to see that your browser is modern enough to support Google maps.

❑ Create a `map` object.

❑ Set a location on the map object.

This example is taken from the Google Maps documentation and will create a map centered around Palo Alto.

```
function load() {
    if (GBrowserIsCompatible()) {
        var map = new GMap2(document.getElementById("map"));
        map.setCenter(new GLatLng(37.4419, -122.1419), 13);
    }
}
```

Already you can see several functions of the API. GBrowserIsCompatible checks to see if the browser is compatible; GMap2 creates a new map object and supplies it with the HTML element that has the ID map. Last, the setCenter API positions the map using latitude and longitude.

Geocode

Google Maps uses latitude and longitude to identify the locations of places on the map. It's simple enough to provide the two coordinates to the GLatLng method. This can prove inconvenient, though, if you (like most of the populace) are unaware of the latitudinal and longitudinal coordinates of the item you are attempting to locate on a map. Google Maps uses the Geocode object to convert addresses into these coordinates, or vice versa.

The Geocode converter is accessed via the GClientGeoCoder object. You create an instance of this, and then you can use the getLatLng method to return a given latitude and longitude for an address. It isn't quite as simple as this because you need to provide an anonymous function as the second argument to the getLatLng method. It is inside this callback function that the conversion to latitude and longitude is performed, as the following code from the Google Maps API documentation demonstrates:

```
function showAddress(address) {
  geocoder.getLatLng(
    address,
    function(point) {
      if (!point) {
        alert(address + " not found");
      } else {
        map.setCenter(point, 13);
        var marker = new GMarker(point);
        map.addOverlay(marker);
        marker.openInfoWindowHtml(address);
      }
    }
  );
}
```

First, you must check that the point argument actually returns a set of coordinates. If the parameter is empty, then the address hasn't been found. If it has been found, then you use the setCenter method and set it to the point parameter and a second parameter to value 13 (which is the code for using this object). Additionally, this example code creates a marker on the map. This takes a further three lines of code (one to create the marker, then two more to add it to the map) using the addOverlay method.

The XMLHttpRequest Factory Method

Last, there is the case of how Google Maps makes use of the XMLHttpRequest object. It does this via a "factory" method. This method creates the object for you and returns the methods and properties of the object for you, without the need for you to have to explicitly create it first. The example code from Google's API documentation shows how it can be called:

```
var request = GXmlHttp.create();
request.open("GET", "myfile.txt", true);
request.onreadystatechange = function() {
  if (request.readyState == 4) {
    alert(request.responseText);
  }
}
request.send(null);
```

201

You call the `create` method of the `GXmlHttp` object. Then you can treat it just like a normal `XMLHttpRequest` object. Interestingly, there is a second API called `GDownloadURL` that eliminates the need to check the `readystate` option of the `XMLHttpRequest` object:

```
GDownloadUrl("myfile.txt", function(data, responseCode) {
  alert(data);
});
```

It does it for you. This sums up the basic mechanics of embedding Google Maps in your pages.

Let's create a small example where you use the Google Maps API. Rather than just regurgitating the samples on that site, let's add some extra functionality, namely the ability to dynamically create your own bookmarks. This ability will be useful when you see the final example in the chapter.

First, you will invite the user to input an address into a text box. You will convert this address into a marker on the map. Even if the user closes the browser, when the user comes back to the map, the marker will still be present. This requires a two-step process. You add an address that must be converted to a Geocode location and written to an XML file. The application then must scan the XML file and place the markers it finds in it on the map. It saves the information to the XML file. This requires some server-side interaction because JavaScript is not capable of writing directly to a file on your machine without some lengthy kludges. It's much easier to get a short piece of server-side code to write the XML file to your machine instead.

Try It Out   An Example Application Using Google Maps

In the following example, the `XMLHttpRequest` object is made use of twice, once behind the scenes when using Google Maps and once to handle the writing of the marker data to the XML file.

1.   Go to the following URL:

```
http://www.google.com/apis/maps/signup.html
```

Sign up for a Google Maps API key. You must specify a URL to use with the example. Use the following because `localhost` can sometimes end up generating an extra port name after it, which will be enough to break the key; using this code also ensures that the case matches exactly:

```
http://127.0.0.1/BegAjax/Chapter7/
```

2.   Write down or copy the key to a text file.

3.   Create the following page called `map.htm`, and add the key to the code:

```
<html xmlns="http://www.w3.org/1999/xhtml">
  <head>
    <meta http-equiv="content-type" content="text/html; charset=utf-8"/>
    <title>Google Maps JavaScript API Example</title>
    <script src="http://maps.google.com/maps?file=api&amp;v=2&amp;key=Add your own
key here"
      type="text/javascript"></script>
    <script src="map.js" type="text/javascript"></script>
  </head>
  <body onload="load()" onunload="GUnload()">
```

```
      <input id="address" name="address" type="text" size="50"/>
      <input type="button" onclick="load('true')" value="Click to Add Marker" />
      <div id="map" style="width: 500px; height: 300px"></div>
   </body>
</html>
```

4. Create the JavaScript file, call it map.js, and add the following code:

```
var map = null;
var geocoder = null;
var xmlhttp = null;
if (window.XMLHttpRequest) {
  xmlhttp = new XMLHttpRequest();
} else if (window.ActiveXObject) {
  xmlhttp = new ActiveXObject("Microsoft.XMLHTTP");
}

function load(e)
    {
       if (GBrowserIsCompatible())
       {
         map = new GMap2(document.getElementById("map"));
         geocoder = new GClientGeocoder();
         placeMarkers(document.getElementById("address").value, e);
         geocoder.getLatLng("Paris", function(point){map.setCenter(point, 13)});
       }
    }

    function placeInXmlFile(point)
    {
       var xml = null;
       if (window.ActiveXObject)
       {
           xml = new ActiveXObject("Microsoft.XMLDOM");
           xml.async = false;
           xml.load("data.xml");
       }
       else
       {
           xml = document.implementation.createDocument("","", null);
           xml.async = false;
           xml.load("data.xml");
       }
       var newmarker =  xml.getElementsByTagName("markers")[0];
       newtag = xml.createElement("marker");
       newmarker.appendChild(newtag);
       newtag.setAttribute("lat", point.y);
       newtag.setAttribute("lng", point.x);
       newtag.setAttribute("address", address.value);

       xmlhttp.abort();
       var xmlToSave = xml.xml || (new XMLSerializer().serializeToString(xml))
       var xmlcode = encodeURIComponent(xmlToSave);
       var url = "Save.aspx?xml=" + xmlcode;
       xmlhttp.open("GET", url, true);
```

```
        xmlhttp.setRequestHeader("Content-Type", "text/xml" );
        xmlhttp.send(null);

 }

function placeMarkers(address, e)
{
if (e == "true")
{
geocoder.getLatLng(address, function(point) {
      if (!point) {
        alert(address + " not found");
      } else {
        map.setCenter(point, 13);
       var marker = new GMarker(point);
        map.addOverlay(marker);
        marker.openInfoWindowHtml(address);
        placeInXmlFile(point, address);
      }
    });
}
GDownloadUrl("data.xml", function(data, responseCode) {
  var xml = GXml.parse(data);
  var markers = xml.documentElement.getElementsByTagName("marker");
  for (var i = 0; i < markers.length; i++) {

    point2 = new GLatLng(parseFloat(markers[i].getAttribute("lat")),
                         parseFloat(markers[i].getAttribute("lng")));
                         map.setCenter(point2, 13);
    marker2 = new GMarker(point2);
    map.addOverlay(marker2);
    marker2.openInfoWindowHtml(markers[i].getAttribute("address"));
  }

});
}
```

5. Create the data file `data.xml` that will contain a list of coordinates, but leave it empty at the moment, except for these two elements:

```
<?xml version="1.0"?>
<markers>
</markers>
```

6. Last, create the server-side file to write to the XML file. In ASP.NET, call this `save.aspx`.

```
<%@Page Language = "C#" Debug="true" ValidateRequest="false"%>
<%@ import Namespace="System.Xml" %>
<script language="C#" runat="server">
    void Page_Load()
    {
        XmlDocument Dom = new XmlDocument();
        Dom.InnerXml = Request.QueryString["xml"];
        Dom.Save(Server.MapPath("Data.Xml"));
    }
</script>
```

Ensure that the ASP.NET account has Read and Write access to the folder `BegAjax\Chapter7`. You can do this by opening Windows Explorer and going to this folder on your hard drive, then right-clicking on it and selecting Properties. Select the Security tab, click Add, and type in ASPNET. Click Check Names, and then click OK to confirm. Check the Read and Write boxes in the Allow Column, and click OK again. If, for any reason in Windows XP Home Edition or Windows XP Professional, the Security tab isn't visible, go to Windows Explorer → Tools → Folder Options, select the View tab from the dialog. and scroll down and ensure that the "Use Simple File Sharing (Recommended)" check box is unchecked.

Or, in PHP, save it as `save.php`:

```php
<?php
    $doc = new DomDocument('1.0');
    $qs = $_GET["xml"];
    $doc->loadXML($qs);
    $doc->save('data.xml');
?>
```

7. View the page `map.htm` in the browser, as shown in Figure 7-8.

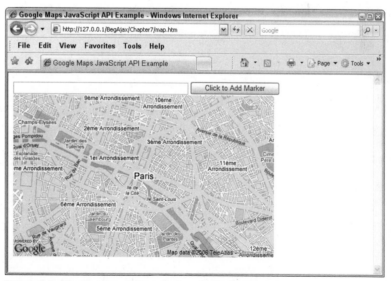

Figure 7-8: Viewing the page `map.htm` in the browser.

8. Now, type in an address you can see (or one you happen to know), and click the Add Marker button. For example, typing in **Champs-Elysees, Paris** will yield the results shown in Figure 7-9.

9. Close the browser, and reopen it. Go to `map.htm`. Scroll back to the location, and the marker will still be present. Open the file `data.xml`, and you should see the following:

```xml
<?xml version="1.0"?>
<markers>
 <marker lat="48.869801" lng="2.307586"address="Champs-Elysees, Paris"/>
</markers>
```

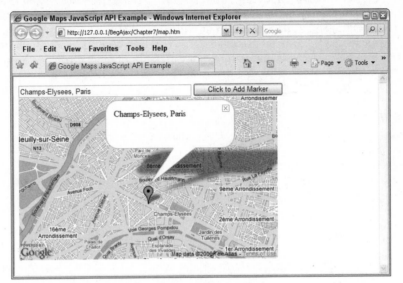

Figure 7-9: Result of entering Champs-Elysees, Paris.

How It Works

This example already uses a lot of the example code on the Google Maps web site previously discussed. You have threaded it together, though, in a new manner to perform the required functions.

The `map.htm` page is almost identical to the example in Google Maps documentation, except that you add a text box called `marker` and a button with an `onclick` event:

```html
<body onload="load()" onunload="GUnload()">
    <input id="address" name="address" type="text" size="50"/>
    <input type="button" onclick="load('true')" value="Click to Add Marker" />
    <div id="map" style="width: 500px; height: 300px"></div>
  </body>
```

This button also calls the `load()` function, but it calls it with an extra parameter. When you first run the application, you determine whether you are running the application for the first time, or whether someone has clicked on the Add Marker button. In this case, you must determine a slightly different course of action. Let's take a look at the script now. `map.js` contains two functions in addition to the `load()` function, but more about those in a minute. You start by creating the `XMLHttpRequest` object to handle the server writing the XML file:

```javascript
var map = null;
var geocoder = null;
var xmlhttp = null;
```

```
if (window.XMLHttpRequest) {
  xmlhttp = new XMLHttpRequest();
} else if (window.ActiveXObject) {
  xmlhttp = new ActiveXObject("Microsoft.XMLHTTP");
}
```

Three small samples have been taken from the documentation, the first of which allows you to type in an address and which will locate that place on the map. This is used in the load() event:

```
if (GBrowserIsCompatible())
  {
    map = new GMap2(document.getElementById("map"));
    geocoder = new GClientGeocoder();
    placeMarkers(document.getElementById("address").value, e);
    geocoder.getLatLng("Paris", function(point){map.setCenter(point, 13)});
  }
}
```

You check to see if the browser can display Google Maps using the GBrowserIsCompatible API. If it can, you create a new map object using GMap2. You then create a Geocode object, using the GClientGeocoder API. You call the placeMarkers function, passing it the address supplied in the text box, and a second parameter that is set only if the user has pressed the button. Then you center the map on Paris.

The placeMarkers will then apply the red marker to the map in the desired location for you. The second piece of sample code uses the getLatLng method, transforms the address into a set of latitude and longitude coordinates, and stores it in the object point for you. First, it assesses whether the user has clicked the Add Marker button. If the user has, then the e parameter will be set to true, and it will add the new marker.

```
if (e == "true")
{
geocoder.getLatLng(address, function(point) {
      if (!point) {
        alert(address + " not found");
      } else {
        map.setCenter(point, 13);
       var marker = new GMarker(point);
        map.addOverlay(marker);
        marker.openInfoWindowHtml(address);
        placeInXmlFile(point, address);
      }
    });
}
```

The map.setCenter centers the map on the new location. The map.AddOverlay adds a marker to the map. Last, the openInforWindowHtml opens up the little speech bubble that accompanies the marker.

You also call the placeInXml method to add the marker to the XML file for you. The third piece of sample code taken from the documentation reads an XML document data.xml that contains the latitude and longitude markers on the map. This is also contained in the placeMarkers function. You download the data from the `data.xml` file and use the factory method to read the XML from the file. You use the DOM to extract the `marker` tags as a set, and you read them into the `markers` variable. Then, you iterate through each `marker` in the set, calling the `GLatLng` method for each one to return the coordinates. Then you use the resulting `point` object to add the marker and the marker information bubble to the map.

```
GDownloadUrl("data.xml", function(data, responseCode) {
  var xml = GXml.parse(data);
  var markers = xml.documentElement.getElementsByTagName("marker");
  for (var i = 0; i < markers.length; i++) {

    point2 = new GLatLng(parseFloat(markers[i].getAttribute("lat")),
                         parseFloat(markers[i].getAttribute("lng")));
                         map.setCenter(point2, 13);
    marker2 = new GMarker(point2);
    map.addOverlay(marker2);
    marker2.openInfoWindowHtml(markers[i].getAttribute("address"));
  }
}
```

Let's jump back slightly to the `placeInXmlFile` method, which does the writing for you. It's fairly straightforward. You pass in the object `point` that contains the latitude and longitude coordinates. You start with some browser-specific code that loads in the contents of `data.xml` for you into either an XMLDOM object or a `document` object, depending on which browser is being used.

```
function placeInXmlFile(point)
{
    var xml = null;
  if (window.ActiveXObject)
  {
      xml = new ActiveXObject("Microsoft.XMLDOM");
      xml.async = false;
      xml.load("data.xml");
  }
  else
  {
      xml = document.implementation.createDocument("","", null);
      xml.async = false;
      xml.load("data.xml");
  }
}
```

You get the root element `markers` and read it into the `newmarker` element. Then you create a new marker object and append it. You set three attributes for this new tag and call the first two `lat` and `lng`, as required by the `data.xml` file. The latitude is contained in the `point.y` property, while the longitude is stored in the `point.x` property. The third is not required, but it stores the `address` property so that you can display the marker information bubble.

```
var newmarker =  xml.getElementsByTagName("markers")[0];
newtag = xml.createElement("marker");
newmarker.appendChild(newtag);
newtag.setAttribute("lat", point.y);
newtag.setAttribute("lng", point.x);
newtag.setAttribute("address", address.value);
```

This has now fully prepared the XML document for you, and you just need to write it to the file. To do this, you clear the existing XMLHttpRequest object. You then URI-encode the XML you have created and read it into a variable xmlcode. This is appended to a querystring, which is passed to the server-side code.

```
xmlhttp.abort();
var xmlToSave = xml.xml || (new XMLSerializer().serializeToString(xml))
var xmlcode = encodeURIComponent(xmlToSave);
var url = "Save.aspx?xml=" + xmlcode;
xmlhttp.open("GET", url, true);
xmlhttp.setRequestHeader("Content-Type", "text/xml" );
xmlhttp.send(null);

}
```

The server-side code creates a new XMLDocument object, retrieves the XML from the querystring, and saves it to the file. It does exactly the same in either PHP or ASP.NET.

```
XmlDocument Dom = new XmlDocument();
Dom.InnerXml = Request.QueryString["xml"];
Dom.Save((Server.MapPath("Data.Xml"));
```

This concludes the cycle. An item is added to the XML file, and the next time you browse it, the marker will be read in by the previous method and added to the map. This gives a good overview of the Google Maps API in action.

Now let's move on to the final subject: how to combine results from two different sets of APIs to create a new application.

Mashups

Mashups are a relatively new phenomenon on the Internet. The term is attributed to a similar concept in pop music where, in its most common form, the vocal tracks of one song were layered over the backing track of a completely different song. The idea was that instead of it being an unlistenable mishmash, you ended up with a radically new take on some old songs. Several chart hits were based on this very technique.

In web terms, though, it has a slightly different meaning. It's about taking APIs or web services from two different sources and combining them into a single application. Common examples of this center around Google Maps. You could have maps showing the locations of photos submitted to flickr.com, for example. Flickr allows you to tag each photo you take, and diligent photographers can also submit the location the photo was taken, via geo-tagging. Another example might be to take music that you have just played (LastFm provides such functionality) and match it to reviews or biographical information about that artist.

Mashups don't have to use APIs, but you are then left with the task of providing the content of one side of the mashup from your application code. It is, therefore, much easier to draw from existing sources of data wherever possible because creation of content is a whole different discipline entirely.

How Ajax Helps Enable the Use of Mashups

With APIs and now mashups, the discussion seems to be straying slightly away from the trail of Ajax, but you're never too far way from it. As you shall see, when creating mashups, there can be a lot of "to-ing" and "fro-ing" from the client to the server and back to the client, as XML files are updated or as web services are called by proxy. Because the advantage of using an application like Google Maps is that it already employs Ajax to provide seamless map scrolling, the last thing you want is for your application to force page refreshes every time you go to the server. Once again, the humble XMLHttpRequest object must be put to work.

Because APIs are called from JavaScript and web services can be launched via a proxy, it makes sense that you control this all from the client side. Indeed, this is what many developers have chosen to do when creating mashups.

The fun thing about mashups is that, with the public opening up of APIs, the ball has been placed squarely in the court of the home and the hobbyist developer. You don't need Visual Studio.NET. You don't need expensive software. Everything can be done for free. Also, with mashups, because you are using JavaScript, your code doesn't have to conform to strong typing; not everything has to be designed and planned to an orthodox methodology beforehand. It doesn't always have to be completely reusable. It's about going back to the days of classic ASP and PHP and just getting things to work, trying things out. That's not to say that structured programming and object orientation are bad things. Of course, they're very important. But for once, and definitely for the novice, half the fun is getting started.

What you will do is use the Flickr API to get a list of photos, and then use the Google Maps API to display the photos next to each marker you have created. Note that Flickr already has its own map that can be used to display geo-tagged photographs. The purpose of this application, though, is to demonstrate how two separate application APIs can be easily combined in one application. Also, the authors personally prefer the Google Maps map to the Flickr one because of its depth of detail, so don't feel as though this is just needlessly reinventing the wheel.

This will require two applications. The first will extract the information from the Flickr site and write it to an XML file. The second application will be an amended version of your Google Maps API application that will be able to display the photos as part of the markers placed on the maps.

Before doing this, let's explore the Flickr API in a little detail.

Using the Flickr API

The Flickr web site (www.flickr.com) is a photograph sharing and archiving site owned by Yahoo!. It has various tools for putting up photos, sorting them, and choosing how to display them, as well as permitting who can see them and who cannot. It also allows users to tag each of their photographs to help with organization. There isn't a formal list of tags in HTML such as <table> and <form>; rather, the tagging system is up to the user. A particular user might choose to tag photographs from Paris with a Paris tag or photos of artworks with a sculpture tag. These tags are labels or keywords that aid the easy sorting and categorization of many disparate groups.

Tag Clouds (Weighted List)

Tagging is another Web 2.0 phenomenon, and tags are commonly displayed in tag clouds, or visual lists where popular tags can be weighted by making them appear bigger. Flickr was the first site to popularize the distinctive appearance, but since then, many more sites (such as `Last.fm`) have used this format. The sans-serif font, blue text on a gray background, and lowercase lettering have become almost an unwritten standard for displaying information in this way.

Figure 7-10 shows a list of Flickr's most popular tags.

You are interested in the tags so that you can use the Flickr APIs to return sets of photographs according to the way they've been tagged. Of course, you depend on people to tag their own photographs correctly. For example, you will notice `newyork` and `newyorkcity` in the Flickr tag cloud, which will overlap and create some confusion about how to locate photographs from New York.

So, how do you actually tag a photo? In Flickr, you just locate your chosen photo, click on the "Add a tag" link next to it, type the appropriate text into the text box, and click the Add button. Flickr lets you create your own tag cloud from your own set of tags.

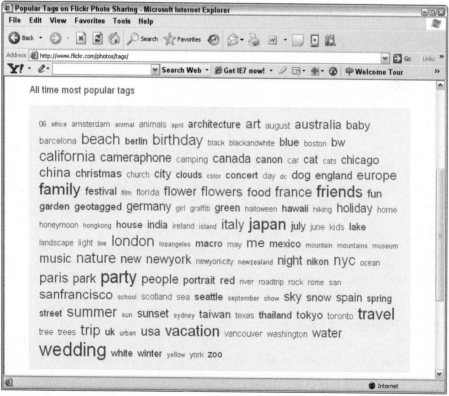

Figure 7-10: List of Flickr's most popular tags.

Using the Flickr API Key

As with Google Maps, you will be required to have a Flickr account to actually be able to use the APIs (and, therefore, run this example). Once again, this account is free. If you read the Flickr API documentation, be warned that it makes it look a little more confusing than it needs to be. If you want to call an API that doesn't require authentication, then all you need to do is apply for an API key.

If you want to use an API that does require authentication, the process is as follows:

1. Apply for an API key.
2. Create a Login link from the API key.
3. Create an Authorization handler.
4. Call the `getToken` method using the handler.
5. Use the token to be able to make an authenticated call to the API.
6. Add the API call to your application.

Fortunately, the APIs you will call don't require authorization; however, the documentation gives the impression that you would have to follow this process to use any API. You can be reassured that this is not the case.

Creating an Example Application

Let's create an example that, when you supply a particular user's ID, will retrieve the public photos of that user and the geographical coordinates for those photos and then write them to an XML file. Following are the particular APIs to focus on:

❑ `getPublicPhotos` API — When supplied with a user ID, it returns a list of photos as an XML file.

❑ `getGeoLocation` API — When supplied with a photo ID, it returns a location with latitude and longitude coordinates.

This means that in this example, you will supply the user ID in a text box. (There is a special WroxTest account ID with a couple of photos in the public domain that will be supplied in the code.) You will use the `getPublicPhotos` API to return an XML list of photos. Then, for each photo in the list, you will use the `getGeoLocation` API to retrieve the latitude and longitude information. You will compile this information into an XML file and save this file.

Geotagging Photos in Flickr

You've learned a little about tagging, but you might be forgiven for wondering how tagging works with regard to location. As you've seen, photos are tagged by hand, by the user, and this can lead to erratic categorization. Fortunately, the locational tagging of photos is done in a much more precise manner.

Within each account on `flickr.com` is a map tab. It is possible to use this map to zoom in on a location, then simply drag and drop your photo or photos onto the map. Once this has been done, your photo will automatically contain the longitude and latitude coordinates that can be retrieved by the `getGeoLocation` API.

The following URL describes the process in more detail:

```
www.flickr.com/groups/geotagging
```

You are now ready to use the Flickr APIs in an application. The Flickr APIs are actually web services so, to call an API from the page, you would call it in just the same way as you'd call a web service. This should make life a bit easier and the code a little more familiar.

Try It Out **Create an Application to Use the Flickr APIs**

This application will ask the user to supply a user ID in the text box and then will scan that user's public photos on Flickr. It will write data about their photos (such as the title, the photo ID, the longitude and latitude) into an XML file.

The XML file, though, will be based on the layout you saw in the Google Maps API example. This will enable the Google Maps application to be able to read the XML file, but you will be able to amend this application to make use of the extra information being sent over as part of the XML file. This won't actually affect the Google Maps API; it will just ignore the superfluous information. This will be used in the second application.

1. First apply for an API key (if you haven't already) at `www.flickr.com/services/api/keys/apply/`. You will have to supply a short description about what it is needed for and confirm that it is for personal use only. You will receive a key and a shared secret. You use the key only for this example.

2. Create the following HTML page, and save it as `flickr.htm`:

```
<html xmlns="http://www.w3.org/1999/xhtml" >
<head>
    <title>Get Photos By Location</title>
      <script src="flickr.js" type="text/javascript"></script>
</head>
  <body>
     <input id="user" name="user" type="text" size="30"/>
     <input type="button" onclick="sendData()" value="Click to Save this User's
Photo Locations" />
  </body>
</html>
```

3. Create a script file called `flickr.js`:

```
var xmlhttp = null;
var finalXML = null;

if (window.ActiveXObject)
{
 finalXML = new ActiveXObject("MSXML2.DOMDocument.3.0");
}
else
{
 finalXML = document.implementation.createDocument("","",null);
}
```

```
finalXML.appendChild(finalXML.createElement("markers"));

countLength = 0;
globalCount=0;
var photoid = new Array();
var phototitleid = new Array();
var photoserverid = new Array();
var photosecret = new Array();


function getRequest()
{
if (window.XMLHttpRequest)
{
  return xmlhttp = new XMLHttpRequest();
}
    else if (window.ActiveXObject)
    {
    return xmlhttp = new ActiveXObject("Microsoft.XMLHTTP");
    }
}

function sendData()
{
     var request = getRequest();
     var url = "flickrproxy.aspx?method=flickr.people.getPublicPhotos&api_key=
your_value_here&parametertype=user_id&parametervalue=" +
document.getElementById("user").value;
     request.open("GET", url, true);
     request.onreadystatechange = function() { getData(request) };
     request.send(null);
}

function getData()
{

  if ((xmlhttp.readyState == 4) &&( xmlhttp.status == 200))
  {

    var xmlobject = xmlhttp.responseXML;
    var photos =  xmlobject.getElementsByTagName("photo");
    countLength = photos.length;

    for (var i = 0; i < photos.length; i++) {
    photoid[i] = photos[i].getAttribute("id");
    phototitleid[i] = photos[i].getAttribute("title");
    photoserverid[i] = photos[i].getAttribute("server");
    photosecret[i] = photos[i].getAttribute("secret");
    }
    sendGeoData();

  }

}
```

```
  function sendGeoData()
  {

    var request = getRequest();
    var url = "flickrproxy.aspx?method=flickr.photos.geo.getLocation&api_key=
your_value_here&parametertype=photo_id&parametervalue=";

    request.open("GET", url + photoid[globalCount], true);
    request.onreadystatechange = function() { getGeoData(request) };
    request.send(null);

 }

function getGeoData(request)
{
  if (request.readyState == 4 &&  request.status == 200)
  {
    xmlobject = request.responseXML;

    var newtag = finalXML.createElement("marker");
    var loc = xmlobject.getElementsByTagName("location")[0];
    var photo = xmlobject.getElementsByTagName("photo")[0];
    newtag.setAttribute("lat", loc.getAttribute("latitude"));
    newtag.setAttribute("lng", loc.getAttribute("longitude"));
    newtag.setAttribute("address", phototitleid[globalCount]);
    newtag.setAttribute("secret", photosecret[globalCount]);
    newtag.setAttribute("server", photoserverid[globalCount]);
    newtag.setAttribute("user_id", document.getElementById("user").value);
    newtag.setAttribute("photo_id", photo.getAttribute("id"));

    finalXML.firstChild.appendChild(newtag);

    globalCount++;

    if (globalCount != countLength)  {
        window.setTimeout(sendGeoData, 10);
    } else {
        saveXml();
    }
  }
}


function saveXml()
{
    var xmlToSave = null;
    if(window.ActiveXObject)
    {
       xmlToSave = finalXML.xml
    }
    else
    {
       xmlToSave = new XMLSerializer().serializeToString(finalXML);
```

```
        }
        var xmlcode = encodeURIComponent(xmlToSave);
        var url = "Save.aspx?xml=" + xmlcode;
        var request = getRequest();
        request.open("GET", url, true);
        request.onreadystatechange = function() {
            if (request.readyState == 4) {
                alert("File saved.");
            }
        };
        if (request.overrideMimeType) {
          request.overrideMimeType("text/plain");
        }
        request.send(null);
}
```

4. Create a server-side file. In ASP.NET, save it as `flickrproxy.aspx`.

```
<%@Page Language = "C#" Debug="true" %>
<%@ import Namespace="System.Xml" %>
<script language="C#" runat="server">
    void Page_Load()
    {
        XmlDocument Dom = new XmlDocument();
        string url = "http://api.flickr.com/services/rest/?method="+
Request.QueryString["method"] + "&api_key=" + Request.QueryString["api_key"] + "&"
+ Request.QueryString["parametertype"] + "=" +
Request.QueryString["parametervalue"];
        Dom.Load(url);
        string abc = Dom.InnerXml;
        Response.ContentType = "text/xml";
        Response.Write(abc);
    }
</script>
```

Or, in PHP, save it as `save.php`.

```
<?php
header('Content-Type: text/xml');
?>
<?php
  $url = 'http://api.flickr.com/services/rest/?method=';
  $method = $_GET["method"];
  $api_key = $_GET["api_key"];
  $parametertype = $_GET["parametertype"];
  $parametervalue = $_GET["parametervalue"];
  $url = $url.$method.'&api_key='.$api_key.'&'.$parametertype.'='.$parametervalue;
  $url = DOMDocument::load($url);
  echo $url->saveXML();
?>
```

5. Ensure that this example is running in the same place as the last example and that the file `save.aspx`/`save.php` is present. The code needs no alteration.

6. Run `flickr.htm` in the browser, and enter the number of the WroxTest user, **64002153@N00,** as shown in Figure 7-11. This will retrieve a set of photos for the WroxTest user and save them to the `data.xml` file.

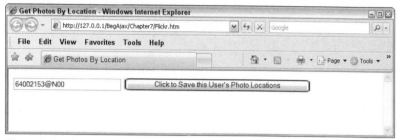

Figure 7-11: Entering the number of the WroxTest user.

7. View the contents of the `data.xml` file. It should look like this:

```xml
<?xml version="1.0"?>
<markers>
  <marker lat="48.85359" lng="2.292366" address="eiffel" secret="c5bdad7cc1"
server="89" user_id="64002153@N00" photo_id="277502325"/>
  <marker lat="48.880634" lng="2.282752" address="champselysees"
secret="1080ee2ca6" server="119" user_id="64002153@N00" photo_id="277437193"/>
</markers>
```

How It Works

This example used the Flickr API to extract photos from the WroxTest user on Flickr's database and then to write the details that you need to display them (as well as their geographical latitude and longitude information) into an XML file. The XML takes the format of the XML file required by Google Maps. This is how you will achieve the interaction between the two separate APIs with two applications. This application has only created the `data.xml` file; the second application will read it.

The HTML file takes the normal format. The button is used to call the `sendData()` event in the JavaScript `flickr.js`. The JavaScript file doesn't start by creating the `XMLHttpRequest` object as normal, though. This time, you must create a separate `XMLHttpRequest` object for each interaction. It's not enough to call `abort()` and reuse this because this causes strange behavior in Firefox. Instead, you create a `getRequest()` function that allows you to create a new `XMLHttpRequest` object with each function call and to return it to the calling function. Also you needed to define some extra global variables to hold information, such as a set of arrays that will hold the tags and, among those, a `finalXML` variable to hold the XML document that is generated:

```javascript
if (window.ActiveXObject)
{
  finalXML = new ActiveXObject("MSXML2.DOMDocument.3.0");
}
else
{
  finalXML = document.implementation.createDocument("","",null);
}
```

```
finalXML.appendChild(finalXML.createElement("markers"));

countLength = 0;
globalCount=0;
var photoid = new Array();
var phototitleid = new Array();
var photoserverid = new Array();
var photosecret = new Array();


function getRequest()
{
if (window.XMLHttpRequest)
{
  return xmlhttp = new XMLHttpRequest();
}
    else if (window.ActiveXObject)
    {
    return xmlhttp = new ActiveXObject("Microsoft.XMLHTTP");
    }
}
```

The `sendData()` function clears the `XMLHttpRequest` object, then creates a URL that contains the method you wish to call. Once again, you use a server-side proxy code to avoid the problem of cross-domain calling.

In the server-side code, you call the `getPublicPhotos` API method, along with the API key, and a parameter type and parameter value. This API takes a `user_id` and will return a set of values in the following format:

```
<photos page="2" pages="89" perpage="10" total="881">
    <photo id="2636" owner="47058503995@N01"
        secret="a123456" server="2" title="test_04"
        ispublic="1" isfriend="0" isfamily="0" />
    <photo id="2635" owner="47058503995@N01"
        secret="b123456" server="2" title="test_03"
        ispublic="0" isfriend="1" isfamily="1" />
    <photo id="2633" owner="47058503995@N01"
        secret="c123456" server="2" title="test_01"
        ispublic="1" isfriend="0" isfamily="0" />
    <photo id="2610" owner="12037949754@N01"
        secret="d123456" server="2" title="00_tall"
        ispublic="1" isfriend="0" isfamily="0" />
</photos>
```

You will need the photo ID, the title, the server, and the secret values to be able to display the photos ultimately. So, you will need to save them in the XML file for the time being. How to display photos from Flickr will be examined later in this chapter when you create the next application.

One thing to note is that the `sendData` *function will work only for Flickr API methods that require single parameters. Because all the methods you wish to call only take one compulsory parameter, this isn't a problem. It might be if you wanted to adapt the code to call a Flickr API method that used more than one.*

The URL is passed to the XMLHttpRequest object, and the getData function is called in the event of the onreadystatechange event firing. You send the object as normal to the server, after calling the new getRequest() method:

```
function sendData()
{
  var request = getRequest();
    var url =
"flickrproxy.aspx?method=flickr.people.getPublicPhotos&api_key=your_value_here&para
metertype=user_id&parametervalue=" + document.getElementById("user").value;
    request.open("GET", url, true);
    request.onreadystatechange = function() { getData(request) };
    request.send(null);
}
```

The getData() function provides the callback function for the server-side code. You load the contents of the responseXML method into a variable:

```
function getData()
{

  if ((xmlhttp.readyState == 4) &&( xmlhttp.status == 200))
  {

    var xmlobject = xmlhttp.responseXML;
    var photos =  xmlobject.getElementsByTagName("photo");
    countLength = photos.length;

    for (var i = 0; i < photos.length; i++) {
    photoid[i] = photos[i].getAttribute("id");
    phototitleid[i] = photos[i].getAttribute("title");
    photoserverid[i] = photos[i].getAttribute("server");
    photosecret[i] = photos[i].getAttribute("secret");
    }
    sendGeoData();

  }

}
```

Because you called the getPublicPhotos API method, you know that you will be receiving the id, title, server, and secret attributes for each photo tag. You store these in the arrays you created at the head of the JavaScript. Last, you call another function, sendGeoData(), once the arrays have been populated.

Let's take a quick recap at this point. You have called the getPublicPhotos API with a user_id. You have received an XML document listing all of the photos that this user has in the public domain. This XML document isn't suitable, though, and you still don't have any location data, namely the longitude and latitude. What you do have is the photo ID that you must supply to the getGeoLocation API method now. You have a number of photos, however, so you must call the method to retrieve the location for as many times as you have photos.

The sendGeoData function uses the global variable photoid, which is an array of photoids. You will be using each individual item in the array to call the getGeoLocation API method. It isn't possible to set up a loop to do this inside your function, though, so your function structure just shows a single call to the flickrproxy server-side page and a single callback function, getGeoData.

```
function sendGeoData(photoid)
{

    var request = getRequest();
    var url =
"flickrproxy.aspx?method=flickr.photos.geo.getLocation&api_key=your_value_here&para
metertype=photo_id&parametervalue=";

    request.open("GET", url + photoid[globalCount], true);
    request.onreadystatechange = function() { getGeoData(request) };
    request.send(null);
}
```

You should be able to start discerning the purpose of this rather untidy set of global variables. While you can't call the getGeoLocation API from inside a loop and then wait for several replies, what you have to do is call it once, get the reply, add the reply to your document, call the API again, get the reply again, and add it to the document. This is exactly what the callback function enables you to do.

```
function getGeoData(request)
{
  if (request.readyState == 4 &&  request.status == 200)
  {
    xmlobject = request.responseXML;

    var newtag = finalXML.createElement("marker");
    var loc = xmlobject.getElementsByTagName("location")[0];
    var photo = xmlobject.getElementsByTagName("photo")[0];
    newtag.setAttribute("lat", loc.getAttribute("latitude"));
    newtag.setAttribute("lng", loc.getAttribute("longitude"));
    newtag.setAttribute("address", phototitleid[globalCount]);
    newtag.setAttribute("secret", photosecret[globalCount]);
    newtag.setAttribute("server", photoserverid[globalCount]);
    newtag.setAttribute("user_id", document.getElementById("user").value);
    newtag.setAttribute("photo_id", photo.getAttribute("id"));

    finalXML.firstChild.appendChild(newtag);

    globalCount++;

    if (globalCount != countLength)  {
        window.setTimeout(sendGeoData, 10);
    } else {
        saveXml();
    }
  }
}
```

The getGeoData function is similar to the getData function in that, once again, you get the responseXML method result and read the XML into an XML document. This time, rather than storing the data in global arrays, you must get ready to put it into an XML document. As you know, this function could be called several times. You just need to dynamically create a marker tag for each photo.

What you will do is create a single marker tag that contains the latitude, longitude, address (title), secret, server, user_id, and photo_id tags:

```
<marker lat="48.85359" lng="2.292366" address="eiffel" secret="c5bdad7cc1"
server="89" user_id="64002153@N00" photo_id="277502325"/>
```

This is both the information you need to geographically display a marker on the map and the information needed by the next application to display the map. You take the information for the address, secret, and server from the global arrays, and you extract the latitude and longitude and photo_id attributes from the XML document returned by the getGeoLocation API method. You append this information into the finalXML array, which contains an array of each marker tag you have created.

As mentioned previously, you know that you must shuffle backward and forward between the sendGeoData and getGeoData functions as many times as there are photos. You use the globalCount variable to keep count of how many photos there are. You also save the total number of photos in the global countLength variable, so when these two are equal, you know that you have called the getGeoLocation API for each photo the user has. If you haven't, you add 1 to the count and call sendGeoData again. If you have, then you call the final function, saveXML.

The saveXML function creates a root element called markers and then appends each one of the marker tags in the finalXML array to the root element. You then URI-encode this XML, append it as a query-string, and send it to the same server-side code that you used in the previous example. This saves the information as an XML document, called data.xml.

```
function saveXml()
{

    var xmlToSave = null;
    if(window.ActiveXObject)
    {
        xmlToSave = finalXML.xml
    }
    else
    {
        xmlToSave = new XMLSerializer().serializeToString(finalXML);
    }
    var xmlcode = encodeURIComponent(xmlToSave);
    var url = "Save.aspx?xml=" + xmlcode;
    var request = getRequest();
    request.open("GET", url, true);
    request.onreadystatechange = function() {
        if (request.readyState == 4) {
            alert("File saved.");
        }
    };
    if (request.overrideMimeType) {
      request.overrideMimeType("text/plain");
    }
    request.send(null);
}
```

You haven't displayed anything to the screen here, but writing to the XML file has allowed you to lay the groundwork to be able to. The data.xml file is in a legal format for the Google Maps API to be able to use, so that all you must do now is retrieve the information from it and display the photos from Flickr.

Displaying Photos from Flickr

The crux of the matter is being able to display the photos. It isn't as straightforward as just displaying a simple URL. The URLs are dynamically created and stored on different servers, so you need to dynamically create them each time.

The URL can take several formats, but the one of interest here is as follows:

```
http://static.flickr.com/{server-id}/{photo_id}_{secret}.jpg
```

You need the `server-id`, the `photo_id`, and the `secret` key. All of these items are returned as attributes when we use the `getPublicPhotos` API method. So, as long as you have stored them somewhere, then to display the photo all you must do is assemble the URL as a string correctly.

So, if you have a `server-id` of 89, a `photo_id` of 277502325, and a `secret` key of c5bdad7cc1, then the following URL should display the photo:

```
http://static.flickr.com/89/277502325_c5bdad7cc1.jpg
```

Of course, this will display a full-sized photo. If you want to display a thumbnail or a different size, you can append a size code as follows:

```
http://static.flickr.com/{server-id}/{photo_id}_{secret}_[mstb].jpg
```

where the following is true:

- ❑   s — small square 75x75
- ❑   t — thumbnail, 100 on longest side
- ❑   m — small, 240 on longest side
- ❑   - — medium, 500 on longest side
- ❑   b — large, 1024 on longest side (only exists for very large original images)
- ❑   o — original image, a jpg, gif, or png, depending on the source format

A small version of the image could be called by the following URL:

```
http://static.flickr.com/89/277502325_c5bdad7cc1_s.jpg
```

Look at the following URL for more details:

```
http://www.flickr.com/services/api/misc.urls.html
```

Try It Out   Creating the Mashup

Let's now return to the maps example and make some changes so that it works in tandem with the Flickr application. Let's exploit the `openWindowInfoHtml` API and pass it more than just simple text this time. You've already done 90 percent of the work, so don't be surprised to find that this example requires rather less code than the previous two.

1. Copy `maps.htm` into a new file called `mashup.htm`, and remove the text box and button lines. Also, change the `script` tag so that it now references the file `mashup.js`. It should now look like:

```
<script
src="http://maps.google.com/maps?file=api&amp;v=2&amp;key=ABQIAAAA2VWtIiYkkrFt6uptB
ppqpRQ-nq7HHFDIgV4kpixi_vFUjvLLkxTADPZAsa_8fbnH5iUxIH47AOnELA"
type="text/javascript"></script>
should be:
<script
src="http://maps.google.com/maps?file=api&amp;v=2&amp;key=add_your_own_key_here"
type="text/javascript"></script>
```

2. Copy `maps.js` into a new file called `mashup.js`. Alter the function `placeMarkers` so that it now reads as follows:

```
function placeMarkers(address, e)
{
    GDownloadUrl("data.xml", function(data, responseCode) {
    var xml = GXml.parse(data);
    var markers = xml.documentElement.getElementsByTagName("marker");
    for (var i = 0; i < markers.length; i++) {

        point2 = new GLatLng(parseFloat(markers[i].getAttribute("lat")),
                            parseFloat(markers[i].getAttribute("lng")));
                            map.setCenter(point2, 13);
        marker2 = new GMarker(point2);
        map.addOverlay(marker2);
        attr = markers[i].getAttribute("address");
        aurl = "http://www.flickr.com/photos/"+ markers[i].getAttribute("user_id") +"/"
+ markers[i].getAttribute("photo_id");
        imageurl = "http://static.flickr.com/" + markers[i].getAttribute("server")+ "/"
+ markers[i].getAttribute("photo_id") +"_" + markers[i].getAttribute("secret") +
"_s.jpg";

        GEvent.addListener(marker2, "click", (function(marker, pAurl, pAttr,
pImageurl) {
            return function() { marker.openInfoWindowHtml("<a href='" + pAurl
+"/'><img alt='" + pAttr + "' src= '" + pImageurl +"'/></a> <span>" + pAttr +
"</span>" ,new GSize(200,200)); }
        })(marker2, aurl, attr, imageurl));
    }
});
}
```

3. Change function `load()` on one line by removing the second argument used to call `placeMarkers` as follows:

```
function load(e)
    {
        if (GBrowserIsCompatible())
```

```
    {
        map = new GMap2(document.getElementById("map"));
        geocoder = new GClientGeocoder();
        placeMarkers();
        geocoder.getLatLng("Paris", function(point){map.setCenter(point, 13)});
    }
}
```

4.   Open `mashup.htm` in your browser. Scroll to a marker (there is one just to the west for Eiffel Tower), and click on the marker. You will now see a photo from the Flickr site display on a Google Maps map (Figure 7-12).

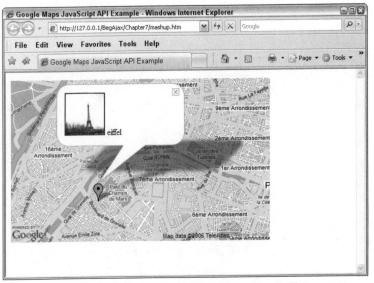

Figure 7-12: Photo from Flickr site displayed on a Google Maps map.

How It Works

In the final example, you have tied together your two applications. After all the hard work of the previous applications, you've not had to add too much more. You have removed the button and the text box from the HTML because you don't need to accept any input from the user. (This can be provided by the Flickr application now.) You've had to update the `load()` and `placemarker()` functions to do this.

In fact, the only new code that you've had to add has been in `placemarkers`:

```
    marker2 = new GMarker(point2);
    map.addOverlay(marker2);
    attr = markers[i].getAttribute("address");
    aurl = "http://www.flickr.com/photos/"+ markers[i].getAttribute("user_id") +"/"
  + markers[i].getAttribute("photo_id");
```

```
        imageurl = "http://static.flickr.com/" + markers[i].getAttribute("server")+ "/"
+ markers[i].getAttribute("photo_id") +"_" + markers[i].getAttribute("secret") +
"_s.jpg";

        GEvent.addListener(marker2, "click", (function(marker, pAurl, pAttr,
pImageurl) {
            return function() {  marker.openInfoWindowHtml("<a href='" + pAurl
+"/'><img alt='" + pAttr + "' src= '" + pImageurl +"'/></a> <span>" + pAttr +
"</span>" ,new GSize(200,200));     }
        })(marker2, aurl, attr, imageurl));
```

Here the code creates a new marker on the map as before. The difference is that the
openInfoWindowHtml method doesn't have to only take text. You can pass it an <img> element, and
you can construct the <img> element's src attribute according to the rules described prior to this "Try It
Out" section. You also create an anchor tag that links back to the page on Flickr where this photo can be
accessed. The URL to do this is simply the following:

```
http://www.flickr.com/{user_id}/{photo_id}
```

You also send the address/title of the photo and write that as a span tag. You've constructed this minia-
ture HTML fragment and supplied it to the openInfoWindowHtml API method as a parameter. This
ensures that the marker creates a bubble that displays the image and associated information. You return
the contents of the anonymous function, which opens the window for each marker point. Once you open
one window for a marker, any previously existing windows are closed. You now have a mashup application that combines Flickr's photographs and displays them on a Google Maps map. Better still, it uses
Ajax to make the whole process as seamless as possible.

Summary

This chapter has touched on a lot of different subjects. The discussion started with web services and
looked at how you can use a browser to consume a simple web service using REST. The discussion then
compared the REST paradigm to the SOAP one, and it talked a little about why you would use one
rather than the other. This chapter then looked at how you could incorporate a web service into an Ajax
application, and it showed the problems involved with calling a web service from one domain when in
another. Two solutions were presented, one that involved using a server-side proxy and the other that
involved pointing the <script> tag's src attribute to the web service, and returning the information in
JSON instead of in XML.

Next, the chapter examined APIs and the fairly arbitrary definition of an API compared to a web service.
You used Google Maps APIs as a simple example. Then the discussion introduced the idea of mashups
and combining calls from the Google Maps API with the Yahoo Flickr API to provide a final sample
application.

Chapter 8 looks at the XSLT and XPath languages (which are used to help select information from documents and web services with a greater degree of granularity) and how they can be used to control the
presentation in Ajax applications.

Exercises

Suggested solutions to these questions can be found in Appendix A.

1. Alter the first example `webservice.htm` so that it no longer asks the use for input and instead just returns a list of five prices for Microsoft (MSFT), Oracle (ORCL), Sun (SUNW), IBM (IBM), and Apple (AAPL).

2. Go to the Google Maps API application, and alter it so that it now centers on the first `<marker>` element in the `data.xml` file.

   Hint: You will need to check that there is a `<marker>` *element in the file.*

8

XSLT and XPath

One of the major additions in the last five years to modern browsers has been that of an Extensible Stylesheet Language Transformation (XSLT) processor. XSLT is primarily used to transform one XML document into another. Transformations can be used to select specific items or sections of the document. XSLT promotes the separation of document structure from the presentation and content of the web page.

Most attractively, XSLT allows you to use other XML languages (such as XPath) to query XML documents. Instead of having to go back to the database each time and hit it with a query, now you're in the position of extracting a single XML document from the server, then deciding which data you want from it on the client side. XPath can select and query data from an XML document more simply and efficiently than using JavaScript. XSLT can also be used to add styles using cascading style sheets (CSS), in the same way that style sheets are used to control the presentation of HTML pages. You can use XSLT to transform your vanilla-text XML document into a presentational tour de force.

For all that, XSLT has been given a lukewarm reception in some quarters. Just about everything you can do in XSLT you can already do with JavaScript and the DOM. It increases the sizes of files sent back to the client. Its programmatic structures can baffle designers used to working with nothing more than HTML and CSS files. Perhaps more problematically, the ugly question of browser compatibility rears its head again. The XSLT engines of Internet Explorer (IE) and Firefox must be called in different ways by the JavaScript code, and worse still, the main elements of XSLT aren't always used or rendered in the same way by the two main browsers, despite the fact that there is a standard governing XSLT.

Despite these drawbacks, XSLT still occupies an important place in the Web developer's toolkit when it comes to rendering XML data in your applications. XSLT also enters the Ajax equation because often when the server returns its data to the client it will be in the form of an XML document. Your applications don't have to do this, but more often than not, it's a good idea because XML preserves the structure of the data, and XML's text format is ideal for data transmission that all applications can understand.

In this chapter, you will learn about the following:

- ❏ What XSLT is
- ❏ XSLT tags
- ❏ What XPath is
- ❏ Performing a transform
- ❏ Passing parameters into an XSLT document

XSLT and Its Purpose

XML, the language for transforming one XML document to another can be used to perform many of the programmatic functions of a language such as JavaScript, PHP, or C#, or it can also be used to provide style information to XML documents. Neither of these functions is really what XSLT does best.

One of the problems with XML data is that anyone can create a schema. Even in relatively restricted fields (such as music notation, chemical elements, or stocks and shares) there will be multiple schemas. With XSLT, you have something that can take documents from multiple sources and transform them with a common structure. XSLT can produce output in a number of different formats: XML, HTML, or pure text.

What exactly is XSLT? XSLT style sheets are XML documents themselves, and, therefore, the rules of XML (such as documents having to be well formed and valid, have single root elements, elements have to be correctly nested, and so on) also apply to XSLT. XSLT is built on a set of templates. Templates can be thought of as similar to functions in JavaScript, and they are reusable in the same way. The processor must also know where to begin, which template to start processing first. This is done via the `match` attribute. Inside the templates is a mixture of XSLT tags and XML data, HTML tags, or text.

When XSLT produces output in HTML, it creates a hybrid XML document of HTML elements and XSLT directives. The HTML elements are interpreted by the browser in the normal way, but the XSLT directives function a bit like the way classic ASP or PHP commands do. For example, consider the following classic ASP snippet:

```
<% if  (x ==5 )  { %>
 <span id="name"> William Shakespeare </span>
<% } else { %>
 <span id="name"> Arthur Miller </span>
<% } %>
```

Now, consider a PHP snippet:

```
<?php if  ($x ==5 )  { ?>
 <span id="name"> William Shakespeare </span>
<?php } else { ?>
 <span id="name"> Arthur Miller </span>
<?php } ?>
```

The items in bold are never displayed. Also, depending on the value of the variable x, only one of the two span tags is displayed as well. From this point of view, XSLT is already looking a little familiar:

```
<xsl:choose>
<xsl:when test="x=5">
<span id="name"> William Shakespeare </span>
</xsl:when>
<xsl:otherwise>
<span id="name"> Arthur Miller </span>
</xsl:otherwise>
</xsl:choose>
```

The XSL directives aren't displayed by the browser, but they are directives to ultimately create HTML elements or text content that can be displayed by the browser. The most important difference, though, is that the XSLT engine is part of the browser, so any XSLT directives are handled on the client and never have go to the browser.

On top of this, though, is the fact that the ASP.NET server-side programming technology also has an XSLT processor, while PHP can have an XSLT processor added via the Sablotron library at the Ginger Alliance. (More details can be found at: http://uk2.php.net/xslt.)

An important thing to note is that XSLT doesn't provide any new functionality with transformations. It provides a more flexible and structured way of performing them. This means that users are no longer hamstrung by having to navigate through the nodes of an XML document. They can use XPath to locate elements and attributes in the document and use XSLT to provide a structure to the document. It's also worth mentioning that XSLT doesn't provide the inline styling itself in the way that CSS does. Instead, it relies on CSS and HTML to look after these aspects. So, XSLT is an intermediary and helps keep the content and structure of your web pages separate.

XSLT isn't universally popular, though, and, as with most Web technologies, there is a time and a place for it, reasons why and where you might consider using it, and reasons why you wouldn't use it. Let's consider some of the main reasons for using XSLT:

❑ It is more difficult in the DOM using JavaScript to transform one XML document into another.

❑ Document structure can be separated from design and content in XSLT, although this does depend on the design being done correctly.

❑ XSLT uses XPath to access nodes. This is better for performing queries and can enhance performance.

❑ XSLT is particularly well suited to convert data from non-XML formats into XML.

The reasons against XSLT are also quite persuasive:

❑ XSLT has a tendency to cause bloat in your applications. XSLT documents can be many thousands of lines long in more complex applications.

❑ It is quite complex. Whereas a designer can easily update the CSS without any programming knowledge, with XSLT, the designer is forced to come to grips with common programming structures. While your design and content are separated, the tasks a designer and developer perform become blurred.

❑   Despite the fact that using XPath to query documents can yield performance benefits, if you create large XSLT documents, then you are shovelling the load back on the client, which might
otherwise have been dealt with on the server. This can negatively affect performance

You are left with having to make a trade-off. XSLT can be of benefit when dealing with XML documents
returned from the server, but the moment they start becoming large and unwieldy is perhaps the
moment you should start to consider creating your XML documents on the server in a way that means
they require less manipulation.

XSLT Elements

XSLT has an element-based structure rather like all of the other mark-up languages you will be familiar
with (such as HTML and XML). A number of predefined elements can be used to create an XSLT style
sheet. Unfortunately, there's no quick way around them, and you do need to learn them to be able build
XSLT style sheets. This discussion provides a quick overview of each of the main elements that you will
need to use when building XSLT style sheets before you see an example of how to use them.

xsl:stylesheet

Every XSLT template begins with an XML declaration because they are all XML documents. After that,
there is an XSL style sheet declaration that contains the whole of the page. All other `xsl:directives`
should be contained in this element.

The `xsl:stylesheet` format is as follows:

```
<xsl:stylesheet version="1.0" xmlns:xsl="http://www.w3.org/1999/XSL/Transform">
   ... Page Content here ...
</xsl:stylesheet>
```

The `xsl:stylesheet` element specifies the version of XSLT being used and typically the namespace.
The version attribute is compulsory.

> The `xsl:transform` **tag can be used in place of the** `xsl:stylesheet` **element and
> works in exactly the same way.**

xsl:output

The next element commonly found in an XSLT document is the `xsl:output` element. The `xsl:output`
element is an optional element that is used to specify the format the document is transformed into. Here
is an example of the `<xsl:output>` element being used to create an XML document:

```
<xsl:output
     method="xml"
     omit-xml-declaration="yes"
     version="1.0"
```

```
        indent="no"
        encoding="UTF-8"
/>
```

You are able to specify such things as whether the XML declaration is added and the version attribute in the XML declaration. All of the attributes are optional. Table 8-1 describes the attributes.

Attribute Name	Description
method	Specifies the output format as XML, HTML, text, or name. The default is XML, unless the first child of the root is HTML (then it becomes HTML).
version	Specifies the version of the HTML or XML standard.
encoding	Specifies the type of encoding.
omit-xml-declaration	Specifies if the XML declaration should be included. The default is no.
standalone	Set to yes or no and defines whether the standalone declaration appears in the output.
doctype-public	Specifies the Public attribute of the DOCTYPE declaration.
doctype-system	Specifies the System attribute of the DOCTYPE declaration.
cdata-section-elements	Specifies a list of elements whose contents should be written in CDATA sections.
indent	Set to yes or no and specifies whether the document should be indented according to the nesting of the tags.
media-type	Specifies the MIME type of the output, normally text/xml.

You can just as easily use this element to specify a HTML document:

```
<xsl:output
    method="html"
    doctype-public="-//W3C//DTD HTML 4.01//EN"
    doctype-system="http://www.w3.org/TR/html4/strict.dtd"
/>
```

These directives are used to create the XML and DOCTYPE declarations that are present at the top of XML or HTML documents. Of course, you already have an XML declaration for the XSLT style sheet itself, but the xsl:output creates the declarations for the transformed document.

xsl:includes

If you want to include other XSL files in your XSL style sheet (such as classic ASP includes or PHP includes), then you can use the xsl:include format as follows:

```
<xsl:include href="../../../includes/var.xsl"/>
```

xsl:template, xsl:apply-templates, and xsl:call-template

So far, you have an XML declaration, a style sheet element, and an optional output element in the XSLT style sheet. None of these deal with the actual processing of the XML document. XSLT is a template-based language, and it uses a series of reusable templates in which fragments of the HTML or XML documents are created. Every document, though, needs a starting point at which the XSLT processor can begin. This will depend on how the `<xsl:template>` tags are specified. An `<xsl:template>` must either have a `match` attribute or a `name` attribute.

The Match Attribute

If the `<xsl:template>` has a `match` attribute, then it can be invoked with the `<xsl:apply-templates>` instruction. Quite commonly, if there is only one template that processes all nodes, then the `<xsl:apply-templates>` element is omitted and the page will work without it.

If you want to create the equivalent of a C#/VB.NET/`Page_Load()` method, or a script that is always executed, then you can set the `match` pattern to "/". This following fragment could be used to process every node in the XML document (depending on the content of the element):

```
<xsl:template match="/">
    ...
</xsl:template>
```

The match pattern can also be set to process only particular nodes in a document. Let's say that you want this to apply to a subsection of nodes using the following XML document:

```
<?xml version="1.0"?>
<cart>
  <book>
    <title>Beginning ASP.NET with CSharp</title>
    <quantity>1</quantity>
    <authors>Hart, Kauffman, Sussman, Ullman</authors>
    <ISBN>0764588508</ISBN>
    <price>39.99</price>
  </book>
  <book>
    <title>Beginning JavaScript 2nd Edition</title>
    <quantity>2</quantity>
    <authors>Wilton</authors>
    <ISBN>076455871</ISBN>
    <price>39.99</price>
  </book>
  <Total>119.97</Total>
</cart>
```

Then you could use the following setting of the `match` attribute:

```
<xsl:template match="book">
    ...
</xsl:template>
```

This means that the `book` elements in the cart would be processed by the template rule, and the `Total` element would be ignored. Anything that goes inside this element will automatically be processed according to the `match` pattern. With an HTML document you would place the outermost HTML tags that go in every document such as `<html>`, `<head>`, and `<body>`:

Most XSLT style sheets you will create will have the following format:

```
<?xml version="1.0"?>
<xsl:stylesheet version="1.0" xmlns:xsl="http://www.w3.org/1999/XSL/Transform">

    <xsl:output method="html" doctype-public="-//W3C//DTD HTML 4.01//EN"
        doctype-system="http://www.w3.org/TR/html4/strict.dtd" />

  <xsl:template match="/">
    <html>
        <head></head>
        <body>
            ... Content goes here ...
        </body>
    </html>
  </xsl:template>

</xsl:stylesheet>
```

The Name Attribute

XSLT can also reuse modular sections of code via templates. These templates are defined by setting the `name` attribute as follows:

```
<xsl:template name="MyTemplate">
    ...
</xsl:template>
```

If you want to call that particular template at any point, you would insert the following call to it:

```
<xsl:call-template name="MyTemplate"></xsl:call-template>
```

The two sets of templates are commonly used together in the page. The `match` attribute will specify an entry point into the document, and `<xsl:call-template>` will be placed inside the "main" template. It is quite common for one template then to call another one, and, in this way, many templates can be nested. It can, though, make the code very difficult to follow.

XSLT Parameters

With reusable sections of code such as methods and functions, you also need the ability to pass information into the structure. XSLT templates are no different. Parameters are defined using the `xsl:param` element:

```
<xsl:param name="MyParameter" />
```

Parameters can then be referenced in the document as follows:

```
$MyParameter
```

You are also able to pass parameters to templates using the `xsl:with-param` element:

```
<xsl:with-param name="current">
    ...
</xsl:with-param>
```

xsl:if

XSLT has a decision-making structure using the `xsl:if` element. The `xsl:if` element takes a single parameter `test`. Inside the `test` attribute, you specify an expression that determines whether to display that particular fragment of code.

The `xsl:if` format is as follows:

```
<xsl:if test="price &gt; 0">
    ...
</xsl:if>
```

The `test` can also contain more complex XPath instructions, as you will see later in this chapter in the discussion of XPath.

xsl:choose

XSLT doesn't have an `if-else` element format. Instead, for decision-making branches where you want to take either one branch or the other, it uses a different set of elements, `<xsl:choose>`, `<xsl:when>`, and `<xsl:otherwise>`. The `<xsl:choose>` element contains the other two elements. The `<xsl:when>` is used like the `<xsl:if>` tag and specifies the test. The `<xsl:otherwise>` element is used to specify the `else` case.

The `xsl:choose` format is as follows:

```
<xsl:choose>
    <xsl:when test="price &gt; 0">
        ...
    </xsl:when>
    <xsl:otherwise>
        ...
    </xsl:otherwise>
</xsl:choose>
```

If you want to emulate the `if {} else if {} else {}` structure, then you can simply place more `xsl:when` elements within the `<xsl:choose>` structure, as shown here:

```
<xsl:choose>
    <xsl:when test="price &lt; 5">
        ...
    </xsl:when>
    <xsl:when test="price &gt; 10">
        ...
    </xsl:when>
```

```
        <xsl:otherwise>
            ...
        </xsl:otherwise>
    </xsl:choose>
```

Here, the first condition is triggered if the value condition in `price` is less than 5, while the second condition is triggered if the price is greater than 10. The conditions where the price is between 5 and 10 will be handled by the `xsl:otherwise` clause.

Escaping XSLT Special Characters

One thing to note about the previous example is that XSLT follows XML rules for special characters. It is, therefore, quite fussy about some characters, and they will need escaping. There are only five, as shown in Table 8-2.

Character	Escape Code
&	&
<	<
>	>
"	"
'	'

xsl:for-each

XSL has a looping structure using `for-each`. This is especially useful for processing nodes in an XML document, given that you might not know how many particular elements there are.

The `xsl:for-each` structure has the following format:

```
<xsl:for-each select="//book">
    ...
</xsl:for-each>
```

The `xsl:for-each` element takes a `select` attribute. This again can take an XPath expression. Here, you have made a call to every `book` element. The `//` notation is what makes the call.

The `xsl:for-each` construct is commonly used in tandem with the `<xsl:if>` element. It has the same effect as saying for every tag in the document, if a particular condition is true, then display this tag. For example, if you wanted to display only the books whose `price` was above 35 dollars, you could use the following:

```
<xsl:for-each select="//book">
    <xsl:if test="price &gt; 35">
        ... Display Content here ...
    </xsl:if>
</xsl:for-each>
```

The `xsl:for-each` structure works for all intents and purposes like the `foreach` construct of C# or PHP.

xsl:value-of

One of the most frequently used tags in an XSL style sheet is the `xsl:value-of` tag. This is used to display the contents of a particular element or variable.

The `xsl:value-of` format takes the `select` attribute. You specify the name of the XML element or variable you want to display, as shown here:

```
<xsl:value-of select="price">
```

If this were done in the context of an `xsl:for-each` loop, then this would display the contents of every element with this element or attribute. For example, the following would display every `price` element for a `book` element:

```
<xsl:for-each select="//book">
      <xsl:value-of select="price"/>
</xsl:for-each>
```

You can also intersperse this code with HTML elements, so that it would insert the text into a table cell, as shown here:

```
<xsl:for-each select="//book">
      <td>
    <xsl:value-of select="price"/>
 </td>
</xsl:for-each>
```

xsl:sort

If you want to order the data you get back from an XML document, then you can use the `xsl:sort` tag and specify a particular element. For example, the following would return a list of books sorted according to `price`:

```
<xsl:for-each select="book">
 <xsl:sort select="price" />
   ... Page Content here ...
</xsl:for-each>
```

xsl:variable

Last, you are able to declare variables in XSLT that can then be referenced later in the template. Variables are created in the same way as with normal programming languages. You create a name and assign it a value. For example, to create a variable called `myvar` with a value of the `price` element multiplied by 10, you would use the following:

```
<xsl:variable name="myvar" select="price * 10" />
```

Then, to use it, you prefix it with a $ sign. To display the value of the variable, you would use the following:

```
<xsl:value-of select="$myvar" />
```

This concludes all the XSLT elements you need to get off the ground. There are plenty more, but to create simple style sheets and couple them with the XPath functionality this chapter examines, this will be more than enough.

XSLT relies on XPath to perform its arithmetic operations and to do its string formatting. XPath has a set of functions that can be called on to provide this functionality. These will be examined later in this chapter.

XSLT Support in the Main Browsers

As intimated in the introduction to this chapter, XSLT support has been a thorny issue when using the XSLT engines of the two main browsers. While they both support XSLT, the engines remain a little divergent in how they interpret the language. This is similar to the situation that persists with CSS, and it isn't helped by the fact that the XSLT standard is larger and more complex than the CSS one.

The current range of support is as follows:

❑   IE versions 5.5, 6, and 7

❑   Firefox 1 and 2, Netscape 6 (limited), 7, and 8

❑   Opera 9

All examples in this chapter will work in IE and Firefox, except where noted. These examples have not been tested on Opera.

Performing a Transform

While the XSLT language is the same for all browsers, despite the quirks an individual browser might have in the way it implements the semantics of the language, the act of transforming one document to another is where the two browsers diverge somewhat. The process of how the documents are transformed is broadly the same, but the JavaScript needed to perform the transform is different.

The steps are as follows:

1.   Load the XSL document.

2.   Load the XML document.

3.   Call a method to transform the XML document using the XSL style sheet.

Let's start by looking at how IE conducts this operation.

Performing a Transform Using IE

In IE, you must create two `ActiveXObjects`. For the examples in this chapter, these will both be of type `XMLDOM`, although there are alternative ActiveX objects such as

`MSXML2.FreeThreadedDomDocument.3.0` and `MSXML2.XSLTemplate`, which confer extra abilities such as the ability to pass parameters.

The first you load with an XML document, and the second with an XSL document (although, strictly speaking, the order in which you do this doesn't matter). You don't want them loaded asynchronously, so you set the `async` property to `false`.

There is a `transformNode` property of the `XMLDOM` object that takes a node (in this case, the `Document` object), processes it using the XSL style sheet, and returns the transformed XML document. The argument to the `transformNode` method can either be an XML document or a node of an XSL style sheet. Once you have saved the resulting transformation, you can write it to the screen, if desired.

The following code fragment loads an XML document called `Example.xml`, loads an XSL style sheet called `Example.xsl`, performs the transformation on the XML document using the style sheet, and saves the document in the variable `transform`. The code then searches the web page for an element with the `id` attribute `example` and replaces its `innerHTML` property with the transformed document.

```
//Load XML
var xml = new ActiveXObject("Microsoft.XMLDOM");
xml.async = false;
xml.load("Example.xml");

//Load XSL
var xsl = new ActiveXObject("Microsoft.XMLDOM");
xsl.async = false;
xsl.load("Example.xsl");

//Transform
var transform = xml.transformNode(xsl);

 //Write to screen
var spantag = document.getElementById("example");
spantag.innerHTML = transform;
```

Try It Out   Performing a Transform in IE

Let's run a quick example now in which you take a very simple XML document, perform a transform, and return the transformation as part of the web page. This example takes a list of hotels from an XML document and displays the name of the hotel and the price in an HTML table. If the price is under 175, then the price is highlighted in red.

You need four different items to do this: the XML document (and XSLT style sheet), an HTML web page, and a script. You'll want to concentrate primarily on the transformation that is performed. Note that this example will work only in IE; the next example will work in Mozilla.

1. Create an HTML page with the following code, and save it as `IETransform.htm`:

```
<html>
<head>
  <title>IE Transformation</title>
  <script type="text/javascript" src="IETransform.js"></script>
</head>
```

```
<body onload="Transform()">
<span id="example"></span>
</body>
</html>
```

2. Create a JavaScript page with the following code, and save it as `IETransform.js`:

```
function Transform()
{
        //Load XML
        var xml = new ActiveXObject("Microsoft.XMLDOM");
        xml.async = false;
        xml.load("Example.xml");

        //Load XSL
        var xsl = new ActiveXObject("Microsoft.XMLDOM");
        xsl.async = false;
        xsl.load("Example.xsl");

        //Transform
        var transform = xml.transformNode(xsl);

        //Insert item into web page
        var spantag = document.getElementById("example");
        spantag.innerHTML = transform;
}
```

3. Create an XML document with the following format, and save it as `Example.xml`:

```
<?xml version="1.0"?>
<hotels>
  <hotel>
    <name>La Splendide</name>
    <city>Paris</city>
    <price>200</price>
  </hotel>
  <hotel>
    <name>The Imperial</name>
    <city>New York</city>
    <price>150</price>
  </hotel>
</hotels>
```

4. Create an XSL document with the following format, and save it as `Example.xsl`:

```
<?xml version="1.0" encoding="utf-8"?>

<xsl:stylesheet version="1.0"
    xmlns:xsl="http://www.w3.org/1999/XSL/Transform">

  <xsl:output
    method="html"
    indent="yes"
    version="4.0" />

  <xsl:template match="/">
```

```
<table border="1">
   <xsl:for-each select="//hotel">
      <xsl:choose>
         <xsl:when test="number(price)&lt; 175">
            <tr >
               <td>
                  <xsl:value-of select="name"/>
               </td>
               <td style="background:red">
                  <xsl:value-of select="price"/>
               </td>
            </tr>
         </xsl:when>
         <xsl:otherwise>
            <tr>
               <td>
                  <xsl:value-of select="name"/>
               </td>
               <td>
                  <xsl:value-of select="price"/>
               </td>
            </tr>
         </xsl:otherwise>
      </xsl:choose>
   </xsl:for-each>
</table>

   </xsl:template>
</xsl:stylesheet>
```

5. Open `Transform.htm`, and view it in IE (Figure 8-1).

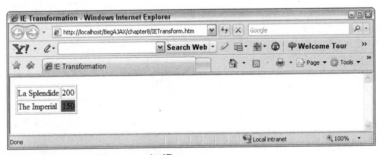

Figure 8-1: `Transform.htm` **in IE.**

How It Works

The JavaScript code follows four steps:

1. Load the XML document.

2. Load the XSLT style sheet.

3. Perform the transform.

4. Insert the contents of the transformation into the web page.

You have already learned about what the JavaScript code does, so now let's focus on the point where the transformation is performed. The call on the following lines of JavaScript takes you out of the JavaScript code and into the XSLT engine:

```
//Transform
var transform = xml.transformNode(xsl);
```

The first thing the XSLT engine encounters after the `output` tag is the `xsl:template` element. This has a `match` attribute, which matches the root element in the document. Next, you create a table with a border immediately inside the `xsl:template`:

```
<xsl:template match="/">
    <table border="1">
```

Then, you start with the `xsl:for-each` loop. You specify every `hotel` element, and inside that you position an `xsl:choose` structure. You say that when the content of the `price` element is smaller than 175, then you create a new table row with two cells in it. The first shows the name of the hotel, while the second displays the price with a red background.

```
<xsl:for-each select="//hotel">
  <xsl:choose>
    <xsl:when test="number(price)&lt; 175">
      <tr >
        <td>
          <xsl:value-of select="name"/>
        </td>
        <td style="background:red">
          <xsl:value-of select="price"/>
        </td>
      </tr>
    </xsl:when>
```

Otherwise, if the `price` element contains a value greater than 175, then you just display a table row and two table cells with the hotel name and price without any background color.

```
<xsl:otherwise>
  <tr>
    <td>
      <xsl:value-of select="name"/>
    </td>
    <td>
      <xsl:value-of select="price"/>
    </td>
  </tr>
</xsl:otherwise>
  </xsl:choose>
  </xsl:for-each>
  </table>
</xsl:template>
```

If you jump to the XML document, you can see that for the first `<hotel>` element, the price is 200, so this won't be displayed with a red background.

```
<hotel>
  <name>La Splendide</name>
  <city>Paris</city>
  <price>200</price>
</hotel>
```

For the second element, the price is less than 175, so it will be displayed with the background.

```
<hotel>
  <name>The Imperial</name>
  <city>New York</city>
  <price>150</price>
</hotel>
```

As the XSLT processor works through the page, it compiles a transformed version of the document. The final transformed document is as follows:

```
<!DOCTYPE html PUBLIC "-//W3C//DTD HTML 4.01//EN"
"http://www.w3.org/TR/html4/strict.dtd">
<table border="1\>
<tr>
<td>La Splendide</td>
<td>200</td>
</tr>
<tr>
<td>The Imperial</td>
<td style="background:red">150</td>
</tr>
</table>
```

Then, this is the HTML you assign to the `<span>` element, which is displayed on the page.

Performing a Transform in Firefox

To perform a transform using Firefox, you must use a slightly different method. Firefox doesn't support the ActiveX objects, and while it doesn't have a native XMLDOM object, it does support a native Document object, so you can use either this or the XMLHttpRequest object to load the XML document and XSL style sheets. As a result, the Firefox version is slightly longer, but not really any more complicated.

You start by creating a new instance of the XSLTProcessor object to process the style sheet. Then you create a new instance of the XMLHttpRequest object and load the XSL document. It doesn't matter whether you load the XML or XSL document first. The crucial difference is that you want the document loaded synchronously here. You don't want to have to wait and come back at a later point, as you need both the XML document and XSL style sheet fully loaded before you can do anything else. The XSL document is created and loaded in an identical way using Firefox's native DOM document object. The XSL style sheet is loaded using the importStylesheet method, which takes just one parameter, the style sheet itself.

Having imported the style sheet successfully, the transformation is performed using the `transformToFragment` method, which takes two parameters. The first is the XML document, and the second is the document object that "owns" the fragment. When placing the new fragment into the current web page, you can pass in the current `document` object.

```
var xsltProcessor = new XSLTProcessor();

//Load XSL
xslStylesheet = document.implementation.createDocument("", "doc",
null);

xslStylesheet.async = false;
xslStylesheet.load("Example.xsl");
xsltProcessor.importStylesheet(xslStylesheet);

//Load XML
xmlDoc = document.implementation.createDocument("", "doc", null);
xmlDoc.async = false;
xmlDoc.load("Example.xml");


//Transform
var fragment = xsltProcessor.transformToFragment(xmlDoc, document);
document.getElementById("example").appendChild(fragment);
```

The `appendChild` method can be used to add the fragment to an element on the web page in a true DOM-centric way.

As mentioned previously, the XSLT processor in Firefox doesn't function in exactly the same way as the one in IE. This means that the document resulting from a transformation performed in IE might be different from the exact same transformation performed in Firefox. This is something to bear in mind. Ensure that you construct your XSLT style sheets as simply as possible. The list of elements and functions that the Mozilla XSLT engine supports can be found at the following URL:

```
http://developer.mozilla.org/en/docs/Transforming_XML_with_XSLT
```

Further details can be found at the following URL:

```
http://developer.mozilla.org/en/docs/Using_the_Mozilla_JavaScript_interface_to_XSL_
Transformations
```

Try It Out   Performing a Transform in Firefox

This example takes the previous XML document and XSL style sheet and uses the Firefox XSLT processor to perform the transformation instead.

1. Open the web page `Transform` from the previous example; change it so that it now uses a script called `FFTransform.js`, and save it as `FFTransform.htm`.

```
<html>
<head>
```

```
<title>Firefox Transformation</title>
<script type="text/javascript" src="FFTransform.js"></script>
</head>
...
```

2. Create a new script called `FFTransform.js`, and add the following:

```
function Transform()
{
            var xsltProcessor = new XSLTProcessor();

        //Load XSL
        xslStylesheet = document.implementation.createDocument("", "doc",
null);

        xslStylesheet.async = false;
        xslStylesheet.load("Example.xsl");
        xsltProcessor.importStylesheet(xslStylesheet);

        //Load XML
        xmlDoc = document.implementation.createDocument("", "doc", null);
        xmlDoc.async = false;
        xmlDoc.load("Example.xml");


        //Transform
        var fragment = xsltProcessor.transformToFragment(xmlDoc, document);
        document.getElementById("example").appendChild(fragment);
}
```

3. Open `FFTransform.htm` in Firefox, and view it (Figure 8-2).

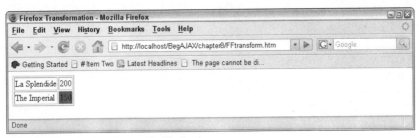

Figure 8-2: `Transform.htm` **in Firefox.**

How It Works

As you can see, the Firefox display is identical to the IE one. With simple style sheets, you are unlikely to run into differences between the two main browsers.

To create a cross-browser-compatible version of the code, you can simply append the two scripts together and use the `if (Window.ActiveXobject)` check that you have been using for the `XMLHttpRequest` object throughout this book.

Performing a Transform on the Server Side

One alternative to having to worry about cross-browser compatibility is to perform the transformation on the server side instead. The .NET Framework has its own native XSLT processor. Unfortunately, PHP doesn't natively support XSLT, although you can download an extension that uses Sablotron and expat libraries. These can both be found at www.gingerall.org/sablotron.html. Binaries are provided as well as source. Because you don't want to (whenever possible) download and install extra extensions, let's create an example version in .NET only.

Before creating an example, it's worth noting some points about the .NET Framework XSLT processor. The .NET Framework has two different versions, and these different versions support different processors. .NET Framework 1.0 and 1.1 support only `XslTransform`, which has been *deprecated* in .NET 2.0. .NET 2.0 introduces the `XslCompiledTransform` class, which is more pedantic in terms of how it parses and displays the XSL style sheet, but it allows step-by-step debugging of the XSLT style sheet in Visual Studio.NET.

> **"Deprecated" means that it has been marked for removal from future versions of .NET and that its use is discouraged. It doesn't mean that you can't use the method, however.**

The `XslCompiledTransform` is a faster engine and is to be preferred. There have been some problems with memory leaks and performance issues, though, that might need a patch from Microsoft. In the following example, you shouldn't encounter any such problems.

Try It Out   Performing a Transform Using .NET

Let's take the style sheet and XML document from the previous two examples and use .NET 2.0 to create an Ajax application that calls the .NET XSLT processor for you. It returns the example in a format that can be handled by the `XMLHttpRequest` object.

1. Open the web page `Transform` from the previous example, and change it so that it now uses a script called `NETTransform.js`.

```
<html>
<head>
  <title>.NET Transformation</title>
  <script type="text/javascript" src="NETTransform.js"></script>
</head>
...
```

2. Create a new script called `NETTransform.js`, save it as `NETTransform.htm`, and add the following:

```
var xHRObject = false;

if (window.XMLHttpRequest)
{
xHRObject = new XMLHttpRequest();
}
else if (window.ActiveXObject)
{
xHRObject = new ActiveXObject("Microsoft.XMLHTTP");
```

```
}

function Transform()
{
        xHRObject.open("GET", "NETTransform.aspx", true);
        xHRObject.onreadystatechange = getData;
        xHRObject.send(null);
}

function getData()
{
    if ((xHRObject.readyState == 4) &&(xHRObject.status == 200))
    {

        var spantag = document.getElementById("example").innerHTML =
xHRObject.responseText;
    }
}
```

3. Create a server-side page `NETTransform.aspx`, and add the following:

```
<%@ Page Language="C#" %>
<%@ import Namespace="System.Net" %>
<%@ import Namespace="System.IO" %>
<%@ import Namespace="System.Xml" %>
<%@ import Namespace="System.Xml.XPath" %>
<%@ import Namespace="System.Xml.Xsl" %>
<script language="C#" runat="server">

    void Page_Load(Object Sender, EventArgs e)
    {
        //Create the XslCompiledTransform object
        XslCompiledTransform xslDoc = new XslCompiledTransform();

        //Load the Xsl Stylesheet
        xslDoc.Load(Server.MapPath("Example.xsl"));

        //Perform the transformation
        xslDoc.Transform(Server.MapPath("Example.xml"), null, Response.Output);
    }
</script>
```

4. View the page `NETTransform.htm` in the browser (Figure 8-3).

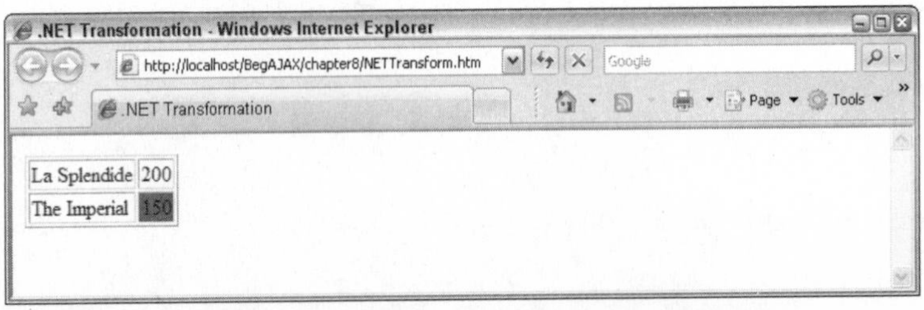

Figure 8-3: Viewing the page `Transform.htm` **in the browser.**

How It Works

This example doesn't have to use Ajax. It would be possible to simply call the NETTransform.aspx page directly and have it display the results to the page. Because this is an alternative to calling the client-side XSLT processors, however, the XMLHttpRequest object has been used to call the server and manage the results.

Using the .NET XSLT processor isn't that different from the previous client-side engines. You still have to follow the same steps. In .NET, it is necessary to create an XslCompiledTransform object first to read the XML document into. This is the object you will load the XSL style sheet into, using the Load method.

```
//Create the XslTransform object
XslCompiledTransform xslDoc = new XslCompiledTransform();

//Load the Xsl Stylesheet
xslDoc.Load(Server.MapPath("Example.xsl"));
```

Last, you perform the transform.

```
xslDoc.Transform(Server.MapPath("Example.xml"), null, Response.Output);
```

The Transform method of the XSL takes three arguments:

❑   The XML document (with the document name)

❑   The XSLTArgumentList object (which is empty)

❑   The location where to put the transformed document

Because you want it written to the Response.Stream, you set it to Response.Output. Once again, you can see that the document produced by the XSLT engine is identical to the ones produced by the IE and Mozilla XSLT processors. This won't always necessarily be the case. One option is that if the two client-side ones differ, you can create a server-side proxy to perform the transformations for you.

Now, let's create a more impressive example.

Creating an XSLT Style Sheet for a Shopping Cart

The shopping cart example in Chapter 3 was really rather rudimentary. You returned the title of the book and the quantity, but you didn't return any pricing information, and you didn't attempt to even title the products in the shopping cart.

You should go back and revisit that example. You are going to add information to the XML document such as the price, the ISBN number, and the authors. Now, you are not going to need all of this information (such as the ISBN number and the authors), but you will need some of it (such as the price), which you are going to want to total.

Ajax won't be used in this example because the intent is to concentrate on the XSL syntax first and the way in which it is used. Once you have mastered that, you will put these techniques into use in an improved version of the Ajax application. In this example, you will just generate a static version of the XML document, then display it using XSL.

Try It Out   **XSLT Shopping Cart Example**

You will need to create a `Chapter8` folder in the `BegAjax` directory for examples in this chapter. A couple of small graphics are being provided to go with these examples: `sbasket.gif` and `button.jpg`. These should be downloaded from the `www.wrox.com` site first and included in the same folder.

1. Create an HTML page, call it `staticxslt.htm`, and add the following code:

```
<html xmlns="http://www.w3.org/1999/xhtml" >
<head>
  <script type="text/javascript" src="StaticXslt.js"></script>
    <link id="Link1" rel="stylesheet"  href="Cart.css" type="text/css" />
</head>
<body>
<a href="javascript:GenerateCart();" >Add to Shopping Cart</a>
<br /><br />
<span id="cart" ></span>
</body>
</html>
```

2. Create a JavaScript page, call it `staticxslt.js`, and add the following code:

```
function loadDocument(fileName)
{
    var xmlDoc = window.ActiveXObject ? new ActiveXObject("MSXML2.DOMDocument.3.0")
:

document.implementation.createDocument("","",null);
    xmlDoc.async = false;
    xmlDoc.load(fileName);
    return xmlDoc;
}

function getTransformedHTML(xmlDoc, xslDoc) {
    var html = "";
    if (window.XSLTProcessor)
    {
        var xsltProc = new XSLTProcessor();
        xsltProc.importStylesheet(xslDoc);
        var fragment = xsltProc.transformToFragment(xmlDoc, document);
        html = new XMLSerializer().serializeToString(fragment);
    }
    else if (window.ActiveXObject)
    {
        html = xmlDoc.transformNode(xslDoc);
    }
    return html;
```

```
}

Function AddRemoveItem() {}

function GenerateCart()
{
    var xmlDoc = loadDocument("cart.xml");
    var xslDoc = loadDocument("cart.xsl");
    document.getElementById("cart").innerHTML = getTransformedHTML(xmlDoc, xslDoc);
}
```

3. Create the following XML page, and save it as `cart.xml`:

```
<?xml version="1.0"?>
<cart>
  <book>
    <Title>Beginning ASP.NET with CSharp</Title>
    <Quantity>1</Quantity>
    <Authors>Hart, Kauffman, Sussman, Ullman</Authors>
    <ISBN>0764588508</ISBN>
    <Price>39.99</Price>
  </book>
  <book>
    <Title>Beginning JavaScript 2nd Edition</Title>
    <Quantity>2</Quantity>
    <Authors>Wilton</Authors>
    <ISBN>076455871</ISBN>
    <Price>39.99</Price>
  </book>
  <Total>119.97</Total>
</cart>
```

4. Create the following XSL page, and save it as `cart.xsl`:

```
<?xml version="1.0" encoding="utf-8"?>

<xsl:stylesheet version="1.0"
    xmlns:xsl="http://www.w3.org/1999/XSL/Transform">

  <xsl:output
    method="html"
    indent="yes"
    version="4.0" />

  <xsl:template match="/">
    <table id="shoppingcart">
      <xsl:call-template name="DisplayCart"></xsl:call-template>
    </table>
  </xsl:template>

  <xsl:template name="DisplayCart">

      <thead class="head">
        <tr>
```

```
            <td colspan="4" align="center">Shopping Basket <img
              src="sbasket.gif"></img>
            </td>
          </tr>
      </thead>
<xsl:if test="sum(//book/Quantity)&gt;0">
  <tr>
  <td class="border">Item</td>
  <td class="border">Qty</td>
  <td class="border">Price</td>
  <td></td>
  </tr>
</xsl:if>

<xsl:for-each select="//book">
  <tr>
    <td class="border2" width="75px">
      <xsl:value-of select="Title"/>
    </td>
    <td class="border2" align="center">
      <xsl:value-of select="Quantity"/>
    </td>
    <td class="border2">
      $<xsl:value-of select="(Price) * (Quantity)"/>
    </td>
    <td class="border2">
      <a href="javascript:AddRemoveItem('Remove');">
        <img src='button.jpg'/>
      </a>
    </td>
  </tr>
</xsl:for-each>
<tr >
  <td colspan='4' class="border2"> </td>

</tr>
<xsl:choose>
  <xsl:when test="number(//book/Quantity)>0">
    <tr>
      <td colspan="2" class="border2">Total:</td>

      <td class="border">
        $
        <xsl:value-of select="(//Total)"/>
      </td>
      <td class="border2"> </td>
    </tr>
  </xsl:when>
  <xsl:otherwise>
    <tr>
      <td colspan = "4" class="border2">Your Basket Is Empty</td>
    </tr>
  </xsl:otherwise>
```

```
        </xsl:choose>
      <tr >
        <td colspan="4" class="border2"> </td>

      </tr>
    </xsl:template>
  </xsl:stylesheet>
```

5. Create a CSS page called `cart.css`, and add the following code:

```
table
{
     background-color: beige;
     border: 1px solid #e4ddca;
}
A IMG
{
     border:0px;
}
tr, td
{
     font-family: Verdana;
     height:15px;
     font-size:75%;
     margin:2px 0px 0px 0px;
     padding:0px 0px 0px 5px;
}
.border
{
     font-weight: bold;
     text-align:center;
}
.border2
{
     background: beige;
}
.head
{
     font-family: Verdana;
     height:15px;
     vertical-align:middle;
     background:#665D43;
     color: beige;
     font-weight: bold;
}
```

6. Open `staticXSLT.htm` in the browser, and click the Add to Shopping Cart button (Figure 8-4).

7. Now, go back to `cart.xml`, remove all of the lines except the following, and then save it:

```
<?xml version="1.0"?>
  <cart>
  </cart>
```

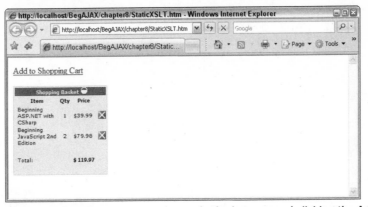

Figure 8-4: Opening `staticXSLT.htm` in the browser and clicking the Add to Shopping Cart button.

8. Open `staticXSLT.htm` in the browser again, and click the Add to Shopping Cart button once more (Figure 8-5).

Figure 8-5: Clicking the Add to Shopping Cart button again.

How It Works

You've created a style sheet that displays the shopping cart as a component. You have used both XSLT and CSS to provide a more sympathetic front end to the shopping cart.

What happens is that the HTML page has a link that calls the `GenerateCart()` function in the JavaScript code. The code loads the XML and XSL files, performs a transformation on them, and writes the results back to the web page. The code has a couple more functions in it. The first function provides a very quick way to load an XML document and XSL document in a browser-compatible way:

```
function loadDocument(fileName)
{
    var xmlDoc = window.ActiveXObject ? new ActiveXObject("MSXML2.DOMDocument.3.0")
    :

document.implementation.createDocument("","",null);
    xmlDoc.async = false;
```

```
        xmlDoc.load(fileName);
        return xmlDoc;
    }
```

You pass the filename in as parameter, and, depending on whether you are using IE or Firefox to browse the page, you create either an `MSXML2.DOMDocument` object or Firefox's native `Document` object. These are loaded synchronously, as before.

The final function is used to extract the transformed HTML. The Firefox implementation requires you to create an instance of the processor and import the style sheets, then serialize the HTML to a string before you can add it to the page, whereas the IE version allows you to simply transform the node:

```
function getTransformedHTML(xmlDoc, xslDoc) {
    var html = "";
    if (window.XSLTProcessor)
    {
        var xsltProc = new XSLTProcessor();
        xsltProc.importStylesheet(xslDoc);
        var fragment = xsltProc.transformToFragment(xmlDoc, document);
        html = new XMLSerializer().serializeToString(fragment);
    } else if (window.ActiveXObject) {
        html = xmlDoc.transformNode(xslDoc);
    }
    return html;
}
```

Let's concentrate now on the transformation that is performed because it is rather more complex than the previous ones. After the XML declaration comes the `xsl:stylesheet` root element that contains all the other XSLT elements and the `xsl:output` element that specifies the output as HTML. The first template is the general template that matches the root node. Inside this, you create an HTML table. Inside the table, you have a call to another template, `DisplayCart`.

```
<xsl:template match="/">
    <table id="shoppingcart">
      <xsl:call-template name="DisplayCart"></xsl:call-template>
    </table>
  </xsl:template>
```

The table has corresponding reference in CSS. This is the set of styles you use to create a small beige box with a 1-pixel-wide border around the edges.

```
table
{
    background-color: beige;
    border: 1px solid #e4ddca;
}
```

Between them, the `DisplayCart` template and the CSS do all the actual work. The first item in the `DisplayCart` template is the table header, `<thead>` element, which contains the olive green header for the shopping basket.

```
        <thead class="head">
          <tr>
```

```
            <td colspan="4" align="center">Shopping Basket <img
              src="sbasket.gif"></img>
            </td>
          </tr>
        </thead>
```

The `<thead>` element references the style sheet class `head`.

```
.head
{
 font-family: Verdana;
      height:15px;
      vertical-align:middle;
      background:#665D43;
      color: beige;
      font-weight: bold;
}
```

The `head` element sets the font size, font color, font height, vertical alignment, background color, and weighting of the heading. You create a single row in the `<thead>` element, a single cell containing the text, and a shopping basket image. There are no XSL declarations in this section.

The next section of the XSLT style sheet deals with the subheader that is displayed only in the event that there is something in the basket.

```
<xsl:if test="sum(//book/Quantity)&gt;0">
<tr>
        <td class="border">Item</td>
        <td class="border">Qty</td>
        <td class="border">Price</td>
        <td></td>
</tr>
</xsl:if>
```

The subheader displays the words "Item," "Qty," and "Price" in the table columns conditionally if there is something in the basket. To test that there is something in the basket, you use a simple XPath expression. The expression sums all the numbers in the `<Quantity>` element belonging to a `<book>` element. If it returns a number that is greater than zero, then you can deduce there is something in the basket and then display the subheader. Logically speaking, this means that if there is one item with a quantity greater than zero, then there must be something in the basket. You know this to be true because if there aren't any items in the basket, then there are no `<book>` or `<quantity>` elements. Creating XPath expressions will be examined in much more detail after this example.

Once you have displayed the header and subheader, you can get down to the task of displaying each of the items in the shopping basket. This is done using an `xsl:for-each` loop. You assign the `select` attribute an XPath expression that references every book node in the XML document. It says, for each node, display a single table row with four columns.

```
<xsl:for-each select="//book">
    <tr>
      <td class="border2" width="75px">
        <xsl:value-of select="Title"/>
```

```
        </td>
        <td class="border2" align="center">
          <xsl:value-of select="Quantity"/>
        </td>
        <td class="border2">
          $<xsl:value-of select="(Price) * (Quantity)"/>
        </td>
        <td class="border2">
          <a href="javascript:AddRemoveItem('Remove');">
            <img src='button.jpg'/>
          </a>
        </td>
      </tr>
  </xsl:for-each>
```

The first column displays the book title. You use the xsl:value-of element to display the contents of each <title> element. The table cell has a style attached to it, border2, which simply sets the table cell's background color to beige. The second column displays the quantity of the item you have in the basket, using the xsl:value-of element. Once again, the same style is applied.

The third column displays the total price of that particular item in the basket. This value isn't directly available from the XML document, but it is indirectly available. You want to display the total price in that row of the books, so if there were one book, it would be 39.99, and if there were two, it would be 79.98, and so on. To do this, you create an XPath expression that takes the Price element and the Quantity element and multiplies them. The xsl:value-of element is used to display the final result.

In the last column, you display the link to remove an item. Rather than displaying a text hyperlink, to keep the shopping cart small and unobtrusive, a small button image has been created with a cross that should intuitively indicate to anyone that this will remove an item from the basket. The <a> link calls the AddRemoveItem method in the JavaScript. This link is not functional in this example because you haven't plugged it back into the main Ajax application yet.

At the bottom of the cart, you have another decision to make. Depending on whether there is anything in the shopping cart, you will choose to display a total of the items or a message indicating that the shopping basket is empty. To do this, an xsl:choose construct has been used. Inside the xsl:choose statement are two possible outcomes. In the xsl:when tag, you perform the same test as you did earlier in the code to see if there are any values in the <Quantity> element. If there are, you display a total using the Total element from the XML document.

```
        <xsl:choose>
          <xsl:when test="sum(//book/Quantity)&gt;0">
            <tr>
              <td colspan="2" class="border2">Total:</td>

              <td class="border">
                $
                <xsl:value-of select="(//Total)"/>
              </td>
              <td class="border2"> </td>
            </tr>
          </xsl:when>
          <xsl:otherwise>
```

```
        <tr>
          <td colspan = "4" class="border2">Your Basket Is Empty</td>
        </tr>
      </xsl:otherwise>
    </xsl:choose>
    <tr >
      <td colspan="4" class="border2"> </td>

    </tr>
  </xsl:template>
```

The xsl:otherwise case handles all other possibilities and displays a table row and single cell containing the "your basket is empty" message. After that, you display a single blank row underneath the row containing the total for aesthetic purposes, and you close the template.

Note that you did not use XPath here to derive the total, even though you can. What is contained in the Price element is not the value you want to use, and using XPath to perform anything more than the most basic arithmetic functions can create a logistical headache in the XSLT (such as how do you multiply two values taken from other transient XPath expressions). In other words, when you multiplied the price * quantity to get the price for a particular row, it wasn't stored anywhere, and retrieving it from the XPath is more complex than just calculating it on the server side and writing the value as a new element into the XML document.

Because this discussion seems to be running more and more into XPath expressions, it's time to consider exactly how to create them and what they can be used for.

XPath and Its Purpose

XSLT is used primarily to select parts of an input document for formatting by the XSLT style sheet. In addition, it can be used to provide arithmetic functions and string formatting and to add Boolean conditions to an expression. XPath's role is somewhat analogous to SQL, in that you create a short expression used to retrieve data from the existing data source.

The XPath specification found at www.w3.org/TR/xpath describes XPath as an expression language (in other words, not a full-fledged programming language). XPath doesn't allow you to create or manipulate the existing data. It is simply used to query it.

XPath, like XSLT, has an important role to play in Ajax applications. The code used in Chapter 3 to select parts of the XML using JavaScript and the DOM took the following format:

```
var header = serverResponse.getElementsByTagName("book");
...
spantag.innerHTML += " " + header[0].firstChild.text;
spantag.innerHTML += " " + header[0].lastChild.text + " " + "<a
            href='javascript:AddRemoveItem(\"Remove\");'>Remove Item</a>";
```

You were restricted to selecting elements via either the getElementById method or getElementsByTagName, then using the firstChild, lastChild and nextSibling methods to find your way around the DOM. Now, while these methods undoubtedly work, it's a little like being blindfolded and getting someone to direct you to take a walk. It can be a little clumsy and inefficient, to put it mildly. XPath is very useful in quickly isolating and ascertaining elements (or subsets of elements) and the values they contain, and returning these results directly to the XSLT style sheet rather than the JavaScript or web page. This, in turn, can lead to a page being more quickly created and increasing your application's performance. XPath contains excellent facilities for retaining the context of where you are in an XML document with regard to other elements and nodes.

As with XSLT, this discussion only skims the surface and demonstrates just a small set of functions to allow you to get around in it.

Basic XPath Functionality

You've already learned a bit about XPath in the XSLT examples. It's unavoidable because when you use one language, you end up having to use the other. The examples that follow also use XSLT to demonstrate the workings of XPath.

This examination splits up the discussion of XPath into two broad sections. The first is the terminology needed to use XPath expressions, and the second goes through some of the most useful of the XPath functions.

XPath Expressions

The Microsoft Developer's Network (MSDN) documentation divides the XPath expressions into five basic types:

❑ Current context

❑ Document root

❑ Root element

❑ Recursive descent

❑ Specific element

Let's have a look very briefly at each. Because it makes it easier to visualize, let's use the following XML document from the XML shopping cart to provide examples:

```xml
<?xml version="1.0"?>
<cart>
  <book>
    <Title>Beginning ASP.NET with CSharp</Title>
    <Quantity>1</Quantity>
    <Authors>Hart, Kauffman, Sussman, Ullman</Authors>
    <ISBN>0764588508</ISBN>
    <Price>$39.99</Price>
  </book>
  <book>
    <Title>Beginning JavaScript 2nd Edition</Title>
    <Quantity>2</Quantity>
```

```
      <ISBN>076455871</ISBN>
      <Price>$39.99</Price>
    </book>
    <Total>119.97</Total>
  </cart>
```

Each of the elements in the XML document can be referred to individually in an XPath expression.

Current Context

The *current context* is the current element you are looking at or dealing with. This, as you've already seen, is referenced using just the node name. For example, to use the current value of the `Price` element, you would use the following:

```
Price
```

It can also be referenced using the following syntax with a period followed by a forward slash as well:

```
./Price
```

The XPath expression to select the current value of the `Price` element in the `xsl:value-of` tag, for example, would be as follows:

```
<xsl:value-of select="Price">
...
```

If there were many `Price` elements in the XML document and this expression were called outside of any `xsl:for-each` loops, then this would return the value in the first `price` element ($39.99). If it were called in an `xsl:for-each` construct, then it would return the value of each element in turn, depending on where in the loop you were.

Document Root

The *document root* is a node. To reference the document root node, you would use a single slash in front of the node and indicate that you want to select the node at the root of the tree to be used as the current context.

```
/cart
```

This would return the `<cart>` with the `<book />` element with the `<Title />` child element, which, in turn, contains the "`Beginning ASP.NET with CSharp`" text node.

Root Element

To use the *root element* as your context, the XPath expression is a single slash followed by an asterisk.

```
/*
```

This would return a reference to the `<cart>` element in the example XML document because this is the root element.

Recursive Descent

Recursive descent might sound like a rather worrying term, but you've already seen this in action when you used an `xsl:for-each` loop. You used it to indicate each item in the loop as follows:

```
//book
```

It is used to include zero or more levels of hierarchy in a search, and it depends on the context of where it is used in the document. So, it will include all of the book elements within the XML document.

It can also be used to isolate groups of elements further down the hierarchy. If you were interested in only the `<Price>` elements of each book, you could use the following:

```
//book/Price
```

You could insert this into an `xsl:if` term, for example, to test each `<price>` element to see whether it was greater than zero:

```
<xsl:if test="sum(//book/Price) &gt; 0">
```

Specific Elements or Items

If you want to use XPath to specify an individual item or element, again, you've already seen an example of this in action. If you want to specify a particular item where there may be one or more items, then use the following terminology:

```
book/Price
```

Each of these items is to be used in the context of an XSLT tag attribute.

XPath Functions

In addition to the syntax for expression handling, XPath also provides a number of functions. These are often what you will be using XPath for. Let's look at some of the most commonly used functions now.

The number Function

The `number` function is used to convert a value to a double-precision floating-point number, the equivalent of a double data type. This is useful if you have a variable that has a numerical value (such as a Boolean value), but that is not immediately recognizable as a number. Sometimes it can be used as a fail-safe in your code, if you're not 100 percent sure about the format of data being returned in the XML document.

For example, you could use it as follows to confirm whether a `price` element had returned a numerical value. The `number` function will return the value NaN (not a number) if the value isn't numerical.

```
<xsl:if test="string(number(Price)) = 'NaN'">
```

Then, you would display the `Price` only if there were a value for the price. If, for example, a particular book had been deleted, then there might be no given price, so you could use this to display a "Not

Applicable" or "Not Available" message instead. The XPath `string` function is used to convert the result of the `number` function into a string. There is a similar function called `boolean` that converts the result of an expression into a Boolean value.

The position Function

The `position` function can be used to see whether you are at the beginning or the end of a particular sequence. The function returns the position of the context node in context node-set. While the `position` function has many uses, one useful function it provides is that it can be used within loops, to discover where you are in a particular loop:

If you wanted, for example, to add a series of words (such as in a menu), each delimited by a "|" (pipe) character, then you could create an XSLT function to test to see if your current context in the loop wasn't last, and then to display the pipe character, as shown here:

```
<xsl:for-each select="//book">
 <xsl:if test="position() != last()">
                    |

    </xsl:if>
</xsl:for-each>
```

The count Function

The `count` function takes a node-set as its argument and returns the number of nodes in the node-set. For example, if you wanted to return the number of book elements in the document (2), then you would use the following example:

```
<xsl:value-of select="count(//book)"/>
```

String Formatting

Here's a not-too-well-kept secret for you. XPath isn't one of the best languages for performing string formatting. You're better off trying to do the formatting elsewhere, such as on the server beforehand, if possible. Most of XPath's functionality for locating sections of strings boils down to the single `substring` function, and it can make performing slice-ups of your strings like a tough crossword or logic puzzle. Some commonly used XPath string expressions are as follows:

❑   `substring` — Returns part of a string value

❑   `concat` — Takes two or more string arguments and appends them end to end

XPath 2.0 also introduces a `replace()` function, but currently no modern browser supports this standard.

To create a substring of "concat" that contains just the word "cat," you would use the following:

```
substring("concat", 4,3)
```

Arithmetic Functions

You can use the normal arithmetic operators such as plus, minus, multiplication, and division operators, as well as using brackets to denominate precedence or operations in XPath expressions. In addition, here is a list of some of XPath's most useful arithmetic functions:

❑ sum — Returns the total of numbers from a node-set of numbers

❑ round — Rounds a number to the closest integer (for example, 3.3 goes to 3 and 4.7 goes to 5)

❑ ceiling — Rounds a number to the closest higher integer (for example, 1.2 goes to 2)

❑ floor — Rounds a number to the closest lower integer (for example, 3.9 goes to 3)

The arithmetic functions are all fairly self-explanatory. Consider the following use of the sum function:

```
sum (//Price)
```

This will be a sum of the price elements in the XML document.

You could use these on the contents of elements. If, for example, you wanted to offer a discount to users who spent more than $100, then you could construct the following XSLT branch to bracket the desired functionality:

```
<xsl:if test="sum(//Total) &gt; 100">
...
</xsl:if>
```

XPath 2.0 adds the following functions:

❑ max — Returns the maximum value from a node-set

❑ min — Returns the minimum value from a node-set

❑ avg — Returns the average value from a node-set

These functions, though, are not supported in IE.

Logical Functions

In XPath, the logical operators are simply the words that represent the operations, and the logical values are the words themselves.

❑ not — Returns true if the value is false, and vice versa

❑ true — Returns true

❑ false — Returns false

The logical operators in XPath are used in the same way as they are in normal programming languages: to join together series of expressions, to provide more complex sets of queries.

❑ and

❑ or

For example, if you wanted to add a further discount to the customers who bought more than three separate items and $100 worth of books, then the following XSLT joins two expressions:

```
<xsl:if test="(price &gt; 100) and (quantity &gt; 3)">
...
</xsl:if>
```

Querying in an XML Document Using XPath

You've already compiled a reasonable set of XPath functions for your toolkit. Let's dive in and create a quick example that relies on XPath to do the work for you.

Using Xpath to Query an XML Document

In this short example, you are going to use XPath to perform some quick manipulation of some runners' results in a race (such as working out the average time and ensuring that the data is formatted to show the times correctly). To make matters a little more difficult, the results are supplied only in a value of total seconds for each runner. This might make it slightly artificial, but it allows you to use some extra processing with XPath to display the data as you want to see it.

1. Create a new HTML file called XPath.htm, and add the following:

```html
<html>
<head>
  <title>XPath Example</title>
  <script type="text/javascript" src="Xpath.js"></script>
</head>
<body onload="Transform()">
<span id="example"></span>
</body>
</html>
```

2. Create a JavaScript file called Xpath.js, and add the following:

```javascript
function loadDocument(fileName)
{
    var xmlDoc = window.ActiveXObject ? new ActiveXObject("MSXML2.DOMDocument.3.0")
:

document.implementation.createDocument("","",null);
    xmlDoc.async = false;
    xmlDoc.load(fileName);
    return xmlDoc;
}

function getTransformedHTML(xmlDoc, xslDoc) {
    var html = "";
    if (window.XSLTProcessor)
    {
        var xsltProc = new XSLTProcessor();
        xsltProc.importStylesheet(xslDoc);
        var fragment = xsltProc.transformToFragment(xmlDoc, document);
        html = new XMLSerializer().serializeToString(fragment);
    }
    else if (window.ActiveXObject)
    {
        html = xmlDoc.transformNode(xslDoc);
    }
```

```
      return html;
}

function Transform()
{
   var xmlDoc = loadDocument("runners.xml");
   var xslDoc = loadDocument("runners.xsl");
   document.getElementById("example").innerHTML = getTransformedHTML(xmlDoc,
xslDoc);
}
```

3. Create an XML file called `runners.xml`:

```
<?xml version="1.0"?>
<runners>
  <runner>
    <name>John Doe</name>
    <totalseconds>3274</totalseconds>
  </runner>
  <runner>
    <name>Joe Bloggs</name>
    <totalseconds>3314</totalseconds>
  </runner>
  <runner>
    <name>Jean Blanc</name>
    <totalseconds>3305</totalseconds>
  </runner>
  <runner>
    <name>Hans Schwarz</name>
    <totalseconds>3256</totalseconds>
  </runner>
  <runner>
    <name>Pedro Blanco</name>
    <totalseconds>3301</totalseconds>
  </runner>
</runners>
```

4. Create an XSLT style sheet called `runners.xsl`, and add the following:

```
<?xml version="1.0" encoding="utf-8"?>

<xsl:stylesheet version="1.0"
    xmlns:xsl="http://www.w3.org/1999/XSL/Transform">

  <xsl:output
    method="html"
    indent="yes"
    version="4.0" />

  <xsl:template match="/">
    <table border="1">
      <thead>
```

```
      <tr>
        <td>Position</td>
        <td>Name</td>
        <td>Time</td>
      </tr>
    </thead>
    <xsl:for-each select="//runner">
      <xsl:sort select="totalseconds"/>
      <tr>
        <td>
          <xsl:value-of select="position()"/>
        </td>
        <td>
          <xsl:value-of select="name"/>
        </td>
        <td>
          <xsl:value-of select="floor(totalseconds div 60)"/>.
          <xsl:choose>
            <xsl:when test ="(totalseconds mod 60) &gt; 9">
              <xsl:value-of select="(totalseconds mod 60)"/>
            </xsl:when>
            <xsl:otherwise>
                0<xsl:value-of select="(totalseconds mod 60)"/>
            </xsl:otherwise>
          </xsl:choose>
        </td>
      </tr>
    </xsl:for-each>
    <tr>
      <td>Average Time:</td>
      <td>
      </td>
      <td>
        <xsl:variable name="avgtime" select="sum(//totalseconds) div
        count(//runner)"/>
        <xsl:value-of select="floor($avgtime div 60)"/>.
          <xsl:choose>
            <xsl:when test ="($avgtime mod 60) &gt; 9">
              <xsl:value-of select="($avgtime mod 60)"/>
            </xsl:when>
            <xsl:otherwise>
                0<xsl:value-of select="($avgtime mod 60)"/>
            </xsl:otherwise>
          </xsl:choose>
      </td>
    </tr>
  </table>
  </xsl:template>

</xsl:stylesheet>
```

5. View Xpath.htm in your browser (Figure 8-6).

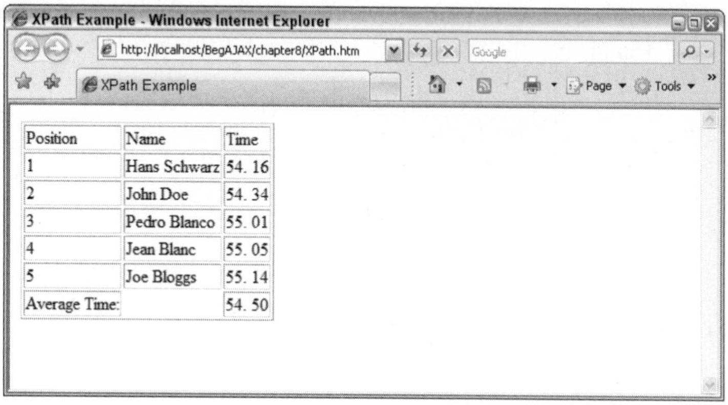

Figure 8-6: Viewing `Xpath.htm` **in the browser.**

How It Works

The JavaScript and HTML you have used to create the page and perform the transform are the same as the previous example, so let's not discuss them any further. Let's look at the XSLT style sheet from an XPath point of view. You start by using the recursive descent notation to specify each and every `<runner>` element in the XML document. XPath has no capability to sort results, so you've had to borrow an XSLT sort tag, using the `totalseconds` element.

```
<xsl:for-each select="//runner">
  <xsl:sort select="totalseconds"/>
```

In the first column, you want to display positioning information. No information like this exists in the XML document, however. You know that the sort will display the runners in order in the `xsl:for-each` loop, so you simply use the XPath `position()` function to return the numerical position in the loop:

```
<tr>
  <td>
    <xsl:value-of select="position()"/>
  </td>
```

In the second cell, you use the XPath current context notation to display the current value of the `name` element. This will change for each element in the document.

```
<td>
  <xsl:value-of select="name"/>
</td>
```

The third column displays the time of the runner. Of course, to display the time of the runner as a total of seconds isn't particularly useful, so you need to change that to display the minutes and seconds. You have to obtain these two values separately.

To obtain the minutes value, the `totalseconds` element was divided by 60 and you used the `floor` function to provide the lowest number of minutes. Most programming languages have an operator that does this for you, and, indeed, XPath 2.0 introduces the `idiv` operator. For IE, though, this isn't an option.

The second value is the seconds, which is just the leftover number of seconds calculated via the `modulo` operator. One last hiccup stands in the way, which is that if the number of seconds is less than 10, you can end up displaying the time such as 54.9 instead of 54.09. To get around this, you check to see if the remainder left over from `totalseconds` calculation divided by 60 is less than or equal to 9. If it is, you append an extra zero; otherwise, you do nothing.

```
<td>
   <xsl:value-of select="floor(totalseconds div 60)"/>.
   <xsl:choose>
     <xsl:when test ="(totalseconds mod 60) &gt; 9">
        <xsl:value-of select="(totalseconds mod 60)"/>
     </xsl:when>
     <xsl:otherwise>
          0<xsl:value-of select="(totalseconds mod 60)"/>
     </xsl:otherwise>
   </xsl:choose>
 </td>
</tr>
</xsl:for-each>
```

XPath 2.0 also provides an `avg` function, but again, as no current browser supports it, you don't have access to this function. This means you have to be slightly more elaborate about how you calculate the average. The average is calculated by taking the value from each and every `totalseconds` element and dividing it by the number of runners. You can return the number of runners by using the `count()` function of XPath to count all the elements. Both times, you use the recursive descent (`//`) notation to identify all elements in the document. Then, once you have the average `totalseconds` per runner, you can use the same process as before to extract the minutes and the seconds, then display them in the table.

```
<tr>
  <td>Average Time:</td>
  <td>
  </td>
  <td>
    <xsl:variable name="avgtime" select="sum(//totalseconds) div
     count(//runner)"/>
    <xsl:value-of select="floor($avgtime div 60)"/>.
      <xsl:choose>
        <xsl:when test ="($avgtime mod 60) &gt; 9">
          <xsl:value-of select="($avgtime mod 60)"/>
        </xsl:when>
        <xsl:otherwise>
            0<xsl:value-of select="($avgtime mod 60)"/>
        </xsl:otherwise>
      </xsl:choose>
```

As you can see, XPath's limitations mean that even providing straightforward functions such as displaying the time can prove quite troublesome. Sometimes, though, developers are not in a position to argue. They just receive the XML data, and they have to make do. In these cases, developers can choose to manipulate it in the XSLT or in the JavaScript, and quite often, many opt to use XPath to process it in the XSLT.

Amending the Shopping Cart Example to Use XSLT and Ajax

You are now at the point where you can combine these languages in the shopping cart example to enable the shopping cart as a working application that allows you to add and remove items, and that uses the XSLT style sheet and CSS rules to render the shopping cart in a more impressive design.

Try It Out   **Making the Shopping Cart Example Interactive**

You will combine code used from Chapter 3, the original shopping cart, and amend some code presented earlier in this chapter to create your working Ajax application.

1. Open `Catalogue1.htm` that you created in Chapter 3. (If you didn't, don't worry because the whole code is provided here.)

```html
<html xmlns="http://www.w3.org/1999/xhtml" >
<head>
    <link id="Link1" rel="stylesheet"  href="Cart.css" type="text/css" />
    <script type="text/javascript" src="ShoppingCart.js"></script>
</head>
<body>
<form id="form1" method="post" action="cartdisplay.aspx">
<br/>
<img id="cover" src="begaspnet.jpg" />
<br />
<br />
<b>Book:</b><span id="book">Beginning ASP.NET with CSharp</span><br />
<b>Authors: </b><span id="authors"> Hart, Kauffman, Sussman, Ullman</span>
<br /><b>ISBN: </b><span id="ISBN">0764588508</span>
<br /><b>Price: </b><span id="price">$39.99</span>
<br /><br />
<a href=" "onclick="AddRemoveItem('Add');" >Add to Shopping Cart</a>
<br /><br />
<span id="cart" ></span>
</form>
</body>
</html>
```

2. Open `Cart.js` that you created earlier in this chapter, and amend the following. Save it as `ShoppingCart.js`. Note that you use this version because it uses the POST method to send its data, and to enable the functionality, it is easier in this case to use the POST method.

```javascript
var xHRObject = false;

if (window.ActiveXObject)
{
xHRObject = new ActiveXObject("Microsoft.XMLHTTP");
}
else if (window.XMLHttpRequest)
{
xHRObject = new XMLHttpRequest();
}
```

```
function getBody(action)
{
      var argument = "book=";
      argument += encodeURI(document.getElementById("book").innerHTML);
      argument += "&ISBN=";
      argument += encodeURI(document.getElementById("ISBN").innerHTML);
      argument += "&authors=";
      argument += encodeURI(document.getElementById("authors").innerHTML);
      argument += "&price=";
      argument += encodeURI(document.getElementById("price").innerHTML);
      argument += "&action=";
      argument += encodeURI(action);
      return argument;
}

function getData()
{
    if ((xHRObject.readyState == 4) && (xHRObject.status == 200))
    {
        if (window.ActiveXObject)
        {
            //Load XML
            var xml = xHRObject.responseXML;

            //Load XSL
            var xsl = new ActiveXObject("Microsoft.XMLDOM");
            xsl.async = false;
            xsl.load("Cart.xsl");

            //Transform
            var transform = xml.transformNode(xsl);
            var spanb = document.getElementById("cart");
            spanb.innerHTML = transform;
        }
        else
        {
            var xsltProcessor = new XSLTProcessor();

            //Load XSL
            xslStylesheet = document.implementation.createDocument("", "doc",
null);
            xslStylesheet.async = false;
            xslStylesheet.load("Cart.xsl");
            xsltProcessor.importStylesheet(xslStylesheet);

            //Load XML
            xmlDoc = xHRObject.responseXML;

            //Transform
            var fragment = xsltProcessor.transformToFragment(xmlDoc, document);
            document.getElementById("cart").innerHTML = new
XMLSerializer().serializeToString(fragment);
        }
    }
}
```

```
function AddRemoveItem(action)
{
        var book  = document.getElementById("book").innerHTML;
        var bodyofform = getBody( action);
        xHRObject.open("POST", "cartdisplay.aspx", true);
        xHRObject.setRequestHeader("Content-Type", "application/x-www-form-
urlencoded");
        xHRObject.onreadystatechange = getData;
        xHRObject.send(bodyofform);

}
```

3.   Next, open up the server-side code `cartdisplay.aspx`, and add the following namespace:

```
<%@ import Namespace="System.Globalization" %>
```

4.   Remaining in the server-side code, make the following amendment to the `toXML` function. In the ASP.NET, this would be as follows:

```
string toXml(Hashtable ht)
    {
        XmlDocument XmlDoc = new XmlDocument();
        XmlNode versionNode = XmlDoc.CreateXmlDeclaration("1.0","ISO-
8859-1","yes");
        XmlNode mainNode = XmlDoc.CreateElement("cart");
        XmlDoc.AppendChild(versionNode);
        XmlDoc.AppendChild(mainNode);
        decimal total = 0;
        XmlNode TotalNode = XmlDoc.CreateElement("Total");

        foreach (string key in ht.Keys)
        {
            XmlNode childNode = XmlDoc.CreateElement("book");
            XmlNode TitleNode = XmlDoc.CreateElement("Title");
            XmlNode QuantityNode = XmlDoc.CreateElement("Quantity");
            XmlNode AuthorNode = XmlDoc.CreateElement("Author");
            XmlNode ISBNNode = XmlDoc.CreateElement("ISBN");
            XmlNode PriceNode = XmlDoc.CreateElement("Price");

            TitleNode.AppendChild(XmlDoc.CreateTextNode(key));
            QuantityNode.AppendChild(XmlDoc.CreateTextNode(ht[key].ToString()));
            AuthorNode.AppendChild(XmlDoc.CreateTextNode(Request.Form["authors"]));
            ISBNNode.AppendChild(XmlDoc.CreateTextNode(Request.Form["ISBN"]));
            string price = Request.Form["price"].Replace("$","");
            PriceNode.AppendChild(XmlDoc.CreateTextNode(price));
            int quantity = int.Parse(ht[key].ToString());
            total += decimal.Parse(price, new CultureInfo("en-US")) * quantity;
            childNode.AppendChild(TitleNode);
            childNode.AppendChild(QuantityNode);
            childNode.AppendChild(AuthorNode);
            childNode.AppendChild(ISBNNode);
            childNode.AppendChild(PriceNode);
            mainNode.AppendChild(childNode);

        }
```

```
        TotalNode.AppendChild(XmlDoc.CreateTextNode(total.ToString()));
        mainNode.AppendChild(TotalNode);
        string strXml = XmlDoc.InnerXml;

        return strXml;
    }
```

In the PHP, it would be as follows:

```
function toXml($MDA)
{
    $doc = new DomDocument('1.0');
    $cart = $doc->appendChild($doc->createElement('cart'));
    $total = 0;

    foreach ($MDA as $Item => $ItemName)
    {
        $book = $cart->appendChild($doc->createElement('book'));

        $title = $doc->appendChild($doc->createElement('Title'));
        $title->appendChild($doc->createTextNode($Item));

        $authors = $book->appendChild($doc->createElement('Authors'));
        $authors->appendChild($doc->createTextNode($_POST['authors']));

        $isbn = $book->appendChild($doc->createElement('ISBN'));
        $isbn->appendChild($doc->createTextNode($_POST['ISBN']));

        $price = str_replace("$","",$_POST['price']);
        $priceNode = $book->appendChild($doc->createElement('Price'));
        $priceNode->appendChild($doc->createTextNode($price));

        $quantity = $book->appendChild($doc->createElement('Quantity'));
        $quantity->appendChild($doc->createTextNode($ItemName));

        $book->appendChild($title);
        $book->appendChild($quantity);
        $book->appendChild($authors);
        $book->appendChild($isbn);
        $book->appendChild($priceNode);

        $total = $price * $ItemName;
    }

    $totalNode =  $cart->appendChild($doc->createElement('Total'));
    $totalNode->appendChild($doc->createTextNode($total));

    $strXml = $doc->saveXML();
    return $strXml;
}
```

5. Open `Catalogue1.htm` in the browser, and click on Add to Cart (Figure 8-7).

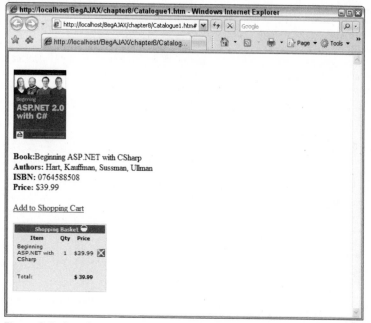

Figure 8-7: Opening `Catalogue1.htm` in the browser and clicking on Add to Cart.

6. If you click on Add to Shopping Cart again, the total increases. If you click on the cross, all items are removed, as shown in Figure 8-8.

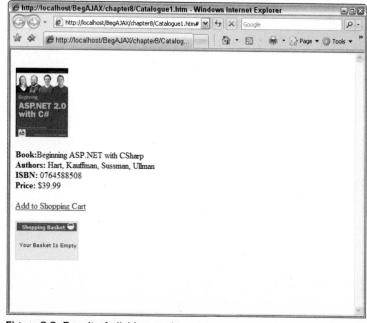

Figure 8-8: Result of clicking on the cross.

How It Works

Nothing dramatically new has been introduced in this example. You've just made use of existing code to enable the shopping cart and make it work dynamically, instead of using it as a glorified static page. You added the script to perform the transform in either IE or Mozilla from the earlier cart examples, and then you added an extra parameter called `action`. This extra parameter is used to determine whether you are intending to add items to the shopping cart or to remove them. Because you are passing your data from the `XMLHttpRequest` object using the `POST` method, you must wrap the extra parameter up in the form using the `getBody` function.

```
function getBody(action)
{
        var argument = "book=";
        argument += encodeURI(document.getElementById("book").innerHTML);
        argument += "&ISBN=";
        argument += encodeURI(document.getElementById("ISBN").innerHTML);
        argument += "&authors=";
        argument += encodeURI(document.getElementById("authors").innerHTML);
        argument += "&price=";
        argument += encodeURI(document.getElementById("price").innerHTML);
        argument += "&action=";
        argument += encodeURI(action);
        return argument;
}
```

This entails adding an extra two lines to the code and passing the value of the `action` parameter into the function. If the user has clicked on "Add to Shopping Cart," then this parameter contains the word "Add."

In the server-side code, all you have done is to add an extra element to the XML document to record the total. This means that when you create the XML document, you now have to ensure that this node is created and that you sum the prices of the items correctly into this node. In ASP.Net, this entailed creating a decimal variable to hold the total and creating an element.

```
decimal total = 0;
XmlNode TotalNode = XmlDoc.CreateElement("Total");
```

Then, during the loop, you can add the price * quantity of each item:

```
total += decimal.Parse(price, new CultureInfo("en-US")) * quantity;
total += decimal.Parse(price, new CultureInfo("en-US")) * quantity;
```

Because some countries have a culture-specific decimal point, there is an extra piece of information specifying the particular decimal point symbol you are using.

Finally, at the end of the loop, you can append the total value to the element, and you can append the new `total` element to the XML document.

```
TotalNode.AppendChild(XmlDoc.CreateTextNode(total.ToString()));
        mainNode.AppendChild(TotalNode);
```

This is sent back as part of the XML document. The XMLHttpRequest object receives a response and makes the XML document available using responseXML. You use the XSLT and XPath to render the shopping cart and its items.

Summary

This chapter has been a whirlwind tour through two languages: XSLT and XPath. You can find entire books devoted to either subject, so this chapter skipped a lot of detail.

XSLT is the language for transforming one XML document into another. XPath is the sublanguage that helps you query and locate specific nodes or elements in the document.

You were able to use these to transform XML documents and return the output to the responseXML method of the XMLHttpRequest object. XSLT uses elements, but it has a pseudo-programming language structure that features xsl:if branches, loops with xsl:for-each, and reusable templates with xsl:template tags. XPath isn't really a language as such, and it provides queries to XSLT attributes that can be used to locate specific document content as an alternative to using the DOM to do it.

The reasons for using XSLT and XPath in Ajax applications are that they help to preserve the separation between design and content, they return content as XML (so they are ideally suited for use with the XMLHttpRequest object), and they provide a simpler (and more effective) way of searching and displaying selective pieces of an XML document on your web pages.

Exercises

Suggested solutions to these questions can be found in Appendix A.

1. Create an XSLT style sheet that takes the Example.xml list of hotels and displays it not in a table, but as a set of list items.

2. Alter the XSLT style sheet of the shopping cart so that it also displays the ISBN number of the book.

Patterns

An important principle of programming is building code that you can reuse throughout your application. If you step back a bit from your application and take a wider view, though, you should see that it's not just small sections of code that must be repeated. The types of problems the code is intended to solve are also repeated. How many times does a developer have to build a shopping cart or implement a secure login algorithm?

Tasks such as form validation are typical chores in the life of a developer, and there's no getting around them. The problem is that it isn't usually possible to take your code from one application and stick it in another. If you're working one week to produce code for a book store and the next week for an accountant, sections of the code might be portable, but a lot might not be. Both sites may require form validation, both may require items such as drag-and-drop lists, and both sites may want errors handled in a graceful way.

In programming, a solution to a common problem is known as a *pattern* or a *design pattern*. It's a template outlining the way you should approach a particular problem. As discussed in Chapter 1, just because you can use Ajax on every web page going doesn't mean you should do so. Just as with any discipline from sports to engineering, there is a right way and a wrong way to do things. In sports, if you don't warm up and cool down correctly, or follow a sensible training schedule, you're likely to get no fitter or, worse, you could injure yourself. In engineering, if you don't follow the correct techniques for building a bridge, then there's a good chance your bridge will fall down (or sway from side to side, as one notorious bridge in London did for a while!). In Ajax applications, if you don't follow a particular pattern, then there's a good chance your application won't work as you intend, if it works at all.

Although some people don't always like to follow instructions and learn the lessons from mistakes made by other people, it is pointless to reinvent the wheel, especially when it comes down to something as tedious as form validation. If there were a better way of doing it, someone would have already invented it! This chapter examines five simple design patterns that Ajax can be applied to, and you will create some example code using each.

This chapter discusses the following topics:

❑   Design pattern background

❑   The form validation design pattern

❑   Extra information on mouseover pattern

❑   The refresh pattern

❑   Drag-and-drop lists

❑   Handling errors

Design Pattern Background

Patterns (or design patterns) are tried-and-tested techniques or approaches to particular commonly occurring problems.

One of the first attempts to document design patterns was made by the programmer Michael Mahemoff on his web site, www.ajaxpatterns.org. Like most things on the Web, a million other people followed suit, and so you'll find plenty of other sites with similar patterns, all providing very similar (if not identical) sets of patterns.

This chapter takes a different approach than other chapters in this book. Each problem is approached individually. The discussion explains how Ajax can be used to solve a problem, then how to implement the solution. There are hundreds of available patterns, and it's just not possible to cover all of them, so this chapter takes a selection of some common ones, and some quite useful ones. If you don't find what you're looking for, then it's worth checking the web site mentioned earlier for a pattern because there is a tremendous collection of them. Because the patterns are quite simple, this chapter won't spend too much time discussing them; the code itself will be of more value.

The first problem is that of form validation.

Form Validation

Form validation is not a favorite activity of many developers. It is a very necessary activity, however, if you want to filter out a lot of the accidental or malicious junk that users tend to throw at forms.

Problem

Waiting for users to enter a whole page of data before attempting to validate what they have entered is a bottleneck that developers have been looking for ways to improve for years. If you do validation only on the client side, then you can't access the database for details. If you do validation only on the server side, then it isn't very responsive. Quite often, the developer ends up doing validation on both the client and the server.

Pattern

There are two variants of patterns that can be used with form validation:

❏ Submit each field when the value changes or when the focus for the field is lost

❏ Periodically submit the contents of the form for validation

Which solution you should employ really depends on the kind of scenario. Remember that form validation is an area of which you should be wary. If you attempt to validate a form after every keypress, you are asking for trouble, and this will run against the rich and seamless user experience that you are trying to create.

Let's begin the first scenario by creating an example whereby the user is asked for a set of details, and among these details is a username. As mentioned in Chapter 1, Ajax techniques can be very obtrusive, so this example deliberately does not use it to validate every detail on the form. You will take the UserName and, when the focus is lost (you'll know this when the onblur event fires), the contents of the UserName box will be submitted to the server, which will query an Access database containing the list of names. This will then display a message to the user letting him or her know whether the preferred username is already taken.

This example will change the form text depending on whether the user has chosen the US option or the UK option in the country. This isn't performed by Ajax, but rather merely by some dynamic JavaScript. The idea is to use Ajax only when it's really needed.

Try It Out   Submitting Values When the Focus Is Lost

To practice submitting values when the focus is lost, follow these steps:

1. Create a HTML page called FormValidation.htm as follows:

```
<html xmlns="http://www.w3.org/1999/xhtml" >
<head>
    <title>Form Validation Example</title>
    <link id="Link1" rel="stylesheet"  href="FormValidation.css" type="text/css" />
    <script type="text/javascript" src="FormValidation.js"></script>
</head>
<body>
Preferred User Name: <input id="UserName" type="text"
onblur="Validate('UserName')" />
<br/>
<span id="span"></span>
<br/>
First Name:<input id="FirstName" class="textbox" type="text" />
<br /><br />
Last Name:<input id="LastName" class="textbox" type="text" />
<br /><br />
Address:<input id="Address" class="textbox" type="text" />
<br /><br />
Town/City:<input id="TownCity" class="textbox" type="text" />
<br /><br />
Country:<select id="Country" class="textbox" onchange="Change()">
<option>US</option>
<option>UK</option>
```

```
</select>
<br /><br />
<span id="state">State:</span><input id="Text1" class="textbox" type="text" />
<br /><br/>
<span id="zipcode">ZipCode:</span>
<input id="Text2" class="textbox" type="text" />
<br /><br />
<input type="button" onclick="submit('UserName')" value="Click here to submit
details" />
</body>
</html>
```

2. Create a script called `FormValidation.js` as follows:

```
var xHRObject = false;

if (window.XMLHttpRequest)
{
xHRObject = new XMLHttpRequest();
}
else if (window.ActiveXObject)
{
xHRObject = new ActiveXObject("Microsoft.XMLHTTP");
}

var NameTaken = "False";

function getData()
{
    if ((xHRObject.readyState == 4) && (xHRObject.status == 200))
     {
         var serverText = xHRObject.responseText;
         if (serverText == "True")
         {
            span.innerHTML = "This user name has already been taken";
            NameTaken = "True";
         }
         if (serverText == "False")
         {
            span.innerHTML = "This user name is available";
            NameTaken = "False";
         }
    }
}

function getBody(newform, data)
{
    var argument = data + "=";
    argument += encodeURIComponent(document.getElementById(data).value)
    return argument;
}

function Validate(data)
{
    var newform = document.forms[0];
    var bodyofform = getBody(newform, data);
```

```
    if (bodyofform != "UserName=")
    {
    xHRObject.open("POST", "Validate.php", true);
    xHRObject.setRequestHeader("Content-Type", "application/x-www-form-urlencoded");
    HRObject.onreadystatechange = getData;
    xHRObject.send(bodyofform); ;
    }
    else
    {
        span.innerHTML = "Blank user names not allowed";
    }
}

function submit(data)
{
    if (NameTaken == "False")
    {
    var newform = document.forms[0];
    var bodyofform = getBody(newform, data);
    if (bodyofform != "UserName=")
    {
    window.location = "formcheck.php"
    }
    else
    {
        span.innerHTML = "Blank user names not allowed";
    }
    }
}

function Change()
{
    if(state.innerHTML == "State:")
    {
     state.innerHTML = "County:"
     zipcode.innerHTML = "Postcode:"
    }
    else
    {
     state.innerHTML = "State:"
     zipcode.innerHTML = "Zipcode:"
    }
}
```

3. Create an ASP.NET page called `Validate.aspx`, as shown here:

```
<%@Page Language = "C#" Debug="true"  ValidateRequest="false"%>
<%@ import Namespace="System.Xml" %>
<%@ import Namespace="System.Data.OleDb" %>
<script language="C#" runat="server">
    void Page_Load()
    {
        bool check = false;
        OleDbConnection SourceDb = new OleDbConnection("PROVIDER=Microsoft
.Jet.OLEDB.4.0;Data Source=" + Server.MapPath("chapter9.mdb") + ";");
```

```
        SourceDb.Open();

        OleDbCommand myOleDbCommand = new OleDbCommand("SELECT * from Users;",
SourceDb);
        OleDbDataReader oleDbReader = myOleDbCommand.ExecuteReader();
        while (oleDbReader.Read())
        {

            if (Request.Form["UserName"] != null)
            {
                if (Request.Form["UserName"] ==
oleDbReader["UserName"].ToString())
                {
                    check = true;
                }
            }
        }

        //clean up database connection
        SourceDb.Close();
        SourceDb.Dispose();
        Response.Write(check);

    }
</script>
```

Or, you can create a PHP script as follows:

```php
<?php
$conn = new COM('ADODB.Connection') or exit('Cannot start ADO.');
$rs = new COM('ADODB.Recordset') or die('Could not make rs');
$connstring = "Provider=Microsoft.Jet.OLEDB.4.0; Data
Source=".realpath('chapter9.mdb').";";
$conn->Open($connstring);
$sql = 'SELECT * from Users';
$rs->Open($sql, $conn, 1, 3);
$rs = $conn->Execute($sql);
$check = "False";
while (!$rs->EOF)
  {
        if ($rs->Fields['UserName']->value == $_POST["UserName"])
        {
            $check = "True";
        }
        $rs->MoveNext();
  }
  $rs->Close();

$conn->Close();

$rs=null;
$conn=null;

echo $check;
?>
```

4. Create a small style sheet called `FormValidation.css`:

```css
.textbox
{
    position: absolute;
    left: 100px;
}
span#span
{
    color: Red;
}
```

5. Finally, add a dummy stub page to ensure that the program doesn't error when you click Submit. Call this `formcheck.aspx`.

```
<%@Page Language = "C#" Debug="true" ValidateRequest="false"%>
<%@ import Namespace="System.Xml" %>
<%@ import Namespace="System.Data.OleDb" %>
<script language="C#" runat="server">
    void Page_Load()
    {
            Response.Write("Your form details have been received");
    }
</script>
```

Or, use the following in PHP, and call it `formcheck.php`:

```php
<?php
echo " Your form details have been received";
?>
```

6. Open `FormValidation.htm` in the browser. Type in the name **Chris** as shown in Figure 9-1, and then move down to the next field. Don't submit the form!

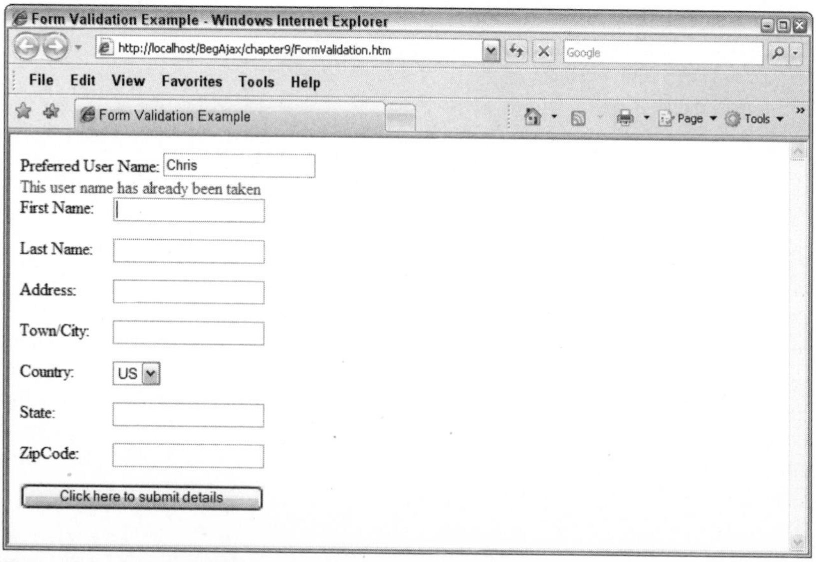

Figure 9-1: Entering data in `FormValidation.htm`.

How It Works

This example should have a very familiar feel to it. You're using the POST method to submit data. The text box for the UserName contains a call to the Validate function in JavaScript. This is called only when the onblur event is fired. onblur is the opposite of onfocus, so it is fired only when the user has moved into a control that has gained focus and then moved out again so that it has lost focus.

```
onblur="Validate('UserName')"
```

In the JavaScript, you initialize an XMLHttpRequest object outside of any functions, making it globally available:

```
var xHRObject = false;

if (window.XMLHttpRequest)
{
xHRObject = new XMLHttpRequest();
}
else if (window.ActiveXObject)
{
xHRObject = new ActiveXObject("Microsoft.XMLHTTP");
}
```

Then, in the Validate function, you pass in the name of the control across to the server-side code. You use the POST mechanism (as is customary with most forms) and use the getBody function to URI-encode the data.

```
function Validate(data)
{
    var newform = document.forms[0];
    var bodyofform = getBody(newform, data);
    if (bodyofform != "UserName=")
    {
    xHRObject.open("POST", "Validate.php", true);
    xHRObject.setRequestHeader("Content@@hyType",
    "application/x@@hywww@@hyform@@hyurlencoded");
    xHRObject.onreadystatechange = getData;
    xHRObject.send(bodyofform); ;
    }
    else
    {
        span.innerHTML = "Blank user names not allowed";
    }
}
```

You also perform a check to see whether the user has entered a blank name because there will be no point in attempting to validate that at all. If the user hasn't entered a blank name, then you send the contents of the data to either formcheck.aspx or formcheck.php, depending on which server-side technology you are using. The server-side page creates a Boolean variable to indicate whether the username has been matched. You assume at the beginning it hasn't been matched. Next, you create a connection to the Access database, and you Open the database:

```
bool check = false;
OleDbConnection("PROVIDER=Microsoft.Jet.OLEDB.4.0;Data Source=" +
Server.MapPath("chapter9.mdb") + ";");
    SourceDb.Open();
```

You create a SQL statement that selects all of the contents of the Users table. If you open up the Users table, then you will see it contains just two columns, one with a unique ID and one with a set of names in it. You then execute this SQL statement against the database. You iterate through each row in the Users table, checking to see whether the name in the field matches the name the user supplied. Only if it does do you alter the Boolean variable to true.

```
OleDbCommand myOleDbCommand = new OleDbCommand("SELECT * from Users;",
    SourceDb);
OleDbDataReader oleDbReader = myOleDbCommand.ExecuteReader();
while (oleDbReader.Read())
{
    if (Request.Form["UserName"] != null)
    {
        if (Request.Form["UserName"] == oleDbReader["UserName"].ToString())
        {
            check = true;
        }
    }
}
```

Last, you close and dispose of the connection. You write the contents of the Boolean variable to the Response stream.

```
SourceDb.Close();
SourceDb.Dispose();
Response.Write(check);
```

The getData function handles the response from the server. The response coming back will either contain True or False (although, you will see later in this chapter, there is possibly a third scenario you must consider). If the response contains the word true, then you can indicate that the name has been taken to the user immediately, before the user submits the form. Otherwise, you can let the user know that the name is OK.

```
var NameTaken = "False";

function getData()
{
    if ((xHRObject.readyState == 4) && (xHRObject.status == 200))
    {
        var serverText = xHRObject.responseText;
        if (serverText == "True")
        {
            span.innerHTML = "This user name has already been taken";
            NameTaken = "True";
        }
        if (serverText == "False")
        {
            span.innerHTML = "This user name is available";
```

```
            NameTaken = "False";
        }
    }
}
```

A global variable NameTaken is set to create a "memory" of whether or not the user name was available or not, in case further updates to the page yield responses from the responseText variable are neither true or false.

The submission of the form is handled by a separate server-side page, and this can perform separate validation checks on the data. As noted earlier, there are some items of information it is useful to check while the user is typing, and it is better to wait on others until after the user has submitted the form.

One last little section is the Change function, which isn't strictly Ajax at all but nicely complements the UserName check. This example deliberately puts the country above the State and ZipCode information, so that when the user selects the country from the drop-down list, it will automatically replace the labels on the next two text boxes on the form, indicating the County and Postcode for an English submission.

```
if(state.innerHTML == "State:")
    {
     state.innerHTML = "County:"
     zipcode.innerHTML = "Postcode:"
    }
    else
    {
     state.innerHTML = "State:"
     zipcode.innerHTML = "Zipcode:"
    }
```

The Change function just alters the corresponding <span> tag's innerHTML properties, depending on whether they are already set to State or to County.

Extra Information on Mouseover Patterns

Mouseovers have been a popular solution to dynamically showing information on web pages for a long time. While Dynamic HTML techniques mean that you can rearrange a page to show extra information, the concept of moving information around to accommodate new sections dynamically can be a clunky one. The mouseover technique avoids these pitfalls by not affecting the layout of any of the original information on the screen.

Problem

How do you show extra information about an item without cluttering up the presentation or distracting the user from the user's current activity?

Pattern

A partially transparent box pops up with extra information about that particular item. This doesn't disrupt the flow, and the partial transparency means that the original information on the page isn't obscured either.

It's quite common on web sites to display a list of graphics (such as pictures of bands on `Last.fm` or groups of photographs on Flickr). The adage that a picture is worth a thousand words seems to be a popular one in contemporary web development thinking. Hence, with a large number of products in a catalogue, you can find them displayed as a series of images. Popups are used because they are quick and they don't alter the layout of the page at all, which makes them very common.

This example displays the covers of six books. When the user hovers over the cover, he or she will get a larger version of the image, along with some details about the book. This example uses an existing library `boxover.js`, available from `http://boxover.swazz.org`, that is very popular, and it does the hard work of displaying the image. Strictly speaking, this doesn't require Ajax; however, this example grafts on some Ajax code that goes to an XML file, identifies the book you have with a mouseover via the ISBN, and then returns a small selection of information about the book (such as the title, authors, ISBN, and price), all displayed in the mouseover box.

Try It Out   Displaying a Transparent Popup

To practice displaying a transparent popup, follow these steps:

1. Create a page called `MouseOver.htm` as follows:

```
<!DOCTYPE html PUBLIC "-//W3C//DTD XHTML 1.0 Transitional//EN"
"http://www.w3.org/TR/xhtml1/DTD/xhtml1-transitional.dtd">
<html xmlns="http://www.w3.org/1999/xhtml" >
<head>
    <title>Mouse Over Example</title>
    <script type="text/javascript" src="mouse.js"></script>
    <script type="text/javascript" src="boxover.js"></script>
</head>
<body>
    <table>
        <tr>
            <td>
<a title="header=[<img src='begajax.jpg'/>] body=[0470106751]'
href="catalogue1.htm">
<img alt="beginning ajax" src="begajax.jpg" /></a></td>
            <td><a title="header=[<img src='begaspnet.jpg'/>] body=[0764588508]'
href="catalogue2.htm"><img alt="beginning ASP NET" src="begaspnet.jpg" /></a></td>
            <td><a title="header=[<img src='begjavascript.jpg'/>] body=[076455871]'
href="catalogue3.htm"><img alt="beginning JavaScript" src="begjavascript.jpg"
/></a></td>
            <td><a title="header=[<img src='begphp5.jpg'/>] body=[0764557831]'
href="catalogue4.htm"><img alt="beginning php5" src="begphp5.jpg" /></a></td>
            <td><a title="header=[<img src='begxml.jpg'/>] body=[0764570773]'
href="catalogue5.htm"><img alt="beginning xml" src="begxml.jpg" /></a></td>
            <td><a title="header=[<img src='proajax.jpg'/>] body=[076455871]'
href="catalogue6.htm"><img alt="professional ajax" src="proajax.jpg" /></a></td>
        </tr>
    </table>
</body>
</html>
```

2. Download the latest version of `boxover.js` from `http://boxover.swazz.org` into the same folder.

3. Locate the `getParam` function, and amend it as follows by adding the highlighted code:

```
function getParam(param,list) {
    var reg = new RegExp('([^a-zA-Z]' + param + '|^' + param +
')\\s*=\\s*\\[\\s*((((\\[\\[()|(\\]\\]])|([^\\]\\[]))*)\\s*\\]');
    var res = reg.exec(list);
    var returnvar;
    if (param != "body")
    {
    if(res)
        return res[2].replace('[[','[').replace(']]',']');
    else
        return '';
    }
    else
    {
        if (res)
            return mousebox(res[2].replace('[[','[').replace(']]',']'));
        else
            return '';
    }
}
```

4. Create a new script called `mouse.js`, and add the following text:

```
var isbn = null;
var http = null;

function mousebox(isbn)
{
                if (window.ActiveXObject)
                {
                    http = new ActiveXObject("Microsoft.XMLHTTP");
                }
                else if (window.XMLHttpRequest)
                {
                    http = new XMLHttpRequest();
                }
                http.open("GET", "Catalogue.xml", false);
                http.send(null);
                var xml = http.responseXML;

                //Load XSL

                if (window.ActiveXObject)
                {
                var xsl = new ActiveXObject("MSXML2.FreeThreadedDomDocument.3.0");
                xsl.async = false
                xsl.load("Catalogue.xsl")

                var template = new ActiveXObject("MSXML2.XSLTemplate")
                template.stylesheet = xsl
```

```
            processor = template.createProcessor()

            processor.input = xml
            processor.addParameter("ISBN", isbn)
            processor.transform()

             //Transform
            return processor.output;
}
else
{

                var xsltProcessor = new XSLTProcessor();

            //Load XSL
            http = new XMLHttpRequest();
            http.open("GET", "Catalogue.xsl", false);
            http.send(null);

            xslStylesheet = http.responseXML;

            xsltProcessor.importStylesheet(xslStylesheet);
            xsltProcessor.setParameter(null, "ISBN", isbn);

            //Transform
            var fragment = xsltProcessor.transformToDocument(xml, document);
            return new XMLSerializer().serializeToString(fragment);
}

}
```

5. Create a file called `catalogue.xml` with the following data:

```xml
<?xml version="1.0" encoding="utf-8" ?>
<catalog>
  <book>
    <Title>Beginning ASP.NET with CSharp</Title>
    <Authors>Hart, Kauffman, Sussman, Ullman</Authors>
    <ISBN>0764588508</ISBN>
    <Price>$39.99</Price>
  </book>
  <book>
    <Title>Beginning JavaScript 2nd Edition</Title>
    <Authors>Wilton</Authors>
    <ISBN>076455871</ISBN>
    <Price>$39.99</Price>
    </book>
  <book>
    <Title>Beginning Ajax</Title>
    <Authors>Dykes, Ullman</Authors>
    <ISBN>0470106751</ISBN>
    <Price>$39.99</Price>
  </book>
  <book>
    <Title>Beginning XML</Title>
    <Authors>Hunter, Watt, Rafter, Duckett</Authors>
```

```
    <ISBN>0764570773</ISBN>
    <Price>$39.99</Price>
  </book>
  <book>
    <Title>Beginning PHP5</Title>
    <Authors>Squier, Mercer, Kent, Choi</Authors>
    <ISBN>0764557831</ISBN>
    <Price>$39.99</Price>
  </book>
  <book>
    <Title>Professional Ajax</Title>
    <Authors>Zakas, McPeak, Fawcett</Authors>
    <ISBN> 0471777781</ISBN>
    <Price>$39.99</Price>
  </book>
  </catalog>
```

6. Create a new file called `Catalogue.xsl`, and add the following data:

```
<?xml version="1.0" encoding="utf-8"?>

<xsl:stylesheet version="1.0"
    xmlns:xsl="http://www.w3.org/1999/XSL/Transform">

  <xsl:output
    method="html"
    indent="yes"
    version="4.0" />
  <xsl:param name="ISBN" />

  <xsl:template match="/">
      <xsl:for-each select="//book">
        <xsl:if test="ISBN=$ISBN">
          <span>
            <b>Title</b> -
            <xsl:value-of select="Title"/>
          </span>
          <br/>
          <span> <b>Authors</b> -
            <xsl:value-of select="Authors"/>
          </span>
          <br/>
          <span> <b>ISBN</b> -
            <xsl:value-of select="ISBN"/>
          </span>
          <br/>
          <span> <b>Price</b> -
            <xsl:value-of select="Price"/>
          </span>
          <br/>
        </xsl:if>
      </xsl:for-each>
  </xsl:template>
</xsl:stylesheet>
```

7. View `MouseOver.htm` in your browser, and hover your mouse over each of the book covers in turn, as shown in Figure 9-2.

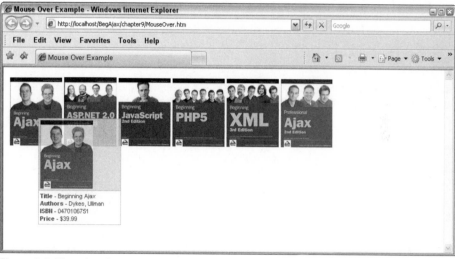

Figure 9-2: Hovering the mouse over a book cover.

How It Works

This example takes a quite large existing library and amends it very slightly so that you can use Ajax to extract the information and display it on the page. Let's not go into detail about what `boxover.js` does because it performs some quite complex handling to ensure that the box follows the mouse as it is switched on and off only when over the correct elements.

The HTML page actually contains the first point of interest. Each of the covers contains some extra information passed into the `title` attribute.

```
<td><a title="header=[<img src='begaspnet.jpg'/>] body=[0764588508]'
href="catalogue2.htm"><img alt="beginning ASP NET" src="begaspnet.jpg" /></a></td>
```

These are parameters that are picked up by the `getParam` method in `boxover.js`. Normally, each parameter (such as `header` and `body`) is identified in turn, and the information has the square brackets stripped from it to return only HTML tags. The code has been altered here to provide a call to a function in the script you created.

```
if (param != "body")
    {
    if(res)
        return res[2].replace('[[','[').replace(']]',']');
    else
        return '';
    }
    else
    {
        if (res)
```

```
            return mousebox(res[2].replace('[[','[').replace(']]',']'));
    else
            return '';
}
```

Instead of passing the HTML as the body of the box to display under the mouseover image, you now call a function that sends the ISBN, returns an XML document, performs a transform via XSL on the document, and returns an HTML fragment as the return value of the function.

The function starts by creating an instance of the XMLHttpRequest object. You immediately open the XML document containing the catalogue data, send it, and store the XML in the xml variable:

```
if (window.ActiveXObject)
{
    http = new ActiveXObject("Microsoft.XMLHTTP");
}
else if (window.XMLHttpRequest)
{
    http = new XMLHttpRequest();
}
http.open("GET", "Catalogue.xml", false);
http.send(null);
var xml = http.responseXML;
```

Next, you load the XSL. This is a browser-specific exercise. You must do a bit more than just load the XSL style sheet, though. You must also pass a parameter (the ISBN number) to the style sheet. Unfortunately, the MSXML.DOMDocument object doesn't possess the functionality to load parameters separately to the style sheet, so instead you use the MSXML2.FreeThreadedDomDocument object. This works in a similar way for the actual loading, but it requires an additional step in the creation of an XSL template object. The template is assigned a style sheet, and the createProcessor method creates an instance of an XSLT style sheet processor for you.

```
if (window.ActiveXObject)
{
var xsl = new ActiveXObject("MSXML2.FreeThreadedDomDocument.3.0");
xsl.async = false
xsl.load("Catalogue.xsl")

var template = new ActiveXObject("MSXML2.XSLTemplate")
template.stylesheet = xsl
processor = template.createProcessor()
```

Next, you assign the style sheet to the processor. Then you create a parameter and pass the isbn variable, which contains the value from the current image that the mouse is hovering over. Then you can perform the transform and return the output.

```
processor.input = xml
processor.addParameter("ISBN", isbn)
processor.transform()

//Transform
return processor.output;
}
```

Fortunately, Mozilla doesn't have any such inflexibilities with its own XSLT processor, which is able to add parameters via the `setParameter` method. Other than that, it works in the familiar way.

```
else
{

                var xsltProcessor = new XSLTProcessor();

            //Load XSL
            http = new XMLHttpRequest();
            http.open("GET", "Catalogue.xsl", false);
            http.send(null);

            xslStylesheet = http.responseXML;

            xsltProcessor.importStylesheet(xslStylesheet);
            xsltProcessor.setParameter(null, "ISBN", isbn);

            //Transform
            var fragment = xsltProcessor.transformToFragment(xml, document);
            return new XMLSerializer().serializeToString(fragment);

}
```

The XSL style sheet defines the parameter `ISBN`. Then, this parameter is referenced in the document by placing a dollar symbol ($) in front of it. You select each book element in the XML document by using XPath. You want to display only information from the book element that is relevant to the one that the mouse is hovering over. So, you use the `xsl:if` test to check the ISBN number of each element against the ISBN number from the book.

```
<xsl:param name="ISBN" />

  <xsl:template match="/">
      <xsl:for-each select="//book">
        <xsl:if test="ISBN=$ISBN">
          <span>
            <b>Title</b> -
            <xsl:value-of select="Title"/>
          </span>
            ...
</xsl:if>
```

Only if the items match do you display the resulting snippet of HTML.

```
                <span><b>Title</b> -
                Beginning Ajax</span><br><span><b>Authors</b> -
                Dykes, Ullman</span><br><span><b>ISBN</b> -
                0470106751</span><br><span><b>Price</b> -
                $39.99</span><br>
```

This event is fired every time the mouse moves over a different image, and it is dynamically populated with information from the XML document each time.

Polling the Server Pattern

A lot of applications make information available as streams (such as news feeds or web services). With applications that read these streams, even though they will be updated every time you refresh the page, you may want the browser display to be updated more frequently, and without the aid of a page refresh.

Problem

How do you check the server not just once for information, but at regular intervals?

Pattern

This kind of asynchronous activity is known as *polling the server*. This kind of pattern is also known as *page streaming* or *service streaming*. To do this, you create a script that runs continuously calling the server/data. Most functions would exit there after the first call, but in this pattern, it will run in a loop, calling the function, then waiting for a set period of time, then calling the function again. As touched upon in Chapter 1, if you use the XMLHttpRequest object with the GET method, Internet Explorer (IE) aggressively caches the XML page that is being called. If the reason for the update is to refresh the page with new data, then displaying the page with cached or out-of-date data will defeat the purpose of polling the server. So, considerations must be made for this as well.

This example creates an XML file with some dummy stock data and some dummy stock prices that are refreshed by random numbers that are emitted to an XML file. You will update the XML file, and you will ensure that the main page is refreshed almost instantaneously.

Try It Out   Polling the Server/Page Streaming

To practice polling the server, follow these steps:

1. Create a page called `polling.htm` as follows:

```
<html xmlns="http://www.w3.org/1999/xhtml" >
<head>
    <title>Polling The Server Example</title>
    <link id="Link1" rel="stylesheet" href="Polling.css" type="text/css" />
    <script type="text/javascript" src="polling.js"></script>
</head>
<body onload="getDocument()">
    <span id="Stocks"></span>
</body>
</html>
```

2. Create a script called `Polling.js` as follows:

```
var xHRObject = false;

if (window.XMLHttpRequest)
{
xHRObject = new XMLHttpRequest();
}
else if (window.ActiveXObject)
{
```

```
xHRObject = new ActiveXObject("Microsoft.XMLHTTP");
}


function loadDocument(fileName) {
    var xmlDoc = null
    if (window.ActiveXObject)
    {
        xmlDoc = new ActiveXObject("MSXML2.DOMDocument.3.0")
    }
    else
    {
        document.implementation.createDocument("","",null);
    }
    xmlDoc.async = false;
    xmlDoc.load(fileName);
    return xmlDoc;
}

function transformToHTML(xmlDoc, xslDoc) {
    var html = "";
    if (window.XSLTProcessor) {
        var xsltProc = new XSLTProcessor();
        xsltProc.importStylesheet(xslDoc);
        var fragment = xsltProc.transformToFragment(xmlDoc, document);
        html = new XMLSerializer().serializeToString(fragment);
    } else if (window.ActiveXObject) {
        html = xmlDoc.transformNode(xslDoc);
    }
    return html;
}



function getData()
{
    //Check to see if the XMlHttpRequest object is ready and whether it has
    //returned a legitimate response
    if (xHRObject.readyState == 4 && xHRObject.status == 200)
    {
        // Load XML
        var xml = loadDocument("Stocks.xml");
        //Load XSL
        var xsl = loadDocument("Stocks.xsl");
         //Transform
        document.getElementById("Stocks").innerHTML = transformToHTML(xml, xsl);
        //Clear the object and call the getDocument function in 5 seconds
        setTimeout("getDocument()", 5000);
    }
}

function getDocument()
{
    xHRObject.open("GET", "GetStocksList.aspx?id=" + Number(new Date()), true);
    xHRObject.onreadystatechange = getData;
```

```
    if (xHRObject.overrideMimeType) {
        xHRObject.overrideMimeType("text/plain");
    }
    xHRObject.send(null);
    }
```

3. Create an XML file called `Stocks.xml` containing the following data:

```xml
<?xml version="1.0" encoding="iso@@hy8859-1" standalone="yes"?>
<stocks>
  <company>
    <name>Isotope International Ltd</name>
    <price>7.8</price>
    <direction>Down</direction>
  </company>
  <company>
    <name>Cartkeys Conglomerates</name>
    <price>29.9</price>
    <direction>Down</direction>
  </company>
  <company>
    <name>Merrible Networks Inc</name>
    <price>53.1</price>
    <direction>Down</direction>
  </company>
  <company>
    <name>Sable Strongholds</name>
    <price>140.4</price>
    <direction>Up</direction>
  </company>
</stocks>
```

4. Create an XSL style sheet called `stocks.xsl` with the following data:

```xml
<?xml version="1.0" encoding="utf-8"?>
<xsl:stylesheet version="1.0"
    xmlns:xsl="http://www.w3.org/1999/XSL/Transform">

  <xsl:output
    method="html"
    indent="yes"
    version="4.0"/>

  <xsl:template match="/">
    <xsl:call-template name="DisplayStocks"></xsl:call-template>

  </xsl:template>


  <xsl:template name="DisplayStocks">

  <table id="stocks">
    <thead class="head">
      <tr>
        <td>Company</td>
        <td>Price</td>
```

```
          <td>Direction</td>
        </tr>
      </thead>
      <tbody>
        <xsl:for-each select="//company">
          <tr>
            <td class="border2">
              <xsl:value-of select="name"/>
            </td>
            <td class="border2" align="center">
              <xsl:value-of select="price"/>
            </td>
            <xsl:choose>
              <xsl:when test="direction='Up'">
                <td class="border2" style="color:blue;">
                  <xsl:value-of select="direction"/>
                </td>
              </xsl:when>
              <xsl:otherwise>
                <td class="border2" style="color:red;">
                  <xsl:value-of select="direction"/>
                </td>
              </xsl:otherwise>
            </xsl:choose>
          </tr>
        </xsl:for-each>
      </tbody>
    </table>
  </xsl:template>

</xsl:stylesheet>
```

5. Create a style sheet called `polling.css` as follows:

```
table
{
    background-color: beige;
    border-top:1px solid #e4ddca;
    border-left:1px solid #e4ddca;
    border-right:1px solid #e4ddca;
    border-bottom :1px solid #e4ddca;
}

tr, td
{
    font-family: Verdana;
    height:15px;
    font-size:75%;
    margin:2px 0px 0px 0px;
    padding:0px 0px 0px 5px;
}

.border
{
    font-weight: bold;
```

```
        text-align:center;
}

.border2
{
    background: beige;
}

.head
{
    font-family: Verdana;
    height:15px;
    vertical-align:middle;
    background:#665D43;
    color: beige;
    font-weight: bold;
}
```

6. Create the server-side page, and call it `GetStocksList.aspx`:

```
<%@Page Language = "C#" Debug="true" %>
<%@ import Namespace="System.Xml" %>
<script language="C#" runat="server">
    void Page_Load()
    {
        XmlDocument CurrentXml = new XmlDocument();
        CurrentXml.Load(Server.MapPath("stocks.xml"));
        XmlNode root = CurrentXml.LastChild;

        Random rc = new Random();
        int RandomNumber;

        for (int i = 0; i < root.ChildNodes.Count; i++)
        {
            RandomNumber = rc.Next(0, 100);
            XmlNode child = root.ChildNodes[i];
            for (int j = 0; j < child.ChildNodes.Count; j++)
            {
                if (child.ChildNodes[j].Name == "price")
                {
                    decimal value = decimal.Parse(child.ChildNodes[j].InnerXml);

                    Random rp = new Random();
                    decimal RandomPrice = rp.Next(0, (int)value);

                    RandomPrice = RandomPrice / 10;
                    string direction = "";
                    if ((RandomNumber % 2) == 1)
                    {
                        direction = "Down";
                        value = value - RandomPrice;
                    }
                    else
                    {
                        direction = "Up";
                        value = value + RandomPrice;
```

```
                    }
                    child.ChildNodes[j].InnerText = value.ToString();
                    child.ChildNodes[j + 1].InnerText = direction;
                }
            }
        }
        CurrentXml.Save(Server.MapPath("stocks.xml"));
    }
</script>
```

Or, if you want to use PHP, use the following and call it `GetStocksList.php`:

```php
<?php
    $dom = new DomDocument('1.0');
    $dom->load('stocks.xml');
    $root = $dom->lastChild;
    srand(time());
    foreach ($root->childNodes As $child)
    {
        $RandomNumber = (rand()%100);
        if ($child->nodeType == 1)
        {
                foreach ($child->childNodes As $subchild)
                {
            if ($subchild->nodeName == "price")
            {
                $value = $subchild->textContent;
                $RandomPrice = (rand()%$value);
                $RandomPrice = $RandomPrice / 10;

                $direction = "";
                if (($RandomNumber % 2) == 1)
                {
                    $direction = "Down";
                    $value = $value - $RandomPrice;

                }
                else
                {
                    $direction = "Up";
                    $value = $value + $RandomPrice;
                }

                            $textNode = $dom->createTextNode($value);
                            $subchild->nodeValue = "";
                $newchild = $subchild->appendChild($textNode);
            }

            if ($subchild->nodeName == "direction")
            {
                            $textNode = $dom->createTextNode($direction);
                            $subchild->nodeValue = "";
                $newchild = $subchild->appendChild($textNode);
            }
```

```
            }
        }
    }
$dom->save('stocks.xml');
?>
```

7. If you're using ASP.NET, then add the ASPNET user via Windows Explorer to the list of users allowed to modify C:\\inetpub\\wwwroot\\BegAjax\\chapter9.

    If you're using PHP with Apache, go to Services, right-click Apache Service, and select Properties. Click the Log On tab, and switch from Local System Account to This Account. Using the browser, choose a local account, and enter the password. Click OK to finish.

    If you're using PHP with IIS, open the IIS console and right-click on "Default web site." Click on Directory Security. Click the Edit button, and switch from the IUSR_yourPcName to a local account (by clicking on the Browse button). Uncheck "Allow IIS to control password" and, in the password field, enter the password for the account you chose. Click OK to finish.

8. Open Polling.htm in the browser, as shown in Figure 9-3.

Figure 9-3: Polling.htm in the browser.

How It Works

This example simulates a stock ticker that moves faster than stock in the real world. However, this is necessary to demonstrate that you have used Ajax to poll the server for an updated XML file.

The body onload attribute is set to getDocument() function. The script starts by creating an XMLHttpRequest object. The getDocument() function assigns the getData function to be called on the event of a change of state of the XMLHttpRequest object. You append a date to the end of GetStocksList.aspx because you know that this will be called over and over, and you don't want IE to cache the file. Then, you send the object's contents to the server.

```
function getDocument()
{
    xHRObject.open("GET", "GetStocksList.aspx?id=" + Number(new Date()), true);
    xHRObject.onreadystatechange = getData;
    if (xHRObject.overrideMimeType) {
        xHRObject.overrideMimeType("text/plain");
    }
    xHRObject.send(null);
    }
```

The receiving page `GetStocksList` has three tasks to perform. The first is to load the existing XML document. The second is to randomly generate some stock data, and the third is to save the new data to the XML document. The first step takes only two lines. After that, you must locate the root of the document (the `<stocks>` element) to perform the iterations on.

```
XmlDocument CurrentXml = new XmlDocument();
CurrentXml.Load(Server.MapPath("stocks.xml"));
XmlNode root = CurrentXml.LastChild;
```

It's the process of generating the random numbers that takes up most of the code. You generate two random numbers. One is used to determine whether the stock is going up or down. You generate a number between 1 and 100, and, if it is odd, then the stock goes down; otherwise, it goes up. The second random number is the amount by which the stock goes up and down. This is a number between 1 and a current value of the stock. You then divide the number by 10 to ensure that the stock can go up or down by at most 10 percent of its value.

```
Random rc = new Random();
int RandomNumber;

for (int i = 0; i < root.ChildNodes.Count; i++)
{
    RandomNumber = rc.Next(0, 100);
    XmlNode child = root.ChildNodes[i];
    for (int j = 0; j < child.ChildNodes.Count; j++)
    {
        if (child.ChildNodes[j].Name == "price")
        {
            decimal value = decimal.Parse(child.ChildNodes[j].InnerXml);

            Random rp = new Random();
            decimal RandomPrice = rp.Next(0, (int)value);

            RandomPrice = RandomPrice / 10;
            string direction = "";
            if ((RandomNumber % 2) == 1)
            {
                direction = "Down";
                value = value - RandomPrice;
            }
            else
            {
                direction = "Up";
                value = value + RandomPrice;
            }
            child.ChildNodes[j].InnerText = value.ToString();
            child.ChildNodes[j + 1].InnerText = direction;
        }
    }
}
```

The values are then reassigned to the `price` and `direction` elements for each item in the document, and the document is then saved.

```
CurrentXml.Save(Server.MapPath("stocks.xml"));
```

Once the document has been saved, JavaScript handles the rest of the operation. The XML is loaded, and the XSL is loaded. The transform is performed on the XML to produce a box showing the latest stock information.

```
var xHRObject = false;

if (window.XMLHttpRequest)
{
xHRObject = new XMLHttpRequest();
}
else if (window.ActiveXObject)
{
xHRObject = new ActiveXObject("Microsoft.XMLHTTP");
}


function loadDocument(fileName) {
    var xmlDoc = null
    if (window.ActiveXObject)
    {
        xmlDoc = new ActiveXObject("MSXML2.DOMDocument.3.0")
    }
    else
    {
        document.implementation.createDocument("","",null);
    }
    xmlDoc.async = false;
    xmlDoc.load(fileName);
    return xmlDoc;
}

function transformToHTML(xmlDoc, xslDoc) {
    var html = "";
    if (window.XSLTProcessor) {
        var xsltProc = new XSLTProcessor();
        xsltProc.importStylesheet(xslDoc);
        var fragment = xsltProc.transformToFragment(xmlDoc, document);
        html = new XMLSerializer().serializeToString(fragment);
    } else if (window.ActiveXObject) {
        html = xmlDoc.transformNode(xslDoc);
    }
    return html;
}
```

This should be fairly familiar. It's just the code at the end of the getData() function that deviates slightly from the normal code. Once you've assigned the results of the transform to the box, you then clear the XMLHttpRequest object and call it again via the JavaScript setTimeout method.

```
                function getData()
{
    //Check to see if the XMlHttpRequest object is ready and whether it has
    //returned a legitimate response
```

```
if (xHRObject.readyState == 4 && xHRObject.status == 200)
{
    // Load XML
    var xml = loadDocument("Stocks.xml");
    //Load XSL
    var xsl = loadDocument("Stocks.xsl");
     //Transform
    document.getElementById("Stocks").innerHTML = transformToHTML(xml, xsl);
    //Clear the object and call the getDocument function in 5 seconds
    setTimeout("getDocument()", 5000);
}
}
```

This ensures that the entire operation continues in a loop, so that the stock ticker will update its results by randomly generating some new figures every five seconds. In reality, it would draw such results from a web service. This possibility is examined in Chapter 7.

Drag-and-Drop Lists Pattern

Drag-and-drop lists are something that have been around since access to the DOM was first granted. They require nothing more than JavaScript and CSS to provide the functionality. If you want to save the contents of your list to a database, then this is where Ajax enters the equation. Two sites that provide this kind of functionality are the online music fraternity www.mog.com and the backpack product of the www.37signals.com web software producers.

Problem

How do you dynamically drag-and-drop list items, then save the order to a file or database so that it will be preserved the next time you go to that screen?

Pattern

Several problems must be considered that make this pattern a little more complex than you might otherwise think. The first is dynamic object movement, which needs to be conducted only on the y-axis (in other words, up and down, and not side to side).

The following code might seem to offer a quick cross-browser alternative to dynamically moving an item:

```
function mouseMoveEvent(e)
{
 if (window.ActiveXObject)
 {
        document.getElementById(ListItemDrag).style.top = event.y;
 }
 else
 {
        document.getElementById(ListItemDrag).style.top = e.layerY;
 }
}
```

The variable `ListItemDrag` contains the ID of the element you want to move. You use the `mousemove` event and simply take the y coordinates generated by the `mouseMoveEvent` and set them to be the y coordinates of the element you are dragging and dropping. This actually works fine in IE, but in Firefox this doesn't work and will cause your mouse cursor to jump erratically up and down the screen because the event target changes, and the object will change, depending on which object is returned by the event handler.

There are quite a few more things that must be taken into consideration, such as which item is being referred to in the event object, and the fact that Mozilla can have quite a few different elements returned (making it more difficult to handle). There are, in fact, already libraries available that solve this problem using custom `drag` events, and this example will be utilizing them.

The second problem is that once you start dragging an item, how do you know when it is over another item? One solution might be to use the `onmouseover` event, but when you use a library that uses `ondrag` to move your element, then `onmouseover` doesn't fire. The solution is to store the positions of the items in an array and then to calculate the position of the element being dragged in relation to the other items on the page. Then, when an element is in close proximity to the drag-and-drop element, perform the swap of the nearest element from its current position to the empty gap.

The pattern is as follows:

1. Handle a mouse-down event, and detect and drag the element.

2. Handle a mouse-move event to move our element dynamically.

3. Detect where the element is in relation to other elements.

4. If there is a static element in the proximity to the drag-and-drop element, then move it to the next available gap. The position of the next available gap will depend on which element is being dragged and dropped, and which element is.

5. Handle a mouse-up event to release and position the dragged element correctly. This will mean realigning it into an available gap. Save this information to the database/XML document via Ajax.

Code for this example will be provided from a couple of libraries so that you can concentrate on the code that actually does the dragging, dropping, sorting, and saving.

This example takes information from an XML document containing a list of five books. You will allow the user to drag and drop each book name in the list to a new position, ensuring that the other book names shuffle correctly to take the place of the dragged-and-dropped book name. Then, when the user clicks a button, this order will be saved, so that when the user comes back to the page, the new order is preserved.

Try It Out   Using Ajax to Save the Order of a Drag-and-Drop List

Follow these steps to use Ajax to save the order of a drag-and-drop list:

1. Create a page called `DragDrop.htm`:

```
<html xmlns="http://www.w3.org/1999/xhtml" >
<head>
        <title>Drag Drop Example</title>
```

```
                <link id="Link1" rel="stylesheet"  href="DragDrop.css" type="text/css" />
        <script type="text/javascript" src="dom-drag.js"></script>
        <script type="text/javascript" src="SaveListOrder.js"></script>
        <script type="text/javascript" src="simple-dnd.js"></script>
</head>
<body>
My Favourite Books:
<br />
<br />
<span id="root">
</span>
<br />
<br />
<input type="button" value="Click to store the sequence" onclick="SaveOrder()" />
</body>
</html>
```

2. As stated earlier, there are libraries available for detecting and dragging elements on the screen. Rather than reinventing the wheel, let's take one of the preexisting ones out there. Download the file dom-drag.js from http://boring.youngpup.net/2001/domdrag or enter the following:

```
/*****************************************************
 * dom-drag.js
 * 09.25.2001
 * www.youngpup.net
 *****************************************************
 * 10.28.2001 - fixed minor bug where events
 * sometimes fired off the handle, not the root.
 *****************************************************/

var Drag = {

    obj : null,

    init : function(o, oRoot, minX, maxX, minY, maxY, bSwapHorzRef, bSwapVertRef,
fXMapper, fYMapper)
    {
    o.onmousedown       = Drag.start;
    o.hmode             = bSwapHorzRef ? false : true ;
    o.vmode             = bSwapVertRef ? false : true ;

    o.root = oRoot && oRoot != null ? oRoot : o ;

    if (o.hmode  && isNaN(parseInt(o.root.style.left  ))) o.root.style.left   =
"0px";
    if (o.vmode  && isNaN(parseInt(o.root.style.top   ))) o.root.style.top    =
"0px";
    if (!o.hmode && isNaN(parseInt(o.root.style.right ))) o.root.style.right  =
"0px";
        if (!o.vmode && isNaN(parseInt(o.root.style.bottom))) o.root.style.bottom =
"0px";

    o.minX     = typeof minX != 'undefined' ? minX : null;
    o.minY     = typeof minY != 'undefined' ? minY : null;
```

```
o.maxX      = typeof maxX != 'undefined' ? maxX : null;
o.maxY      = typeof maxY != 'undefined' ? maxY : null;

o.xMapper = fXMapper ? fXMapper : null;
o.yMapper = fYMapper ? fYMapper : null;

o.root.onDragStart     = new Function();
o.root.onDragEnd       = new Function();
o.root.onDrag          = new Function();
},

start : function(e)
{
var o = Drag.obj = this;
e = Drag.fixE(e);
var y = parseInt(o.vmode ? o.root.style.top  : o.root.style.bottom);
var x = parseInt(o.hmode ? o.root.style.left : o.root.style.right );
o.root.onDragStart(x, y);

o.lastMouseX      = e.clientX;
o.lastMouseY      = e.clientY;

if (o.hmode) {
    if (o.minX != null)     o.minMouseX       = e.clientX - x + o.minX;
    if (o.maxX != null)     o.maxMouseX       = o.minMouseX + o.maxX - o.minX;
    } else {
    if (o.minX != null) o.maxMouseX = -o.minX + e.clientX + x;
    if (o.maxX != null) o.minMouseX = -o.maxX + e.clientX + x;
    }

    if (o.vmode) {
    if (o.minY != null)     o.minMouseY       = e.clientY - y + o.minY;
    if (o.maxY != null)     o.maxMouseY       = o.minMouseY + o.maxY - o.minY;
    } else {
    if (o.minY != null) o.maxMouseY = -o.minY + e.clientY + y;
    if (o.maxY != null) o.minMouseY = -o.maxY + e.clientY + y;
    }

    document.onmousemove      = Drag.drag;
    document.onmouseup        = Drag.end;

    return false;
},

drag : function(e)
{
e = Drag.fixE(e);
var o = Drag.obj;

var ey     = e.clientY;
var ex     = e.clientX;
var y = parseInt(o.vmode ? o.root.style.top  : o.root.style.bottom);
var x = parseInt(o.hmode ? o.root.style.left : o.root.style.right );
```

```
        var nx, ny;

        if (o.minX != null) ex = o.hmode ? Math.max(ex, o.minMouseX) : Math.min(ex,
o.maxMouseX);
        if (o.maxX != null) ex = o.hmode ? Math.min(ex, o.maxMouseX) : Math.max(ex,
o.minMouseX);
        if (o.minY != null) ey = o.vmode ? Math.max(ey, o.minMouseY) : Math.min(ey,
o.maxMouseY);
        if (o.maxY != null) ey = o.vmode ? Math.min(ey, o.maxMouseY) : Math.max(ey,
o.minMouseY);

        nx = x + ((ex - o.lastMouseX) * (o.hmode ? 1 : -1));
        ny = y + ((ey - o.lastMouseY) * (o.vmode ? 1 : -1));

        if (o.xMapper)        nx = o.xMapper(y);
        else if (o.yMapper)   ny = o.yMapper(x);

        Drag.obj.root.style[o.hmode ? "left" : "right"] = nx + "px";
        Drag.obj.root.style[o.vmode ? "top" : "bottom"] = ny + "px";
        Drag.obj.lastMouseX    = ex;
        Drag.obj.lastMouseY    = ey;

        Drag.obj.root.onDrag(nx, ny);
            return false;
        },

    end : function()
    {
    document.onmousemove = null;
    document.onmouseup   = null;
    Drag.obj.root.onDragEnd(      parseInt(Drag.obj.root.style[Drag.obj.hmode ?
"left" : "right"]),

parseInt(Drag.obj.root.style[Drag.obj.vmode ? "top" : "bottom"]));
        Drag.obj = null;
    },

    fixE : function(e)
    {
        if (typeof e == 'undefined') e = window.event;
        if (typeof e.layerX == 'undefined') e.layerX = e.offsetX;
        if (typeof e.layerY == 'undefined') e.layerY = e.offsetY;
        return e;
    }
};
```

3. The second library handles the dragging and dropping of the list. Some global variables have been added here, which are displayed in bold. Save this as `simple-dnd.js`.

```
/*****************************************************************************
 * Simple DnD
 * Copyright (c) 2006 Ben Sherratt
 *
 * Permission is hereby granted, free of charge, to any person obtaining a copy of
 * this software and associated documentation files (the "Software"), to deal in
 * the Software without restriction, including without limitation the rights to
```

```
 * use, copy, modify, merge, publish, distribute, sublicense, and/or sell copies
 * of the Software, and to permit persons to whom the Software is furnished to do
 * so, subject to the following conditions:
 *
 * The above copyright notice and this permission notice shall be included in all
 * copies or substantial portions of the Software.
 *
 * THE SOFTWARE IS PROVIDED "AS IS", WITHOUT WARRANTY OF ANY KIND, EXPRESS OR
 * IMPLIED, INCLUDING BUT NOT LIMITED TO THE WARRANTIES OF MERCHANTABILITY,
 * FITNESS FOR A PARTICULAR PURPOSE AND NONINFRINGEMENT. IN NO EVENT SHALL THE
 * AUTHORS OR COPYRIGHT HOLDERS BE LIABLE FOR ANY CLAIM, DAMAGES OR OTHER
 * LIABILITY, WHETHER IN AN ACTION OF CONTRACT, TORT OR OTHERWISE, ARISING FROM,
 * OUT OF OR IN CONNECTION WITH THE SOFTWARE OR THE USE OR OTHER DEALINGS IN THE
 * SOFTWARE.
 ***********************************************************************************/

if (window.XMLHttpRequest)
{
xHRObject = new XMLHttpRequest();
}
else if (window.ActiveXObject)
{
xHRObject = new ActiveXObject("Microsoft.XMLHTTP");
}


var list = null;
var listItems = null;
Display();

function makeDnD(list) {
    // Get the items of the list
    var listItems = list.getElementsByTagName("div");

    for(var i = 0; i < listItems.length; i++) {
        var listItem = listItems[i];

        // Set up the drag
        Drag.init(listItem, null, 0, 0);

        listItem.onDragStart = function() {
            var listItem = Drag.obj;
            list = listItem.parentNode;

            // Set temp variables
            listItem.items = list.getElementsByTagName("div");

            for(var i = 0; i < listItem.items.length; i++)
                if(listItem.items[i] == listItem)
                    listItem.position = i;

            listItem.originalPosition = listItem.position;

            // Set the style
            listItem.style.opacity = 0.75;
```

```
            listItem.style.filter = "alpha(opacity=75)";
            listItem.style.zIndex = listItem.items.length;
    };

    listItem.onDrag = function(x, y, e) {
        var listItem = Drag.obj;

        var top = listItem.offsetTop + (listItem.offsetHeight / 2);

        if(listItem.position != 0 && listItem.position <=
listItem.originalPosition && top < (listItem.items[listItem.position - 1].offsetTop
+ (listItem.items[listItem.position - 1].offsetHeight / 2))) {
            // Change the position and top
            listItem.position--;
            listItem.items[listItem.position].style.top =
listItem.offsetHeight + "px";
        } else if(listItem.position != 0 && listItem.position >
listItem.originalPosition && top < (listItem.items[listItem.position].offsetTop +
(listItem.items[listItem.position].offsetHeight / 2))) {
            // Change the position and top
            listItem.position--;
            listItem.items[listItem.position + 1].style.top = "0px";
        } else if(listItem.position != listItem.items.length - 1 &&
listItem.position >= listItem.originalPosition && top >
(listItem.items[listItem.position + 1].offsetTop +
(listItem.items[listItem.position + 1].offsetHeight / 2))) {
            // Change the position and top
            listItem.position++;
            listItem.items[listItem.position].style.top = -
listItem.offsetHeight + "px";
        } else if(listItem.position != listItem.items.length - 1 &&
listItem.position < listItem.originalPosition && top >
(listItem.items[listItem.position].offsetTop +
(listItem.items[listItem.position].offsetHeight / 2))) {
            // Change the position and top
            listItem.position++;
            listItem.items[listItem.position - 1].style.top = "0px";
        }
    };

    listItem.onDragEnd = function(x, y, e) {
        var listItem = Drag.obj;

        for(var i = 0; i < listItem.items.length; i++)
            listItem.items[i].style.top = "0px";

        // Remove the item
        list.removeChild(listItem);

        // Re-insert the item
        if(listItem.items[listItem.position])
            list.insertBefore(listItem, listItem.items[listItem.position]);
        else
            list.appendChild(listItem);

        // Unset temp variables
```

```
//      listItem.items = null;
        listItem.position = null;
        listItem.originalPosition = null;

        // Unset the style
        listItem.style.opacity = 1.00;
        listItem.style.filter = "alpha(opacity=100)";
        listItem.style.zIndex = 0;
    };
  }
}
```

4. To this script, add the following function and save it:

```
function Display()
{
     xHRObject.onreadystatechange = getData;
   xHRObject.open("GET", "List.xml?id="+ Number(new Date()),true);
   xHRObject.send(null);
}
```

5. The next script is all new code. Save this as `SaveListOrder.js`.

```
var xHRObject = false;

if (window.XMLHttpRequest)
{
xHRObject = new XMLHttpRequest();
}
else if (window.ActiveXObject)
{
xHRObject = new ActiveXObject("Microsoft.XMLHTTP");
}

function getData()
{
    if ((xHRObject.readyState == 4) &&(xHRObject.status == 200))
    {
        var xmlDoc = xHRObject.responseXML;
            if (window.ActiveXObject)
            {
            // Load XML
            var xml = new ActiveXObject("Microsoft.XMLDOM");
            xml.async = false;
            xml.load("list.xml");

            //Load XSL
            var xsl = new ActiveXObject("Microsoft.XMLDOM");
            xsl.async = false;
            xsl.load("list.xsl");

            //Transform
            var transform = xml.transformNode(xsl);
            var spanb = document.getElementById("root");
            if (spanb != null)
            {
```

```
                            spanb.innerHTML = transform;
                            makeDnD(document.getElementById("root"));
                    }

                    }


                else
                {

                    var xsltProcessor = new XSLTProcessor();

                    //Load XSL
                    var XHRObject = new XMLHttpRequest();
                    XHRObject.open("GET", "list.xsl", false);
                    XHRObject.send(null);

                    xslStylesheet = XHRObject.responseXML;
                    xsltProcessor.importStylesheet(xslStylesheet);

                    //Load XML
                    XHRObject = new XMLHttpRequest();
                    XHRObject.open("GET", "list.xml", false);
                    XHRObject.send(null);

                    xmlDoc = XHRObject.responseXML;

                    //Transform
                    var fragment = xsltProcessor.transformToFragment(xmlDoc, document);
                    if(document.getElementById("root").innerHTML != "")
                    {
                        document.getElementById("root").innerHTML = "";
                    }
                    document.getElementById("root").appendChild(fragment);
                    makeDnD(document.getElementById("root"));

                        }
        }
}

function SaveOrder()
{
    list = document.getElementById("root");
    var newlist= list.getElementsByTagName("div");
    querystring = "";
    for(var i = 0; i < newlist.length; i++) {
            querystring += "booktitle" + (i+1) + "=" + newlist[i].innerHTML;
            if (i!=newlist.length-1) querystring+="&";
    }

    querystring = encodeURI(querystring);
    xHRObject.open("GET", "SaveList.aspx?"+querystring,true);
    xHRObject.send(null);
}
```

6. Save the following as `list.xml`:

```xml
<?xml version="1.0" encoding="ISO-8859-1" standalone="yes"?>
<books>
  <book>
    <title>On The Road</title>
  </book>
  <book>
    <title>Midnight's Children</title>
  </book>
  <book>
    <title>The Corrections</title>
  </book>
  <book>
    <title>At Swim Two Birds </title>
  </book>
  <book>
    <title>Atonement</title>
  </book>
</books>
```

7. Save the following as `list.xsl`:

```xml
<?xml version="1.0" encoding="utf-8"?>

<xsl:stylesheet version="1.0"   xmlns:xsl="http://www.w3.org/1999/XSL/Transform">

    <xsl:template match="/">
      <xsl:for-each select="//book">
        <div>
          <xsl:value-of select="title"></xsl:value-of>
        </div>
        </xsl:for-each>
      </xsl:template>

</xsl:stylesheet>
```

8. Save the following file as `SaveList.aspx`:

```
<%@Page Language = "C#" Debug="true"  ValidateRequest="false"%>
<%@ import Namespace="System.Xml" %>
<script language="C#" runat="server">
    void Page_Load()
    {
        XmlDocument XmlDoc = new XmlDocument();
        XmlNode versionNode = XmlDoc.CreateXmlDeclaration("1.0", "ISO-8859-1",
"yes");
        XmlNode mainNode = XmlDoc.CreateElement("books");
        XmlDoc.AppendChild(versionNode);
        XmlDoc.AppendChild(mainNode);

        foreach (string key in Request.QueryString)
        {
            XmlNode childNode = XmlDoc.CreateElement("book");
            XmlNode TitleNode = XmlDoc.CreateElement("title");
```

```
            TitleNode.AppendChild(XmlDoc.CreateTextNode(Request.QueryString[key]));
            childNode.AppendChild(TitleNode);
            mainNode.AppendChild(childNode);
        }
        XmlDoc.Save(Server.MapPath("List.Xml"));
    }
</script>
```

The PHP version is as follows (and should be saved as SaveList.php):

```php
<?php
        $xmlDoc = new DomDocument('1.0');
        $mainNode = $xmlDoc->createElement('books');
        $mainNode = $xmlDoc->appendChild($mainNode);

        foreach ($_GET as $key=>$value)
        {
            $childNode = $xmlDoc->createElement('book');
            $childNode = $mainNode->appendChild($childNode);

            $titleNode = $xmlDoc->createElement('title');
            $titleNode = $childNode->appendChild($titleNode);

            $textNode = $xmlDoc->createTextNode($value);
            $textNode = $titleNode->appendChild($textNode);
        }

        $xmlDoc->save('List.Xml');
?>
```

9. View the page dragdrop.htm in the browser, as shown in Figure 9-4.

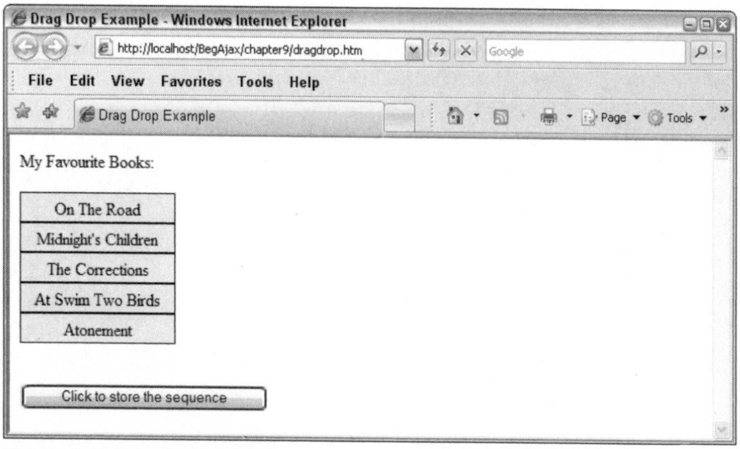

Figure 9-4: Viewing the page dragdrop.htm in the browser.

10. Shuffle the items around in the browser. If you refresh the page, then it reverts to the original sequence. Click on the button, and this code now saves the new order as an XML document. Close the browser, and look at the new sorted sequence, as shown in Figure 9-5.

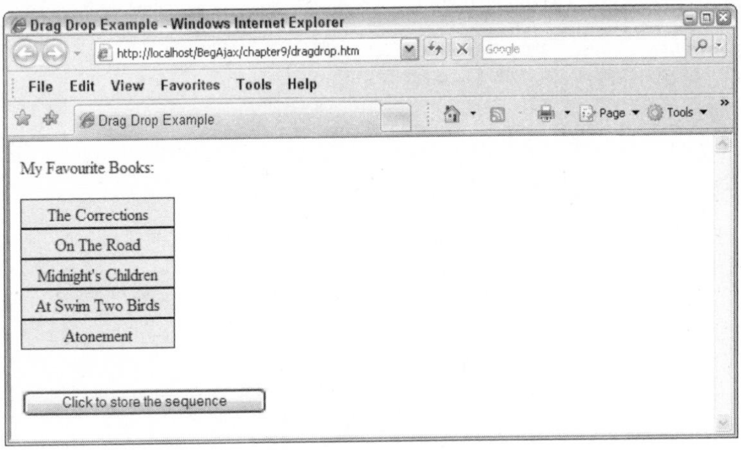

Figure 9-5: The new sorted sequence.

How It Works

This example contains a lot of code, but let's hone in on the JavaScript page that you created from scratch. Don't worry about how the dragging and dropping is handled because this is neatly encapsulated in the `Drag.Init` API. Each element in the list has an `ondrag` event added to it, and this is fired whenever you attempt to drag and drop an element in the list.

Also, let's not consider the actual laborious process of the dragging and dropping of list elements. This is done by calculating the current position of the draggable element, storing the coordinates, and comparing them to the stored coordinates of the other elements in the list. The elements are then shuffled along in turn.

The function `getData()` is used to load the XML document and perform a transform on it once again. It provides a link to the script that handles the dragging and dropping by calling the `makeDnd` method and passing the root element, the element that contains the whole list.

```
function getData()
{
    if ((xHRObject.readyState == 4) &&(xHRObject.status == 200))
    {
        var xmlDoc = xHRObject.responseXML;
            if (window.ActiveXObject)
            {
            // Load XML
            var xml = new ActiveXObject("Microsoft.XMLDOM");
            xml.async = false;
            xml.load("list.xml");

            //Load XSL
            var xsl = new ActiveXObject("Microsoft.XMLDOM");
            xsl.async = false;
            xsl.load("list.xsl");

            //Transform
```

```
var transform = xml.transformNode(xsl);
var spanb = document.getElementById("root");

//If you refresh the page then this tag is sometimes empty.
//This stops it causing an error and redisplays the page.
if (spanb != null)
{
    spanb.innerHTML = transform;
    makeDnD(document.getElementById("root"));
}


}


else
{

    var xsltProcessor = new XSLTProcessor();

    //Load XSL
    var XHRObject = new XMLHttpRequest();
    XHRObject.open("GET", "list.xsl", false);
    XHRObject.send(null);

    xslStylesheet = XHRObject.responseXML;
    xsltProcessor.importStylesheet(xslStylesheet);

    //Load XML
    XHRObject = new XMLHttpRequest();
    XHRObject.open("GET", "list.xml", false);
    XHRObject.send(null);

    xmlDoc = XHRObject.responseXML;

    //Transform
    var fragment = xsltProcessor.transformToFragment(xmlDoc, document);
    if(document.getElementById("root").innerHTML != "")
    {
        document.getElementById("root").innerHTML = "";
    }
    document.getElementById("root").appendChild(fragment);
    makeDnD(document.getElementById("root"));

        }
    }
}
```

When a user clicks on the Save button, the SaveOrder function is called. The SaveOrder function first selects the list on the page, and then it creates an array containing each of the list elements. The text from each element in the list is extracted and added to a dynamically created query string. Each book title has an extra number added to the end, so it can be individually identified. You don't have a callback function because the control will be taken over by the main page; all you want to do is save the file.

```
function SaveOrder()
{
    list = document.getElementById("root");
    var newlist= list.getElementsByTagName("div");
    querystring = "";
    for(var i = 0; i < newlist.length; i++) {
            querystring += "booktitle" + (i+1) + "=" + newlist[i].innerHTML;
            if (i!=newlist.length-1) querystring+="&";
    }


        querystring = encodeURI(querystring);
        xHRObject.open("GET", "SaveList.aspx?"+querystring,true);
        xHRObject.send(null);
}
```

The query string is then passed to the server-side page. The server-side page creates an XML document from which the list order is derived. It creates a `book` element and a `title` element for each separate book. For each separate value in the query string, you create a couple of new elements, passing the contents of the query string as the text node for that element. The query string preserves the order of the list, and so you can be certain when you extract each item in turn, you will be saving the order of the items that the user saved on the screen.

```
XmlDocument XmlDoc = new XmlDocument();
        XmlNode versionNode = XmlDoc.CreateXmlDeclaration("1.0", "ISO-8859-1",
"yes");
        XmlNode mainNode = XmlDoc.CreateElement("books");
        XmlDoc.AppendChild(versionNode);
        XmlDoc.AppendChild(mainNode);

        foreach (string key in Request.QueryString)
        {
            XmlNode childNode = XmlDoc.CreateElement("book");
            XmlNode TitleNode = XmlDoc.CreateElement("title");
            TitleNode.AppendChild(XmlDoc.CreateTextNode(Request.QueryString[key]));
            childNode.AppendChild(TitleNode);
            mainNode.AppendChild(childNode);
        }
        XmlDoc.Save(Server.MapPath("List.Xml"));
```

The XML document is saved, and then this is picked up by the JavaScript to display it once again. In this way, the elements can be shuffled around, but the order is saved only when the user clicks the button.

Handling Errors Pattern

One of the problems with using Ajax is that some of the techniques involved can be a little quirky, to put it mildly! Even in this book, you'll probably encounter either delays in the pages being rendered or the pages not being rendered at all. This could well be caused by a small typing error or the misspelling of a page name, in which case, you'll require your application to be a bit more robust than to fall over at the first hint of trouble. The process of debugging and error handling is discussed in more detail in Chapter 6, but for purposes of this discussion, let's consider some common scenarios that applications should be able to handle. One of the following three outcomes is likely if you have made a mistake:

❑   404 — Page Not Found Error

❑   302 — Found — asks permission for a redirect

❑   200 — No error, but the page doesn't display

Let's address the last kind of error first because it's not something that a pattern can really do much about. It implies there has been a mistake in the server-side code or the code that the XMLHTTPRequest object has called. The responseText and responseXML properties will be blank. This is usually attributable to a logical error in the code. It suggests that the code has executed correctly but not returned an answer. The status property of the XMLHttpRequest object will be 200 in this case. The first two responses, however, are much easier to deal with.

Problem

What action should be taken if the XMLHttpRequest object returns a readyState of 4, but returns status of something other than 200?

Pattern

The XMLHttpRequest object goes through a series of stages where it initializes the object, sends the data, and receives a response back again. It goes from 0 to 4. Generally, you would expect the status property to return 200 at the same time that the readyState returns 4. If this doesn't happen, though, it can cause the script to crash because once the readyState of 4 has been returned, the readyState won't change again unless reset.

There are two possible ways around this. The first is to cancel the request completely; the second is to continue trying for a specified amount of time (or number of requests). Let's look at the practical examples of both scenarios now.

In the first example in this chapter, you performed some form validation using the XMLHttpRequest object by checking the UserName against a database already containing a set of usernames. Transient conditions on the Internet introduce the possibility that you don't get back a status of 200. In this case, some other action must be taken. Let's simulate these conditions by changing the filename that the XMLHTTPRequest object calls to a nonexistent one. In the case of the status not being equal to 200, let's display a third alternative message.

Try It Out   **Cancelling Requests**

To practice cancelling requests, follow these steps:

1.   Go back to formvalidation.htm, amend the code as follows, and save it as Formvalidation2.htm:

```
<head>
    <title>Form Validation Example</title>
    <link id="Link1" rel="stylesheet"  href="FormValidation.css" type="text/css" />
    <script type="text/javascript" src="FormValidation2.js"></script>
</head>
```

2. Open `formvalidation.js`, and amend two functions in it. Change `GetData()` as follows:

```
if ((xHRObject.readyState == 4))
    {
    if (xHRObject.status == 200)
    {
var serverText = xHRObject.responseText;
        if (serverText == "True")
        {
            span.innerHTML = "This user name has already been taken";
            NameTaken = "True";
        }
        if (serverText == "False")
        {
            span.innerHTML = "This user name is available";
            NameTaken = "False";
        }
    }
    else
    {
        span.innerHTML = "We cannot currently assess whether this user name is
    taken or not. It will be checked when you submit the form";
    xHRObject.abort();
    }
    }
}
```

3. Next, find the function `Validate`, and change the code as shown in the following highlighted line. (Be sure that the file you reference doesn't actually exist.)

```
function Validate(data)
{
    var newform = document.forms[0];
    var bodyofform = getBody(newform, data);
    if (bodyofform != "UserName=")
    {
    xHRObject.open("POST", "thisfiledoesntexist.php", true);
        xHRObject.setRequestHeader("Content-Type", "application/x-www-form-
urlencoded");
    xHRObject.onreadystatechange = getData;
    xHRObject.send(bodyofform); ;
    }
    else
    {
        span.innerHTML = "Blank user names not allowed";
    }
}
```

4. Save this as `formvalidation2.js`.

5. Open `formvalidation2.htm` in your browser, type in any username, and then move to another text box without clicking on Submit (Figure 9-6).

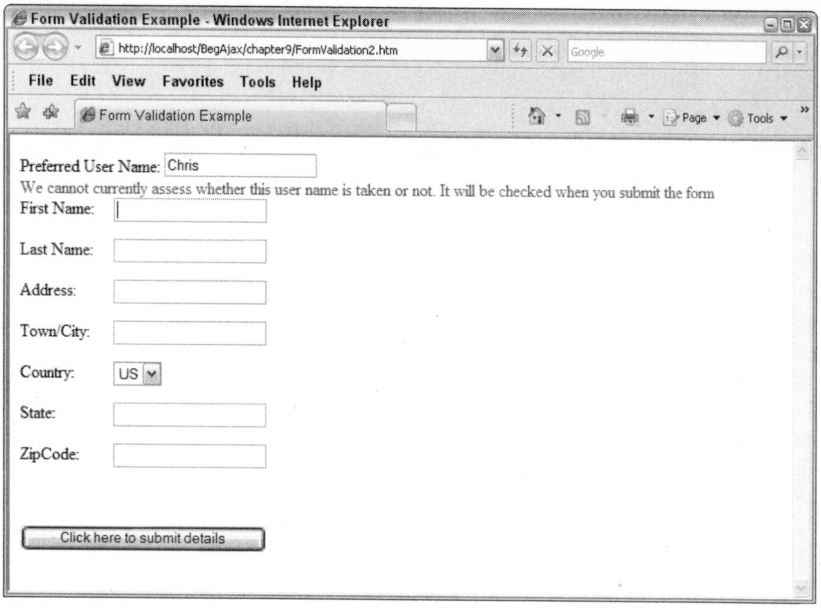

Figure 9-6: Entering a username in the `formvalidation2.htm` page.

How It Works

This example involves the tweaking of the code to deliberately return a status of 404. You also had to amend the code to be able to deal with this.

First, you must split the detection of the `readyState` from the detection of the status. You now evaluate them as two separate `if` clauses, one nested inside the other.

```
if ((xHRObject.readyState == 4))
{
if (xHRObject.status == 200)
{
```

The innermost `if` clause will now have a separate `else` clause. You separate them because the `readyState` will be changed, and this function will be fired several times as the `readyState` changes from 0 to 4. You don't know until the `readyState` of 4 is returned what the status property will return. Hence, you must separate the `if` clauses.

In the `else` clause, you supply a separate message as an `innerHTML` property, and you clear the `XMLHttpRequest` object by calling the `abort` method.

```
else
    {
        span.innerHTML = "We cannot currently assess whether this user name is
    taken or not. It will be checked when you submit the form";
        xHRObject.abort();
    }
```

There's really nothing more to it than that. But what would happen if, for example, you wanted to continue trying to see if the status was equal to 200?

In the server polling example earlier in this chapter, you continually polled the server for a response. In these kinds of situations, it's quite likely that one of the responses coming back from the server might return a status of something other than 200 (if the server goes down, for example). In this situation, you would probably want to continue polling the server and showing the old information, but letting the user know that the information displayed on the screen was out of date. Let's do that now.

Try It Out   Retrying Several Times

To practice retrying several times, follow these steps:

1. Open the page `polling.htm`, change it as follows, and save it as polling2.htm:

```
<head>
    <title>Polling The Server Example</title>
    <link id="Link1" rel="stylesheet"  href="Polling.css" type="text/css" />
    <script type="text/javascript" src="polling2.js"></script>
</head>
```

2. Open the script `polling.js`, amend locate function `GetData`, and amend it as follows, by adding the section highlighted in gray:

```
if (xHRObject.readyState == 4)
{
  if  (xHRObject.status == 200)
        {

            // Load XML
        var xml = loadDocument("Stocks.xml");
        //Load XSL
        var xsl = loadDocument("Stocks.xsl");
         //Transform
        document.getElementById("Stocks").innerHTML = transformToHTML(xml, xsl);
        //Clear the object and call the getDocument function in 5 seconds
        setTimeout("getDocument()", 5000);
        }
        else
        {
            var Stocks = document.getElementById("Stocks");
            if (Stocks.innerHTML.indexOf("available")==-1)
            {
```

```
                        Stocks.innerHTML += "<br/><span>Current stock information not
                   available, currently showing the last available data</span>";
              }
              xHRObject.abort();
              setTimeout("getDocument()", 5000);
         }
    }
```

3. Save this as `polling2.js`.

4. View it in the browser without changing anything. It should be work just as the polling-the-server example did.

5. Next, go to your web server (whether Apache or IIS), and switch off the server for this application. Once you have done this, in IIS you would see the screen shown in Figure 9-7.

Figure 9-7: Stopping the web server from IIS.

6. View `polling2.htm` in the browser, as shown in Figure 9-8

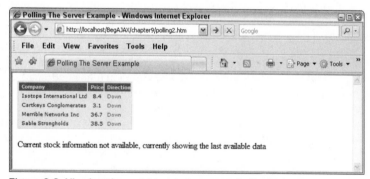

Figure 9-8: Viewing the `polling2.htm` page in the browser.

7. Go back to the server, and switch it back on again. The message will appear, and the information will be updated once more.

How It Works

The functionality allowing you to try again is already present in the page. The `getDocument()` method is polled every five seconds. Instead, what you must do is tack some extra error handling onto the end of the JavaScript handling of the `XMLHttpRequest` objects's response.

Once again, you must separate to the two clauses. The first checks for the `readyState` being equal to 4, while the second checks to see if the status is something other than 200.

```
if (xHRObject.readyState == 4)
{
  if (xHRObject.status == 200)
      {
```

Then, at the foot of the clause, you add an `else` clause. This clause must deal with the fact there has been no information returned from the `XMLHttoRequest` object. You should have the data from the last run. In this case, you scrape the information using the `document.getElementById` method.

```
else
{
            Stocks = document.getElementById("Stocks");
            if (Stocks.innerHTML.indexOf("available")==-1)
            {
                Stocks.innerHTML += "<br/><span>Current stock information not
                available, currently showing the last available data</span>";
            }
            xHRObject.abort();
            setTimeout("getDocument()", 5000);
}
```

Next, you have a small catch to deal with. You want to add a message on to the bottom of the existing information; however, you also want to poll the server at the end of the `else` clause. If the `XMLHttpRequest` object returns no data for several iterations, then you will be continually printing out a new version of that message. Instead, you check to see if the information printed already contains the word "available." (Note it doesn't have to be this word, but it seems like an easy one to scan for.) If it doesn't, then you append the message about the old information to the bottom of the stock data using the `innerHTML` routine. If it does, then you just skip that section.

At the end, you call `abort()` to clear the object, and then you call `getDocument()` via a timeout of 5,000 milliseconds to start the whole loop once again.

Summary

This chapter hasn't been theoretical because a lot of the patterns involved are very simple.

The discussion looked at the form validation pattern first, which used the `onblur` event to trigger a script that uses Ajax to identify whether the `UserName` was already taken in an Access database. In this way, you could display extra information to the user about the preferred choice of a username.

The second example used a mouseover library to query an XML document (although it quite as easily could have been a database) and then injected this into the mouseover box.

The third example showed how you could continually poll a server page using the XMLHTTPRequest object and how this information could be streamed back to the page to update without a refresh.

The fourth example used two more libraries to provide drag-and-drop functionality to a list, and it used Ajax to store the saved order of the list to an XML document.

Last, this chapter considered a couple of error-handling patterns that enabled you to handle occurrences when the XMLHttpRequest object returns something other than a 200 status.

Chapter 10 examines in more detail how you can use Ajax to utilize external resources such as news feeds.

Exercises

Suggested solutions to these questions can be found in Appendix A.

1. Change the form validation example so that it is now no longer possible to submit the form if the UserName that the user has requested has already been taken.

2. Amend the final retry example so that, instead of displaying a message, it counts to 10 times and then doesn't display any stock information at all. It then displays a new message telling the user that the information is currently unavailable.

10

Working with External Data

One of the most widely used formats for sharing data on the Web today is XML files that are formatted in a specific way and syndicated as news feeds. These XML files can be used to give visitors a preview of the latest content on a web site or blog, including descriptions and links for the newest information. Although these XML files are most commonly used for news, they can be used for any content that can be separated into distinct items of information.

One way to access these XML files is to use a desktop reader and subscribe to available feeds for sites and blogs you're interested in. If your own site content changes frequently, you can create XML feeds for your site and register them with an RSS directory.

You can also use Ajax to create an online feed reader on your own site by retrieving data from XML feeds. When you make an Ajax request to a server, you can retrieve the data from the server response in two different ways:

❑ You can access the data in XML format using the `responseXML` property of the `XMLHttpRequest` object.

❑ You can access the data in string format using the `responseText` property of this object.

The choice depends on what you want to do with the data. If you want to retrieve a single variable value, you can extract a value from an XML file using JavaScript's `getElementsByTagName` method, which works for XML tags as well as HTML/XHTML tags. If you want to retrieve HTML or JavaScript code to add to your page, you can extract the code as string data.

This chapter provides a close look at the different types of XML formats used for feeds, including how to extract data from these files and add it to your web pages, and how to use Ajax and PHP to add a feed reader to your site.

In this chapter, you learn about

❑ **Syndication and XML feeds** — RSS 0.9x, RSS 2.0, RSS 1.0, Atom 1.0

❑ **Extracting data from an XML feed** — Extracting XML data and extracting string data

❑ **Constructing an online feed reader** — Creating an Ajax request, parsing the server response, and displaying data from the response on a web page

Working with XML News Feeds

Like many aspects of the Web, XML news feeds have evolved and changed since the time they were first introduced as Active Channels in 1998 in Internet Explorer 4.0. Active Channels were the first way that updates about site content were syndicated and made available to users by online subscription. Channels didn't really catch on, largely because the content was laden with advertising and heavy on bandwidth. Then, in 1999, Netscape introduced the My Netscape portal, designed to gather a customized collection of the latest news from selected sites and provide access to this information via links and descriptions on a My Netscape portal page. As part of the MyNetscape project, Netscape developed an XML format named *RDF Site Summary* (*RSS*). This version of RSS, later known as RSS 0.9, was based on the World Wide Web Consortium (W3C) recommendation for an XML language called *Resource Description Framework* (*RDF*).

The RSS 0.9 format was modified by Dave Winer of UserLand for use as a news format for his site, Scripting News. Later that year (1999), Blogger introduced a free, Web-based tool for creating RSS files so that users no longer needed to create the XML files for news feeds by hand. In fact, users didn't need to know how to code at all to use this tool successfully. The modification of the RSS format and the introduction of tools such as Blogger were major forces in the evolution of blogs (web *logs*) into the short journal form that's popular today.

Two separate lines of RSS development then occurred: one line (RSS 1.0) based closely on RDF, and the other (including RSS 0.9x and RSS 2.0) designed to exclude many of the complexities of the RDF format.

Along with the different forms of RSS came different meanings for the RSS acronym, including the following:

❑ *Rich Site Summary* (RSS 0.91)

❑ *RDF Site Summary* (RSS 0.9 and RSS 1.0)

❑ *Really Simple Syndication* (RSS 2.0)

In 2003, Dave Winer transferred the RSS 2.0 copyright to Harvard University, and development of this line was intentionally stopped at this point. Dissatisfaction with RSS 2.0, and the inability for further modifications to it, prompted the birth and development of another XML syndication language named Atom. The Atom project was eventually moved to the *Internet Engineering Task Force* (*IETF*), and Atom 1.0 was issued as a proposed IETF standard in December 2005.

Currently, RSS 2.0 is the most widely used XML format for news feeds. Atom 1.0 is the newest contender, and it has been adopted as an RSS replacement by Google and by Movable Type, as well as many others. Many blogs (such as Peter-Paul Koch's Elsewhere on the 'Net blog) offer feeds in either RSS or Atom, as shown in Figure 10-1. It's useful to understand the structure of these formats if you want to extract data from news feeds.

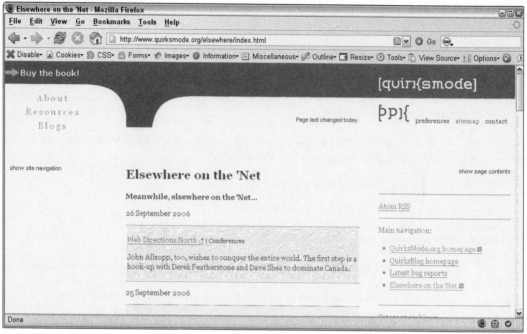

Figure 10-1: Elsewhere on the 'Net.

For more information on the convoluted and contentious history of XML news feeds, see "History of RSS" at www.rss-specifications.com/history-rss.htm *and "The Myth of RSS Compatibility" at* http://diveintomark.org/archives/2004/02/04/incompatible-rss.

RSS 0.9x

All RSS files are XML files, and they start with an XML declaration:

```
<?xml version="1.0"?>
```

For more information on XML structure and syntax, see Chapter 5, "Working with XML."

RSS 0.9x (in other words, RSS 0.91, RSS 0.92, RSS 0.93, and RSS 0.94) files have an `rss` root element that contains one `channel` element that contains the rest of the document:

```
<rss version="0.91">
  <channel>
  ...
  </channel>
</rss>
```

There are five required child elements of `channel`:

❑   `title` — The name of the feed

❑   `link` — The URL of the web site associated with the feed

- ❑   `description` — A text description of the channel

- ❑   `language` — The code for the language the feed is written in

- ❑   `image` — A description of the graphic icon for the feed

There are also several optional child elements of the `channel` element (such as the `copyright` element) that are important if you are creating an RSS file. Generally, these elements don't contain data that you want to extract from the file, however.

Although not required in RSS 0.9x, the most important part of an XML news feed is the `item` element. The `item` element contains two required child elements:

- ❑   `title` — Contains the headline of the content item

- ❑   `link` — Contains the URL of the content item

The `item` element also includes an optional element:

- ❑   `description` — Contains a text summary of the item content, with a maximum of 500 characters

The following code is an RSS 0.91 file for an imaginary news feed with one `item` element.

This file is in Userland RSS 0.91 format. There is also a Netscape RSS 0.91 format that uses a Document Type Definition (DTD).

```
<?xml version="1.0"?>
  <rss version="0.91">
    <channel>
      <title>My Channel</title>
      <link>http://www.mySite.com/</link>
      <description>My News</description>
      <language>en</language>
      <copyright>2006, Lucinda Dykes</copyright>
      <image>
        <title>My Logo</title>
        <url>http://www.silkcreek.net/graphics/sc_logo.jpg</url>
        <link>http://www.wilkcreek.net</link>
        <width>90</width>
        <height>67</height>
      </image>
      <item>
        <title>Earth Headed for Warmest Temps in a Million Years</title>
        <link>http://dailynews.att.net</link>
 <description>In about 45 years, temperatures on Earth will be hotter than at
anytime during the past one million years, says the U.S. government's top
climatologist in a new report released today.
        </description>
      </item>
    </channel>
  </rss>
```

Generally, the information you want to extract from an RSS file includes the titles, links, and descriptions of the item elements:

```
<item>
    <title>Earth Headed for Warmest Temps in a Million Years</title>
    <link>http://dailynews.att.net</link>
 <description>In about 45 years, temperatures on Earth will be hotter than at
anytime during the past one million years, says the U.S. government's top
climatologist in a new report released today.
    </description>
    </item>
```

For RSS 0.9x, the item element(s) are children of the channel element.

The last version in the RSS 0.9x series was RSS 0.94, released in August 2002. It was soon followed in September 2002 by the release of the most popular version of RSS, 2.0.

To add to the overall confusion of RSS history, the numbering of the versions is not always in chronological order. RSS 0.93 and RSS 0.94 were both released after RSS 1.0.

RSS 2.0

RSS 2.0 is very similar to RSS 0.9x. One major addition in RSS 2.0 is optional namespace modules. A *namespace* is a vocabulary of XML elements as defined in a specific XML document. Namespaces provide a means to use elements with the same name that are defined in different XML files. The namespaces that are used in the feed file are declared in the rss element. The namespace declaration includes a prefix that identifies elements from that namespace, as shown in the following example:

```
<?xml version="1.0"?>
<rss version="2.0" xmlns:radio="http://backend.userland.com/radioWeblogPostModule">
```

Adding this namespace to the rss element enables you to add elements from the radioWeblogPostModule namespace. Elements from that namespace are identified in the feed file with a radio prefix. For example, the radioWeblogPostModule includes an id element:

```
<item>
  <title>Earth Headed for Warmest Temps in a Million Years</title>
  <link>http://dailynews.att.net</link>
  <description>In about 45 years, temperatures on Earth will be hotter than at
anytime during the past one million years, says the U.S. government's top
climatologist in a new report released today.</description>
    <radio:id>68795874989</radio:id>
</item>
```

Note that the radio prefix that's included in the namespace declaration (xmlns:radio) is also included in the opening and closing tags for any elements from this namespace (radio:id) that are used in the feed document. The prefix identifies the element as a member of the radioWeblogPostModule namespace.

For more information on RSS 2.0/2.01 namespace modules, see http://blogs.law.harvard. edu/tech/directory/5/specifications/rss20ModulesNamespaces.

In RSS 2.0, the overall structure of an RSS file is somewhat different from earlier versions. RSS 2.0 files still include an `rss` root element that contains one `channel` element enclosing the rest of the document, but the only required child elements of `channel` are `title`, `link`, and `description`. Any number of `item` elements can be included in a `channel` element. At least one `title` or `description` element must be included in every `item` element, but otherwise there are no required child elements of an `item` element.

Several additional optional child elements for both the `channel` element and the `item` element are included in RSS 2.0. For more details, see the RSS 2.0 specification at `http://blogs.law.harvard.edu/tech/rss`.

Following is an imaginary news feed in RSS 2.0. The `image` element is now optional, so it's not included, and a new optional element, `comments`, has been added to specify the URL of the comments page for the item. Otherwise, the file is almost exactly the same as the RSS 0.91 version.

```xml
<?xml version="1.0"?>
  <rss version="2.0">
    <channel>
      <title>My Channel</title>
      <link>http://www.mySite.com/</link>
      <description>My News</description>
      <language>en</language>
      <copyright>2006, Lucinda Dykes</copyright>
      <item>
        <title>Earth Headed for Warmest Temps in a Million Years</title>
        <link>http://dailynews.att.net</link>
        <description>In about 45 years, temperatures on Earth will be hotter than
at anytime during the past one million years, says the U.S. government's top
climatologist in a new report released today.
        </description>
        <comments>http://myNews.com/entry/6743/notes</comments>
      </item>
    </channel>
  </rss>
```

> RSS 2.0's optional `enclosure` element can be used to create podcast feed files. An RSS 2.0 *podcast* is a feed that uses the RSS 2.0 `enclosure` element to specify the location of an online media file. A podcast reader is used to subscribe to podcast feeds and download media files at the URLs included in the feed. Although Atom 1.0 can also be used for podcasts, RSS 2.0 currently remains the preferred podcast format.

RSS 1.0

RSS 1.0 is a W3C specification that was released in 2000. RSS 1.0 is based on the W3C specification for *Resource Description Framework* (*RDF*). RDF is an XML language that's used for providing *meta data* about resources on the Web. Meta data is data that describes and models other data.

RSS 1.0 is a lightweight version of RDF, but it is more complex than RSS 0.9x or 2.0.

```
<?xml version="1.0"?>
  <rdf:RDF xmlns:rdf="http://www.w3.org/1999/02/22-rdf-syntax-ns#"
xmlns="http://purl.org/rss/1.0">
    <channel rdf:about="http://www.mySite.com/mySite.rdf">
      <title>My Channel</title>
      <link>http://www.mySite.com/</link>
      <description>My News</description>
      <image rdf:resource="http://www.silkcreek.net/graphics/sc_logo.jpg" />
      <items>
        <rdf:Seq>
          <li rdf:resource="http://dailynews.att.net" />
        </rdf:Seq>
      </items>
    </channel>
    <image rdf:about="http://www.silkcreek.net/graphics/sc_logo.jpg">
      <title>My Logo</title>
      <url>http://www.silkcreek.net/graphics/sc_logo.jpg</url>
      <link>http://www.wilkcreek.net</link>
    </image>
    <item rdf:about="http://dailynews.att.net">
      <title>Earth Headed for Warmest Temps in a Million Years</title>
      <link>http://dailynews.att.net</link>
 <description>In about 45 years, temperatures on Earth will be hotter than at
anytime during the past one million years, says the U.S. government's top
climatologist in a new report released today.
      </description>
    </item>
  </rdf:RDF>
```

The imaginary news feed in RSS 1.0 is quite different from the RSS 0.9x or 2.0 versions. The root element is rdf:RDF, and several attributes from the rdf namespace are used to specify the location of resources related to the feed item. The item element isn't contained in the channel element. Instead, the channel, image, and item elements are all children of the root element, rdf:RDF.

RSS 1.0's complexity is likely the main reason it's the least popular of the RSS formats for XML feeds.

Atom

The Atom 1.0 Syndication Format is the newest entry to the XML syndication languages, and it is very different from any version of RSS. Because Atom is also XML, the basic structure is similar to any XML file, but Atom uses a different root element (feed) than RSS and includes other important differences.

```
<?xml version="1.0"?>
<feed xmlns="http://www.w3.org/2005/Atom" xml:lang="en">
```

The feed element includes three required child elements:

❑   id — The permanent URL for the feed

❑   title — The name of the feed

❑   updated — The last time the feed was updated

```
<feed xmlns="http://www.w3.org/2005/Atom" xml:lang="en">
   <id>http://www.mySite.com</id>
   <title>My News</title>
   <updated>2006-09-13T12:00:00Z</updated>
```

In place of `item`, an `entry` element is used. This element includes three required child elements:

❑   `id` — The URL for the entry

❑   `title` — The name of the entry

❑   `updated` — The last time the entry was modified

The `summary` element is an optional child element of `entry`, similar to the `description` element used in an RSS `item`.

```
<entry>
   <id>http://mySite.com/entry/6743/</id>
   <title>Earth Headed for Warmest Temps in a Million Years</title>
   <updated>2005-07-15T12:00:00Z</updated>
   <summary>In about 45 years, temperatures on Earth will be hotter than at anytime
during the past one million years, says the U.S. government's top climatologist in
a new report released today.</summary>
</entry>
```

Many other optional elements are available in the Atom Syndication Format, but an Atom file can be as simple as this Atom 1.0 file for the imaginary news feed:

```
<?xml version="1.0"?>
   <feed xmlns="http://www.w3.org/2005/Atom" xml:lang="en">
     <id>http://www.mySite.com</id>
     <title>My News</title>
     <updated>2006-09-13T12:00:00Z</updated>
   <entry>
     <id>http://mySite.com/entry/6743/</id>
     <title>Earth Headed for Warmest Temps in a Million Years</title>
     <updated>2005-07-15T12:00:00Z</updated>
     <summary>In about 45 years, temperatures on Earth will be hotter than at
anytime during the past one million years, says the U.S. government's top
climatologist in a new report released today.</summary>
   </entry>
   </feed>
```

Atom 1.0 supports plain text, HTML, XHTML, XML, and base-64 encoded binary content such as that used as a transfer encoding for e-mail documents. Atom also includes accessibility features and its own MIME media type, `application/atom+xml`. For more details on the Atom 1.0 format, see "The Atom Syndication Format" at www.atomenabled.org/developers/syndication/.

Extracting Data from an XML Feed

An XML news feed (whether it's in RSS format or Atom format) is an XML file. You have the option of extracting the data in the feed as XML or as string data, using either the `responseXML` or `responseText` property of the `XMLHttpRequest` object when you process the server's response to your Ajax request.

Extracting XML Data

In this section, you'll use the RSS 2.0 version of the imaginary news feed file, and you'll extract the data from this file as XML. In the "Create an Ajax Feed Reader" Try It Out section later in this chapter, you'll learn how to use PHP to load an actual XML feed file into an online Ajax feed reader application.

Try it Out   Extracting XML Data from an XML Feed

In this example, you create an `XMLHttpRequest` object to retrieve an XML document in RSS 2.0 format (`feed.xml`) from the server. Type the following code into your text editor, and save it as `ch10_examp1.htm`. When the user clicks the Extract button (Figure 10-2), the item data from the feed file for `title`, `link`, and `description` is added to selected `span` elements on the page, as shown in Figure 10-3.

```
<!DOCTYPE html PUBLIC "-//W3C//DTD XHTML 1.0 Transitional//EN"
"http://www.w3.org/TR/xhtml1/DTD/xhtml1-transitional.dtd">
<html xmlns="http://www.w3.org/1999/xhtml">
<head>
<meta http-equiv="Content-Type" content="text/html; charset=iso-8859-1" />
<title>Extracting XML from a news feed</title>
<script language = "javascript">
var request = makeHTR();

function makeHTR()
{
  var request;
  if(window.XMLHttpRequest)
  {
    try
    {
      request = new XMLHttpRequest();
    }
    catch (e)
    {
      request = null;
    }
  }
  else
  {
    try
    {
      request = new ActiveXObject("Microsoft.XMLHTTP");
    }
    catch (e)
    {
      request = null;
    }
  }
```

```
  if (!request)

    alert("Error creating the XMLHttpRequest object.");
  else
    return request;
}

function sendRequest()
{
if (request.readyState == 4 || request.readyState == 0) {

 request.open("GET", "feed.xml", true);
    request.onreadystatechange = processResults;
    request.send(null);
  }
}

function processResults() {
  if (request.readyState == 4)
  {
    if (request.status == 200)
    {
   var xmlDocument = request.responseXML;
   var channelNodes = xmlDocument.documentElement.firstChild.childNodes;
   var item = channelNodes[5].childNodes;
   var title = item[0].firstChild.nodeValue;
   document.getElementById('title').innerHTML = title;
   var link = item[1].firstChild.nodeValue;
   document.getElementById('link').innerHTML = link;
   var description = item[2].firstChild.nodeValue;
   document.getElementById('description').innerHTML = description;
    }
    else
    {
      alert("There was a problem accessing the server: " + request.statusText);
    }
  }
}
  </script>
  </head>
 <body>

 <h1>Get Feed Results</h1>
    <form>
      <input type="button" id="feedR" value = "Extract">
    </form>

 <h4>Title: <span id="title"></span></h4>
 <h4>Link: <span id="link"></span></h4>
 <h4>Description: <span id="description"></span></h4>
<script type="text/javascript">
var myDoc = document.getElementById('feedR');
myDoc.onclick = sendRequest;
</script>
 </body>
</html>
```

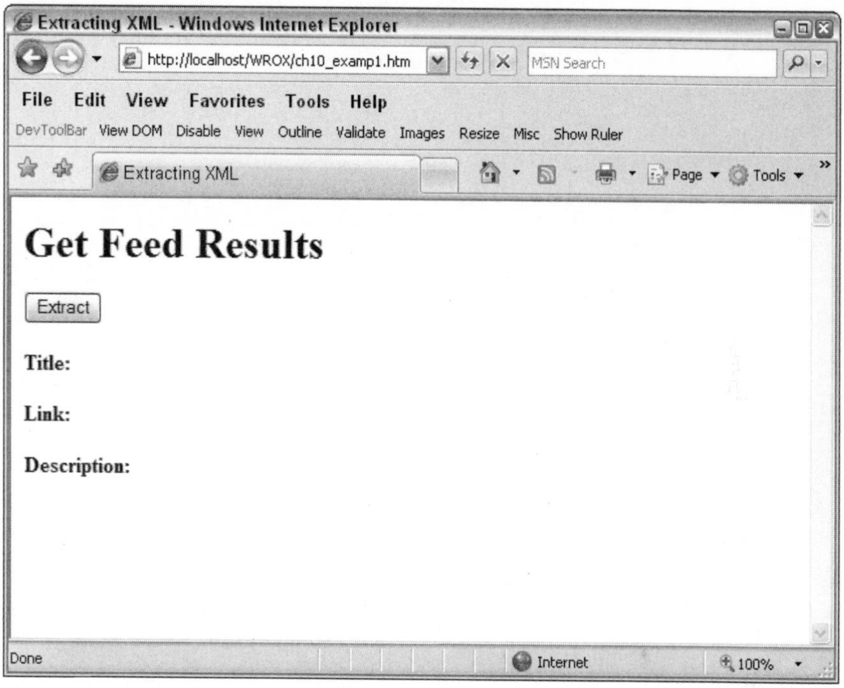

Figure 10-2: Selecting the Extract button.

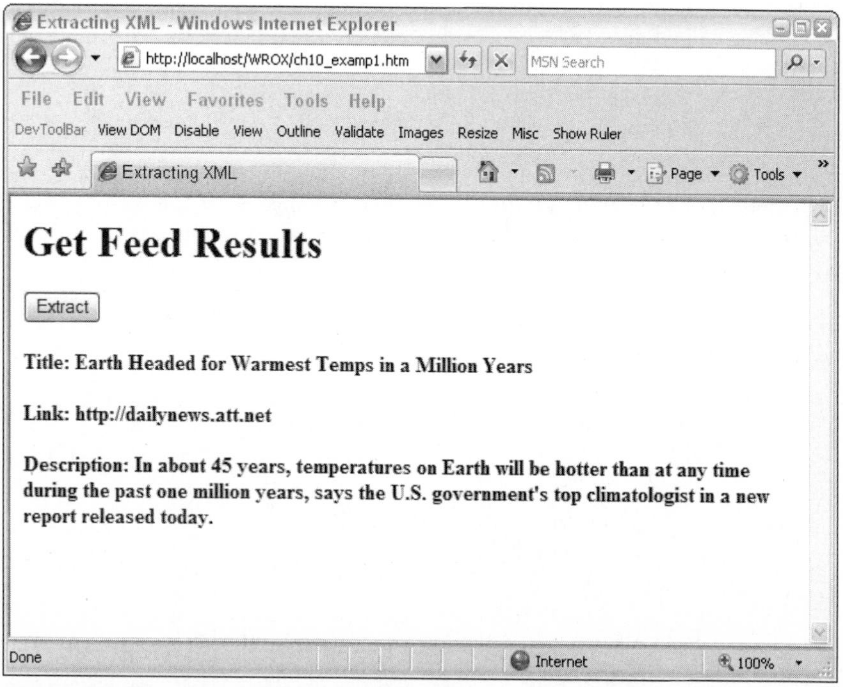

Figure 10-3: Item data from the feed file added to selected span elements.

Type the following code into your text editor, and save it as `feed.xml`:

```xml
<?xml version="1.0"?>
  <rss version="2.0">
    <channel>
      <title>My Channel</title>
      <link>http://www.mySite.com/</link>
      <description>My News</description>
      <language>en</language>
      <copyright>2006, Lucinda Dykes</copyright>
      <item>
        <title>Earth Headed for Warmest Temps in a Million Years</title>
        <link>http://dailynews.att.net</link>
        <description>In about 45 years, temperatures on Earth will be hotter than
at any time during the past one million years, says the U.S. government's top
climatologist in a new report released today.</description>
        <comments>http://myNews.com/entry/6743/notes</comments>
      </item>
    </channel>
  </rss>
```

Both `Ch10_examp1.htm` and `feed.xml` need to be on your server for the Ajax request to work. Copy both these files to the `Chapter10` subfolder of the `BegAjax` folder in the root folder of your web server (for example, the root folder is the `wwwroot` folder if you're using IIS or the `htdocs` folder if you're using Apache).

How It Works

When the `Ch10_examp1.htm` page is parsed by a browser, the `makeHTR()` function is called as soon as the script block in the `head` section of the page is read, and an instance of `XMLHttpRequest` is stored in the global variable named `request`.

```
<script language = "javascript">
var request = makeHTR();
```

The `makeHTR()` function creates a local variable named `request`, then checks to see if the browser supports the `XMLHttpRequest` object. If it does, then a new instance of the `XMLHttpRequest` object is created. If the new instance is not created, the value of the `request` variable is set to `null` in the `catch` statement block.

For more details on error handling and using `try` statements and `catch` clauses, see Chapter 6, "Debugging and Error Handling."

```javascript
var request;
  if(window.XMLHttpRequest)
  {
    try
    {
      request = new XMLHttpRequest();
    }
    catch (e)
    {
```

```
        request = null;
      }
    }
```

If the browser is Internet Explorer 5 or 6, it doesn't support the XMLHttpRequest object; the next part of the makeHTR() function creates a new instance of the ActiveXObject. If the new instance is not created, the value of the request variable is set to null in the catch statement block.

```
    else
    {
      try
      {
        request = new ActiveXObject("Microsoft.XMLHTTP");
      }
      catch (e)
      {
        request = null;
      }
```

The makeHTR() function then checks to see if the new object instance (request) was created. If request wasn't created, an alert is used to display an error message. Otherwise, the new object is returned.

```
    if (!request)

      alert("Error creating the XMLHttpRequest object.");
    else
      return request;
  }
```

Three placeholders are created in the body of the page using span elements with id attributes. These placeholders will be used to display the data that's extracted from the feed.

```
<h4>Title: <span id="title"></span></h4>
 <h4>Link: <span id="link"></span></h4>
  <h4>Description: <span id="description"></span></h4>
```

The page includes a form with a button labeled "Extract." When the user clicks the button, the sendRequest() function is called.

```
    <form>
       <input type="button" id="feedR" value = "Extract">
    </form>
```

Traditional event registration is used to register the click event rather than including an onclick attribute in the input tag.

```
<script type="text/javascript">
var myDoc = document.getElementById('feedR');
myDoc.onclick = sendRequest;
</script>
```

When the user clicks the Extract button and the `sendRequest()` function is called, an `if` statement is used to check the status of the `request` object. If the `readyState` property of the `request` object has a value of 4 (complete) or 0 (uninitialized), then the request object is available, and a new HTTP request is initiated. The `open` method of the `XMLHttpRequest` object is used to request data from the XML document, `feed.xml`. This method uses three parameters:

❑ The HTTP method used for the request (`"GET"`)

❑ The URL of the document (`"feed.xml"`)

❑ A Boolean value of `true` to indicate that the call is asynchronous

```
function sendRequest()
{
if (request.readyState == 4 || request.readyState == 0) {
 request.open("GET", "feed.xml", true);
```

When the `readyState` property of the `XMLHttpRequest` object changes (that is, when the data starts to download), the `processResults()` function will be called to process the data that's returned from the server.

```
request.onreadystatechange = processResults;
```

The actual request to the server is made using the `send` method of the `XMLHttpRequest` object. When you use the `GET` method, you include a `null` parameter with this method.

```
request.send(null);
```

Once the `readyState` property of the `request` object changes, the `processResults()` function is called. If the `readyState` property is equal to 4, the download from the server is complete. As an additional check, a `status` property equal to 200 also indicates that the request was processed successfully.

```
function processResults() {
   if (request.readyState == 4)
   {
      if (request.status == 200)
      {
```

Once the download is complete, the `responseXML` property is used to store the data as XML in a variable named `xmlDocument`.

```
var xmlDocument = request.responseXML;
```

DOM methods are then used to traverse the XML document and extract the `title`, `link`, and `description` data from the `item` element in the `feed.xml` document.

```
var channelNodes = xmlDocument.documentElement.firstChild.childNodes;
var item = channelNodes[5].childNodes;
```

The `documentElement` is the root element of the XML document. In this case, that's the `rss` element. The first child of the `rss` element is the `channel` element. The `channel` element contains an array of six child nodes, with array index values from 0 to 5. The last child node of the `channel` element, the `item` element, has an array index value of 5. The item element also contains an array of four child nodes, with array index values from 0 to 3.

> This example works fine in Internet Explorer; however, Mozilla-based browsers treat white space in XML documents as text nodes. When you access the `firstChild` of the `rss` element in a Mozilla-based browser, you access the white space text node instead of the `channel` element. You can take the white space into account and skip over these white space text nodes using family relationships. For more information on this approach, see Chapter 5.
>
> You can also add code to remove all the white space from the XML document, rather than dealing with these increasingly cumbersome family relationships.
>
> Another way to get around the white-space issues in Mozilla-based browsers is to use a server-side language such as PHP for extracting the data from an XML document, rather than traversing the DOM with JavaScript, as you'll see in the online Ajax feed reader example later in this chapter.

```
var title = item[0].firstChild.nodeValue;
document.getElementById('title').innerHTML = title;
var link = item[1].firstChild.nodeValue;
document.getElementById('link').innerHTML = link;
var description = item[2].firstChild.nodeValue;
document.getElementById('description').innerHTML = description;
```

The first child node of the `item` element is the `title` element. The first child of the `title` element is the `text` node that contains the content of the `title` element. The value of this node is assigned to the `title` variable. The `document.getElementById()` method is used to locate the `span` element with an `id` value of `title`, and the `innerHTML` property is used to assign the data from the `title` element to this span element. The same sequence is used for the `link` element and the `description` element.

```
else
{
   alert("There was a problem accessing the server: " + request.statusText);
}
```

If the `status` is not equal to `200`, the download was not successful, and an alert is used to display an error message using the `statusText` property of the `XMLHttpRequest` object that contains the HTTP response status text.

Extracting String Data

You can use the `responseText` property of the `XMLHttpRequest` object for extracting string data from an XML news feed file. It's difficult, though, to process this data with JavaScript and extract specific pieces of data to add to your page. For example, in the `Ch10_examp1.htm` file that was used in the previous example, if you change the `responseXML` property to `responseText` and attempt to add that data to a span on the page using the `innerHTML` property, you end up with an undifferentiated string that contains most of the text content of the XML file, as shown in Figures 10-4 and 10-5.

```
var xmlDocument = request.responseText;
document.getElementById('response').innerHTML = xmlDocument;
...
<h4>Response: <span id="response"></span></h4>
```

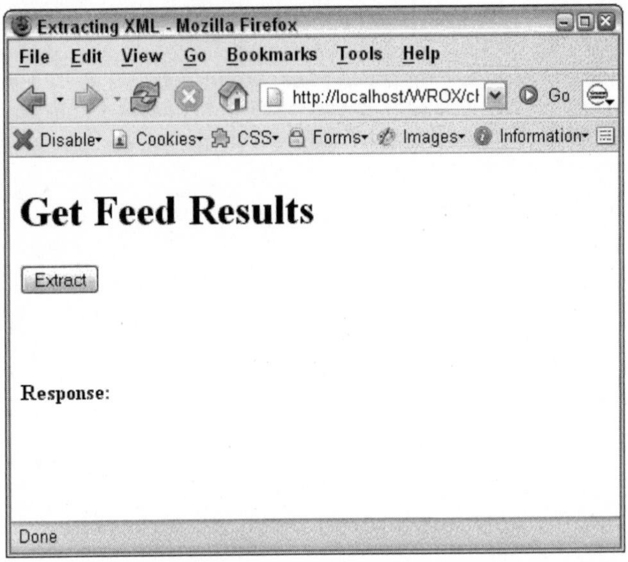

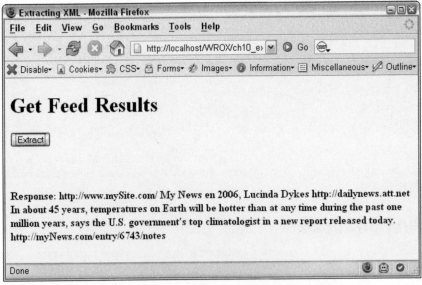

Figure 10-4: Extracting the data using `responseText`.

Figure 10-5: Using `responseText` returns an undifferentiated string.

Although you could manipulate this string with JavaScript string functions, it would be a cumbersome and difficult endeavor to extract just that string data from the XML news feed that you were interested in adding to your page.

The `responseText` property can be very useful when you're making an HTTP request for a text file or when you use a server-side language such as PHP to process the data from the server's response to an HTTP request, as you'll see in the feed reader example in the following section. It can also be useful if the XML file that you're requesting from the server consists of HTML code that you can then add directly to a page dynamically. If the XML file you're requesting is an XML news feed, though, it's much easier to use the `responseXML` property to return XML data to process, rather than string data, unless you're using a server-side language to assist in the processing of the data returned from the HTTP request.

Building an Online Feed Reader with Ajax

The main reason for using news feeds and feed readers is to provide a means to access online content that changes frequently. You can create an Ajax application that includes JavaScript to make the request for the XML news feed file, PHP to extract and process the data from the news feed before you add it to your page, and XHTML and CSS to display the extracted data on your page. For this application, you'll use a separate file for each of these pieces of the application: XHTML, CSS, JavaScript, and PHP. This application works in Internet Explorer 6 and 7, as well as Firefox.

Try It Out   **Create an Ajax Feed Reader**

In this example, you'll use an external JavaScript file to create an `XMLHttpRequest` object that is used to request a PHP file. The PHP file uses PHP 5's `simpleXML` extension to load an XML news feed file, then extracts data for the `title`, `link`, and `publication date` from the feed. The data is added to the XHTML page using a `div` and `innerHTML`, and it is formatted with CSS. The feed data can be updated at any time by clicking a button that generates a new instance of the `XMLHttpRequest` object.

This application includes four files: `ch10_examp2.htm`, `feed.js`, `feed.css`, and `FeedRead3.php`. All of these files need to be on your server for the Ajax request to work. Copy all four files to the `Chapter10` subfolder of the `BegAjax` folder in the root folder of your web server (for example, the root folder is `wwwroot` if you're using IIS or `htdocs` if you're using Apache).

Figure 10-6 shows the application in Firefox.

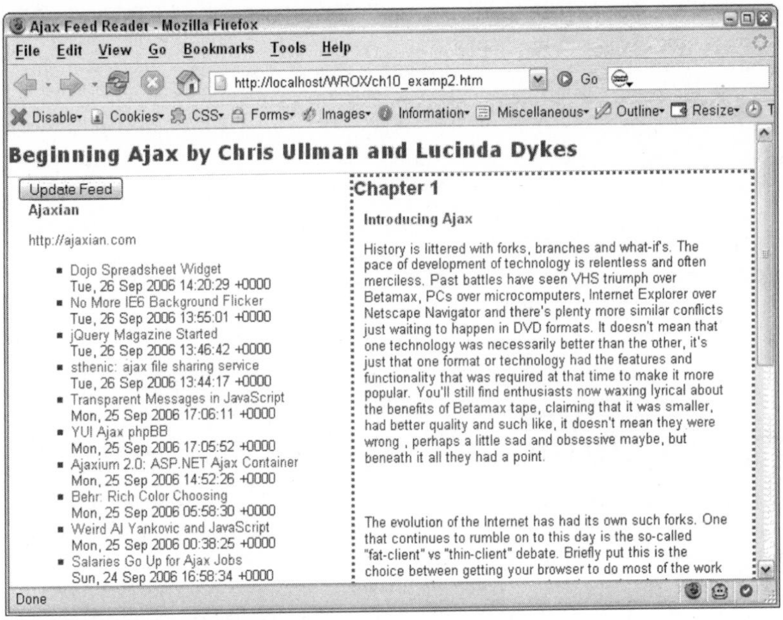

Figure 10-6: Application in Firefox.

Type the following code into your text editor, and save it as `ch10_examp2.htm`:

```
<!DOCTYPE html PUBLIC "-//W3C//DTD XHTML 1.0 Transitional//EN"
"http://www.w3.org/TR/xhtml1/DTD/xhtml1-transitional.dtd">
<html xmlns="http://www.w3.org/1999/xhtml">
<head>
<meta http-equiv="Content-Type" content="text/html; charset=iso-8859-1" />
<title>Ajax Feed Reader</title>
<link rel="stylesheet" href="feed.css" type="text/css" />
<script type="text/javascript" src="feed.js"></script>
</head>
<body onload="sendRequest()">
<div id="masthead">
  <h1 id="siteName">Beginning Ajax by Chris Ullman and Lucinda Dykes </h1>
</div>
<div id="content">
  <h2 id="pageName">Chapter 1</h2>
  <div class="story">
    <h3>Introducing Ajax</h3>
    <p> History is littered with forks, branches and what-if's. The pace of
development of technology is relentless and often merciless. Past battles have seen
VHS triumph over Betamax, PCs over microcomputers, Internet Explorer over Netscape
Navigator and there's plenty more similar conflicts just waiting to happen in DVD
formats. It doesn't mean that one technology was necessarily better than the other,
it's just that one format or technology had the features and functionality that
were required at that time to make it more popular. You'll still find enthusiasts
now waxing lyrical about the benefits of  Betamax tape, claiming that it was
smaller, had better quality and such like, it doesn't mean they were wrong ,
perhaps a little sad and obsessive maybe, but beneath it all they had a point.</p>
```

```
    </div>
    <div class="story">
        <p> The evolution of the Internet has had its own such forks. One that
continues to rumble on to this day is the so-called "fat-client" vs "thin-client"
debate. Briefly put this is the choice between getting your browser to do most of
the work as opposed to get a server at the other end to do the processing.
Initially in the mid-90s it looked as if the "fat-client" ideology was going to win
out.  The introduction of Internet Explorer 4 and Netscape Navigator 4 brought with
them the advent of Dynamic HTML, which used scripting languages to alter pages so
that you could drag and drop items or make menus appear and disappear without
requiring a page refresh. However within a year there was a rush towards the "thin-
client", with the introduction of server-side technologies such as Active Server
Pages and PHP. The client-side techniques still exist, but the model of current
Internet and web page usage is broadly based upon the server-side method of "enter
your data, send the page to the server and wait for a response" model. </p>
    </div>
</div>
<div class="feedResults">
<form>
<input type="button" value="Update Feed" name="update" id="update" />
</form>
<script type="text/javascript">
var updateFeed = document.getElementById('update');
updateFeed.onclick = sendRequest;
</script>
<div class="feedResults" id="displayResults"> 
</div>
<br />
</body>
</html>
```

Type the following code into your text editor, and save it as feed.js:

```
var request = makeHTR();

function makeHTR()
{
  var request;
  if(window.XMLHttpRequest)
  {
    try
    {
      request = new XMLHttpRequest();
    }
    catch (e)
    {
      request = null;
    }
  }
  else
  {
    try
    {
      request = new ActiveXObject("Microsoft.XMLHTTP");
    }
```

```
      catch (e)
      {
        request = null;
      }
    }
    if (!request)
      alert("Error creating the XMLHttpRequest object.");
    else
      return request;
}

function sendRequest()
{
if (request.readyState == 4 || request.readyState == 0) {
    num = Math.round(Math.random()*999999);
    request.open("GET", "FeedRead3.php?id="+num, true);
    request.onreadystatechange = processResults;
    request.send(null);
  }
  else
    setTimeout('sendRequest()', 1000);
}

function processResults()
{
  if (request.readyState == 4)
  {
    if (request.status == 200)
    {
     var textResponse = request.responseText;
     alert('Updating the Feed');
     document.getElementById('displayResults').innerHTML = textResponse;


    }
    else
    {
      alert("There was a problem accessing the server: " + request.statusText);
    }
  }
}
```

Type the following code into your text editor, and save it as `FeedRead3.php`:

```php
<?php
$feed = simplexml_load_file('http://feeds.feedburner.com/ajaxian');

foreach($feed->channel as $channel) {
 echo '<h3>' . htmlentities($channel->title) . '</h3>';
 echo '<p><a href="' . htmlentities($channel->link) . '">' . htmlentities($channel-
>link) . '</a></p>';
 echo '<ul>';
         foreach ($channel->item as $item) {
                 echo '<li><a href="' . htmlentities($item->link) . '">';
                 echo htmlentities($item->title) . '</a><br />';
                 echo htmlentities($item->pubDate) .'<br /></li>';
```

```
            }
         echo '</ul>';
      }
 ?>
```

Type the following code into your text editor, and save it as `feed.css`:

```css
body {
  font-family: Arial,sans-serif;
  color: #333333;
  line-height: 1.166;
  margin: 0px;
  padding: 0px;
}

a:link, a:visited, a:hover {
  color: #006699;
  text-decoration: none;
}

a:hover {
  text-decoration: underline;
}


h1, h2, h3, h4, h5, h6 {
  font-family: Arial,sans-serif;
  margin: 0px;
  padding: 0px;
}

h1{
  font-family: Verdana,Arial,sans-serif;
  font-size: 120%;
  color: #334d55;
}

h2{
  font-size: 114%;
  color: #006699;
}

h3{
  font-size: 100%;
  color: #334d55;
}

h4{
  font-size: 100%;
  font-weight: normal;
  color: #333333;
}

h5{
  font-size: 100%;
```

```css
    color: #334d55;
}

ul{
   list-style-type: square;
}

ul ul{
   list-style-type: disc;
}

ul ul ul{
   list-style-type: none;
}

#masthead{
   margin: 0;
   padding: 10px 0px;
   border-bottom: 1px solid #cccccc;
   width: 100%;
}

#content{
   float:right;
   width: 50%;
   margin: 0;
   padding: 0 3% 0 0;
   border: medium dotted #0066CC;
}

.story{
   clear: both;
   padding: 10px 0px 0px 10px;
   font-size: 80%;
}

.story p{
   padding: 0px 0px 10px 0px;
}

.feedResults{
   margin: 0px;
   padding: 0px 0px 10px 10px;
   font-size: 90%;
}
```

How It Works

The `feed.js` file contains the JavaScript that creates a new instance of the `XMLHttpRequest` object. The initial part of this JavaScript code is exactly the same as the code included in `Ch10_examp1.htm`. When the `feed.js` page is parsed by a browser, the `makeHTR()` function is called in the first line, and an instance of `XMLHttpRequest` is stored in the global variable named `request`.

```
var request = makeHTR();
```

The `makeHTR()` function creates a local variable named `request`, then checks to see if the browser supports the `XMLHttpRequest` object. If it does, then a new instance of the `XMLHttpRequest` object is created. If the new instance is not created, the value of the `request` variable is set to `null` in the `catch` statement block.

```
function makeHTR()
{
  var request;
  if(window.XMLHttpRequest)
  {
    try
    {
      request = new XMLHttpRequest();
    }
    catch (e)
    {
      request = null;
    }
  }
}
```

If the browser is Internet Explorer 5 or 6, it doesn't support the `XMLHttpRequest` object, and the next part of the `makeHTR()` function creates a new instance of the `ActiveXObject`. If the new instance is not created, the value of the `request` variable is set to `null` in the `catch` statement block.

```
  else
  {
    try
    {
      request = new ActiveXObject("Microsoft.XMLHTTP");
    }
    catch (e)
    {
      request = null;
    }
```

The `makeHTR()` function then checks to see if the new object instance (`request`) was created. If the `request` wasn't created, an alert is used to display an error message. Otherwise, the new object is returned.

```
  if (!request)

    alert("Error creating the XMLHttpRequest object.");
  else
    return request;
}
```

When the `ch10_examp2.htm` page has finished loading in the browser, the `sendRequest()` function is called. If the `readyState` property of the `request` object has a value of 4 (complete) or 0 (uninitialized), then the request object is available, and a new HTTP request is initiated.

```
function sendRequest()
{
if (request.readyState == 4 || request.readyState == 0) {
```

Before the HTTP request is initiated, a random number is generated to add to the URL in the GET request. Internet Explorer caches the request and doesn't update it each time a new request is made. As a workaround for this issue, this code generates a new number each time a new request is made, so that each request is distinct. For more information about this issue, see this post on the Ajaxian blog at http://ajaxian.com/archives/ajax-ie-caching-issue.

```
num = Math.round(Math.random()*999999);
```

Figure 10-7 shows the Firebug console and a list of consecutive GET requests. Each request has a different id value.

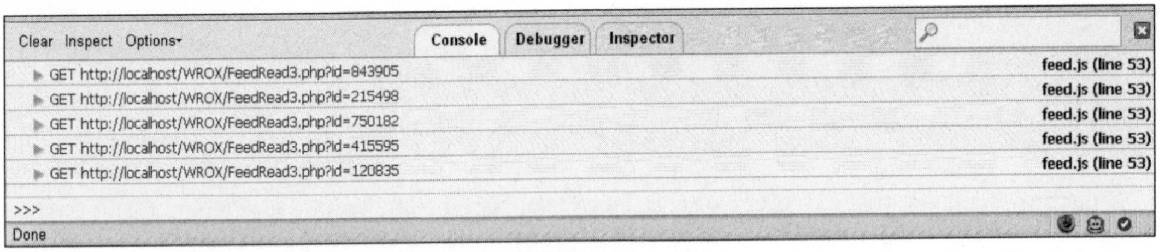

Figure 10-7: Firebug console with list of GET requests.

The open method of the XMLHttpRequest object is used to request data from the PHP file that has loaded the latest version of the XML news feed and extracted data for the title, link, and publication date of each item in the feed. The open method uses three parameters:

❏ The HTTP method used for the request ("GET")

❏ The URL of the document ("FeedRead3.php?id="+num) with a query string added to the URL that includes an id variable that has a value equal to the random number generated in the previous line of code (num)

❏ A Boolean value of true to indicate that the call is asynchronous

```
request.open("GET", "FeedRead3.php?id="+num, true);
```

When the readyState property of the XMLHttpRequest object changes (that is, when the data starts to download), the processResults() function will be called to process the data that's returned from the server.

```
request.onreadystatechange = processResults;
```

The actual request to the server is made using the send method of the XMLHttpRequest object. When you use the GET method, you include a null parameter with this method.

```
request.send(null);
```

An `else` condition is included so that if the connection is busy, the `sendRequest` function is called again in 1000 milliseconds (1 second).

```
else
    setTimeout('sendRequest()', 1000);
}
```

Once the `readyState` property of the `request` object changes, the `processResults()` function is called. If the `readyState` property is equal to `4`, the download from the server is complete. As an additional check, a `status` property equal to `200` also indicates that the request was processed successfully.

```
function processResults() {
  if (request.readyState == 4)
  {
     if (request.status == 200)
     {
```

Once the download is complete, the `responseText` property is used to store the string data in a variable named `textResponse`. In this case, `responseText` is used rather than `responseXML` because the request is being made for a PHP page, which will process the XML, extract the data, and return a string. An alert displays to let the user know that the feed data has been updated—otherwise, if the data has not changed, the user may not know if the request was successful. The string data is then added to the XHTML page using the `getElementById` method, a `div` with an `id` value of `displayResults`, and the `innerHTML` property that replaces the contents of the `div` with the contents of the `textResponse` variable.

```
var textResponse = request.responseText;
alert('Updating the Feed');
document.getElementById('displayResults').innerHTML = textResponse;
```

If the `status` is not equal to `200`, the download was not successful, and an alert is used to display an error message using the `statusText` property of the `XMLHttpRequest` object that contains the HTTP response status text.

```
else
{
  alert("There was a problem accessing the server: " + request.statusText);
 }
```

The page includes a form with a button labeled "Update Feed." When the user clicks the button, the `sendRequest()` function is called. This function is called when the page initially loads, but it can be called again at any time by clicking the button.

```
<form>
  <input type="button" value="Update Feed" name="update" id="update" />
</form>
```

Traditional event registration is used to register the click event rather than including an `onclick` attribute in the `input` tag.

```
<script type="text/javascript">
var updateFeed = document.getElementById('update');
updateFeed.onclick = sendRequest;
</script>
```

The PHP file uses the `simpleXML` extension (enabled by default in PHP 5) to load the URL for the feed. The `simpleXML` extension is enabled by default when you install PHP 5. This URL is for the XML news feed file for the Ajaxian blog (an excellent source of Ajax news), but it can be changed to another URL. Although this application uses only one news feed, it could be expanded to include additional feeds by using a PHP array to load several XML files.

For more information on using simpleXML, see "Using PHP 5's SimpleXML" at www.onlamp.com/pub/a/php/2004/01/15/simplexml.html.

```php
<?php
$feed = simplexml_load_file('http://feeds.feedburner.com/ajaxian');
```

The XML file is read, and two `foreach` loops are used to extract data from the `title` and `link` elements in the `channel` element in the feed, and the data from the `title`, `link`, and `pubDate` (publication date) elements from each `item` element in the feed.

Each time a new `XMLHttpRequest` is created, the PHP file loads the newest version of the feed file and extracts the current data, which is then added to the XHTML page.

In Figure 10-8, the Firebug console shows the data returned from the PHP page. You can see that it's HTML code that can be directly added to the page using `innerHTML`.

For more information on using Firebug, see Chapter 6, "Debugging and Error Handling."

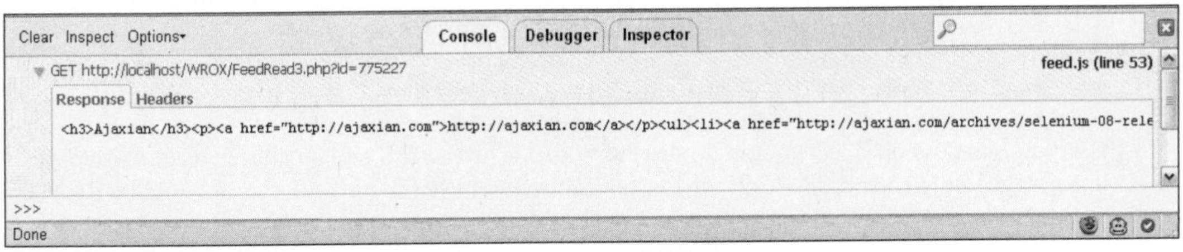

Figure 10-8: Firebug console with data returned from the PHP page.

Summary

XML news feeds are a widely available source of external XML data that can be added to web pages using Ajax techniques.

This chapter included the following points:

❑ Although there are several different XML formats in use for news feeds, the most widely used format now is RSS 2.0.

❑ The Atom 1.0 Syndication format includes many more features than RSS 2.0, is being used by Google and Movable Type, among many others, and is becoming a very popular format.

❑ Mozilla-based browsers treat white space as text nodes, and they make it difficult to traverse the DOM to extract data from an XML news feed file.

❑   Internet Explorer caches Ajax requests, so it's necessary to add a workaround for this issue to make repeated requests.

❑   Although you can return either XML or string data from an XMLHttpRequest, when the request is for an XML news feed, it's easier to process and extract XML data rather than string data.

❑   You can process and extract XML data using an application server such as PHP 5 and return string data as HTML code that can be directly added to your page.

As you've seen, it can be difficult to parse XML and extract the data you want to add to a page. Extracting data from an undifferentiated string can also be problematic. In Chapter 11, you'll learn about an alternative data format named JavaScript Object Notation (JSON). JSON can be used with the responseText property of the XMLHttpRequest object to return data to your page that can be easily extracted with additional JavaScript.

Exercise

Suggested solutions to this question can be found in Appendix A.

1.   Add JavaScript to ch10_examp1.htm to convert the link text to an actual link when the data is displayed on the page.

```
var link = item[1].firstChild.nodeValue;
document.getElementById('link').innerHTML = link;
```

JSON

As you probably know from reading Chapter 3, when you make an Ajax request to a server, you can retrieve the data from the server response in two different ways. You can access the data in XML format using the `responseXML` property of the `XMLHttpRequest` object, or you can access the data in string format using the `responseText` property of this object. XML is currently the standard language for data transmission, but one of the disadvantages of using XML is that it can be difficult to parse XML and extract the data that you want to add to your page.

Douglas Crockford has created an alternative data transmission format named *JavaScript Object Notation (JSON)*. One of the advantages of using JSON for data transmission is that JSON is actually JavaScript — it's a text format based on a subset of JavaScript object-literal syntax from the third edition of ECMAScript. This means you can use `responseText` to retrieve JSON data from a server, and then you can use JavaScript's `eval()` method to convert a JSON string into a JavaScript object. You can then easily extract the data from this object using additional JavaScript — and no DOM manipulation is needed.

There are also JSON libraries available for most programming languages, including C++, C#, ColdFusion, Java, Perl, PHP, and Python, among others. These libraries enable you to convert data formatted in these languages into JSON format. For more details, visit the JSON site at `www.json.org`.

This chapter takes a close look at using JSON, including the basics of JSON syntax, a comparison of using JSON and XML for data transmission, and details of retrieving and extracting JSON data using the `XMLHttpRequest` object.

In this chapter, you learn about the following:

- ❑ JSON syntax (`object literals`, `array literals`, `datatypes`)
- ❑ Data transmission formats (readability, speed, data extraction)
- ❑ Using JSON data (creating an Ajax request for JSON data, parsing the server response, using a JSON parser, and displaying data from the response on a web page)
- ❑ Using JSON with PHP

JSON Syntax

JSON consists of two data structures:

- ❏ **Objects** — An unordered collection of name/value pairs
- ❏ **Arrays** — An ordered collection of values

There are no variables or other control structures in JSON. It's designed solely for transmitting data.

JSON syntax is based on JavaScript syntax for object literals and array literals. When you use literals, you include the data itself, rather than an expression that generates the data. For example, in the following code block, the value that's assigned to the variable x is a literal (15), while the value that's assigned to the variable y is an expression (3*x) that must be evaluated before the assignment is complete.

```
var x = 15;
var y = 3 * x;
```

JSON Datatypes

JSON data structures can include any of the following types of data:

- ❏ String
- ❏ Number
- ❏ Boolean value (true/false)
- ❏ null
- ❏ Object
- ❏ Array

JSON strings must be double-quoted. They use standard JavaScript escape codes and add a backslash before the following characters:

- ❏ " (quotation marks)
- ❏ b (backspace)
- ❏ n (new line)
- ❏ f (form feed)
- ❏ r (carriage return)
- ❏ t (horizontal tab)
- ❏ u (plus 4 digits for a Unicode character)
- ❏ \ (backslash)
- ❏ / (forward slash)

For example, to represent the string `I feel "funny"`, you escape both sets of quotation marks around the word `funny`:

```
"I feel \"funny\""
```

Object Literals

JavaScript objects can be defined using an object constructor or an object literal. To define a new object with a constructor, you use the Object constructor function with the `new` keyword.

```
var member = new Object();
```

Then you can add properties to the object using dot notation.

```
member.name = "Jobo";
member.address = "325 Smith Rd";
member.isRegistered = true;
```

You can also add properties to the object using array syntax.

```
member["name"] = "Jobo";
member["address"] = "325 Smith Rd";
member["isRegistered"] = true;
```

You can create the same object more efficiently by using an object literal.

```
var member =
{name: "Jobo",
address: "325 Smith Road",
isRegistered: true
};
```

JSON doesn't use constructors, only literals. The following code shows the `member` object formulated as JSON text:

```
{"name": "Jobo",
 "address": "325 Smith Road",
 "isRegistered": true
}
```

Note that there is no semicolon at the end of a JSON object definition.

If there is more than one member object, you could represent it in JSON as an object that contains an array of two objects.

```
{"member": [
{"name": "Jobo",
 "address": "325 Smith Road",
 "isRegistered": true
},
```

```
{"name": "Rico",
 "address": "30 Ocean Drive",
 "isRegistered": false
 }
 ]
 }
```

For more details on JavaScript objects, see Chapter 2.

Array Literals

JavaScript arrays can also be created using a constructor or using an array literal. To define a new array with a constructor, you use the Array constructor function with the new keyword.

```
var myArray = new Array();
```

Then, you can add members to the array using square brackets and an index value that indicates the position in the array.

```
myArray[0] = 1218;
myArray[1] = "Crawford"
myArray[2] = "Drive";
```

You can create the same object more efficiently using an array literal.

```
var myArray = [1218, "Crawford", "Drive"];
```

The following code shows this array formulated as JSON text:

```
[1218, "Crawford", "Drive"]
```

Using a JSON Parser

You can use a JSON parser to create JSON text from objects and arrays, and to create objects and arrays from JSON text. A JSON parser is provided on the JSON site at www.json.org/json.js. You can copy this JavaScript file and reference it in your page by including this code in the head section of the page:

```
<script type="text/javascript" src="json.js"></script>
```

It defines two functions:

❑   toJSONString()

❑   parseJSON()

The toJSONString() method is added to the JavaScript Object and Array definitions, and it enables you to convert a JavaScript object or array to JSON text. The object or array doesn't need to be preformulated as a literal in order to use this method. For example, the following code for the member object uses the Object constructor:

```
<script type="text/javascript">
var member = new Object();
member.name = "Jobo";
member.address = "325 Smith Rd";
member.isRegistered = true;
member = member.toJSONString();
alert("The member object as a JSON data structure: \n" + member);
</script>
```

Figure 11-1 shows the result of this conversion in an alert dialog in IE 7.

Figure 11-1: Alert dialog in IE 7.

The parseJSON() method is added to the JavaScript String definition and enables you to create an object or array from JSON text. You'll use this method in the section "Ajax and JSON," later in this chapter.

Data Transmission Formats

Either JSON or XML can be used for data transmission in Ajax applications. The major factor in choosing a data transmission format is the type of data you want to transmit. XML has a much more complex structure than JSON, and it can be used for transmitting almost any type of data. Many desktop applications (such as Microsoft Word, Excel, and Access) now allow you to import and export data as XML; however, JSON's simple data structure may be all you need to transmit the data in your Ajax application, and using JSON has several advantages:

❑ **JSON is JavaScript.** — JSON text can be easily converted into JavaScript objects and arrays using JavaScript's eval() method. You can then extract the data from the server response using JavaScript. This means JSON is especially easy to use if you're already familiar with JavaScript.

❑ **JSON is typed.** — A JSON object already has a JavaScript datatype: string, number, Boolean, null, array, or object. Datatypes for XML content can be included by using a DTD or XML schema to define an XML document's structure, but JavaScript datatypes are not a built-in feature of XML.

❑ **JSON can be parsed as JavaScript.** — JSON represents JavaScript in a text format. Using JavaScript itself, you can convert JSON text to JavaScript. For additional security, you can use a JSON parser for the conversion. Returning data as XML means that you need to parse the XML. This usually requires DOM methods and DOM manipulation. As you've seen in earlier chapters, this can become quite complex, even for simple data.

Both XML and JSON are easily readable by both people and machines. The following code shows the XML file from Chapter 5, `classes.xml`:

```xml
<?xml version="1.0"?>
<classes>
  <class>
    <classID>CS115</classID>
    <department>ComputerScience</department>
    <credits req="yes">3</credits>
    <instructor>Adams</instructor>
    <title>Programming Concepts</title>
  </class>
  <class>
    <classID semester="fall">CS205</classID>
    <department>ComputerScience</department>
    <credits req="yes">3</credits>
    <instructor>Dykes</instructor>
    <title>JavaScript</title>
  </class>
  <class>
    <classID semester="fall">CS255</classID>
    <department>ComputerScience</department>
    <credits req="yes">3</credits>
    <instructor>Brunner</instructor>
    <title>Java</title>
  </class>
</classes>
```

This is the same data in JSON format (`classes.txt`):

```json
{"class1": [
    {
      "classID": "CS115",
      "department": "Computer Science",
      "credits": 3,
      "req": "yes",
      "instructor" : "Adams",
      "title" : "Programming Concepts"
    },
    {
      "classID": "CS205",
      "semester": "fall",
      "department": "Computer Science",
      "credits": 3,
      "req": "yes",
      "instructor" : "Dykes",
      "title" : "JavaScript"
    },
    {
      "classID": "CS255",
      "semester": "fall",
      "department": "Computer Science",
      "credits": 3,
      "req": "yes",
      "instructor" : "Brunner",
```

```
        "title" : "Java"
      }
    ]
}
```

The name of the object has been changed from class *to* class1 *because* class *is a reserved word in JavaScript. Reserved words are set aside for future extensions of the JavaScript language.*

XML uses elements, attributes, entities, and other structures. JSON isn't a document format, so it doesn't need these additional structures. Because JSON data includes only name-value pairs (object) or just values (array), JSON data has a smaller size than equivalent XML data. For example, classes.xml is 690 bytes, and classes.txt is 647 bytes. Although this is a trivial difference in this case, in a large application, the size difference between XML and JSON data could make a significant speed difference.

For additional details on the comparison between XML and JSON, see "JSON: The Fat-Free Alternative to XML," at www.json.org/xml.html.

Ajax and JSON

In the same way you create any Ajax request for text data, you can use the XMLHttpRequest object to create a request for JSON data.

Creating the Request

If you're requesting JSON data directly from a JSON file on the server (in other words, not using a server-side language such as PHP as an intermediary to obtain the data), you can simply request the JSON file by name.

```
request.open("GET", "classes.txt", true);
```

In this case, classes.txt is the name of the JSON data file, and request is the variable created to hold the XMLHttpRequest object.

Figure 11-2 shows the server response in the Firebug console. As you can see in Figure 11-3, the content-type of the response is text/plain.

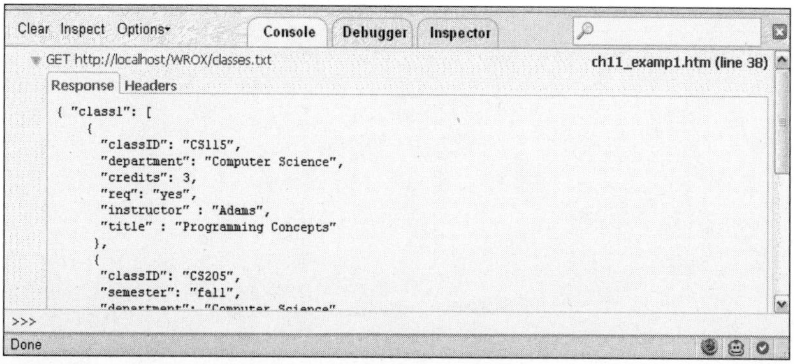

Figure 11-2: Server response in the Firebug console.

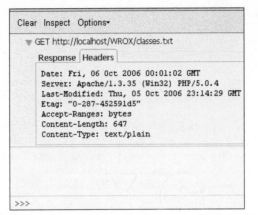

Figure 11-3: Content-type of the response is `text/plain`.

For more information on using the Firebug extension for Firefox, see Chapter 6.

If you request XML data directly from an XML file on the server, you also request the XML file by name.

```
request.open("GET", "classes.xml", true);
```

Figure 11-4 shows the server response in the Firebug console. As you can see in Figure 11-5, because we're using an Apache web server, the `content-type` of the response is `application/xml`. If the web server is IIS, the `content-type` of the response is `text/xml`.

Figure 11-4: Server response again in the Firebug console.

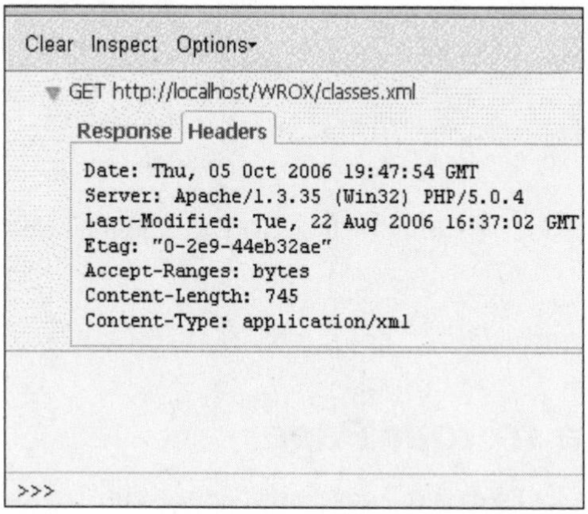

Figure 11-5: Content-type of the response is `application/xml`.

Parsing the Response

Once you receive the JSON data from the server, you can parse this response in two different ways. You can use JavaScript's built-in `eval()` function, or, for extra security, you can use a JSON parser instead.

Using eval()

The `eval()` method takes a JavaScript string as an argument and converts the string into an object or runs the string as a command. For example, you could use `eval()` to create a new variable that holds the current date and time.

```
eval("var myDate = new Date();");
```

If you're making a request for JSON data, use the `responseText` property of the `XMLHttpRequest` object, then use `eval()` to convert the JSON text string into a JavaScript object.

```
var jsonResp = request.responseText;
jsonResp = eval("(" + jsonResp + ")");
```

> Because JSON strings often include curly braces (such as those used with JavaScript for or if statements), extra parentheses are used around the JSON string to indicate that it's an expression to be evaluated, rather than a command to be run.

Using parseJSON()

If your web server is providing both the JSON data and the requesting page, using `eval()` is fine. If security is a concern, though, use a JSON parser. A JSON parser will act only on JSON text and won't execute any other JavaScript.

In this case, you use `responseText`, but you use the `parseJSON()` method to convert the JSON text string into a JavaScript object.

```
var jsonResp = request.responseText;
jsonResp = jsonResp.parseJSON();
```

In order to access the `parseJSON()` function, you also need to include a script tag referencing the `json.js` file.

```
<script type="text/javascript" src="json.js"></script>
```

Adding JSON Data to Your Page

Once you've converted the JSON data to a JavaScript object, you can use JavaScript to extract the data from the object. For example, if the variable `jsonResp` contains a JavaScript array, you can use a `for` loop to iterate through the members of the array.

```
for (i=0; i < jsonResp.class1.length; i++) {
...
```

You won't need to use the DOM to extract the data from the response, but you're likely to use DOM methods such as `createElement()` to dynamically add the response data to your page, as shown in the following example.

Try It Out   Making an XMLHttpRequest for JSON Data

In this example, an `XMLHttpRequest` is created and opened for the `classes.txt` file, the JSON data version of the `classes.xml` file. The data is then dynamically displayed to the page using DOM methods. Type the following code into your text editor, and save it as `ch11_examp1.htm`.

```
<!DOCTYPE html PUBLIC "-//W3C//DTD XHTML 1.0 Transitional//EN"
"http://www.w3.org/TR/xhtml1/DTD/xhtml1-transitional.dtd">
<html xmlns="http://www.w3.org/1999/xhtml">
<head>
<meta http-equiv="Content-Type" content="text/html; charset=iso-8859-1" />
<title>Checking Courses</title>
<script type="text/javascript">
  function getDoc()
  {
    var request;
    if (window.XMLHttpRequest) {
      request = new XMLHttpRequest();
    }
    else if (window.ActiveXObject) {
      request = new ActiveXObject("Microsoft.XMLHTTP");
    }
    if(request) {
      request.open("GET", "classes.txt", true);
      request.onreadystatechange = function()

      if ((request.readyState == 4) && (request.status == 200)) {
        var jsonResp = request.responseText;
        jsonResp = eval("(" + jsonResp + ")");
```

```
        findClass(jsonResp);
      }

  }

    request.send(null);
  }

    function findClass(jsonResp) {
      for (i=0; i < jsonResp.class1.length; i++) {
        var title = jsonResp.class1[i].title;
        var req = jsonResp.class1[i].req;
        var myEl = document.createElement('p');
        var newText = title + " is the name of a course in the Computer Science
department.";
        var myTx = document.createTextNode(newText);
        myEl.appendChild(myTx);
        var course = document.getElementById('title');
        course.appendChild(myEl);

        if (req == 'yes') {
          var addlText = " This is a required course.";
          var addlText2 = document.createTextNode(addlText);
          myEl.appendChild(addlText2);
        }

        else {
          var addlText = " This is not a required course.";
          var addlText2 = document.createTextNode(addlText);
          myEl.appendChild(addlText2);
        }
      }

    }
</script>
</head>
<body>

<h1>Checking courses</h1>
  <form>
    <input type = "button" id="reqDoc" value = "Check courses" />
  </form>
<script type="text/javascript">
var myDoc = document.getElementById('reqDoc');
myDoc.onclick = getDoc;
</script>
<div id="title"></div>
</body>
</html>
```

Both `Ch11_examp1.htm` and `classes.txt` need to be on your server for the Ajax request to work. Copy both these files to the `Chapter11` subfolder of the `BegAjax` folder in the root folder of your web server (for example, the root folder is the `wwwroot` folder, if you're using IIS, or the `htdocs` folder, if you're using Apache).

How It Works

This page includes a form with a button labeled "Check Courses." When the user clicks the button, the `getDoc()` function is called.

```
<form>
<input type = "button" id="reqDoc" value = "Make request">
</form>
```

Traditional event registration is used to register the click event rather than including an `onclick` attribute in the `input` tag.

```
<script type="text/javascript">
var myDoc = document.getElementById('reqDoc');
myDoc.onclick = getDoc;
</script>
```

The `getDoc()` function uses an if statement to test if the browser supports `XMLHttpRequest` directly. If so, a new `XMLHttpRequest` object is created and stored in the variable named request.

```
if (window.XMLHttpRequest) {
   request = new XMLHttpRequest();
}
```

If the browser is IE 5 or IE 6, a new `ActiveXObject` is created and stored in the request variable.

```
else if (window.ActiveXObject) {
   request = new ActiveXObject("Microsoft.XMLHTTP");
}
```

If the object has been created, the open method of the `XMLHttpRequest` object is used to request data from the JSON document, `classes.txt`. This method uses three parameters: the HTTP method used for the request (`"GET"`), the URL of the document (`"classes.txt"`), and a Boolean value of `true` to indicate that the call is asynchronous.

```
if(request) {
   request.open("GET", "classes.txt", true);
```

The `request` variable is declared even though it's not initially assigned a value. Using an undeclared variable in an expression generates an error.

```
var request;
```

When the `readyState` property of the `XMLHttpRequest` object changes (when the data starts to download), an `anonymous` function is called.

```
request.onreadystatechange = function()
   {
   if ((request.readyState == 4) && (request.status == 200)) {
```

If the `readyState` property is equal to 4, the download is complete. As an additional check, a `status` property equal to 200 also indicates that the request was processed successfully.

```
var jsonResp = request.responseText;
jsonResp = eval("(" + jsonResp + ")");
findClass(jsonResp);
```

Once the download is complete, the `responseText` property is used to store the JSON data in a variable named `jsonResp`. The `eval()` method is then used to convert the JSON data to a JavaScript object. This object is sent as a parameter to the `findClass()` function.

```
function findClass(jsonResp) {
        for (i=0; i < jsonResp.class1.length; i++) {
```

The `findClass()` function uses a for loop that iterates through the `class1` array until data has been extracted from each member of the array. The length of this array is used in the test condition of the `for` loop:

```
i < jsonResp.class1.length;
```

The `title` and `req` data are extracted from the array.

```
        var title = jsonResp.class1[i].title;
        var req = jsonResp.class1[i].req;
```

The value of the title is added to the existing page using `createElement`, `createTextNode`, and `appendChild`.

```
    var myEl = document.createElement('p');
    var newText = title + " is the name of a course in the Computer Science
department.";
    var myTx = document.createTextNode(newText);
    myEl.appendChild(myTx);
    var course = document.getElementById('title');
    course.appendChild(myEl);
```

This value is added to the div element with an id value of title, which is identified by `getElementById('title')`.

```
<div id="title"></div>
```

The value of `req` is used in an `if/else` statement, and an additional text node is added to the `myEl` element.

```
        if (req == 'yes') {
          var addlText = " This is a required course.";
          var addlText2 = document.createTextNode(addlText);
          myEl.appendChild(addlText2);
        }
        else {
    var addlText = " This is not a required course.";
          var addlText2 = document.createTextNode(addlText);
          myEl.appendChild(addlText2);
        }
```

If you use the JSON parser rather than `eval()`, you need to change only two lines in this code. Add the following line in the head section of the page so that you can access the `parseJSON()` function. Also, be sure to copy the `json.js` file to the same location as `ch11_examp1.htm`.

```
<script type="text/javascript" src="json.js"></script>
```

Substitute this line of code for the line of code that calls the `eval()` method:

```
jsonResp = jsonResp.parseJSON();
```

The rest of the code is exactly the same, and it functions in the same way.

Using JSON with PHP

JSON is available for many server-side frameworks, including PHP, Java, C#, Ruby, Python, Perl, and ColdFusion. For the full list, see the JSON homepage at `www.json.org`.

JSON-PHP is a PHP library that enables PHP to work with JSON data. It's available for free download at `http://mike.teczno.com/JSON/JSON.phps`. To use JSON-PHP with a PHP file, follow these steps:

1. Copy and save the `JSON.phps` file as `JSON.php`.

2. Make sure this file is loaded and available to your PHP page by including this line of code in your PHP file:

```
require_once('JSON.php');
```

3. Create a new instance of the `Services_JSON()` class, and assign it to a PHP variable. The `Services_JSON` class is defined in `JSON.php`.

```
$myJSON = new Services_JSON();
```

4. Convert your PHP object to JSON format with the `encode()` method.

```
$response = $myJSON -> encode($response);
```

5. Send the JSON data to the client.

```
print($response);
```

For example, the following PHP code (`array.php`) creates a PHP array with three members, then sends the array data as JSON to the requesting browser:

```php
<?php
require_once('JSON.php');
$myJSON = new Services_JSON();
$av1 = array(1, 3, 'x');
$response = $myJSON-> encode($av1);
echo ($response);
?>
```

Use the following to make an Ajax request for this JSON data:

```
request.open("GET", "array.php", true);
```

Use a `div` with an `id` value of `"display"` to show the server response on the page using `innerHTML`.

```
var jsonResp = request.responseText;
jsonResp = eval("(" + jsonResp + ")");
var display1 = document.getElementById('display');
display1.innerHTML = jsonResp;
```

Figure 11-6 shows the response in the Firebug console.

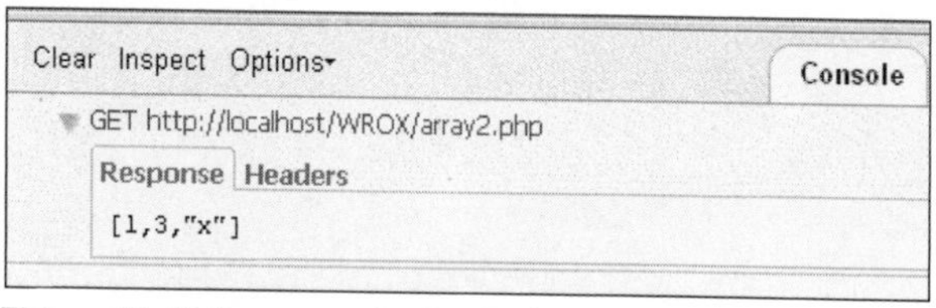

Figure 11-6: Response in the Firebug console.

For more information on using JSON-PHP, see the documentation at `http://mike.teczno.com/JSON/doc/`.

Summary

JSON is a subset of JavaScript object and array literals that can be used for data transmission. JSON is less complex than XML, and it can speed up performance because of its smaller file size than comparable XML documents.

This chapter included the following points:

- ❑ JSON is a text format that uses two structures for data transmission: JavaScript object literals containing name-value pairs and JavaScript array literals containing values.

- ❑ Unlike XML, JSON is designed only for data transmission, not as a document format.

- ❑ Douglas Crockford's JSON parser is a JavaScript file (`json.js`) that can be used to add methods to JavaScript to convert between JSON data and JavaScript objects.

- ❑ The `responseText` property can be used to return a string of JSON data from an Ajax request.

- ❑ JSON data can be parsed by converting the string to a JavaScript object using `eval()` or `parseJSON()`.

In Chapter 12, you can use what you've learned about Ajax to create a real-world Ajax application: a sortable list created with a MySQL database and PHP.

Exercises

Suggested solutions to these questions can be found in Appendix A.

1. Convert the following JavaScript object definition to an object literal:

```
var myObject = new Object();
myObject.name = "Cessna";
myObject.model = "152";
myObject.year = "1984";
myObject.color1 = "white";
myObject.color2 = "blue";
```

2. Convert the JavaScript object from Exercise 1 into JSON format using the JSON parser, json.js.

In-Depth Example: Sortable List

In previous chapters, you learned all about Ajax, including techniques, patterns, cross-browser issues, server-side and client-side technologies, and the roles of JavaScript, XML, XSLT, and JSON in Ajax applications. In this chapter, you get the opportunity to use what you've learned about Ajax to create a real-world Ajax application.

This Ajax application is a sortable list created with a MySQL database and PHP. You can drag and drop the list items to create a new order of items on the web page, which is then saved in the database. When you close the page, the order of the items is preserved in the database, and the order will be the same when you reopen the page. You can also add and delete list items on the page, and you can add and delete them from the database at the same time. The ability to sort list items in this way is very useful for lists that have a custom and changeable order, such as a to-do list.

In this chapter, you learn about the following:

- ❑ Creating a MySQL database table
- ❑ Using PHP to create a connection to a MySQL database
- ❑ Using the Prototype and Scriptaculous JavaScript libraries
- ❑ Creating an Ajax request with Prototype
- ❑ Making items sortable and droppable with Scriptaculous
- ❑ Using Ajax and PHP to interact with a MySQL database

The application in this chapter uses the following versions of software on Windows XP:

- ❑ **PHP 5.0.4.4.**
- ❑ **MySQL Server 4.1**
- ❑ **Scriptaculous 1.6.4**
- ❑ **Prototype 1.5.0_rcl (included as part of Scriptaculous 1.6.4. download)**

Using MySQL

A *database* is a collection of information that's stored in an organized way. The term "database" is also sometimes used to refer to database software, but database software is actually a database management system (DBMS). A database can be created and manipulated via a DBMS. A common type of DBMS used for web applications is a relational database management system (RDBMS), such as Microsoft Access or MySQL.

You can use almost any DBMS with a web application, depending on your experience with database design, your projected number of site visitors, and your budget. MySQL was chosen for this application because it's easy to use with PHP, and it is a good compromise between a file-based database system (such as Microsoft Access) and a high-end commercial server-based system (such as Oracle). MySQL is now available in both an Open Source free developer version (MySQL Community Server) and a commercial version for production use (MySQL Enterprise Server). For more information, see the MySQL homepage at www.mysql.com.

In a file-based system, data is processed on the client side. When a user makes a request for data from a database table, the entire table is copied to the user's computer and the request is processed there. In a server-based system, the request is processed on the server-side and then the filtered data is sent to the user's computer. Server-based systems transmit much less data and can provide data more efficiently and to more users than a file-based system. MySQL is a server-based system.

Creating a MySQL Table

An easy way to interact with MySQL in Windows is via the MySQL Monitor (Figure 12-1). The MySQL Monitor is installed as part of the Windows installation of MySQL, and it provides a command-line interface for interacting with MySQL databases. To open the MySQL Monitor, choose Start → All Programs → MySQL → My SQL Server → MySQL Command Line Client. You'll need the password you chose when you installed MySQL to start the monitor.

The Mac OS X equivalent of Window's MySQL Monitor is the MySQL daemon. You can access it via the Terminal window. Double-click the Macintosh hard drive icon on the Mac desktop, then select Applications → Utilities → Terminal. The specifics of connecting with MySQL via the Terminal window vary depending on the MySQL installation. See the MySQL documentation for more details.

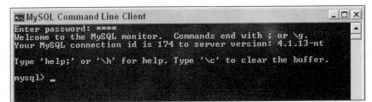

Figure 12-1: MySQL Monitor.

Once you've opened the MySQL Monitor and entered your password, create the tasks database by entering the following code at the mysql prompt:

```
CREATE DATABASE tasks;
```

Select the `tasks` database by entering the following code at the `mysql` prompt:

```
USE tasks;
```

The database table for this application is very simple. It consists of the following three fields:

❑   `task_id` — The ID of the list item and the primary key of the table

❑   `task` — The text content of the list item

❑   `rank` — The current order of the item in the list

The following code creates the table named `tasks` (Figure 12-2):

```
CREATE TABLE tasks (
      task_id int not null auto_increment,
      task varchar(100) not null,
      rank int,
      primary key (task_id)
      );
```

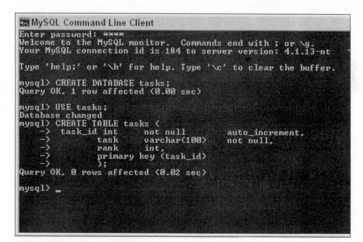

Figure 12-2: `tasks` **table.**

The `task_id` and `task` fields must contain a value (not null). The `task_id` field contains an integer that's auto-incremented (that is, a value for this field is automatically created when a new record is added to the database table). This field is used as the `id` of the list item (`li`) when it's displayed on the web page, and it is used to uniquely identify this item when adding or deleting records from the database. The `task` field contains the content of the list item, and it can include up to 100 alphanumeric characters. The `rank` field contains an integer. This field has an initial value of `NULL` when a new item is added to the list, but an integer value is assigned whenever the list items are sorted.

Adding Data to the Table

After you have created the table, add some values for list items using INSERT INTO statements, such as the following:

```
INSERT INTO tasks (task) VALUES ("New forecast dates for Med3 Project");
INSERT INTO tasks (task) VALUES ("Call Joe Smith and schedule meeting");
INSERT INTO tasks (task) VALUES ("Get estimates from Laura");
```

INSERT INTO is followed by the name of the database table (tasks). Because you're adding values for only one field in the table, follow the name of the table with the name of that field, and enclose it in parentheses , such as (task). This is followed by VALUES and then the content for the task field in quotation marks and enclosed in parentheses, such as ("Get estimates from Laura").

You can use a SELECT * statement to view the contents of the table, as shown in Figure 12-3.

```
SELECT * FROM tasks;
```

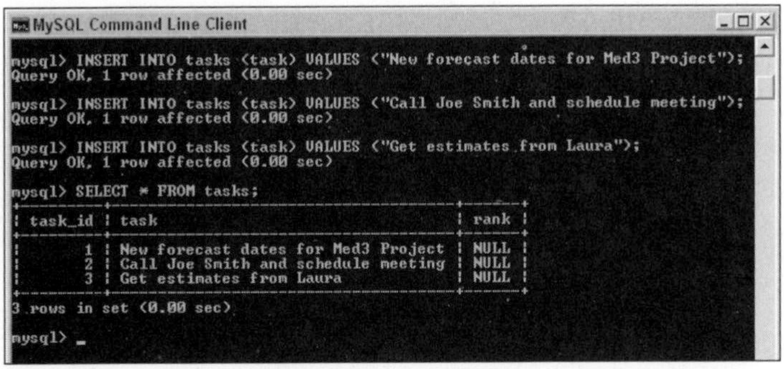

Figure 12-3: Viewing the contents of the table.

The * character is a wildcard character that selects all the fields in the table. You can see that the task_id field has automatically been assigned incremental values, and the values for the rank field are NULL so far because the list has not yet been sorted.

> The MySQL Monitor will prove to be a very useful tool as you develop this application. If you keep the Monitor open while you're working on the application files, you can check the current content of the table at any time using a SELECT * statement. This is a great way to figure out what's actually happening in the database.

Creating a Database Connection

To interact with the MySQL database from the application, you must create a connection to the database. You can save all the connection details in one PHP file, then use that file as an external file that can be called from other PHP files using the require_once function.

You must supply four pieces of information to make a database connection from your application:

❑ Host name

❑ Username

❑ Password

❑ Database name

Once values are set for the host, user, and password, you can make a connection to MySQL using the `mysql_connect` function.

Save the following code as `connect.php`. You'll reference it as an external PHP file in several of the other PHP files included in this application, and you'll call it whenever you must create a connection to MySQL.

```php
<?php
define ("MYSQLHOST", "localhost");
define ("MYSQLUSER", "root");
define ("MYSQLPASS", "****");
define ("MYSQLDB", "tasks");
function dbConnect() {
$db = mysql_connect(MYSQLHOST, MYSQLUSER, MYSQLPASS);
if (!$db) {
    return false;
    }
else {
    mysql_select_db (MYSQLDB, $db);
    }
return $db;
}
?>
```

Change these values to those that work with your MySQL database. Once the connection is created, the `mysql_select_db` function tells MySQL the name of the database (`tasks`) to use for queries.

Creating Database Queries

Database queries are used to provide the data to create the list dynamically on the web page. They're also used for dynamically ordering the list. Two PHP functions are used to create database queries and return a results array, as shown in the following code. Save this file as `tasks.php`.

```php
<?php
    function getTasks()
    {   $query = 'SELECT task_id, task FROM tasks ORDER BY rank';
        $result = mysql_query($query);
        $tasks = array();
        while ($row = mysql_fetch_object($result)) {
            $tasks[$row->task_id] = $row->task;
        }
```

```
            return $tasks;
    }
    function taskOrder($key)
    {
        if (!isset($_POST[$key]))
            return;
        $tasks = getTasks();
        $queries = array();
        $rank = 1;
        foreach ($_POST[$key] as $task_id) {
            if (!array_key_exists($task_id, $tasks))
                continue;
            $query = sprintf('UPDATE tasks SET rank = %d WHERE task_id = %d',
                            $rank,
                            $task_id);

            mysql_query($query);
            $rank++;
        }
    }
?>
```

Obtaining Current Field Values

The first function on this page, getTasks, is used to extract the current values for task_id and task for all the records in the tasks table in the database and to sort them in ascending order by the value of the rank field:

```
$query = 'SELECT task_id, task FROM tasks ORDER BY rank';
```

The mysql_query function is used to make the actual query:

```
$result = mysql_query($query);
```

An array named tasks is created, and a while loop and the mysql_fetch_object function are used to populate the array with data:

```
        $tasks = array();
        while ($row = mysql_fetch_object($result)) {
            $tasks[$row->task_id] = $row->task;
        }
```

The mysql_fetch_object function returns a row as an object. When you use this function, you access the data in each row of the database table by the field names (for example, task_id and task).

The getTasks function is used by the application to query the database and supply the information to dynamically display the current database values in a list. It will be used to create the list values when the index page of the application (index.php) is loaded in a browser. It's also used by the second function on the tasks.php page, the taskOrder function.

Ordering the List

The taskOrder function is invoked to create a database query whenever the list order is changed. An Ajax request on the index page uses the POST method to call the order.php file. This file calls the taskOrder function. By calling the order.php file via an Ajax request, JavaScript is used to invoke a PHP function.

Because the POST method is used in the request, the taskOrder function first checks to see if the element with $key index value of the $_POST array has been set. If not, the function ends at this point with a return statement.

```
if (!isset($_POST[$key]))
    return;
```

If the element with $key index value has been set, the getTasks function is called and returns the current values of the database table fields.

```
$tasks = getTasks();
```

A foreach loop creates a query that generates an array of task_id values in their current order in the database table. A value for the rank field is then assigned in consecutive order to each row of the table.

```
foreach ($_POST[$key] as $task_id) {
    if (!array_key_exists($task_id, $tasks))
        continue;
    $query = sprintf('UPDATE tasks SET rank = %d WHERE task_id = %d',
                     $rank,
                     $task_id);
```

The sprintf function creates a string for the database query by supplying values for rank and task_id to the query string. This query updates the values for rank in the table.

```
mysql_query($query);
$rank++;
```

The query is made using the mysql_query function, and the value of rank is incremented by 1.

The taskOrder function is called from the order.php file, as shown in the following code. Save this file as order.php.

```php
<?php
    require_once('connect.php');
    require_once('tasks.php');
    if (!dbConnect()) {
        echo 'Unable to establish database connection';
        exit;
    }
    $tasks = taskOrder('task_list');
?>
```

This file calls `connect.php` to make a connection to the database and `tasks.php` to invoke the `taskOrder` function. The `'task_list'` parameter value is the `id` of the unordered list (`ul`) used on index page.

The `tasks.php` file supplies the functions for querying the database to display the list on the index page and to add rank values to the list when the order is changed. You must also create PHP files that create database queries to add or delete a list item.

Editing Database Records

The `insert.php` and `delete.php` files use database queries to add or delete list items and the corresponding database records. Ajax requests are used to call each of these files. The list display and the database records are dynamically updated.

Inserting a Record

The index page includes an HTML form for adding a new task to the task list. When the user clicks the button to submit the new task, a JavaScript function is called that creates an Ajax request. This request uses the POST method and calls the `insert.php` file, as shown in the following code. Save this file as `insert.php`.

```php
<?php
require_once('connect.php');
if (!dbConnect()) {
   echo "Unable to establish database connection";
   exit;
}
$task = $_POST['task'];
$task = mysql_real_escape_string($task);
if ((isset($_POST['task']))) {
   $sql = mysql_query("INSERT INTO tasks (task)" . "VALUES ('$task')");
}
$result = mysql_query("SELECT task_id, task FROM tasks ORDER BY rank");
if(!$result) {
   die("Query Failed.");
}
echo '<ul id="task_list" class="sortable">';
while($row = mysql_fetch_row($result)) {
   $task_id = $row[0];
   $task = $row[1];
   echo '<li id="task_';
   echo $task_id;
   echo '">' . $task . '</li>';
}
echo '</ul>'
?>
```

This file calls `connect.php` to make a connection to the database. The element with `task` index of the `$_POST` array is assigned to the `$task` variable. The `mysql_real_escape_string` function escapes any special characters in the string data typed in the form field by the user before the string is used in a query. This is one way to prevent *SQL injection*, which is a technique whereby a SQL query is tampered with to provide access to hidden data or to execute system commands on a database host. For more information on SQL injection and additional methods for preventing it, see the SQL injection section of the PHP manual at http://us3.php.net/manual/en/security.database.sql-injection.php.

```
$task = $_POST['task'];
$task = mysql_real_escape_string($task);
```

If the element with task index of $_POST array has been set, a database query is created to add the new task to the task list. A value for task_id is automatically generated when the new record is inserted in the database table, and the user's input is used for the value of the task field. The initial value for rank will be NULL until the list is sorted.

```
if ((isset($_POST['task']))) {
$sql = mysql_query("INSERT INTO tasks (task)" . "VALUES ('$task')");
}
```

A second query is created to obtain the current information from the database table.

```
$result = mysql_query("SELECT task_id, task FROM tasks ORDER BY rank");
```

PHP's echo function is used to send a response to the Ajax request. The callback function for the Ajax request uses this response to refresh the display of the list and include the new list item.

```
echo '<ul id="task_list" class="sortable">';
while($row = mysql_fetch_row($result)) {
    $task_id = $row[0];
    $task = $row[1];
    echo '<li id="task_';
    echo $task_id;
    echo '">' . $task . '</li>';
}
echo '</ul>'
```

The mysql_fetch_row function returns a row as an array. By assigning array values to the list variables, the returned data includes values for the data rather than array references. This makes it possible to continue to use the task_id value to indicate a unique item in the list. This value is used for sorting the list, as well as for adding and deleting items from the list. For example, assume that the third item you added to the table is still in the last position on the list:

```
INSERT INTO tasks (task) VALUES ("New forecast dates for Med3 Project");
```

The string created by the echo function for this item would be as follows:

```
<li id="task_3">New forecast dates for Med3 Project</li>
```

Deleting a Record

The index page of the application contains a droppable region. When a list item is dragged and dropped on this area of the page, a JavaScript function is called that creates an Ajax request. This request uses the GET method and calls the delete.php file, as shown in the following code. Save this file as delete.php.

```php
<?php
require_once('connect.php');
if (!dbConnect()) {
  echo "Unable to establish database connection";
  exit;
}
$task_id = $_GET['task_id'];
if ((isset($_GET['task_id']))) {
  $sql = mysql_query("DELETE FROM tasks WHERE task_id = " . $task_id);
}
$result = mysql_query("SELECT * FROM tasks ORDER BY rank");
if(!$result) die("Query Failed.");
echo '<ul id="task_list" class="sortable">';
while($row = mysql_fetch_row($result)) {

  $task_id = $row[0];
  $task = $row[1];
  echo '<li id="task_';
  echo $task_id;
  echo '">' . $task . '</li>';
}
echo '</ul>'
?>
```

The `delete.php` file is almost exactly the same as the `insert.php` file, except that the first query string is used to delete a record. Also, it uses a GET variable rather than a POST variable. The `task_id` value is sent as part of the query string when the Ajax request is created, and it supplies the unique `id` value for the record to be deleted.

```php
$sql = mysql_query("DELETE FROM tasks WHERE task_id = " . $task_id);
```

As in `insert.php`, a second query is used to obtain current information from the database table.

```php
$result = mysql_query("SELECT task_id, task FROM tasks ORDER BY rank");
```

PHP's `echo` function is used to send a response to the Ajax request. The callback function for the Ajax request uses this response to refresh the display of the list and exclude the deleted item.

Using Scriptaculous for Drag and Drop

An important aspect of using Ajax is including a way to let the user know that an area of the page has been refreshed. One way to do this is by using the Scriptaculous JavaScript library for visual effects and drag-and-drop capabilities.

Scriptaculous is a collection of user-interface components built on top of the Prototype JavaScript library. To use Scriptaculous in your application, you will also need to include Prototype. Prototype is included in the Scriptaculous download, so this is not difficult to do. This chapter focuses on using Scriptaculous for drag and drop, but it includes many visual effects, as well as auto-completion functions. For more information on Scriptaculous and other JavaScript libraries and Ajax frameworks, see Appendix B. You can also find out more about Scriptaculous at http://script.aculo.us/.

Creating a Droppable Element

On the index page of the application, Scriptaculous is used to create a Droppable div element. When a list item is dragged and dropped on the display area of this div, an onDrop callback is used to call an anonymous function, which confirms that the user wants to delete the item. It then hides the item and calls a JavaScript function that makes an Ajax request to delete.php.

The Droppable div is created with the delTask function:

```
function delTask () {
    Droppables.add ('dropZone',
      {onDrop: function (element) {
          var myDelete = confirm("Do you want to delete this task?");
          if (myDelete) {
            Element.hide(element);
            removeTask(element.id);
          }
        }
      });
}
```

The delTask function is called when the page is loaded and creates a Droppable element. The id of the div element (dropZone) is the first parameter of the Droppables.add function. An onDrop callback calls a function when a list item is dropped on the div. This function first checks to ensure that the user wants to delete the list item. If the user responds with a Yes to the confirm message, the list item is hidden using the hide method of Prototype's Element object. This method sets the style.display value for the dropped element to none.

```
Element.hide(element);
```

The id of the dropped element is used as a parameter when the removeTask function is called to create an Ajax request to delete.php.

```
removeTask(element.id);
```

CSS is used to create the appearance of the drop zone, as shown in Figure 12-4.

```
#dropZone
{
  border: 1px dotted #ff0000;
  width: 300px;
  padding: 10px;
}
```

Droppable elements can include several other options in addition to the onDrop callback. For more details, see the documentation on the Scriptaculous wiki at http://wiki.script.aculo.us/scriptaculous/show/Droppables.add.

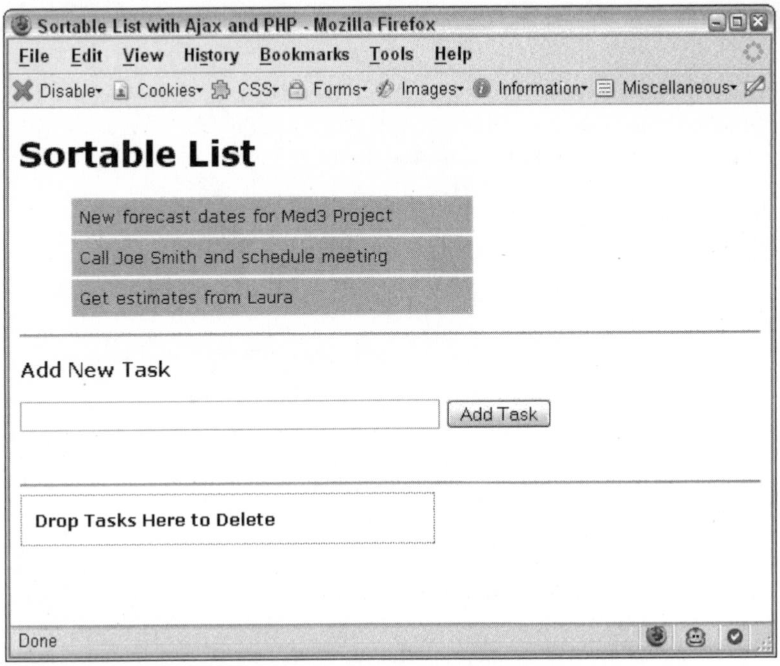

Figure 12-4: Using CSS to create the appearance of the drop zone.

Creating a Sortable Element

On the index page of the application, Scriptaculous is used to create a sortable unordered list element.

```
Sortable.create('task_list', { tag: "li", onUpdate : updateList });
```

`Sortable.create` initializes a sortable element. The first parameter of this function is the `id` value (`task_list`) of the sortable element (the unordered list element with this `id` value). Additional options include `tag` (which specifies the tag name of the items that will be made sortable) and an `onUpdate` callback (which calls the `updateList` function whenever the sort order changes while an element is dragged).

When you move the mouse over a sortable item, it changes into a handle that can be used to drag the item, as shown in Figure 12-5.

Following are two important details about using `Sortable.create`:

❑ You must call `Sortable.create` whenever the list changes in any way (additions, deletions, or changes to the order) to maintain the list as a sortable element.

❑ The sortable elements must have `id` attributes that are in this form: `string_identifier`, for example, `task_list` or `task_1`. Otherwise, you won't be able to use `Sortable.serialize` to format the information so that it's suitable for an HTTP GET or POST request.

Figure 12-5: Handle used to drag the item.

Sortable.create can include several other options in addition to tag and the onUpdate callback. For more details, see the documentation on the Scriptaculous wiki at http://wiki.script.aculo.us/scriptaculous/show/Sortable.create.

In the application, the onUpdate callback function, updateList, uses Sortable.serialize to serialize the data for an Ajax request using the POST method. Figure 12-6 shows an alert message that displays an example of serialized data sent to the Ajax target URL when a list item is moved.

```
function updateList()
{
        new Ajax.Request('order.php', {method : 'post',
        parameters : Sortable.serialize('task_list')});
}
```

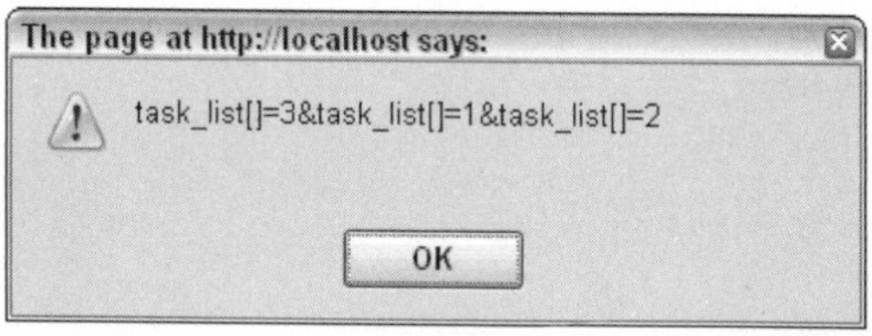

Figure 12-6: Alert message displaying serialized data sent to the Ajax target URL.

The `updateList` function uses the Prototype `Ajax` object and `Ajax.Request` class to create an Ajax request. The first parameter, `order.php`, specifies the URL targeted by the Ajax request. Additional arguments include `method` and `parameters`. The `parameters` are a formatted list of values. In this case, `Sortable.serialize` is used to create a serialized form of the list data for the `ul` element with the ID `task_list`. This sets the element with `$key` index of the `$_POST` array that's used in the `taskOrder` function included in the `tasks.php` file. Because you must include the Prototype library when you use the Scriptaculous library in your application, this means that you can also use include Prototype library items in your application. For more information on Prototype, see Appendix B. You can also learn more about Prototype at the Prototype web site at `http://prototype.conio.net/` and the Prototype wiki at `http://wiki.script.aculo.us/scriptaculous/show/Prototype`.

Interaction with the User: The Index Page

The index page of this application, `index.php`, includes the code for the list display, a form for adding a list item, and a droppable area for deleting a list item. Although the application includes eight files (not counting the Scriptaculous and Prototype files), the user's interaction with the application is through `index.php`, shown in the following code. Save this file as `index.php`.

```php
<?php
    require_once('connect.php');
    require_once('tasks.php');
    if (!dbConnect()) {
        echo 'Unable to establish database connection';
        exit;
    }
    $tasks = getTasks();
?>
<!DOCTYPE html PUBLIC "-//W3C//DTD XHTML 1.0 Strict//EN" "DTD/xhtml1-strict.dtd">
<html>
    <head>
        <title>Sortable List with Ajax and PHP</title>
         <link rel="stylesheet" type="text/css" href="sortable.css" />
        <script type="text/javascript" src="scriptaculous-js-
1.6.4/lib/prototype.js"></script>
        <script type="text/javascript" src="scriptaculous-js-
1.6.4/src/scriptaculous.js"></script>
            <script type="text/javascript" src="tasks.js"></script>
    </head>
    <body onload="delTask()">
        <h1>Sortable List</h1>
        <div id="newList">
        <ul id="task_list" class="sortable">
            <?php foreach ($tasks as $task_id => $task) { ?>
                <li id="task_<?= $task_id ?>"><?= $task ?></li>
            <?php } ?>
        </ul>
          </div>
          <hr />
<h3>Add New Task</h3>
<form>
<input type="text" name="newTask" id="newTask" size="50" maxlength="100" />
```

```
<input type="button" name="addTask" id="addTask" value="Add Task"
onclick="appendTask()"/>
</form>
<br /><br />
<hr />
<div id="dropZone"><strong>
Drop Tasks Here to Delete</strong></div>
<script type="text/javascript">
var id = 0;
function delTask () {
     Droppables.add ('dropZone',
       {onDrop: function (element) {
             var myDelete = confirm("Do you want to delete this task?");
           if (myDelete) {
               Element.hide(element);
            removeTask(element.id);
            }
           }
       });
}
function updateList()
{
         new Ajax.Request('order.php', {method : 'post',
         parameters : Sortable.serialize('task_list')});
}
Sortable.create('task_list', { tag: "li", onUpdate : updateList });
</script>
</body>
</html>
```

The index page starts off with a call to connect.php. Once a database connection is established, the current data for the list items is obtained via a call to the getTasks function included in tasks.php. This information will be used for the initial display of the list on this page.

```
<?php
    require_once('connect.php');
    require_once('tasks.php');
    if (!dbConnect()) {
        echo 'Unable to establish database connection';
        exit;
    }
    $tasks = getTasks();
?>
```

A link to an external CSS file (sortable.css) and three JavaScript files are included in the head section of the page.

```
        <link rel="stylesheet" type="text/css" href="sortable.css" />
        <script type="text/javascript" src="scriptaculous-js-
1.6.4/lib/prototype.js"></script>
        <script type="text/javascript" src="scriptaculous-js-
1.6.4/src/scriptaculous.js"></script>
          <script type="text/javascript" src="tasks.js"></script>
    </head>
```

The JavaScript files include `prototype.js`, `scriptaculous.js`, and the `tasks.js` file. All these files must be available for the application to function correctly, so modify the locations to point to the files for your version of this application. Note that `prototype.js` is included in the `scriptaculous` directory.

Once the page is fully loaded, the `delTask` function is called and creates a `Droppable` element from the `div` with the `id` value of `dropZone`.

```
<body onload="delTask()">
...
<div id="dropZone"><strong>
Drop Tasks Here to Delete</strong></div>
...
function delTask () {
     Droppables.add ('dropZone',
        {onDrop: function (element) {
            var myDelete = confirm("Do you want to delete this task?");
            if (myDelete) {
               Element.hide(element);
               removeTask(element.id);
             }
           }
        });
}
```

The data returned from the `getTasks` function is used to supply data for the initial display of the list.

```
<h1>Sortable List</h1>
        <div id="newList">
        <ul id="task_list" class="sortable">
            <?php foreach ($tasks as $task_id => $task) { ?>
                <li id="task_<?= $task_id ?>"><?= $task ?></li>
            <?php } ?>
        </ul>
          </div>
```

A PHP `foreach` loop is used to access the `$tasks` array data returned by `getTasks`. This loop iterates through each element in the array and accesses both the array key (`$task_id`) and values (`$task`) to create the list items.

An HTML form is used to provide a way to add new list items to the list.

```
<form>
<input type="text" name="newTask" id="newTask" size="50" maxlength="100" />
<input type="button" name="addTask" id="addTask" value="Add Task"
onclick="appendTask()"/>
</form>
```

This form includes a text field and a button. Note that the `form` element does not include any attributes such as `name`, `id`, `method`, or `action`. Also, the form uses a simple button instead of a Submit button. When the user clicks the button, a JavaScript function named `appendTask` is called. This function creates an Ajax request to `insert.php`, using the POST method.

The updateList function and Sortable.create statement complete the index page.

```
function updateList()
{
        new Ajax.Request('order.php', {method : 'post',
        parameters : Sortable.serialize('task_list')});
}
Sortable.create('task_list', { tag: "li", onUpdate : updateList });
```

The Sortable.create statement makes the list sortable and calls the updateList function whenever list items are dragged into a different order.

The final piece of the application is the tasks.js file, which contains the code for the Ajax requests for inserting and deleting items in the list and in the database, and the sortable.css file, which includes the page and the list styles.

Using Ajax for Updates

The tasks.js page includes four JavaScript functions that create an XMLHttpRequest object, generate Ajax requests for inserting or deleting a list item, and process the server response, as shown in the following code. Save this file as tasks.js.

```
function makeRequest ()
    {
    var request;

    if (window.XMLHttpRequest) {
        request = new XMLHttpRequest();
    }
    else if (window.ActiveXObject) {
        request = new ActiveXObject("Microsoft.XMLHTTP");
    }

    return request;
    }

function appendTask()
    {
    var request = makeRequest();
    if(request) {
        var str_1 = document.getElementById('newTask').value;
        str_1 = encodeURIComponent(str_1);
        var str = "task=" + str_1;
        document.forms[0].newTask.value = "";
        request.open("POST", "insert.php", true);
        request.setRequestHeader("Content-Type", "application/x-www-form-
urlencoded");
        request.onreadystatechange = function()
        {
```

```
            if ((request.readyState == 4) && (request.status == 200)) {
            var doc = request.responseText;
            processResults(doc);
              }
          }
        request.send(str);
          }
    }
    function removeTask(id)
          {
        var request = makeRequest();
        if(request) {
            var task_id = (id).substring(5);
            request.open("GET", "delete.php?task_id=" + task_id, true);
            request.onreadystatechange = function()
            {
              if ((request.readyState == 4) && (request.status == 200)) {
                var doc = request.responseText;
                processResults(doc);
              }
            }
            request.send(null);
            }
    }

    function processResults(doc)
          {
            document.getElementById('newList').innerHTML = doc;
            updateList();
            Sortable.create('task_list', { tag: "li", onUpdate : updateList });
    }
```

The first function, makeRequest, creates an XMLHttpRequest object. The appendTask function uses form data and the POST method to make an Ajax request to insert.php. The removeTask function uses the GET method and the task_id of the dropped element to make an Ajax request to delete.php. A fourth JavaScript function, processResults, is called when the Ajax requests are complete. This function processes the response returned by the server to the Ajax request.

Much of this code is probably familiar from earlier chapters. The makeRequest function creates an XMLHttpRequest object. The code includes options for browsers that support XMLHttpRequest directly and those that use an ActiveX object for the request.

```
        if (window.XMLHttpRequest) {
            request = new XMLHttpRequest();
        }
          else if (window.ActiveXObject) {
            request = new ActiveXObject("Microsoft.XMLHTTP");
          }
```

The new objects are stored in the request variable, which is returned from the function.

Creating POST Requests

There are differences between an Ajax request using the POST method and an Ajax request using the GET method. In addition, there are some other differences between appendTask and removeTask, since the Ajax request in appendTask uses data from the HTML form in index.php.

The appendTask function creates a local variable named request and assigns it the value returned from invoking the makeRequest function.

var request = makeRequest(); If a request variable has been created, the getElementById function is used to access the user's input in the form text field. This information is stored in the str_1 variable. The encodeURIComponent function is used to replace certain characters with the escape sequences representing the UTF-8 encoding of the character. For example, %40 is the escape sequence for the @ character. The string task= is added to the value of the str_1 variable to create a name-value pair for the task.

```
if(request) {
    var str_1 = document.getElementById('newTask').value;
    str_1 = encodeURIComponent(str_1);
    var str = "task=" + str_1;
```

Once the value of the text field is stored in the str variable, the value is cleared from the index.php page by setting it equal to an empty string.

```
document.forms[0].newTask.value = "";
```

The request is opened with the POST method and the insert.php target. Because this request uses form data, the setRequestHeader method is used to set the Content-Type to application/x-www-form-urlencoded.

```
request.open("POST", "insert.php", true);
request.setRequestHeader("Content-Type", "application/x-www-form-urlencoded");
```

When the readyState property of the request object changes (that is, when the data starts to download), an anonymous function is called. Once the download is complete, the responseText property is used to store the data as a string in a variable named doc. The processResults function is then called to process the server response.

```
request.onreadystatechange = function()
    {
    if ((request.readyState == 4) && (request.status == 200)) {
    var doc = request.responseText;
        processResults(doc);
    }
```

Because this request uses the POST method, the str variable containing the data is used as a parameter for the send method.

```
request.send(str);
```

Firebug is a great tool for troubleshooting Ajax applications because you can see the content of requests and responses in the console. Figure 12-7 shows that a new list item has been added to the top of the list. The Firebug console shows the encoded content of the item in the Post tab, and Figure 12-8 shows the server's response in the Response tab. For more information on the Firebug extension to Firefox, see Chapter 6.

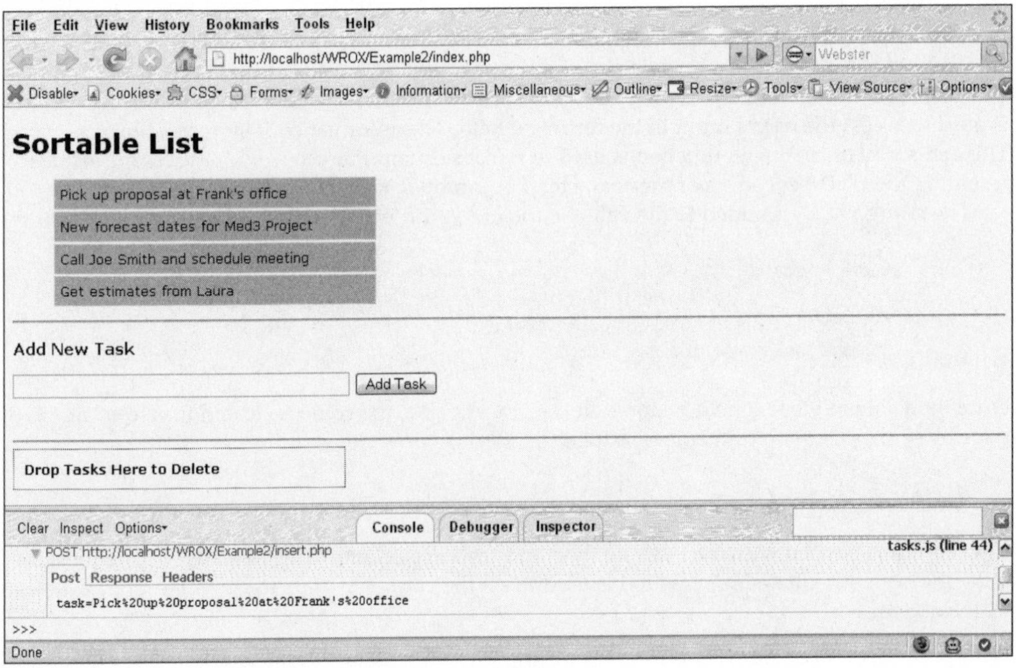

Figure 12-7: A new list item added to the top of the list.

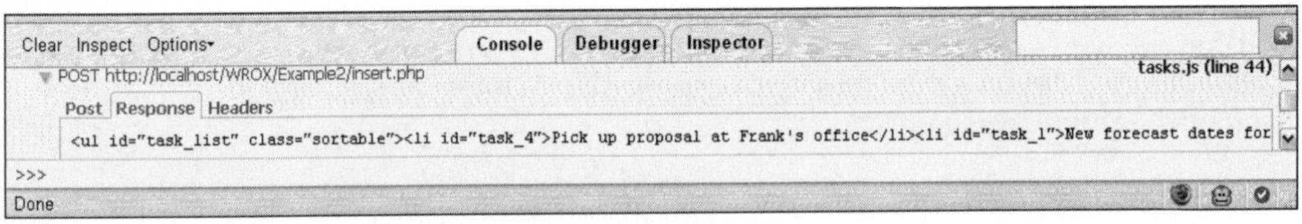

Figure 12-8: The server's response in the Response tab.

Creating GET Requests

The removeTask function uses data from the delTask function in index.php. The removeTask function call in delTask includes an id parameter. This is the id of the list item that was dropped on the dropZone div.

```
var task_id = (id).substring(5);
```

Because this id value is in the format task, followed by the value of task_id (so that it can be serialized for the updating the list order), you use JavaScript's substring method to extract the substring containing the value of task_id.

```
request.open("GET", "delete.php?task_id=" + task_id, true);
```

The request is opened using the GET method and a query string containing the task_id value is appended to the URL for delete.php. This value will be used by delete.php to identify the database record to delete.

Figure 12-9 shows the Firebug console display for a GET request. The query string is displayed in the URL, and the content of the response is shown in the Response tab.

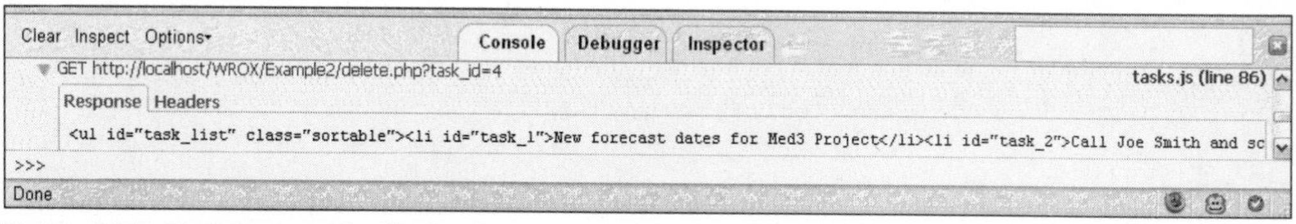

Figure 12-9: Firebug console display for a GET request.

```
request.send(null);
```

Because this request uses the GET method, the parameter for the send method has a value of null.

Processing the Results

Both the appendTask and removeTask functions use the processResults function to process the server response.

```
var doc = request.responseText;
processResults(doc);
```

This function is called from both appendTask and removeTask with a doc parameter, which is a variable that contains the server response text.

```
document.getElementById('newList').innerHTML = doc;
```

The server response replaces the contents of the newList div and displays the new list on the index.php page.

```
            updateList();
            Sortable.create('task_list', { tag: "li", onUpdate : updateList });
```

The updateList function is called to add rank values to the new list, and Sortable.create is used to make the new list sortable.

Adding Style

The `sortable.css` file contains CSS styles for the list items and the `dropZone div`.

```css
.sortable {
    list-style-type : none;
}
.sortable li {
        border : thin solid #ccc;
        cursor : move;
        margin : 2px 0 2px 0;
        padding : 5px;
        width : 300px;
        font-family: Verdana, Arial, Helvetica, sans-serif;
        font-size: small;
        background-color: #99CC99;
}
#dropZone
{
    border: 1px dotted #ff0000;
    width: 300px;
    padding: 10px;
}
body {
        font-family: Verdana, Arial, Helvetica, sans-serif;
        font-size: small;
}
```

Additional styles could be added for the display of any of these items on `index.php`.

The Files

This application includes the following eight files (in addition to `scriptaculous.js` and `prototype.js`):

- ❑ `index.php`
- ❑ `connect.php`
- ❑ `tasks.php`
- ❑ `insert.php`
- ❑ `delete.php`
- ❑ `order.php`
- ❑ `tasks.js`
- ❑ `sortable.css`

All the code for these eight files is included in this chapter. Be sure to include the Scriptaculous and Prototype files when you test these files on your server.

Summary

In this chapter, you learned to create an Ajax application to make a sortable list. Developing this application required many techniques that were discussed in the previous chapters of this book. It demonstrates that even a very simple Ajax application may require lots of code, and it illustrates a variety of different types of Ajax requests.

This chapter included the following points:

❑ The MySQL Monitor can be used to track what's actually occurring in the database when you use an application that interacts with a database.

❑ It's important to pay attention to security issues when you have an application that interacts with a database. If your application includes user input that's added to a database, ensure that you take the appropriate steps to prevent SQL injection.

❑ You can call a PHP (or other server-side language) function from JavaScript by using an Ajax request that targets a PHP page that calls the PHP function.

❑ External JavaScript libraries can be used to add functionality to your Ajax application. Scriptaculous is particularly useful for interactive effects such as visual effects and drag-and-drop capabilities.

❑ The Firebug extension to Firefox can be used to troubleshoot Ajax applications and view the content of requests, responses, and headers.

Exercise Solutions

This appendix provides answers to selected exercises presented throughout the book.

Chapter 1

Exercise 1

What are the defining points that will make a web application into an Ajax application?

Solution

The ability to refresh a page or a section of a page, without requiring a full screen refresh.

Exercise 2

Why might Ajax be considered a misleading acronym?

Solution

Ajax nominally stands for "Asynchronous JavaScript and XML," yet an Ajax application doesn't have to be asynchronous or necessarily use XML.

Chapter 2

This chapter focuses on JavaScript as a language and the interaction between JavaScript and the browser.

Exercise 1

Use a `for` loop to create a running total of numbers from 1 to 10. Display the subtotals on the page using `document.write`.

Appendix A: Exercise Solutions

Solution

```
<!DOCTYPE html PUBLIC "-//W3C//DTD XHTML 1.0 Transitional//EN"
"http://www.w3.org/TR/xhtml1/DTD/xhtml1-transitional.dtd">
<html xmlns="http://www.w3.org/1999/xhtml">
<head>
<meta http-equiv="Content-Type" content="text/html; charset=iso-8859-1" />
<title>Subtotals</title>
<script type="text/javascript">
j = 0;
for (i=1; i<=10; i++) {
  j+= i;
  document.write('j equals ' + j + '<br />');
}
</script>
</head>
<body>
</body>
</html>
```

A `for` loop is used to add numbers from 1 to 10 and display subtotals on the page using document .write. The loop iterator is i++. A separate variable, j, is used to keep a running subtotal by using the += operator.

Exercise 2

Create a function to change the `backgroundColor` style of the page. Call the function using a button.

Solution

```
<!DOCTYPE html PUBLIC "-//W3C//DTD XHTML 1.0 Transitional//EN"
"http://www.w3.org/TR/xhtml1/DTD/xhtml1-transitional.dtd">
<html xmlns="http://www.w3.org/1999/xhtml">
<head>
<meta http-equiv="Content-Type" content="text/html; charset=iso-8859-1" />
<title>Subtotals</title>
<script type="text/javascript">
function myColor () {
  document.body.style.backgroundColor = "blue";
}
</script>
</head>
<body>
<form>
  <input type="button" value="Color Me" onclick="myColor()" />
</form>
</body>
</html>
```

When the button is clicked, the `myColor` function is called. This function uses the `style` property to change the background color of the page to blue.

Chapter 3

Exercise 1

Add the ISBN to the XML document. Why might this be useful?

Solution

It might be useful to uniquely identify a particular book in the catalogue and also in your shopping cart.

Following is `Cart.js`:

```
var xHRObject = false;
if (window.XMLHttpRequest)
{
xHRObject = new XMLHttpRequest();
}
else if (window.ActiveXObject)
{
xHRObject = new ActiveXObject("Microsoft.XMLHTTP");
}


function getData()
{
    if ((xHRObject.readyState == 4) &&(xHRObject.status == 200))
    {
        var serverResponse = xHRObject.responseXML;
        var header = serverResponse.getElementsByTagName("book");
        var spantag = document.getElementById("cart");
        spantag.innerHTML = "";

        if (window.ActiveXObject)
        {
            spantag.innerHTML += " " +header[0].firstChild.text;
            spantag.innerHTML += " " + header[0].lastChild.text + " " + "<a
href='#' onclick='AddRemoveItem(\"Remove\");'>Remove Item</a>";
        }
        else
        {
            spantag.innerHTML += " " +header[0].firstChild.textContent;
            spantag.innerHTML += " " + header[0].lastChild.textContent + " " + "<a
href='#' onclick='AddRemoveItem(\"Remove\");'>Remove Item</a>";
        }


    }
}

function AddRemoveItem(action)
{
        var book  = document.getElementById("book").innerHTML;
        var ISBN  = document.getElementById("ISBN").innerHTML;
```

```
            xHRObject.open("GET", "ManageCart.aspx?action=" + action + "&book=" +
encodeURIComponent(book) +  "&ISBN=" + encodeURIComponent(ISBN) + "&value=" +
Number(new Date), true);
        xHRObject.onreadystatechange = getData;
        xHRObject.send(null);
}
```

Following is `ManageCart.aspx`:

```
<%@Page Language = "C#" Debug="true" %>

<%@ import Namespace="System.Xml" %>
<script language="C#" runat="server">
    string ISBN="";

    void Page_Load()
    {
        string newitem = Request.Params["book"];
        ISBN = Request.Params["ISBN"];
        string action = Request.Params["action"];
        Hashtable ht = new Hashtable();
        if (Session["Cart"] != null)
        {
            ht = (Hashtable)Session["Cart"];
            if (action == "Add")
            {
                if (ht.ContainsKey(newitem))
                {
                    int value = int.Parse(ht[newitem].ToString());
                    ht.Remove(newitem);
                    value++;
                    ht.Add(newitem, value);
                    Session["Cart"] = ht;
                    Response.ContentType = "text/xml";
                    Response.Write(toXml(ht));
                }
                else
                {
                    ht.Add(newitem, 1);
                    Session["Cart"] = ht;
                    Response.ContentType = "text/xml";
                    Response.Write(toXml(ht));
                }
            }
            else
            {
                ht.Remove(newitem);
                Session["Cart"] = null;
                Response.ContentType = "text/xml";
                Response.Write(toXml(ht));
            }
        }
        else
```

```
        {
            ht.Add(newitem, 1);
            Session["Cart"] = ht;
            Response.ContentType = "text/xml";
            Response.Write(toXml(ht));

        }

    }

    string toXml(Hashtable ht)
    {
        XmlDocument XmlDoc = new XmlDocument();
        XmlNode versionNode = XmlDoc.CreateXmlDeclaration("1.0","ISO-
8859-1","yes");
        XmlNode mainNode = XmlDoc.CreateElement("cart");
        XmlDoc.AppendChild(versionNode);
        XmlDoc.AppendChild(mainNode);

        foreach (string key in ht.Keys)
        {
            XmlNode childNode = XmlDoc.CreateElement("book");
            XmlNode TitleNode = XmlDoc.CreateElement("Title");
            XmlNode QuantityNode = XmlDoc.CreateElement("Quantity");
            XmlNode ISBNNode = XmlDoc.CreateElement("ISBN");
            TitleNode.AppendChild(XmlDoc.CreateTextNode(key));
            QuantityNode.AppendChild(XmlDoc.CreateTextNode(ht[key].ToString()));
            ISBNNode.AppendChild(XmlDoc.CreateTextNode(ISBN));
            childNode.AppendChild(TitleNode);
            childNode.AppendChild(QuantityNode);
            childNode.AppendChild(ISBNNode);
            mainNode.AppendChild(childNode);
        }

        string strXml = XmlDoc.InnerXml;

        return strXml;
    }
</script>
```

Following is `ManageCart.php`:

```
<?php
session_register('Cart');
header('Content-Type: text/xml');
?>
<?php
        $newitem = $_GET["book"];
        $ISBNNo = $_REQUEST["ISBN"];
        $action = $_GET["action"];
        if ($_SESSION["Cart"] != "")
        {
            $MDA = $_SESSION["Cart"];
```

```
            if ($action == "Add")
            {
                if ($MDA[$newitem] != "")
                {
                    $value = $MDA[$newitem] + 1;
                    $MDA[$newitem] = $value;
                    $_SESSION["Cart"] = $MDA;
                    ECHO (toXml($MDA));
                }
                else
                {
                    $MDA[$newitem] = "";
                    $_SESSION["Cart"] = $MDA;
                    ECHO (toXml($MDA));
                }
            }
            else
            {
                unset($MDA[$newitem]);
                $_SESSION["Cart"] = "";
                ECHO (toXml($MDA));
            }
        }
        else
        {
            $MDA[$newitem] = "1";
            $_SESSION["Cart"] = $MDA;
            ECHO (toXml($MDA));
        }


    function toXml($MDA)
    {
        $doc = new DomDocument('1.0');
        $cart = $doc->createElement('cart');
        $cart = $doc->appendChild($cart);

        foreach ($MDA as $Item => $ItemName)
        {

        $book = $doc->createElement('book');
        $book = $cart->appendChild($book);

        $title = $doc->createElement('title');
        $title = $book->appendChild($title);
        $value = $doc->createTextNode($Item);
        $value = $title->appendChild($value);


$ISBN = $doc->createElement('ISBN');
        $ISBN->appendChild($doc->createTextNode($_GET["ISBN"]));
        $book->appendChild($ISBN);

    $quantity = $doc->createElement('quantity');
```

```
            $quantity = $book->appendChild($quantity);


            $value2 = $doc->createTextNode($ItemName);
            $value2 = $quantity->appendChild($value2);

        }

        $strXml = $doc->saveXML();
        return $strXml;
    }
?>
```

Exercise 2

Amend the cart so that the ISBN is now visible in the cart display.

Solution

Change the following lines in Cart.js:

```
    if (window.ActiveXObject)
        {
            spantag.innerHTML += " " +header[0].childNodes[0].text;
            spantag.innerHTML += " " +header[0].childNodes[1].text;
            spantag.innerHTML += " " + header[0].lastChild.text + " " + "<a
href='#' onclick='AddRemoveItem(\"Remove\");'>Remove Item</a>";
        }
        else
        {
            spantag.innerHTML += " " +header[0].childNodes[0].textContent;
            spantag.innerHTML += " " +header[0].childNodes[1].textContent;
            spantag.innerHTML += " " + header[0].lastChild.textContent + " " + "<a
href='#' onclick='AddRemoveItem(\"Remove\");'>Remove Item</a>";
        }
```

Chapter 4

Exercise 1

Amend the XMLHttpRequest object example so that it "works" synchronously. How does its behavior change (if at all)? Why do you think this is?

Solution

Change the following line to:

```
xHRObject.open("GET", "display.php?id=" + Number(new Date) +"&value=" + data,
false);
```

The behavior does not change for IE (though it is not the way synchronous requests are usually handled). The sequence of `readystatechange` events is fired, and response is processed correctly. In Firefox, the example stops working because `readystatechange` events are not fired for a synchronous request and the response is not processed at all.

Exercise 2

The dynamic script tag can also be used to load web services. Create an example that uses the following web service call to display five images of William Shakespeare at the press of a button:

```
http://api.search.yahoo.com/ImageSearchService/V1/imageSearch?appid=YahooDemo&query
=Shakespeare&output=json&callback=getImages
```

Hint: The result will be returned as a JSON object. You create a callback function and return this object as follows in your JavaScript:

```
function getImages(JSONData)
{
    ...
}
```

The JSON object contains all the images of Shakespeare on the Web. You can retrieve an image URL from the object as follows, where I is the number of the image:

```
JSONData.ResultSet.Result[i].Url
```

These are the only references you will need to the JSON object.

Solution

Following is the HTML:

```
<html xmlns="http://www.w3.org/1999/xhtml" >
<head>
    <title>Dynamic Script Tag Example</title>
<script type="text/javascript" src="dynamictag.js"></script>
</head>
<body>
<input type="button" onclick="dynamicTag();" value="Get Shakespeare" />
<br />
<div id="PlaceImages"></div>
</body>
</html>
```

Following is the JavaScript (`dynamictag.js`)

```
function dynamicTag()
{
    var request =
"http://api.search.yahoo.com/ImageSearchService/V1/imageSearch?appid=YahooDemo&quer
y=Shakespeare&output=json&callback=getImages";
    var head = document.getElementsByTagName("head").item(0);
    var script = document.createElement("script");
```

```
        script.setAttribute("type", "text/javascript");
        script.setAttribute("src", request);
        head.appendChild(script);
    }

    function getImages(JSONData) {
        if (JSONData != null)
        {
          var div = document.getElementById("PlaceImages");
          for (i=0; i<5; i++)
          {
            var image = document.createElement("image");
            image.setAttribute("src", JSONData.ResultSet.Result[i].Url);
            image.setAttribute("width", 100);
            image.setAttribute("height", 100);
            div.appendChild(image);
          }
        }
    }
```

Chapter 5

This chapter focuses on processing XML returned from the server in response to an Ajax request. The XML data that you add to your page can be styled dynamically using JavaScript and CSS.

Exercise 1

Create an XML document that organizes sales data for one day into three categories: date, amount, salesperson. Include a `salesID` attribute in the salesperson element. Once you've created the document structure (elements and attributes), add the following content to the document:

❑   `date`: Today's date

❑   `amount`: Any amounts from $20 to $500

❑   `salesperson`: Marie (salesID = 225), Joan (salesID = 198), and Ron (salesID = 304)

Solution

```xml
<?xml version="1.0" encoding="iso-8859-1"?>
<totalSales>
    <sales>
        <date>Aug 21</date>
        <amount>45</amount>
        <salesperson salesID="225">Marie</salesperson>
    </sales>
    <sales>
        <date>Aug 21</date>
        <amount>395</amount>
        <salesperson salesID="198">Joan</salesperson>
    </sales>
    <sales>
        <date>Aug 21</date>
        <amount>160</amount>
```

```
            <salesperson salesID="304">Ron</salesperson>
        </sales>
    </totalSales>
```

Exercise 2

Use JavaScript's `style` property to apply a dynamic style to a paragraph that consists of a single word (flower). Change the background color and text color, and specify the Arial font family with a bold font weight.

Solution

```
<!DOCTYPE html PUBLIC "-//W3C//DTD XHTML 1.0 Transitional//EN"
"http://www.w3.org/TR/xhtml11/DTD/xhtml1-transitional.dtd">
<html xmlns="http://www.w3.org/1999/xhtml">
<head>
<meta http-equiv="Content-Type" content="text/html; charset=iso-8859-1" />
<title>Dynamic Styles</title>
<script type="text/javascript">
  function changeFlower() {
    flower.style.backgroundColor = "silver";
    flower.style.color = "red";
    flower.style.fontFamily = "Arial";
    flower.style.fontWeight = "bold";
  }
  function changeBack() {
    flower.style.backgroundColor = "";
    flower.style.color = "black";
    flower.style.fontFamily = "Times";
    flower.style.fontWeight = "normal";
  }
</script>
</head>
<body>
<p id="fl">flower</p>
<script type="text/javascript">
var flower=document.getElementById('fl');
flower.onmouseover = changeFlower;
flower.onmouseout = changeBack;
</script>
</body>
</html>
```

When a user moves the mouse over the paragraph, the `changeFlower` function is called and dynamically changes the style properties applied to this paragraph. When the user moves the mouse off the paragraph, the `changeBack` function is called and the style changes are removed.

Chapter 6

This chapter focuses on debugging and error handling in Ajax applications. This includes debugging JavaScript, inspecting the DOM tree, and viewing HTTP Header information.

Exercise 1

Use the tools of your choice to find the four errors in the JavaScript code in this document (ch6
_exercise1.html).

```
<!DOCTYPE html PUBLIC "-//W3C//DTD XHTML 1.0 Transitional//EN"
"http://www.w3.org/TR/xhtml1/DTD/xhtml1-transitional.dtd">
<html xmlns="http://www.w3.org/1999/xhtml">
<head>
<meta http-equiv="Content-Type" content="text/html; charset=iso-8859-1" />
<title>Debugging JavaScript</title>
<script type="text/javascript">
  function myErrors () {
    alert ("There's an error!');
  }
</script>
</head>

<body>
<script type="text/javascript">
onerror=myErrors;
var x = a;
x = x * 3;
alert ('x = ' + x;
</body>
</html>
```

Solution

Line 8: unterminated string literal — Two different types of quotation marks were used in this alert. The
quotation marks should be a matched pair of either single or double quotation marks.

```
alert ("There's an error!');
```

Line 14-18: no closing script tag for this script block — When the script tag isn't closed, the code is displayed on the page as plain text.

```
<script type="text/javascript">
onerror=myErrors;
var x = a;
x = x * 3;
alert ('x = ' + x;
```

Line 18: missing) after argument list — The closing parenthesis is missing from the alert statement.

```
alert ('x = ' + x;
```

Line 16: x is not defined — The variable x is assigned an undefined value. Either change the value or
delete this line.

```
var x = a;
```

The complete code for the corrected file (`ch6_exercise1_corrected.html`) follows.

Solution

```
<!DOCTYPE html PUBLIC "-//W3C//DTD XHTML 1.0 Transitional//EN"
"http://www.w3.org/TR/xhtml1/DTD/xhtml1-transitional.dtd">
<html xmlns="http://www.w3.org/1999/xhtml">
<head>
<meta http-equiv="Content-Type" content="text/html; charset=iso-8859-1" />
<title>Debugging JavaScript</title>
<script type="text/javascript">
  function myErrors () {
    alert ("There's an error!");
  }
</script>
</head>

<body>
<script type="text/javascript">
onerror=myErrors;
var x = 5;
x = x * 3;
alert ('x = ' + x);
</script>
</body>
</html>
```

Exercise 2

Create an HTML file with JavaScript code that uses a `try` statement and a `catch` clause. Include an error in the block of code in the `try` statement. The code in the `catch` clause should consist of one line only, and it should consist of an alert that displays the error name and message.

Solution

```
<!DOCTYPE html PUBLIC "-//W3C//DTD XHTML 1.0 Transitional//EN"
"http://www.w3.org/TR/xhtml1/DTD/xhtml1-transitional.dtd">
<html xmlns="http://www.w3.org/1999/xhtml">
<head>
<meta http-equiv="Content-Type" content="text/html; charset=iso-8859-1" />
<title>Try and Catch</title>
<script type="text/javascript">
try {
  var x = a;
  alert (x);
}
catch (err) {
  alert ('A ' + err.name + ' occurred: ' + err.message);
}
</script>
</head>

<body>
</body>
</html>
```

This is one possible solution to this exercise. If you open this file in Firefox, the error is identified as a `ReferenceError`. If you open this file in IE, the error is identified as a `TypeError`.

Chapter 7

Exercise 1

Alter the first example `webservice.htm` so that it no longer asks the user for input and instead just returns a list of five prices for Microsoft (MSFT), Oracle (ORCL), Sun (SUNW), IBM (IBM), and Apple (AAPL).

Solution

Following is `WebService.htm`:

```
<html xmlns="http://www.w3.org/1999/xhtml" >
<head>
    <title>Untitled Page</title>
<script type="text/javascript" src="webservice.js"></script>
</head>
<body>
<form id="form1" name="form1">

<table id="table1">
</table>
</form>
</body>
</html>
```

Following is `WebService.js`:

```
var xmlhttp = null;
if (window.XMLHttpRequest) {
  xmlhttp = new XMLHttpRequest();
} else if (window.ActiveXObject) {
  xmlhttp = new ActiveXObject("Microsoft.XMLHTTP");
}

var stockList = new Array("MSFT", "ORCL", "SUNW", "IBM", "AAPL");
var i=0;

    xmlhttprequest = getRequest();
    var url = "applicationproxy.aspx?symbol=" + stockList[i];
    xmlhttprequest.open("GET", url, true);
    xmlhttprequest.onreadystatechange = getData;
    xmlhttprequest.send(null);

function getRequest()
{
if (window.XMLHttpRequest)
{
  return xmlhttp = new XMLHttpRequest();
}
    else if (window.ActiveXObject)
    {
```

```
        return xmlhttp = new ActiveXObject("Microsoft.XMLHTTP");
        }
}

function getData()
{
  if ((xmlhttp.readyState == 4) &&( xmlhttp.status == 200))
  {
    var myXml = xmlhttp.responseXML;
    var xmlobject = null;
    var XMLDoc = null;
    if (window.ActiveXObject)
    {
        XMLDoc = myXml.childNodes[1].firstChild.nodeValue;
        var xmlobject = new ActiveXObject("Microsoft.XMLDOM");
        xmlobject.async="false";
        xmlobject.loadXML(XMLDoc);
    }
    else
    {
        XMLDoc = myXml.childNodes[0].firstChild.nodeValue;
        var parser = new DOMParser();
        xmlobject = parser.parseFromString(XMLDoc, "text/xml");
    }

    var table = document.getElementById("table1");
    var row = table.insertRow(table.rows.length);

    var cell1 = row.insertCell(row.cells.length);
    cell1.appendChild(getText("Name",xmlobject));
    var cell2 = row.insertCell(row.cells.length);
    cell2.appendChild(getText("Last",xmlobject));
    var cell3 = row.insertCell(row.cells.length);
    cell3.appendChild(getText("Date",xmlobject));

    table.setAttribute("border", "2");
    i++;
    if (i<5)
    {
  xmlhttprequest = getRequest();
    var url = "applicationproxy.aspx?symbol=" + stockList[i];
    xmlhttprequest.open("GET", url, true);
    xmlhttprequest.onreadystatechange = getData;
    xmlhttprequest.send(null);
    }
  }
}

function getText(tagName, xmlobject)
{
 var tags = xmlobject.getElementsByTagName(tagName);
        var txtNode = null;
        if (window.ActiveXObject)
        {
```

```
                txtNode = document.createTextNode(tags[0].firstChild.text);
        }
        else
        {
                txtNode = document.createTextNode(tags[0].firstChild.textContent);
        }
        return txtNode;
}
```

Exercise 2

Go to the Google Maps API application, and alter it so that it now centers on the first `<marker>` element in the data.xml file.

Hint: You will need to check that there is a `<marker>` element in the file.

Solution

Change the `onclick` event on the button to `onclick="find()";`

Change `load()` function to the following:

```
function load()
    {
       if (GBrowserIsCompatible())
       {
         map = new GMap2(document.getElementById("map"));
         geocoder = new GClientGeocoder();
GDownloadUrl("data.xml", function(data, responseCode) {
            var xml = GXml.parse(data);
            var markers = xml.documentElement.getElementsByTagName("marker");
            for (var i = 0; i < markers.length; i++) {
                point2 = new GLatLng(parseFloat(markers[i].getAttribute("lat")),
                parseFloat(markers[i].getAttribute("lng")));
                map.setCenter(point2, 13);
                var marker2 = new GMarker(point2);
                map.addOverlay(marker2);
                if( i == 0 )
marker2.openInfoWindowHtml(markers[i].getAttribute("address"));
            }
            if (markers.length > 0)
            {
                point2 = new
GLatLng(parseFloat(markers[0].getAttribute("lat")),parseFloat(markers[0]
.getAttribute("lng")));
                map.setCenter(point2, 13);
            }
            else
            {
                geocoder.getLatLng("Paris", function(point){map.setCenter(point,
                13)}});
            }
        });
```

```
        }
    }

Rename the placeMarkers method to find() and rewrite as follows:

function find()
{
    var address = document.getElementById("address").value;

    geocoder.getLatLng(address, function(point) {
        if (!point) {
            alert(address + " not found");
        } else {
            map.setCenter(point, 13);
            var marker = new GMarker(point);
            map.addOverlay(marker);
            marker.openInfoWindowHtml(address);
            placeInXmlFile(point, address);
        }
    });
}
```

Chapter 8

Exercise 1

Create an XSLT style sheet that takes the Example.xml list of hotels and displays it not in a table, but as a set of list items.

Solution

```
<?xml version="1.0" encoding="utf-8"?>

<xsl:stylesheet version="1.0"
    xmlns:xsl="http://www.w3.org/1999/XSL/Transform">

  <xsl:output
    method="html"
    indent="yes"
    version="4.0" />

  <xsl:template match="/">
    <ul>
      <xsl:for-each select="//hotel">
        <xsl:choose>
          <xsl:when test="sum(price)&lt; 175">
            <li>
                <xsl:value-of select="name"/>
                -
                <xsl:value-of select="price"/>
            </li>

          </xsl:when>
```

```
                <xsl:otherwise>

                    <li>
                      <xsl:value-of select="name"/>
                      -
                      <xsl:value-of select="price"/>
                    </li>

                </xsl:otherwise>
              </xsl:choose>
          </xsl:for-each>
      </ul>
    </xsl:template>

</xsl:stylesheet>
```

Alter the XSLT style sheet of the shopping cart so that it also displays the ISBN number of the book.

Solution

```
<?xml version="1.0" encoding="utf-8"?>

<xsl:stylesheet version="1.0"
    xmlns:xsl="http://www.w3.org/1999/XSL/Transform">

  <xsl:output
    method="html"
    indent="yes"
    version="4.0"
    doctype-public="-//W3C//DTD HTML 4.01//EN"
    doctype-system="http://www.w3.org/TR/html4/strict.dtd"/>

  <xsl:template match="/">
    <table id="shoppingcart">
      <xsl:call-template name="DisplayCart"></xsl:call-template>
    </table>
  </xsl:template>


  <xsl:template name="DisplayCart">



        <tr class="head">
          <td colspan="4" align="center">Shopping Basket <img
src="sbasket.gif"></img>
          </td>
        </tr>

    <xsl:if test="number(//book/Quantity)>0">
      <tr>
        <td class="border">Item</td>
        <td class="border">ISBN</td>
        <td class="border">Qty</td>
```

```
            <td class="border">Price</td>
            <td></td>
          </tr>
      </xsl:if>
      <xsl:for-each select="//book">
          <tr>
            <td class="border2" width="75px">
              <xsl:value-of select="Title"/>
            </td>
            <td class="border2" align="center">
              <xsl:value-of select="ISBN"/>
            </td>
            <td class="border2" align="center">
              <xsl:value-of select="Quantity"/>
            </td>
            <td class="border2">
              $<xsl:value-of select="Price * Quantity"/>
            </td>
            <td class="border2">
              <a href="javascript:AddRemoveItem('Remove');">
                <img src='button.jpg'/>
              </a>
            </td>
          </tr>
      </xsl:for-each>
      <tr >
          <td colspan='4' class="border2"> </td>

      </tr>
      <xsl:choose>
        <xsl:when test="sum(//book/Quantity)&gt;0">
          <tr>
            <td colspan="2" class="border2">Total:</td>

            <td class="border">
              $
              <xsl:value-of select="(//Total)"/>
            </td>
            <td class="border2"> </td>
          </tr>
        </xsl:when>
        <xsl:otherwise>
          <tr>
            <td colspan = "4" class="border2">Your Basket Is Empty</td>
          </tr>
        </xsl:otherwise>
      </xsl:choose>
      <tr >
          <td colspan="4" class="border2"> </td>

      </tr>
  </xsl:template>
</xsl:stylesheet>
```

Chapter 9

Exercise 1

Change the form validation example so that it is now no longer possible to submit the form if the UserName that the user has requested has already been taken.

Solution

Change `formvalidation.htm` as follows:

```
<html xmlns="http://www.w3.org/1999/xhtml" >
<head>
    <title>Form Validation Example</title>
    <link id="Link1" rel="stylesheet"  href="FormValidation.css" type="text/css" />
    <script type="text/javascript" src="FormValidation.js"></script>
</head>
<body>
Preferred User Name: <input id="UserName" type="text"
onblur="Validate('UserName')" />
<br/>
<span id="span"></span>
<br/>
First Name:<input id="FirstName" class="textbox" type="text" />
<br /><br />
Last Name:<input id="LastName" class="textbox" type="text" />
<br /><br />
Address:<input id="Address" class="textbox" type="text" />
<br /><br />
Town/City:<input id="TownCity" class="textbox" type="text" />
<br /><br />
Country:<select id="Country" class="textbox" onchange="Change()">
<option>US</option>
<option>UK</option>
</select>
<br /><br />
<span id="state">State:</span><input id="Text1" class="textbox" type="text" />
<br /><br/>
<span id="zipcode">ZipCode:</span>
<input id="Text2" class="textbox" type="text" />
<br /><br />
<input type="button" onclick="submit('UserName')" value="Click here to submit
details" />
</body>
</html>
```

Add a global variable to `FormValidation.js`:

```
var NameTaken = "False";
```

Amend the `getData` function as follows:

```
function getData()
{
    if ((xHRObject.readyState == 4) && (xHRObject.status == 200))
    {
        var serverText = xHRObject.responseText;
        if (serverText == "True")
        {
            span.innerHTML = "This user name has already been taken";
            NameTaken = "True";
        }
        if (serverText == "False")
        {
            span.innerHTML = "This user name is available";
            NameTaken = "False";
        }
    }
}
```

Add this new function to `FormValidation.js`:

```
function submit(data)
{
    if (NameTaken == "False")
    {
    var newform = document.forms[0];
    var bodyofform = getBody(newform, data);
    if (bodyofform != "UserName=")
    {
    window.location = "formcheck.php";
    }
    else
    {
        span.innerHTML = "Blank user names not allowed";
    }
    }
}
```

Amend the final retry example so that, instead of displaying a message, it counts to 10 times and then doesn't display any stock information at all. It then displays a new message telling the user that the information is currently unavailable.

Solution

Add the following global variable:

```
var Count =0;
```

Change `getData()` as follows:

```
function getData()
{
    //Check to see if the XMlHttpRequest object is ready and whether it has
    //returned a legitimate response
    if (xHRObject.readyState == 4)
    {
 if  (xHRObject.status == 200)
        {

        // Load XML
        var xml = loadDocument("Stocks.xml");
        //Load XSL
        var xsl = loadDocument("Stocks.xsl");
         //Transform
        document.getElementById("Stocks").innerHTML = transformToHTML(xml, xsl);
        //Clear the object and call the getDocument function in 5 seconds
        setTimeout("getDocument()", 5000);
    }
            else
        {
          var Stocks = document.getElementById("Stocks");
          if (Stocks.innerHTML.indexOf("available")==-1)
          {
              Count++;

          }
          if (Count>=10)
          {
           Stocks.innerHTML = "<br/><span>Current stock information not
available</span>";
          }
          xHRObject.abort();
          setTimeout("getDocument()", 5000);
        }
    }
    }
```

Chapter 10

This chapter focuses on using Ajax to obtain external data from XML news feeds, extract the data, process the data, and display it on web pages.

Exercise 1

Add JavaScript to ch10_examp1.htm to convert the link text to an actual link when the data is displayed on the page.

```
    var link = item[1].firstChild.nodeValue;
    document.getElementById('link').innerHTML = link;
```

Solution

```
var link = item[1].firstChild.nodeValue;
var link2 = "<a href='" + link + "'>" + link + "</a>";
document.getElementById('link2').innerHTML = link2;

...
  <h4>Link: <span id="link2"></span></h4>
```

Use JavaScript to add HTML code to the link variable.

Create a new variable named link2, then add the beginning of an opening a tag with an href attribute. The HTML is treated as a string, so it needs to be in quotation marks. The single quotation mark after the = sign will be used for the URL value. You need to use a single quotation mark here to make it distinct from the double quotation mark that ends this string. Otherwise, the second quotation mark will be misinterpreted as the end of the string.

```
"<a href='"
```

The link variable is added to the string using the concatenation operator (+), and then more HTML is added to close the opening a tag with a single quotation mark at the end of the URL value and a closing angle bracket.

```
"<a href='" + link + "'>"
```

The link variable is added again. In this case, it will be used for the link text that displays on the page. Finally, add a string with a closing a tag.

```
var link2 = "<a href='" + link + "'>" + link + "</a>";
```

Be sure to change the name of the variable in this line of code from link to link2. You must change it in two places in this line.

```
document.getElementById('link2').innerHTML = link2;
```

Change the value of the id in the span from link to link2.

```
<h4>Link: <span id="link2"></span></h4>
```

Ch10_examp1b.htm contains the revised code.

Chapter 11

This chapter focuses on using Ajax with JSON.

Exercise 1

Convert the following JavaScript object definition to an object literal:

```
var myObject = new Object();
myObject.name = "Cessna";
myObject.model = "152";
myObject.year = "1984";
myObject.color1 = "white";
myObject.color2 = "blue";
```

Solution

```
var myObject =
{name: "Cessna",
 model: "152",
 year: "1984",
 color1: "white",
 color2: "blue"
};
```

Exercise 2

Convert the JavaScript object from Exercise 1 into JSON format using the JSON parser, json.js.

Solution

```
<!DOCTYPE html PUBLIC "-//W3C//DTD XHTML 1.0 Transitional//EN"
"http://www.w3.org/TR/xhtml1/DTD/xhtml1-transitional.dtd">
<html xmlns="http://www.w3.org/1999/xhtml">
<head>
<meta http-equiv="Content-Type" content="text/html; charset=iso-8859-1" />
<title>Stringify</title>
<script type="text/javascript" src="json.js"></script>
</head>
<body>
<script type="text/javascript">
var myObject = new Object();
myObject.name = "Cessna";
myObject.model = "152";
myObject.year = "1984";
myObject.color1 = "white";
myObject.color2 = "blue";
myObject = myObject.toJSONString();
alert("myObject as a JSON data structure: \n" + myObject);
</script>
</body>
</html>
```

The file named stringify.html contains the code.

Include a script tag that references the external JavaScript file, json.js. Ensure that this file is in the same folder as stringify.html.

```
<script type="text/javascript">
```

Use the toJSONString() method to convert the JavaScript object named myObject to JSON data.

```
myObject = myObject.toJSONString();
```

B

Ajax Resources:
Frameworks and Libraries

Frameworks and libraries provide reusable code for common functions and reduce the amount of custom coding that's needed to create an Ajax application. Although you'll hear the term "framework" used to describe almost anything associated with Ajax development, there's a difference between a framework and a library. A *framework* includes programs, libraries, and a scripting language, and it usually includes an underlying structure for organizing projects. A *library* is a collection of functions that are easy to access because they're gathered together in one location.

Many client-side frameworks and libraries include JavaScript functions for creating and sending an Ajax request and extracting the results. Some also include visual effects and widgets for displaying the results. *Widgets* allow the user to interact with the page using a graphic interface such as a button, menu, or toggle switch. Because Ajax requests occur in the background without a complete page refresh, *visual effects* let the user know that a request is complete and that information from the request is available on the page.

Server-side frameworks contain functions for processing an Ajax request and transmitting a response to the browser. Some frameworks also generate HTML and JavaScript.

There's a wide range of size and functionality available. A framework such as Ruby on Rails offers a comprehensive programming environment, while a library such as Scriptaculous specializes in visual effects. There's also a wide range of documentation for these frameworks and libraries, from nearly none for some to comprehensive documentation for others.

Right now there are more than 100 Ajax-related frameworks and libraries, and new ones appear weekly. In addition, many of these frameworks and libraries have developed through several versions. The details are changing too fast to make it useful to include them here. Instead, this appendix focuses on the Ajax-related features of the major frameworks and libraries.

Client-Side

As of this writing, the major client-side libraries related to Ajax application development are Prototype, Scriptaculous, Dojo, Yahoo! User Interface, and MochiKit.

Prototype

Prototype is a general-purpose JavaScript library that extends the JavaScript language to include more object-oriented programming capabilities. Prototype is included in the installation of the Ruby on Rails framework, but it can be used in any environment.

You can download Prototype from the Prototype site at `http://prototype.conio.net/`. The current version, 1.4.0, is a 54KB JavaScript file. You can access the Prototype library by including a `script` tag in your page that references the location of `prototype.js` on your Web server:

```
<script type="text/javascript" src="prototype.js"></script>
```

One of Prototype's most powerful functions is `Object.extend`, which allows a second object to "extend" the first object by adding the second object's properties and methods to the first object:

```
myObj = {name: "reservation", required: "yes"};
myObj2 = {deposit: "one night"};
Object.extend(myObj, myObj2);
```

`myObj` now includes the properties of `myObj2` in addition to its own properties. In addition to supporting the creation of custom objects with `Object.extend`, Prototype includes several methods that extend JavaScript's built-in objects. For example, the `camelize` method can be used with instances of `String` objects to convert a hyphen-delimited string into a `camelCaseString`. This is useful for converting CSS property names into JavaScript format.

Prototype includes a built-in `Ajax` object that can be used to make cross-browser XMLHTTP requests. It can be used with the `Request` method and the `new` keyword to create an Ajax.Request object that takes a URL and `options` object that includes properties such as the `onComplete` property that specifies a callback function. For example, to create an XMLHTTP request to `ajax.php`, and to call a function named `process` when the request is completed, you could use the following code:

```
new Ajax.Request('ajax.php', {method: 'get', onComplete: process});
```

If the server response is HTML, you can use `Ajax.Updater` to add the response to a specific element on the page identified by its `id` value. For example, you could use the following to add the HTML to a `div` element with an ID value of `myDiv`:

```
new Ajax.Updater('myDiv', 'ajax.php', {method: 'get', onComplete: process});
```

`Ajax.PeriodicalUpdater` is similar to `Ajax.Updater`, but it makes the request at an interval that you specify. You can include a decay option that compares the latest response with the previous response, and if the values are the same, it changes the interval for repeating the request.

Prototype's `Element` object includes several methods for DOM manipulation. Similar to `getElementById`, the `Element` object uses an `id` value to reference a specific element on the page:

```
<p id="p3">My Para</p>
<a href="#" onclick="Element.hide('p3'); return false;">Hide the paragraph</a>
```

A particularly useful method for Ajax development is `Element.cleanWhitespace`. This removes all empty text node children of an element so that they don't interfere with DOM traversal, and it is another solution for the white space issues in parsing Ajax responses in Mozilla-based browsers.

Additional DOM manipulation methods include the `$()`, `$$()`, and the `getElementsByClassName()` methods. The `$` method is similar to `getElementById()`, but it takes it a step further. You can pass more than one `id` value to `$()` and return an array with all the elements with any of the passed `id` values.

The `$$()` method, introduced in Prototype 1.5, enables you to select elements using CSS selector syntax. For example, the following code returns an array of all `select` elements contained in the form whose `id` value is `contactInfo`:

```
var mySelects = $$("#contactInfo select");
```

If you download Prototype itself, the current version is 1.4. If you're using Prototype along with Scriptaculous, however, Prototype 1.5 is included in the current Scriptaculous download.

You can also use `$$()` to access all elements with a particular class name. You could use the following to access all paragraphs with the class name `red`:

```
var myPara = $$("p.red");
```

Or you could use the `getElementsByClassName` method to return an array of all elements with the CSS class name `red`:

```
var myPara = document.getElementsByClassName('red');
```

Prototype includes many more features, and luckily more documentation is becoming available, including the Prototype wiki at `http://wiki.script.aculo.us/scriptaculous/show/Prototype` and Sergio Periera's extensive documentation for Prototype 1.4.0 at `www.sergiopereira.com/articles/prototype.js.html`.

Scriptaculous

Scriptaculous is a collection of user-interface components that is built on top of the Prototype library. You can download Scriptaculous at `http://script.aculo.us/downloads`.

You can access all of Scriptaculous by adding the following code to the head section of your page once you've copied `prototype.js` and `scriptaculous.js` to your Web server:

```
<script src="javascripts/prototype.js" type="text/javascript"></script>
<script src="javascripts/scriptaculous.js" type="text/javascript"></script>
```

You can also include only the scripts you need by specifying them in a comma-separated list. The five scripts are `builder`, `effects`, `dragdrop`, `controls`, and `slider`.

```
<script src="javascripts/prototype.js" type="text/javascript"></script>
<script src="scriptaculous.js?load=effects,dragdrop"
type="text/javascript"></script>
```

The core effects include `Opacity`, `Scale`, `MoveBy`, `Highlight`, and `Parallel`. Several optional parameters are available for effects including `duration` and `startpoint`. You can also specify callback functions to be invoked while an effect is running. A wide variety of combination effects constructed from the five core effects are also available, including effects such as `Appear`, `Fade`, `Grow`, `Pulsate`, and `Shake`. Demos of the combination effects can be seen at `http://wiki.script.aculo.us/scriptaculous/show/CombinationEffectsDemo`.

Scriptaculous incorporates drag-and-drop effects, including sortable lists and sliders, as well as auto-completion. You can view demos of these effects at `http://wiki.script.aculo.us/scriptaculous/show/Demos`.

Scriptaculous documentation is provided via the wiki. Although not all features of Scriptaculous are included in the wiki so far, enough information to get started is provided there. You can access the wiki via the main Scriptaculous site at `http://script.aculo.us/`.

Dojo

Dojo is a powerful JavaScript library that includes a group of core libraries for working with HTML, JavaScript, and the DOM, as well as libraries for data structures, RPC, JSON, animation, drag-and-drop, validation, cryptography, math, and an extensive collection of widgets. You can download one of many special editions of Dojo (for example, an Ajax edition, event edition, or widget edition) from the main Dojo site at `http://dojotoolkit.org`.

Dojo is made up of packages including packages for Ajax, animation, drag-and-drop, events, and widgets. Once you've copied `dojo.js` to your Web server, you can access a Dojo package from your page by including a `script` element with the URL for the `dojo.js` file, also known as the *Dojo bootstrap*:

```
<script type="text/javascript" src="dojo.js"></script>
```

Next, add another `script` element that specifies which Dojo packages you're using in the page:

```
<script type="text/javascript">
  dojo.require("dojo.event.*");
  dojo.require("dojo.widget.*");
</script>
```

Ajax requests are handled using the `dojo.io.bind()` method:

```
dojo.io.bind({
    url: "http://example.com/Data.txt",
    load: processResults,
    mimetype: "text/plain"
});
```

This method includes the URL for the server request, a callback function, and a MIME type for the request. To use this method, you need to include the `io` package, as shown here:

```
<script type="text/javascript">
  dojo.require("dojo.io.*");
</script>
```

The `io.bind()` method can also be used to submit form data. The `formNode` references the form element by its `id` value.

```
dojo.io.bind({
    url: "http://example.com/form.php",
    load: processResults,
    formNode: document.getElementById('myForm')
});
```

Dojo includes several methods for working with the DOM, such as `createDocument()` (which returns an XML document object), `getAncestorsByTag()` (which returns all ancestors with a specific tag name), `copyChildren()` (which copies child nodes from a source node to a destination node and offers the option of trimming text nodes), and many more. For an overview of all of Dojo's DOM methods, see the DOM section in the API at `http://dojotoolkit.org/api/`.

Dojo provides additional usability features for tying in to the browser back and forward buttons by allowing you to specify code to execute when the user clicks these buttons. It also supports bookmarking with the `changeURL` parameter of `io.bind()` This parameter enables you to add a string to the URL:

```
dojo.io.bind({
    url: "http://example.com/form.php",
    load: processResults,
    changeURL: "contactInfo"
});
```

The URL will be changed to `http://example.com/form.php#contactInfo`.

Dojo is a large library with a huge API. Documentation has been sparse in the past, but new documentation for the API has just been added to the Dojo site at `http://dojotoolkit.org/api/`. Although the API documentation is not yet complete, much more information is now available. Another source of information is the Dojo wiki at `http://dojo.jot.com/WikiHome`.

Yahoo! User Interface Library

The Yahoo! UI library (YUI) is a collection of utilities and controls. Originally created by Yahoo! for its own use, it is now available as Open Source. The entire library can be downloaded at `http://sourceforge.net/projects/yui`. Documentation and examples are included in the download. You can also download a zip file of Yahoo! Cheat Sheets (`http://developer.yahoo.com/yui/docs/assets/yui-0.11-cheatsheets.zip`) that includes a cheat sheet for each library that details the methods, properties, and syntax for that library.

The utilities include scripts for animation, Ajax (connection manager), DOM manipulation, drag-and-drop, and events. The user interface controls include scripts for interactive design elements including `AutoComplete`, `Calendar`, `Containers` (panels and dialogs), `Logger` (for logging to a debugging console), `Menu`, `Slider`, and `TreeView` (node tree).

Each of the Yahoo libraries depends on the small (4K) `yahoo.js` file. Once you've downloaded the library and uploaded it to your Web server, you can access any of the YUI libraries from your pages. To reference a library from your page, include both `yahoo.js` and the specific library you want to use. For example, to use the connection library, include these `script` tags in the `head` section of your page:

```
<script type="text/javascript" src="yahoo.js"></script>
<script type="text/javascript" src="connection.js"></script>
```

You can then create a cross-browser asynchronous request with the connection library. If your request uses the `GET` method, create a variable that includes the URL that includes a querystring with the name-value pairs to be sent with the request.

```
var myURL = "ajax.php?username=JBanks&userid=379";
```

Create another variable that holds the `callback` object:

```
var callback = {success: process};
```

The `success` method calls the `process` function if the HTTP response status code is greater than or equal to 200 and less than 300.

```
var request = YAHOO.util.Connect.asyncRequest ('GET', myURL, callback);
```

The `callback` object also includes additional methods for failure, arguments, scope, timeout interval, and file uploads. The `request` returns a transaction object that includes a transaction ID, the HTTP status code, status text, response header, `responseText`, `responseXML`, and arguments from the `callback` object.

You can also make `POST` requests:

```
var myOtherURL = "form.php";
var request = YAHOO.util.Connect.asyncRequest ('POST', myOtherURL, callback,
postInfo);
```

In this case, `postInfo` is a variable that contains the `POST` message.

If you're sending form data, you can use the `setForm` method to send the form data.

```
YAHOO.util.Connect.setForm('contactForm');
var request = YAHOO.util.Connect.asyncRequest ('POST', myOtherURL, callback);
```

This sends the form data from the form with an `id` value of `contactForm` to `form.php` and returns the response to the `callback` object.

The DOM library includes a collection of methods for DOM scripting, including methods for positioning, getting styles, setting styles, getting the size of the document window (viewport), and managing class names. For example, this code uses the `getElementsByClassName` method to return an array of `p` elements with the class name `red`:

```
var myEl = YAHOO.util.Dom.getElementsByClassName('red', 'p');
```

To access the DOM library, include a `script` tag that references the location of the `dom.js` file:

```
<script type="text/javascript" src="dom.js"></script>
```

One of the major strengths of the YUI library is the event library that includes several useful methods (including methods for attaching event listeners, automatically cleaning up event listeners, and scope correction). The event library also supports custom event creation. One particularly useful feature is the deferred attachment of event listeners. If you attempt to attach an event listener to an element before the page is fully loaded, and the element is not yet available, the event utility will periodically check for the element until the page is fully loaded, rather than creating a JavaScript error.

For additional information on the event library, see the documentation included with the library download and check out Dustin Diaz's article, "Forget addEvent, use Yahoo's Event Utility," at `www.dustin diaz.com/yahoo-event-utility/`.

Yahoo's documentation is excellent, and each library can be downloaded and used separately along with the `yahoo.js` file. Some of the libraries are not small, however, and size is certainly a consideration in using some libraries such as drag-and-drop and tree-view. For more details on the size of the files, see Dean Edwards' blog posting at `http://dean.edwards.name/weblog/2006/05/das-bloat`.

For additional information, visit the YUI Library home page at `http://developer.yahoo.com/yui/index.html`.

MochiKit

MochiKit calls itself a "lightweight JavaScript library." It's available as a free-standing download at `www.mochikit.com` and is also bundled with the Python-based TurboGears framework.

MochiKit is a collection of 14 modules. The `MochiKit.Base` module is the foundation for the rest of the modules. `MochiKit.Base` includes functions for manipulating objects and arrays, comparison functions, and functions for JSON serialization and evaluation. `MochiKit.Base` is similar to the Python standard library.

MochiKit also includes modules for asynchronous tasks, DOM manipulation, event handling, and logging, as well as modules for effects and CSS (including drag-and-drop, CSS manipulation, `sortable` objects, and visual effects).

MochiKit methods are well documented, but unless you're well versed in functional programming techniques, you'll likely find it difficult to use.

Server-Side

As of this writing, the major server-side frameworks and libraries related to Ajax application development are Ruby on Rails and ASP.NET Ajax (formerly known as Atlas).

Ruby on Rails

Ruby on Rails is a framework for rapid development of database-driven Web applications based on the Ruby programming language. Ruby is an object-oriented programming language that originated in Japan in the early 1990s and became popular worldwide as English documentation of its features became available. Rails was developed by the 37signals group (www.37signals.com) when they created Basecamp software for project management online.

Rails provides Ajax support through the Prototype library, which is included in the Rails installation. You make Prototype accessible by adding this code to the head section of your web page:

```
<%= javascript_include_tag "prototype" %>
```

Rails includes helper functions specific to Ajax, including `link_to_remote()`, `form_remote_tag()`, and `observe_field()`.

Consider the following example:

```
<%= link_to_remote( "get feed",
    :update => "results",
    :url =>{ :action => :update_feed }) %>
```

The `link_to_remote()` method uses three parameters:

❑ The text to display for the link (`"get feed"`)

❑ The `id` of the DOM element containing content to replace with the results of executing the action (`"results"`)

❑ The URL of the server-side action to call (`update_feed`)

When the user clicks on the link, the browser creates an `XMLHttpRequest` and sends it to the server. The `update_feed` action is invoked, and it returns a response. The response is used to replace the contents of the element with an `id` value of `"results"`.

You can also include an optional `position` parameter with `link_to_remote()` to insert the response content before or after the target element, or at the top or bottom of the element content:

```
<%= link_to_remote("get feed",
    :update => "results",
    :url =>{ :action => :update_feed },
    :position => "after") %>
```

The `form_remote_tag()` method is similar to `link_to_remote()`, except that it sends the contents of an HTML form. The `observe_field()` method is used to monitor a form field and initiate an Ajax request whenever the value of the field changes.

For more information (including links to screencasts and tutorials), see the Ruby on Rails home page at www.rubyonrails.org.

Atlas (ASP.NET Ajax)

ASP.NET Ajax (formerly known in earlier versions as Atlas) is a Microsoft framework designed for Ajax application development by ASP.NET developers, although the Microsoft Ajax library is also available as a standalone library. ASP.NET Ajax contains JavaScript libraries and server components.

Client-side features of this framework include extensions to JavaScript (such as namespaces and object serialization) and extensions to JavaScript's `Array`, `Boolean`, `Error`, `Number`, `Object`, and `String` objects. For more details on these extensions see `http://ajax.asp.net/docs/ClientReference/JavascriptTypeExtensions/default.aspx`. These libraries also feature user-interface components and controls such as an auto-completion text box.

Server-side features of this framework include web services that integrate with Ajax applications, server controls that generate JavaScript code, and integration with Visual Studio.

The asynchronous communication model includes the following:

❑   Data formats including XML, JSON, string, and custom formats, depending on the specified content type

❑   An `XmlHttpExecutor` component

❑   JavaScript Web service proxies

For more information on the ASP.NET AJAX framework, see `http://ajax.asp.net`.

C

JavaScript Resources

There are numerous online resources for learning more about JavaScript, including blogs, web sites, tutorials, and articles. This appendix examines resources that feature coding tips, documentation, tutorials, and articles, rather than those that focus on prebuilt code samples for copy-and-paste scripting.

JavaScript Blogs

Blogs that focus on JavaScript are a great resource for learning more about JavaScript, and they have become a major source of JavaScript information. JavaScript blog postings usually include solutions to common coding problems and cross-browser issues, reviews of new JavaScript tools, information about conferences and other events, or links and comments about review articles on JavaScript topics.

Following are some favorites of the authors:

❑ *Web Standards with Imagination* (www.dustindiaz.com) — Dustin Diaz now offers three different feeds for the WSWI blog, including articles, podcasts, and video tutorials. His site and blogs focus on JavaScript, CSS, XHTML, accessibility, and a wide range of web development topics. Diaz is a user interface engineer for Yahoo!

❑ *Wait Till I Come!* (www.wait-till-i.com) — Christian Heilmann's blog focuses on JavaScript and DOM scripting topics, including scripting best practices, accessibility, cross-browser issues, and integrating CSS and JavaScript. Heilmann is a web developer.

❑ *DOM Scripting* (http://domscripting.com) — Jeremy Keith is a web developer and member of the Web Standards Project and the DOM Scripting Task Force. His DOM Scripting blog focuses on DOM scripting issues, web standards, CSS, JavaScript, and Ajax.

❑ *Quirks Blog* (www.quirksmode.org/blog/) — Peter-Paul Koch (ppk) is a web developer who's been writing about JavaScript and web development topics for many years. His Quirks blog continues his tradition of offering JavaScript code solutions, cross-browser tips, and understandable and useful explorations of JavaScript topics such as events.

❏ *Simon Willison's Weblog* (`http://simon.incutio.com/`) — Simon Willison's blog features several different web development topics, including PHP, Python, CSS, and XML, as well as JavaScript issues. Willison is a web application developer and a member of the Web Standards Project.

❏ *NCZOnline* (`www.nczonline.net/`) — Nicholas Zakas is a software engineer and user interface designer. He is also the author of *Professional JavaScript for Web Developers* (Indianapolis: Wiley, 2005) and lead author of *Professional Ajax, Second Edition* (Indianapolis: Wiley, 2007). Zakas' blog includes JavaScript and Ajax topics, cross-browser issues, and other web development subjects.

JavaScript Web Sites

There are now numerous web sites about JavaScript. The following list includes sites that feature JavaScript coding tips or articles and tutorials on JavaScript topics:

❏ `http://javascript.about.com/` — About.com's Focus on JavaScript site includes daily postings of JavaScript coding tips, as well as JavaScript articles and tutorials.

❏ `www.webdeveloper.com/javascript/` — The JavaScript section of the Webdeveloper.com site features a wide assortment of JavaScript articles that range from JavaScript fundamentals in the JavaScript Diaries and JavaScript Basic series to a multitude of articles on current JavaScript development issues such as using JavaScript with XML.

❏ `www.webreference.com/programming/javascript/index.html` — In addition to JavaScript tutorials and documentation, the JavaScript section of the Webreference.com site includes a large collection of JavaScript articles featuring code solutions and current JavaScript development topics.

❏ `www.javascriptkit.com/` — The JavaScript Kit site features articles, scripts, reference guides, and a wide range of tutorials on JavaScript, CSS, DOM, and other web development topics.

The following list features sites that provide JavaScript documentation:

❏ `www.mozilla.org/js/` — Mozilla's JavaScript page includes information on implementation and JavaScript support in Mozilla-based browsers.

❏ `www.mozilla.org/js/language/` — Mozilla's JavaScript Language Resource page includes links to PDFs of all the versions of ECMAScript, including E4X (ECMAScript for XML) and links to more information about JavaScript 2.0 and ECMAScript Edition 4.

❏ `http://developer.mozilla.org/en/docs/Core_JavaScript_1.5_Guide` — The Core JavaScript 1.5 Guide provides information on the fundamentals of JavaScript 1.5, including operators, statements, functions, and objects. Additional details are available in the Core JavaScript 1.5 Reference at `http://developer.mozilla.org/en/docs/Core_JavaScript_1.5_Reference`.

❏ `http://msdn.microsoft.com/library/default.asp?url=/library/en-us/script56/html/e4fb1cc7-15e0-43e9-bf2e-469fe7b2050c.asp` — The JScript User's Guide on the MSDN site includes information on basic and advanced features of JScript.

In addition, the following two sites each offer comprehensive JavaScript Frequently Asked Questions (FAQs):

❏   www.jibbering.com/faq/

❏   www.faqts.com/knowledge_base/index.phtml/fid/53/

Tutorials

JavaScript tutorials can be divided into two groups: those that focus on JavaScript fundamentals and those that cover current JavaScript development topics.

These tutorials cover JavaScript basics:

❏   www.w3schools.com/js/default.asp — The JavaScript tutorials at W3Schools are short introductions to both basic and advanced JavaScript concepts and techniques.

❏   www.yourhtmlsource.com/javascript/ — The JavaScript section of the HTML Source site offers several tutorials on basic and advanced JavaScript.

❏   www.htmlgoodies.com/primers/jsp/ — The HTML Goodies site includes two series of basic JavaScript tutorials.

These tutorials focus on advanced JavaScript topics, as well as current JavaScript and Ajax development issues:

❏   www.onlinetools.org/articles/unobtrusivejavascript/ — This tutorial by Christian Heilmann looks at JavaScript and accessibility issues.

❏   www.econym.demon.co.uk/googlemaps/ — Mike Williams' tutorial focuses on creating interactive maps using the Google Maps API.

❏   www.javascriptkit.com/javatutors/closures.shtml — This tutorial by Morris Johns explores JavaScript closures.

Articles

In addition to blogs and tutorials, several excellent JavaScript articles can help you learn more about JavaScript development issues, as well as fundamental JavaScript features:

❏   www.digital-web.com/articles/scope_in_javascript/ — In this article, Mike West offers a thorough review of the issue of scope in JavaScript.

❏   www.jibbering.com/faq/faq_notes/closures.html — In addition to a comprehensive look at the issue of closures in JavaScript, this article addresses execution contexts and scope chains.

❏   www.robertnyman.com/2005/04/25/53/ — Robert Nyman's article details a web standards view of three separate layers for content (HTML), presentation (CSS), and behavior (JavaScript).

❑   `www.thinkvitamin.com/features/dev/the-importance-of-maintainable-javascript` — Christian Heilmann presents eight guidelines for keeping your JavaScript code easy to maintain.

❑   `www.bobbyvandersluis.com/articles/goodpractices.php` — In this article, Bobby Vandersluis presents his selection of 10 good practices for writing JavaScript.

❑   `http://javascript.crockford.com/` — This site includes links to several JavaScript articles by Douglas Crockford, the creator of JavaScript Object Notation (JSON), and other JavaScript developers.

❑   `www.litotes.demon.co.uk/js_info/private_static.html` — Richard Cornford's article expands on Douglas Crockford's work on JavaScript closures and shows how closures can be used to create private members of JavaScript objects.

JavaScript libraries are another important JavaScript resource. For more information on libraries and frameworks, see Appendix B.

JavaScript Language Reference

This appendix provides a reference to the JavaScript language. Within this appendix, you will find listings for JavaScript's many language conventions, including its objects, methods, and properties. For more information on using the language, see Chapter 2.

> To appropriately cover standard JavaScript, browser-specific objects, properties, and methods have been omitted from this reference. This appendix covers ECMA-327, third edition (www.ecma-international.org/publications/standards/Ecma-327.htm).

This appendix is based on information originally published in Web Standards Programmer's Reference: HTML, CSS, JavaScript, Perl, Python, and PHP *(Indianapolis: Wiley, 2005) by Steven M. Schafer.*

Constants

Table D-1 shows available constants.

Constant	Description
Infinity	Represents positive infinity. This constant is used in place of a number that exceeds the upper limit of the floating-point type.
NaN	Not a number. This constant is used in place of a number when a legal number cannot be returned when expected. You can use the function isNaN() to test for NaN.

Operators

This section examines available operators and is grouped as follows:

- ❑ Arithmetic operators
- ❑ Assignment operators
- ❑ Comparison operators
- ❑ Logical operators
- ❑ Bitwise operators
- ❑ Miscellaneous operators
- ❑ String operators
- ❑ Escape characters

JavaScript Arithmetic Operators

Table D-2 describes JavaScript arithmetic operators.

Operator	Description
+	Addition (note that the same symbol is used for the string concatenation operator)
–	Subtraction
*	Multiplication
/	Division
%	Modulus
++	Increment
– –	Decrement

JavaScript Assignment Operators

Table D-3 describes JavaScript assignment operators.

Operator	Description
=	Assignment
+=	Increment assignment
-=	Decrement assignment

Operator	Description
*=	Multiplication assignment
/=	Division assignment
%=	Modulus assignment

JavaScript Comparison Operators

Table D-4 describes JavaScript comparison operators.

Operator	Description
==	Is equal to
===	Exactly equal to (in value and type)
!=	Is not equal to
!==	Is not exactly equal to
>	Is greater than
<	Is less than
>=	Is greater than or equal to
<=	Is less than or equal to

JavaScript Logical Operators

Table D-5 describes JavaScript logical operators.

Operator	Description
&&	And
||	Or
!	Not

JavaScript Bitwise Operators

Table D-6 describes JavaScript bitwise operators.

Operator	Description
&	And
|	Or

Operator	Description
^	Xor
~	Not
<<	Left shift
>>	Right shift
>>>	Zero fill right shift

JavaScript Miscellaneous Operators

Table D-7 describes miscellaneous JavaScript operators.

Operator	Description
.	Object/property/method separator (dot notation).

?	Conditional operator (also known as the ternary operator); used for short-hand `if`/`else` statements:
	`if (x ==3) { x = y}`
	`else {x = z}`
	Can be expressed as follows:
	`x ==3 ? x = y : x =z`

,	Specify multiple expressions in place of one expression. For example, you can use this operator to specify two variables to initialize at the beginning of a `for` loop:
	`for (x=0, y=0; x<=20; x++) {`
	`// loop code`
	`}`

delete	Delete specified object.
new	Create new object.
typeof	Returns a string with the datatype of object:: "number" for `Number` type, "string" for `String` type, "boolean" for `Boolean` type, "undefined" for `Undefined` type, "object" for `Null` type or a reference type.

String Operators

Table D-8 describes string operators.

Operator	Use
+	Concatenation (note that the same symbol is used for the addition operator)

Escape Characters

Table D-9 describes escape characters.

Characters	Description
\'	Single quote
\"	Double quote
\\	Backslash
\b	Backspace
\f	Form feed
\n	New line
\r	Carriage return
\t	Tab

The backslash can also be used to escape any character simply by prefixing the character with a backslash.

Statements

Table D-10 describes statements.

Statement	Description
break [label]	Breaks out of the enclosing statement designated by the optional label. The enclosing statement can be a loop or any block of statements contained in curly braces. Program execution continues on the first line outside the enclosing statement. When break is used without specifying a label, it can be used with switch statements as well as loops.
comment (// and /* */)	Use either construct (double-slash or slash-asterisk) to create a comment in the code. The double-slash method can be used for a one-line or end-of-line comment:
	// this is a comment
	i++; // increment I
	The slash-asterisk method can be used for multiline comments:
	/* function circle_area
	arguments: radius
	returns: area of circle */
	Multiline comments (/* */) can't be nested.

Table continued on following page

Statement	Description
`continue [label]`	Causes the current loop, or the loop designated by the optional `label`, to end the current iteration and begin the next. Program execution resumes at the beginning of the appropriate loop, performing any increment or other action as appropriate at the start of another iteration.
`do {`	Performs the loop code while `expr` evaluates to `true`. Note that because the conditional statement is at the end of the loop, the loop code will execute at least once.
`// loop code`	
`} while (expr);`	

`for (init_expr;`
`cond_expr;`
`counter) {`
	The `for` loop is a complex loop structure typically used to iterate over a sequence of numbers. At the start of the loop, the `init_expr` and the `cond_expr` are evaluated. The loop executes as long as `cond_expr` remains `true`. The counter increments or decrements the value of the initial expression each time the loop completes a cycle. For example, the following loop executes 10 times, assigning the variable x values of 1 through 10:

`// loop code`	`for (x = 1; x <= 10; x++) {`
`}`	`// loop code`
	`}`
`for (var_name` `in object) {`	Performs the loop code once for every property in `object`, assigning the variable `var_name` to each property in turn. For example, the following code will output every available property name and value of the `window` object:
`// loop code`	`for (p in window) {`
`}`	`document.write("Property: "+p+" / ");`
	`document.writeln("Value: "+window[p]);`
	`}`
	All user-defined properties will be output with this code, but only some built-in properties and no built-in methods will be included.

`function`
`func_name`
`([arg1,`
`arg2...,argN])`
	Declares and defines a user-defined function. The optional arguments become variables local to the function, and the optional `return` statement provides the function's return value. For example, the following function returns the area of a circle, given the circle's radius:

`{`	`function circle_area (radius) {`
`// function code`	`// area = pi * radius-squared`
`[return (expr);]`	`with (Math) {`
`}`	`var area = PI * pow(radius,2);`
	`}`
	`return area;`

Statement	Description
	`}`
	If the `return` statement is omitted, the function returns a value of `undefined`.
`if (expr) {`	Executes code based on the evaluation of the expression, `expr`. If `expr` evaluates to `true`, the block of code in the `if` section is executed. If `expr` evaluates to `false`, the code in the `if` section is not executed, but the code in the optional `else` section is.
`// code to do` `if expr = true`	
`} [ else {`	
`// code to do` `if expr = false`	
`} ]`	
`label:`	Declares a `label` in the code that can be referenced via a `break` or `continue` statement. The label text (`label`) can be any valid nonreserved name and must end in a colon. For example, the following code utilizes a `label` named `loop1`:
	`loop1:`
	`for (i = 1; i <= 20; i++) {`
	`for (j = i+1; j <= 20; j++) {`
	`// loop code`
	`// if k ever exceeds 20, break out of loops`
	`if (k > 20) { break loop1; }`
	`}`
	`}`
`return [expr]`	Causes current execution of a function to end and returns the optional value of the expression `expr`. Can be used only within a function.
`switch (expr) {`	Performs segments of code based on the value of expression `expr`. At the beginning of the switch construct, `expr` is evaluated and matched against each case `value`. If a match is found, the matching code (in the appropriate `case` section) is executed. If a match is not found, the code in the optional `default` section is executed. For example, the following `switch` construct outputs appropriate text based on the value of the variable `x`:
`case value1:`	`switch (x) {`
`// code to do` `if expr = value1`	`case 1:`

Table continued on following page

Statement	Description
`break;`	`document.write("x = 1");`
`case value2:`	`break;`
`// code to do if expr = value2`	`case 2:`
`break;`	`document.write("x = 2");`
`. . .`	`break;`
`case valueN:`	`default:`
`// code to do if expr = valueN`	`document.write("x != 1 or 2");`
`break;`	`}`
`[default:`	
`// code to do if expr != any values ]`	
`}`	
`throw expression`	Creates an exception that breaks out of the current `try` construct and can be caught by a corresponding `catch` construct. (See the next entry for information about `try` and `catch`.)
`try {`	Creates a testing structure for code. Using `throw` statements in the `try` section can create specific exceptions (errors) that can then be caught by the `catch` construct. An optional `finally` section can also be used to provide code that's always executed, regardless of what happens in the `try` section.
`// code to try`	For example, the following code throws an exception if k = 12 or 24, informing the catch construct of the value of k:
`[ throw value;` `// throw an error]`	`try {`
`}`	`// code to try`
`catch (value) {`	`if (k = 12 || k = 24) { throw k; }`
`// code to diagnose/report error`	`}`
`}`	`catch (err) {`
	`// now err = value of k when exception`
	`// was thrown, handle and/or report`
	`// appropriately`
	`}`

Statement	Description
`finally {`	Optionally used with `try` or with `try` and `catch`, the `finally` statement provides code that is always executed no matter what happens in the `try` block. Generally used for cleanup after the `try` code is executed.

`// code that always`
`executes if try`
`executes`
	`finally {`

`}`	`// code that's always executed if try is executed`
	`}`
`var var_name` `[= value ] |`	Declares a variable and optionally assigns it an initial value. When used with the `new` operator and an object constructor, assigns an object type, or an object type with initial values. For example, the following `var` statements are all valid:
`[= new object_type]`	`var x;`
	`var x = 3;`
	`var myImage = new Image();`
	`var myArray = new Array("dog","cat","ferret");`
`while (expr) {`	Performs the loop code as long as `expr` evaluates to true. Note that because the conditional statement is at the beginning of the loop, the loop code may not execute (if `expr` is initially false). Note that if `expr` always evaluates to true, the loop will be infinite.
`// loop code` `while expr = true`	
`}`	
`with (object) {`	Performs multiple actions using a particular object. If code within the `with` construct calls for an object, an attempt is made to match the `object` specified in the `with` statement. For example, the following code eliminates the need to repeatedly specify the `Math` object for each method and property (`PI` and `pow()`):
`// code using object`	`with (Math) {`
`}`	`var area = PI * pow(radius,2);`
	`}`

Standard Elements

This section details the methods, properties, and events that are common to many objects. The listings in this section explain only the meaning of the items; see the listing for specific objects to determine whether a specific object supports the item listed here.

Standard Methods

Table D-11 shows the standard methods.

Methods	Description
blur()	Removes focus from an object
select()	Highlights all or a portion of the text in form control elements for text (input element with type = "text" or textarea element)
click()	Triggers the object's onclick handler
focus()	Applies focus to an object

Standard Properties

Table D-12 shows the standard properties.

Properties	Description
constructor	A reference to the constructor function that created the object.
prototype	The prototype property of an object's constructor function. It can be referenced using object.constructor.prototype. Additional properties can be added to all instances of an object using the prototype property.

Standard Event Handlers

Names of event handlers in JavaScript are always lowercase (for example, onclick). Names of event handlers in HTML are case insensitive (for example, onclick, onClick, or ONCLICK). Table D-12 lists the standard event handlers.

Event Handlers	Description
onabort	Is triggered whenever an abort event occurs, such as a user navigating away from a page before it completes loading or clicking the Stop button
onblur	Is triggered when an object loses focus
onchange	Is triggered when a form field loses focus and the value of the form field has changed
onclick	Is triggered when an object is clicked
ondblclick	Is triggered when an object is double-clicked
onerror	Is triggered when a JavaScript syntax or runtime error occurs
onfocus	Is triggered when an object obtains focus
onkeydown	Is triggered when a key is pressed

Event Handlers	Description
onkeypress	Is triggered when a key is pressed (follows keydown)
onkeyup	Is triggered when a key is released (follows keypress)
onload	Is triggered when an object (body, img, frameset) finishes loading
onmousedown	Is triggered when a mouse button is pressed
onmousemove	Is triggered when the mouse is moved
onmouseout	Is triggered when the mouse pointer is moved away from an object (after being over the object)
onmouseover	Is triggered when the mouse pointer is placed over an object
onmouseup	Is triggered when a mouse button is released
onreset	Is triggered when the user clicks the Reset button on the corresponding form
onresize	Is triggered when the window size is changed
onselect	Is triggered when text is selected
onsubmit	Is triggered when the user clicks the Submit button on the corresponding form
onunload	Is triggered when a document or frameset is unloaded

Top-Level Functions

Table D-13 describes top-level functions.

Function	Returns	Description
encodeURI(string)	string	This function encodes the supplied string and replaces any characters that are illegal in Uniform Resource Identifiers (URIs) with UTF-8 encoding.
		For example, a space is converted to hexadecimal %20.
		The encodeURIComponent() method also encodes special characters that are part of a URI, such as a forward slash or colon.
		Use the decodeURI() or decodeURIComponent() methods to replace the UTF-8 encoding with the appropriate character.
eval(string)	value of last statement	This method takes a JavaScript string as an argument and parses it. The string is converted to an object, or if valid code is found in the string, the function executes the code and returns the value of the last statement encountered.

Table continued on following page

Function	Returns	Description
isFinite(object)	Boolean	This function evaluates the given object and returns true if the object is a finite number or false if the object is infinite or is not a number.
isNaN(object)	Boolean	This function evaluates the given object and returns true if the object cannot be evaluated as a number or false if the object can be evaluated as a number.
Number(object)	number or NaN	This function evaluates the given object and parses it to obtain a number. If the object can be evaluated as a number, the evaluated number is returned. If the object cannot be evaluated as a number, the function returns NaN. (Note that the Number() function can be used to translate Boolean objects into their numeric equivalents — 0 for false or 1 for true.)
parseFloat(object)	float or NaN	This function evaluates the given object and parses it to obtain a floating-point number. If the object can be evaluated as a floating-point number, the evaluated number is returned. If the object cannot be evaluated as a number, the function returns NaN.
parseInt(object)	integer or NaN	This function evaluates the given object and parses it to obtain an integer. If the object can be evaluated as an integer, the evaluated number is returned. If the object cannot be evaluated as an integer, the function returns NaN.
String(value)	string	This function converts the given value into a string value.

Objects

This section provides details on the multitude of objects available in JavaScript.

Anchor Object

The Anchor object corresponds to an XHTML anchor tag (<a>) that includes a name attribute. You can use this object to create an anchor with the document.write() method, in addition to writing specific code for the anchor. The following examples are identical:

```
var myheader = "Chapter 1";
document.write(myheader.anchor("Chapter_1"));

document.write('<a name="Chapter_1">Chapter 1</a>');
```

Property

Table D-14 shows the property for this object.

Property	Description
name	A string that specifies the anchor's name

Method

Table D-15 shows the method for this object.

Method	Description
focus()	Scrolls the document to the location of the Anchor object

Area Object

An Area object is a type of Link object and has the same attributes. This object corresponds to the XHTML <area> tag. For more information on the Area object, see the Link object.

Properties

There are no properties specific to the Area object.

Methods

There are no methods specific to the Area object.

Array Object

The JavaScript Array object is similar to the array objects of other languages, holding an ordered set of values. The following example creates an array of four string elements:

```
fruits = new Array("banana", "pear", "apple", "strawberry");
```

Elements of an array can be accessed by their numeric index, corresponding to their position in the array, starting with 0. For example, you could access the second element in the preceding array ("pear") as fruits[1].

Property

Table D-16 shows the property for this object.

Property	Description
length	The length of the array (number of elements)

Methods

Table D-17 shows the methods for this object.

Methods	Description
concat(array1, array2, ... arrayN)	Joins multiple Array objects to create a new array.
join(separator)	Joins the elements of an array into a single string separated by the given separator. (The default is a comma.)
pop()	Removes an element from the end of an array.
push()	Adds an element to the end of an array.
reverse()	Reverses the order of the elements in an array.
shift()	Removes an element from the beginning of an array and shifts all the other elements in the array.
slice (begin [,end])	Returns a new array containing the elements from the position begin up to (but not including) the element at the position end.
sort(function)	Sorts the elements of an array via the function specified. If no function is specified, the sort method sorts the array lexicographically. To sort an array numerically, you can define and specify one of the following functions in your code:
	function numAcending(a, b) { return (a-b); }
	function numDecending(a, b) { return (b-a); }
splice(start, number[,el1,el2, [,...]]])	Inserts, deletes, or replaces array elements starting by removing the specified number of elements beginning at start and replacing them with the arguments el1, el2, ... if the arguments are included.
toString()	Converts an array to a comma-separated string.
valueOf()	Converts an array to a comma-separated string.
unshift()	Inserts an element at the beginning of an array and shifts all the other elements in the array.

Boolean Object

The Boolean object is an object wrapper for a Boolean value. The following constructors will all create a Boolean object with a value of false:

```
new Boolean()
new Boolean(0)
new Boolean(-0)
new Boolean(null)
new Boolean(false)
new Boolean("")
```

A constructor with any other value will create a Boolean object with a value of true, even if the argument is the string false.

A `Boolean` object, unlike a Boolean primitive, will always evaluate to `true` when used in a conditional statement:

```
b = new Boolean(false);
if (b) {
  // Always true
}

b = false;
if (b) {
  // Not always true
}
```

Properties

The standard object properties apply. See the section "Standard Properties," earlier in this appendix.

Methods

Table D-17 shows the methods for this object.

Methods	Description
`toString()`	Converts the `Boolean` object to a string (for example, `true` or `false`). This method is called automatically whenever a `Boolean` object is used in a situation requiring a string.
`valueOf()`	Returns the primitive value (`true` or `false`) of the `Boolean` object.

Button Object

A `Button` object is created with every instance of an XHTML `<input type="button">` tag in the document. The objects are stored in the array of the parent form and accessed using the name defined in the XHTML tag, or an integer representing the order in which the element appears in the form (with 0 being the first element).

Properties

Table D-18 shows the properties for this object.

Properties	Description
`form`	Returns a reference to the object's parent form
`name`	Sets or returns the value of the object's `name` attribute
`type`	The value of this property is always `button`
`value`	Sets or returns the object's `value` attribute

Methods

The standard object methods apply. See the section "Standard Methods," earlier in this appendix.

Event Handlers

Following are the event handlers for this object:

- ❑ onblur
- ❑ onclick
- ❑ onfocus
- ❑ onmousedown
- ❑ onmouseup

Checkbox Object

A `Checkbox` object is created with every instance of an XHTML `<input type="checkbox">` tag in the document. The objects are stored in the array of the parent form and accessed using the name defined in the XHTML tag, or an integer representing the order in which the element appears in the form (with 0 being the first element).

Properties

Table D-19 shows the properties for this object.

Properties	Description
checked	A Boolean value that sets or returns the current state of the object (`true` if the box is checked, and `false` if it is not checked)
defaultChecked	A Boolean value that indicates if the checkbox was checked by default
form	Returns a reference to the object's parent form
name	Sets or returns the value of the object's `name` attribute
type	The value of this property is always `checkbox`
value	Sets or returns the value of the object's `value` attribute

Methods

The standard object methods apply. See the section "Standard Methods," earlier in this appendix.

Event Handlers

Following are the event handlers for this object:

- ❑ onblur
- ❑ onclick
- ❑ onfocus

Date Object

The Date object allows you to work with dates and times. You create a Date object using the new operator and the Date constructor:

```
var today = new Date(parameters);
```

The available parameters are shown in Table D-20.

Parameter	Description
milliseconds	An integer specifying the number of milliseconds since 01/01/1970 00:00:00
datestring	A string representing the date in a format that can be recognized by the Date.parse() method
year_num, month_num, day_num	Integers representing year, month, and day
hour_num, min_num, sec_num, ms_num	Integers representing hours, minutes, seconds, and milliseconds

If you don't supply any parameters, JavaScript creates an object using the current time on the local machine.

Properties

The standard object properties apply. See the section "Standard Properties," earlier in this appendix.

Methods

Table D-21 shows the methods for this object.

Methods	Description
getDate()	Returns an integer (between 1 and 31) representing the day of the month for the specified Date object.
getDay()	Returns an integer (between 0 and 6) representing the day of the week for the specified Date object, starting with 0 for Sunday.
getFullYear()	Returns an integer representing the 4-digit year for the specified Date object.
getHours()	Returns an integer (between 0 and 23) that represents the hour for the specified Date object.
getMilliseconds()	Returns an integer (between 0 and 999) that represents the milliseconds for the specified Date object.

Table continued on following page

Methods	Description
getMinutes()	Returns an integer (between 0 and 59) that represents the minutes for the specified Date object.
getMonth()	Returns an integer (between 0 and 11) that represents the month for the specified Date object, starting with 0 for January.
getSeconds()	Returns an integer (between 0 and 59) that represents the seconds for the specified Date object.
getTime()	Returns an integer representing the number of milliseconds since midnight 01/01/1970 for the specified Date object.
getTimezone Offset()	Returns an integer representing the difference in minutes between local time and Universal Time Coordinate (UTC).
getUTCDate()	Returns an integer (between 1 and 31) that represents the day of the month, according to universal time, for the specified Date object.
getUTCDay()	Returns an integer (between 0 and 6) that represents the day of the week, according to universal time, for the specified Date object.
getUTCFullYear()	Returns an integer representing the 4-digit year, according to universal time, for the specified Date object.
getUTCHours()	Returns an integer (between 0 and 23) representing the hours, according to universal time, for the specified Date object.
getUTCMilli-seconds()	Returns an integer (between 0 and 999) representing the milliseconds, according to universal time, for the specified Date object.
getUTCMinutes()	Returns an integer (between 0 and 59) representing the minutes, in universal time, for the specified Date object.
getUTCMonth()	Returns an integer (between 0 and 11) representing the month, according to universal time, for the specified Date object.
getUTCSeconds()	Returns an integer (between 0 and 59) representing the seconds, according to universal time, for the specified Date object.
parse(date_string)	Parses a string representing a date and returns the number of milliseconds since January 1, 1970 00:00:00.
setDate(integer)	Sets the day of the month for the specified Date object.
setFullYear (integer)	Sets the full year for the specified Date object.
setHours(integer)	Sets the hour for the specified Date object.
setMilliseconds (integer)	Sets the milliseconds for the specified Date object.
setMinutes(integer)	Sets the minutes for the specified Date object.
setMonth(integer)	Sets the month for the specified Date object.
setSeconds(integer)	Sets the seconds for the specified Date object.

Methods	Description
setTime(integer)	Sets the time for the specified Date object as the number of milliseconds since January 1, 1970 00:00:00.
setUTCDate (integer)	Sets the day of the month for the specified Date object according to universal time.
setUTCFullYear (integer)	Sets the full year for the specified Date object according to universal time.
setUTCHours (integer)	Sets the hours for the specified Date object according to universal time.
setUTCMilliseconds (integer)	Sets the milliseconds for the specified Date object, according to universal time.
setUTCMinutes (integer)	Sets the minutes for the specified Date object, according to universal time.
setUTCMonth (integer)	Sets the month for the specified Date object, according to universal time.
setUTCSeconds (integer)	Sets the seconds for the specified Date object, according to universal time.
toDateString()	Returns the date portion of the specified Date object as a string.
toLocaleString()	Converts the specified Date object to a string using the relevant locale's date conventions.
toString()	Converts the specified Date object to a string. This method is automatically called whenever a Date object is needed as text.
toUTCString()	Converts the specified Date object to a string using the universal time convention.
UTC()	Returns the number of milliseconds since January 1, 1970 00:00:00, according to universal time.
valueOf()	Returns a primitive value representing the number of milliseconds since January 1, 1970 00:00:00, of the specified Date object.

The non-UTC Date *functions use local date and time conventions when converting or constructing date values.*

Document Object

The Document object provides access to the XHTML elements in a document. This includes properties of forms, links, and anchors, as well as general Document properties.

Properties

Table D-22 shows the properties for this object.

Properties	Description
anchors[ ]	An array containing all the named Anchor objects in the specified document.
bgColor [= "color"]	Returns or sets the background color of the specified document. The color value is either the hexadecimal definition of the color (for example, #FF0000) or its textual description (for example, red).
cookie [= "expression"]	Returns or sets cookies that are associated with the specified document. Note that this property returns only visible and unexpired cookies.
domain [= "domain"]	Returns the domain name from which the specified document originated.
embeds[ ]	An array containing all the embedded objects in the specified document.
forms[ ]	An array containing all the Form objects in the specified document.
images[ ]	An array containing all the Image objects in the specified document.
lastModified	Returns the date that the specified document was last modified.
links[ ]	An array containing all the Area and Link objects in the specified document.
referrer	Returns the referring URL of the specified document.
title	Returns the specified document's title (that is, the text between the <title> tags).
URL	Returns the specified document's full URL.

Methods

Table D-23 shows the methods for this object.

Methods	Description
addEventListener()	Adds an event-handler function to the specified document. Not supported in Internet Explorer (IE).
attachEvent()	Adds an event-handler function to the specified document. Only supported in IE.
close()	Closes the output stream previously opened with the document.open method and forces data from any document.write or document.writeln methods to be displayed.
createAttribute()	Creates a new Attr node with the specified name.
createComment()	Creates a new Comment node containing the specified string.
createElement()	Creates a new Element node with the specified element name.
createTextNode()	Creates a new Text node for the specified text.

Methods	Description
detachEvent()	Removes an event-handler function from the specified document. Only supported in IE.
getElementById ('value')	Returns an element in the specified document that has the specified value for its id attribute.
getElementsByName ('value')	Returns an array of elements with the specified value for name attribute.
getElementsByTagName ('value')	Returns an array of elements with the specified value for tag name.
open()	Used to open an output stream in the specified document for writing.
removeEventListener()	Removes an event handler in the specified document. Not supported in IE.
write("expression(s)")	Used to write text (which may or may not include XHTML or other code) to the specified document.
writeln ("expression(s)")	Identical to the write method, except that writeln ends the write with a newline.

Event Handlers

Following are the event handlers for this object:

- ❏ onclick
- ❏ ondblclick
- ❏ onkeydown
- ❏ onkeypress
- ❏ onkeyup
- ❏ onmousedown
- ❏ onmouseup

Event Object

JavaScript creates an Event object automatically on the occurrence of an event. The object's various properties can provide information about the event (such as event type, the position of the cursor at the time the event occurred, and so on).

Properties

Table D-24 shows the properties for this object.

Properties	Description
screenX / screenY	Returns the position of the cursor relative to the screen (in pixels) when the event occurred
type	Returns a string that represents the type of the event (click, keydown, and so on)

The Event object supports the following types of events:

- abort
- blur
- change
- click
- dblclick
- dragdrop
- error
- focus
- keydown
- keypress
- keyup
- load
- mousedown
- mousemove
- mouseout
- mouseover
- mouseup
- move
- reset
- resize
- select
- submit
- unload

Methods

Table D-25 shows the methods for this object.

Methods	Description
initEvent()	Initializes the properties of a new Event object
preventDefault()	Instructs the browser not to perform the default action for this event
stopPropagation()	Stops the event from propagating any further

FileUpload Object

The FileUpload object is created with every instance of an XHTML `<input type="file">` tag in the document. The objects are stored in the array of the parent form and accessed using the name defined in the XHTML tag, or an integer representing the order in which the element appears in the form (with 0 being the first element).

Properties

Table D-26 shows the properties for this object.

Properties	Description
form	Returns a reference to the object's parent form
name	Sets or returns the value of the object's name attribute
type	The value of this property is always file
value	Sets or returns the value of the object's value attribute

Methods

The standard object methods apply. See the section "Standard Methods," earlier in this appendix.

Event Handlers

Following are the event handlers for this object:

❑ onblur

❑ onselect

❑ onfocus

Form Object

A Form object is created with every instance of an XHTML `<form>` tag within the document. The objects are stored in the Document object and can be accessed using the name defined within the XHTML tag, or an integer representing the order in which the element appears in the document (with 0 being the first element).

Properties

Table D-27 shows the properties for this object.

Properties	Description
`action [= "string"]`	Returns or sets the `action` attribute for the specified form
`elements[ ]`	An array containing objects corresponding to form control elements in the specified form
`encoding [= "string"]`	Returns or sets the `enctype` attribute of the specified form
`length`	Returns the number of elements in the specified form
`method [= "GET	POST"]`	Returns or sets the `method` attribute for the specified form
`name [= "string"]`	Returns or sets the `name` attribute for the specified form
`target [= "string"]`	Returns or sets the `target` attribute for the specified form

Methods

Table D-28 shows the methods for this object.

Methods	Description
`reset()`	Emulates the clicking of a Reset button
`submit()`	Emulates the clicking of a Submit button, but does not trigger a `submit` event

Event Handlers

Following are the event handlers for this object:

❑   onreset

❑   onsubmit

Function Object

The `Function` object corresponds to functions defined in your JavaScript code. Function definitions using the standard `function` statement have the following, basic syntax:

```
function function_name (function_argument(s)) {
  // function code
  return return_value;
}
```

For example, to define a function to add two values, you could use the following code:

```
function add_values (value1, value2) {
  var total = value1 + value2;
```

```
    return total;
}

alert("The sum of 2 and 4 is: "+add_values(2,4));
```

The function can also be defined using the function constructor in the standard object form:

```
var function_name = new Function("argument1", "argument2"...,
    "argumentN", "expression(s)");
```

Converting this example function to this format yields the following:

```
var add_values = new Function("value1","value2",
    "var total=value1+value2; return total;");

alert("The sum of 2 and 4 is: "+add_values(2,4));
```

Properties

Table D-29 shows the properties for this object.

Properties	Description
arguments[ ]	An array containing all the arguments passed to the specified function
arguments.length	Returns the number of arguments passed to the specified function
length	The number of arguments the function expects to be passed

Methods

Table D-30 shows the methods for this object.

Methods	Description
toString()	Returns a string containing the source code of a function
valueOf()	Like toString, this returns a string containing the source code of a function

Hidden Object

A Hidden object is created with every instance of an XHTML <input type="hidden"> tag in the document. The objects are stored in the array of the parent form and accessed using the name defined in the XHTML tag or an integer representing the order in which the element appears in the form (with 0 being the first element).

Properties

Table D-31 shows the properties for this object.

Properties	Description
form	Returns a reference to the object's parent form
name	Sets or returns the value of the object's name attribute
type	The value of this property is always hidden
value	Sets or returns the button's value attribute

Methods

There are no methods specific to the Hidden object.

History Object

The History object is a predefined JavaScript object accessible through the history property of a window object. The window.history property returns an array of URLs as strings, reflecting entries in the History object; these entries correspond to the URLs accessible through the browser's history function.

Property

Table D-32 shows the property for this object.

Property	Description
length	Returns the number of entries in the history list

Methods

Table D-33 shows the methods for this object.

Methods	Description
back()	Causes the browser to move one entry backward in the history list (similar to pressing the browser's Back button).
forward()	Causes the browser to move one entry forward in the history list (similar to pressing the browser's Forward button).
go(delta| can location)	Causes the browser to load a specific entry in the history list. The entry can be specified using a positive or negative delta (negative numbers move back the specified number of entries, positive numbers move forward) or a string containing text to match to the closest URL in the history list (for example, specifying "example.com" will move to the closest entry containing example.com).

Image Object

An `Image` object is created with every instance of an XHTML `<img>` tag. The objects are stored in the array of the `document.images` property and accessed using the name defined in the XHTML tag or an integer representing the order in which the element appears in the document (with 0 being the first element).

You can also use the Image constructor and the new operator to create an Image object, which can then be displayed in an existing displayed element. For example, the following code creates a new Image object called myImage containing the image `cat.gif`:

```
var myImage = new Image()
myImage.src = "cat.gif"
```

You could then have this image replace an existing image when a button is pressed, creating an event linked to code that swaps the source.

Properties

Table D-34 shows the properties for this object.

Properties	Description
border	Returns a string containing the border width of the specified image (in pixels)
complete	Returns a Boolean value indicating whether the browser has finished loading the specified image (read-only)
height	Returns a string containing the `height` attribute of the specified image (in pixels)
hspace	Returns a string containing the `hspace` attribute of the specified image (in pixels)
name	Sets or returns the value of the object's `name` attribute
src	Sets or returns the value of the object's `src` attribute
vspace	Returns a string containing the `vspace` attribute of the specified image (in pixels)
width	Returns a string containing the `width` attribute of the specified image (in pixels)

Methods

There are no methods specific to the `Image` object.

Event Handlers

All of the `Image` object's event handlers have an equivalent property (in lowercase) that can be used with the `Image` constructor.

Following are the event handlers for this object:

- ❏ onabort
- ❏ onerror
- ❏ onload

Link Object

A Link object is created with every instance of an XHTML <a> or <area> tag in the document. The objects are stored in the array of the document.links property and accessed using the name defined in the XHTML tag or an integer representing the order in which the element appears in the document (with 0 being the first element).

A Link object is also a Location object and, therefore, shares the same properties.

Properties

Table D-35 shows the properties for this object.

Properties	Description
hash	Returns the anchor portion (#anchor) of the specified object
host	Returns the host and port portions (for example, www.example.com:80) of the specified object
hostname	Returns the server name and domain name (for example, www.example.com) or IP address of the specified object
href	Returns the entire URL (protocol, hostname, port, and so on) of the specified object
pathname	Returns the path and name (for example, /samples/index.html) of the specified object
port	Returns the port number (for example, 80) of the specified object
protocol	Returns the protocol (for example, http:) of the specified object
search	Returns any query information (also known as GET information, for example, ?name=Steve&id=245) of the specified object
target	Sets or returns the value of the object's target attribute

Methods

There are no methods specific to the Link object.

Event Handlers

Following are the event handlers for this object:

❑   onclick

❑   ondblclick

❑   onkeydown

❑   onkeypress

❑   onkeyup

❑   onmousedown

❑   onmouseout

❑   onmouseup

❑   onmouseover

Location Object

The `Location` object is part of the `Window` object, accessed through the `window.location` property. This object contains the complete URL of a specified `Window` object.

Properties

Table D-36 shows the properties for this object.

Properties	Description
hash	Returns the anchor portion (#anchor) of the specified object
host	Returns the host and port portions (for example, `www.example .com:80`) of the specified object
hostname	Returns the server name and domain name (for example, `www.example .com`) or IP address of the specified object
href	Returns the entire URL (protocol, hostname, port, and so on) of the specified object
pathname	Returns the path and name (for example, `/samples/index.html`) of the specified object
port	Returns the port number (for example, `80`) of the specified object
protocol	Returns the protocol (for example, `http:`) of the specified object
search	Returns any query information (also known as GET information, for example, `?name=Steve&id=245`) of the specified object

Methods

Table D-37 shows the methods for this object.

Methods	Description
`reload()`	Causes the browser to reload the window's current document
`replace(URL)`	Replaces the object's history entry with the specified URL

Math Object

The `Math` object is a top-level, built-in JavaScript object used to perform advanced calculations.

Constants

Table D-38 lists the constants for the Math object.

Constants	Description
`E`	Provides Euler's constant and the base of natural logarithms (approximately 2.7183)
`LN10`	Provides the natural logarithm of 10 (approximately 2.3026)
`LN2`	Provides the natural logarithm of 2 (approximately 0.6931)
`LOG10E`	Provides the base 10 logarithm of E (approximately 0.4343)
`LOG2E`	Provides the base 2 logarithm of E (approximately 1.4427)
`PI`	Provides the value of pi (approximately 3.1416)
`SQRT1_2`	Provides the value of 1 divided by the square root of 2 (approximately 0.7071)
`SQRT2`	Provides the square root of 2 (approximately 1.4142)

Methods

Table D-39 shows the methods for this object.

Methods	Description
`abs(number)`	Returns the absolute value of `number`
`acos(number)`	Returns the arccosine of `number`
`asin(number)`	Returns the arcsine of `number`
`atan(number)`	Returns the arctangent of `number`
`atan2(number1, number2)`	Returns the arctangent of the quotient of its arguments

Methods	Description
`ceil(number)`	Returns an integer equal to or the next integer greater than `number`
`cos(number)`	Returns the cosine of `number`
`exp(number)`	Returns the value of E^{number} where E is Euler's constant
`floor(number)`	Returns an integer equal to or the next integer less than `number`
`log(number)`	Returns the natural logarithm (base E) of `number`
`max(number1,number2)`	Returns the greater of the two supplied numbers
`min(number1,number2)`	Returns the lesser of the two supplied numbers
`pow(number1,number2)`	Returns the value of `number1` to the power of `number2` ($number1^{number2}$), where `number1` is the base and `number2` is the exponent
`random()`	Returns a pseudo-random number between 0 and 1
`round(number)`	Returns `number` rounded to the nearest integer
`sin(number)`	Returns the sine of `number`
`sqrt(number)`	Returns the square root of `number`
`tan(number)`	Returns the tangent of `number`

Navigator Object

The `Navigator` object contains information about the user agent. Designed originally for Netscape Navigator, it can also be used with other browsers.

Properties

Table D-40 shows the properties for this object.

Properties	Description
`appCodeName`	Contains the code name of the browser
`appName`	Contains the name of the browser
`appVersion`	Contains information about the browser version
`platform`	Contains a string containing the machine type on which the browser is running
`userAgent`	Contains a string containing the value of the `User-agent` header sent by the client to the server

Method

Table D-41 shows the method for this object.

Method	Description
javaEnabled	Tests whether Java is enabled, returning true if it is and false if not

Number Object

The Number object is an object wrapper for primitive numeric values.

Constants

Table D-42 lists the constants for the Number object.

Constants	Description
MAX_VALUE	Contains the largest number possible in JavaScript (approximately 1.79769e+308)
MIN_VALUE	Contains the smallest number possible in JavaScript (approximately 5e-324)
NaN	Represents the special value Not a Number (NaN)
POSITIVE_INFINITY	Contains a special value representing infinity, which is returned on overflow

Methods

Table D-43 shows the methods for this object.

Methods	Description
toFixed(n)	Converts a number to a string with a specified number of digits (n) after the decimal place
toString()	Converts a number to a string
valueOf()	Returns the primitive value of a Number object as a number datatype

Object Object

Object is the JavaScript object from which all other objects are derived.

Properties

Table D-44 shows the properties for this object.

Properties	Description
constructor	A reference to the constructor function that created the object.
prototype	The `prototype` property of an object's constructor function. It can be referenced using `object.constructor.prototype`. Additional properties can be added to all instances of an object using the `prototype` property.

Methods

Table D-45 shows the methods for this object.

Methods	Description
toString()	Returns a string representing a specified object
valueOf()	Returns a primitive value for a specified object

Option Object

An `Option` object is created with every instance of an XHTML `<option>` tag in the document. The objects are stored in the array of the parent form and accessed using the name defined in the XHTML tag or an integer representing the order in which the element appears in the form (with 0 being the first element).

Properties

Table D-46 shows the properties for this object.

Properties	Description
defaultSelected	A Boolean value that indicates if the option was selected by default.
selected	Sets or returns the current state of the object (selected returns `true`, not selected returns `false`). A Boolean value that indicates if the option was selected.
text	Sets or returns the value of the text of the object (text that composes the visible portion of the option).
value	Sets or returns the value of the object's `value` attribute.

Methods

There are no methods specific to the `Option` object.

Password Object

A `Password` object is created with every instance of an XHTML `<input type="password">` tag in the document. The objects are stored in the array of the parent form and accessed using the name defined in the XHTML tag or an integer representing the order in which the element appears in the form (with 0 being the first element).

Properties

Table D-47 shows the properties for this object.

Properties	Description
form	Returns a reference to the object's parent form
name	Sets or returns the value of the object's name attribute
type	The value of this property is always password
value	Returns the value entered by the user

Methods

There are no methods specific to the `Password` object.

Event Handlers

Following are the event handlers for this object:

- ❑ onblur
- ❑ onfocus

Radio Object

A `Radio` object is created with every instance of an XHTML `<input type="radio">` tag in the document. The objects are stored in the array of the parent form and accessed using the name defined in the XHTML tag or an integer representing the order in which the element appears in the form (with 0 being the first element). Because radio buttons share the same name, they are stored in an array using the name of the group of buttons.

Properties

Table D-48 shows the properties for this object.

Properties	Description
checked	A Boolean value that indicates if the radio button is checked
defaultChecked	A Boolean value that indicates if the radio button was checked by default
form	Returns a reference to the object's parent form

Properties	Description
name	Sets or returns the value of the object's name attribute
type	The value of this property is always radio
value	Sets or returns the object's value attribute

Methods

There are no methods specific to the Radio object.

Event Handlers

Following are the event handlers for this object:

- ❑ onblur
- ❑ onclick
- ❑ onfocus

RegExp Object

The RegExp object contains a regular expression and is used to match strings using its methods and properties. A RegExp object can be created with the new keyword and the RegExp() constructor. The first parameter of the constructor is a string that contains the regular expression, as shown here:

```
var myExp = new RegExp("\\d{4}");
```

A RegExp object can also be created using literal syntax:

```
var myPattern = /\d{4}/;
```

Both the myExp and myPattern variables contain a regular expression that specifies a pattern of four digits.

A RegExp object includes both static properties (properties of the RegExp constructor) and instance properties (properties of an individual instance of a RegExp object).

Static Property

Table D-49 shows the static properties for this object.

Properties	Description
$1, ..., $9	Strings containing the text of the first nine *backreferences* (parenthesized substrings) — from the most recent pattern match
index	The position of the first character in the most recent pattern match

Table continued on following page

Properties	Description
input	The string to match against the pattern
lastIndex	The position in the string where the next match will be started
lastMatch	The string containing the most recent pattern match
lastParen	The string containing the text of the last parenthesized substring from the most recent pattern match
leftContext	The substring preceding the most recent pattern match
multiline	A Boolean value that specifies whether strings are to be searched across multiple lines
rightContext	The substring following the most recent pattern match

Instance Properties

Table D-50 shows the instance properties for this object.

Properties	Description
global	Specifies whether all matches are to be made or just the first match, corresponds to the g flag
ignoreCase	Specifies if the match is case insensitive, corresponds to the i flag
lastIndex	The position in the string where the next match will be started
multiline	A Boolean value that specifies whether strings are to be searched across multiple lines
source	The string source of the regular expression

Methods

Table D-51 shows the methods for the RegExp object.

Methods	Description
compile(pattern [, flags])	Compiles the specified regular expression; used to replace an expression with a new expression
exec([string])	Executes a search using the specified regular expression in the string and returns a result array
test()	Tests whether a string contains a specific pattern, returns a Boolean value
toString()	Returns a string corresponding to the regular expression

Reset Object

A Reset object is created with every instance of an XHTML `<input type="reset">` tag in the document. The objects are stored in the array of the parent form and accessed using the name definedin the XHTML tag or an integer representing the order in which the element appears in the form (with 0 being the first element).

Properties

Table D-52 shows the properties for this object.

Properties	Description
form	Returns a reference to the object's parent form
name	Sets or returns the value of the object's name attribute
type	The value of this property is always reset
value	Sets or returns the object's value attribute

Methods

There are no methods specific to the Reset object.

Event Handlers

Following are the event handlers for this object:

- ❏ onblur
- ❏ onclick
- ❏ onfocus

Screen Object

The Screen object contains and returns information about the user's display screen.

Properties

Table D-53 shows the properties for this object.

Properties	Description
availHeight()	Returns the usable height of the screen (in pixels), minus operating system (OS) interface features (such as the Windows taskbar)
availWidth()	Returns the usable width of the screen (in pixels), minus OS interface features (such as the Windows taskbar)
colorDepth()	Returns the color bit depth of the palette in use or the bit depth of the screen if no palette is in use

Table continued on following page

Properties	Description
height()	Returns the full height of the screen (in pixels)
pixelDepth()	Returns the color bit depth of the screen
width()	Returns the full width of the screen (in pixels)

Methods

There are no methods specific to the Screen object.

Select Object

A Select object is created with every instance of an XHTML <select> tag in the document. The objects are stored in the array of the parent form and accessed using the name defined in the XHTML tag or an integer representing the order in which the element appears in the form (with 0 being the first element).

Properties

Table D-54 shows the properties for this object.

Properties	Description
form	Returns a reference to the object's parent form.
length	Contains the number of items (options) in the select list.
name	Sets or returns the value of the object's name attribute.
options[ ]	An array containing all of the options in the specified object.
selectedIndex	Returns the index of the currently selected item (option). If the list allows for multiple selections, this property will return the index of only the first item selected.
type	Returns the value of the select object's type. Returns select-one if the list allows only a single selection, or select-multiple if the list allows multiple selections.

Methods

Table D-55 shows the methods for this object.

Methods	Description
add()	Adds a new option
remove(n)	Removes the option at position n in the options array

Event Handler

Following is the event handler for this object:

❑ onchange

String Object

A `String` object represents a series of characters in a string.

Property

Table D-56 shows the property for this object.

Property	Description
length	Returns the number of characters in the string

Methods

Table D-57 shows the methods for this object.

Methods	Description
anchor("name")	Embeds the string in anchor tags (`<a>`) using `name` for the name of the anchor (for example, `<a name="name">string</a>`).
big()	Embeds the string in big tags (`<big>`).
blink()	Embeds the string in blink tags (`<blink>`).
bold()	Embeds the string in bold tags (`<b>`).
charAt(integer)	Returns the character at position `integer` in the string. (Note that the first character in a string has an index of 0.)
charCodeAt(integer)	Returns the Unicode value of the character at position `integer` in the string.
concat(string1, string2..., stringN)	Concatenates the given strings with the specified object and returns the resulting string.
fixed()	Embeds the string in teletype tags (`<tt>`).
fontcolor ("colorvalue")	Embeds the string in font tags using `colorvalue` as the value for the color attribute (for example, `<font color="colorvalue">string</font>`).
fontsize("sizevalue")	Embeds the string in font tags using `sizevalue` as the value for the size attribute (for example, `<font size="sizevalue">string</font>`).

Table continued on following page

Methods	Description
fromCharCode(code1, code2...,codeN)	Returns a string composed of the supplied Unicode values. (Static method does not return an object.)
indexOf (searchstring, [index])	Returns the index of the first occurrence of searchstring in the specified string, starting at the optional index position in the string.
italics()	Embeds the string in italic tags (<i>).
lastIndexOf (searchstring, [index])	Returns the index of the last occurrence of searchstring in the specified string, starting backward at the optional index position in the string.
link(url)	Embeds the string in anchor tags (<a>) using url as the URL in the href attribute (for example, <a href="url">string</a>).
match(regexp)	Matches the regular expression regexp against the specified string. Returns the matched portion of the string or null if no match can be made.
replace(regexp, newstring)	Matches the regular expression regexp against the specified string, replacing any matches with the specified newstring. Returns the string with the replacements.
search(regexp)	Searches the specified string for text matching the regular expression regexp. Returns 1 if a match was found or 0 if a match was not found.
slice(start,end)	Returns a slice of the specified string from index start to index end, inclusive.
small()	Embeds the specified string in small tags (<small>).
split(separator)	Splits the specified string at each occurrence of separator, creating an array containing the resulting substrings. (Note: The separator is discarded and does not appear in the resulting substrings.)
strike()	Embeds the specified string in strikeout tags (<strike>).
sub()	Embeds the specified string in subscript tags (<sub>).
substr(start [,length]);	Returns a substring from the specified string starting at the start index for a total of length characters. If length is not specified, the substring contains the characters from the start index through the end of the string.
substring(start,end)	Returns a substring of the specified string between the start and end indexes, inclusive.
sup()	Embeds the specified string in superscript tags (<sup>).
toLowerCase()	Returns the specified string converted to lowercase.
toString()	Returns the string representation of the specified object.
toUpperCase()	Returns the specified string converted to uppercase.
valueOf()	Returns the primitive value of a String object as a string datatype.

Submit Object

A Submit object is created with every instance of an XHTML `<input type="submit">` tag in the document. The objects are stored in the array of the parent form and accessed using the name defined in the XHTML tag or an integer representing the order in which the element appears in the form (with 0 being the first element).

Properties

Table D-58 shows the properties for this object.

Properties	Description
form	Returns a reference to the object's parent form
name	Sets or returns the value of the object's name attribute
type	The value of this property is always submit
value	Sets or returns the object's value attribute

Methods

There are no methods specific to the Submit object.

Event Handlers

Following are the event handlers for this object:

- ❑ onblur
- ❑ onclick
- ❑ onfocus

Text Object

A Text object is created with every instance of an XHTML `<input type="text">` tag in the document. The objects are stored in the array of the parent form and accessed using the name defined in the XHTML tag or an integer representing the order in which the element appears in the form (with 0 being the first element).

Properties

Table D-59 shows the properties for this object.

Properties	Description
defaultValue	Sets or returns the object's initial value attribute
form	Returns a reference to the object's parent form
name	Sets or returns the value of the object's name attribute

Table continued on following page

Properties	Description
type	The value of this property is always `text`
value	Sets or returns the object's `value` attribute

Method

Table D-60 shows the method for this object.

Method	Description
select()	Highlights the text in the text field

Event Handlers

Following are the event handlers for this object:

- ❑ onblur
- ❑ onchange
- ❑ onfocus
- ❑ onselect

Textarea Object

A `Textarea` object is created with every instance of an XHTML `<textarea>` tag in the document. The objects are stored in the array of the parent form and accessed using the name defined in the XHTML tag or an integer representing the order in which the element appears in the form (with 0 being the first element).

Properties

Table D-61 shows the properties for this object.

Properties	Description
defaultValue	Sets or returns the object's initial `value` attribute
form	Returns a reference to the object's parent form
name	Sets or returns the value of the object's `name` attribute
type	The value of this property is always `textarea`
value	Sets or returns the object's `value` attribute

Method

Table D-62 shows the method for this object.

Method	Description
select	Highlights the text in the text area

Event Handlers

Following are the event handlers for this object:

- ❑ onblur
- ❑ onchange
- ❑ onfocus
- ❑ onkeydown
- ❑ onkeypress
- ❑ onkeyup
- ❑ onselect

Window Object

As the top-level object in the JavaScript client hierarchy, a Window object is created for every window and frame (every instance of an XHTML <body> or <frameset> tag).

Properties

Table D-63 shows the properties for this object.

Properties	Description
closed	Returns a Boolean value corresponding to whether a window has been closed. If the window has been closed, this property is true.
defaultStatus [= "message"]	Returns or sets the message displayed in a window's status bar. This property can be disabled by the user in Firefox.
document	Returns a reference to the document currently displayed in the window. See Document object.
frames[ ]	An array containing all the child frames in the current window.
history	A reference to the window's History object. See the History object.
length	Returns the number of child frames contained in a window.
location	A reference to the window's Location object. See the Location object.
name[="name"]	Returns or sets a window's name attribute.
opener	Returns a reference to the object (usually window) that opened the specified window.

Table continued on following page

Properties	Description
outerheight / outerwidth	Determines the dimensions (in pixels) of the outside boundary of a window (including all interface elements).
pageXOffset / pageYOffset	Returns the X and Y positions (in pixels) of the current document's upper-left corner in relation to the upper-left corner of a window's display area.
parent	Returns a reference to the window or frame that contains the calling frame.
personalbar [.visible = true|false]	Sets the visibility of the window's personal bar (or directories bar).
scrollbars [.visible = true|false]	Sets the visibility of the window's scroll bars.
self	Returns a reference to the current active window or frame.
status[= "message"]	Returns or sets the message displayed in a window's status bar.
statusbar [.visible = true|false]	Sets the visibility of the window's status bar.
toolbar [.visible = true|false]	Sets the visibility of the window's toolbar. Note that this property can be set only prior to the window being opened, and it requires the UniversalBrowserWrite privilege.
top	Returns a reference to the topmost browser window.
window	Returns a reference to the current window or frame.

Methods

Table D-64 shows the methods for this object.

Methods	Description
alert("message")	Displays an alert box containing message and an OK button (to clear the box).
blur()	Removes the focus from the specified window.
captureEvents (event_types)	Instructs the window to capture all events of a particular type. See the Event object for a list of event types.
clearInterval (intervalID)	Used to cancel an interval previously set with the setInterval method.
clearTimeout (timeoutID)	Used to cancel a timeout previously set with the setTimeout method.
close()	Causes the specified window to close.

Methods	Description
confirm("message")	Displays a dialog box containing message, along with OK and Cancel buttons. If the user clicks the OK button, this method returns true; if the user clicks the Cancel button (or otherwise closes the dialog box), the method returns false.
disableExternal Capture()	Disables the capturing of events previously enabled using the enableExternalCapture method.
enableExternal Capture()	Allows a window that contains frames to capture events in documents that are loaded from other servers.
focus()	Assigns focus to the specified window.
forward()	Causes the window to move one entry forward in the history list (similar to pressing the browser's Forward button).
home()	Mimics the user pressing the Home button, causing the window to display the document designated as the user's home page.
moveBy(horizPixels, vertPixels)	Moves the window horizontally by horizPixels and vertically by vertPixels in relation to its current position.
moveTo(Xposition, Yposition)	Moves the window's upper-left corner to the position Xposition (horizontal) and Yposition (vertically).
open(URL, windowname [, features])	Opens a new window named windowname, displaying the document referred to by URL, with the optional specified features. The specified features are contained in a string, with the features separated by commas. Features can include the following:
	toolbar=yes|no — Controls the visibility of the window's toolbar
	location=yes|no — Controls the visibility of the window's location bar
	directories=yes|no — Controls the visibility of the window's directory buttons
	status=yes|no — Controls the visibility of the window's status bar
	menubar=yes|no—Controls the visibility of the window's menu bar
	resizable=yes|no— Controls whether the window can be resized
	scrollbars=yes|no — Controls the visibility of the window's scroll bars
	width=pixels— Sets the width of the new window
	height=pixels— Sets the height of the new window
	For example, to create a new window that is 400 pixels square, is not resizable, and has no scroll bars, you could use the following string for features:
	"height=400,width=400,resizeable=no,scrollbars=no"

Table continued on following page

473

Methods	Description
print()	Calls the print routine for the user agent to print the current document.
prompt(message [, input])	Displays a dialog box containing message and a text box with the default input (if specified). The content of the text box is returned if the user clicks OK. If the user clicks Cancel or otherwise closes the dialog box, the method returns null.
releaseEvents (event_type)	Used to release any captured events of the specified type and to send them on to objects further down the event hierarchy.
resizeBy(horizPixels, vertPixels)	Resizes the specified window by the specified horizontal and vertical pixels. The window retains its upper-left position; the resize moves the lower-right corner appropriately.
resizeTo(horizPixels, vertPixels)	Resizes the specified window to the specified dimensions.
routeEvent(event_type)	Used to send an event further down the normal event hierarchy.
scrollTo(Xposition, Yposition)	Scrolls the specified window to the specified coordinates, with the specified coordinate becoming the top left corner of the viewable area.
setInterval (expression/function, milliseconds)	Causes the expression to be evaluated or the function called every milliseconds. Returns the ID of the interval. Use the clearInterval method to stop the iterations.
setTimeout (expression/function, milliseconds)	Causes the expression to be evaluated or the function called after the specified milliseconds elapse. Returns the ID of the timer. Use the clearTimeout method to stop the iteration.
stop()	Mimics the user clicking the Stop button in a browser.

Event Handlers

Following are the event handlers for this object:

❑   onblur

❑   onerror

❑   onfocus

❑   onload

❑   onresize

❑   onunload

Index

T